STATE AID LAW OF THE EUROPEAN UNION

STATE AID LAW OF THE EUROPEAN UNION

First Edition

By

Peter Vesterdorf

Mogens Uhd Nielsen

Translated from Danish by
Stephen Harris

SWEET & MAXWELL

THOMSON REUTERS

First edition 2008

Published in 2008 by
Thomson Reuters (Legal) Limited (Registered in England & Wales,
Company No 1679046. Registered office and address for service:
100 Avenue Road, London, NW3 3PF) trading as Sweet & Maxwell.
For further information on our products and services,
visit www.sweetandmaxwell.co.uk
Typeset by Servis Filmsetting Ltd, Stockport, Cheshire
Printed and bound in Great Britain by
MPG Books Ltd, Bodmin, Cornwall

No natural forests were destroyed to make this product;
only farmed timber was used and re-planted.

British Library Cataloguing in Publication Data

A CIP catalogue record for this book
is available from the British Library

ISBN 978 1 847 03749 7

FOREWORD

EC State aid law has in many aspects undergone substantial changes during the last years due to the implementation of the State aid Action Plan. This plan introduces a new approach to State aid as a tool to promote economic growth and to create jobs while observing EU policies such as the protection of the environment and the promotion of free and undistorted competition, hence the subtitle of the mentioned plan: less and better targeted State aid.

The book provides an introduction to the EC State aid law as it stands at the beginning of a period with a new State aid law regime.

It is the ambition of the authors to provide the reader with a practical tool that can form the basis for or help solving most questions relating to EC State aid law. Consequently, the book offers an introduction to the provisions of the EC Treaty on State aid generally applicable as well as to the provisions applicable to agriculture, fisheries and transport. The interplay between those provisions is also touched upon. Apart from the mentioned provisions and the case law of the European Court of Justice and the Court of First Instance, the main body of EC State aid law consists of Commission regulations, guidelines, notices, frameworks, etc. Given their practical importance, particular attention has been devoted to those instruments. Finally, the book provides an introduction to the administrative State aid law procedure, the recovery of State aid and the judicial protection in the field of State aid law.

The authors wish to thank Publishing Editor, Ms Amanda Strange, and Sweet & Maxwell for their positive attitude to publishing the book at hand. The authors also wish to express their gratitude to Margot and Thorvald Dreyers Fund, Copenhagen, who so generously sponsored the translation of this book; and Mr Steven Harris, who translated it from the original Danish.

Mogens Uhd Nielsen
Peter Vesterdorf
31 July 2008

CONTENTS

TABLE OF CASES

CASES BEFORE THE ECJ AND CFI – ALPHABETICAL ORDER

Table of Commission Decisions

TABLE OF ECSC DECISIONS

TABLE OF EUROPEAN AND INTERNATIONAL LEGISLATION

SOURCES OF EC LAW

REFERENCES TO SOURCES OF EC LAW AND PUBLICATIONS BY THE COMMISSION

The sources used in this book are primarily accessible at the following web pages:

Generally applicable EC State aid law:
http://ec.europa.eu/comm/competition/state_aid/overview/index_en.cfm (Competition)

EC State aid law applicable to agriculture:
http://ec.europa.eu/agriculture/stateaid/index_en.htm (Agriculture and Rural Development)

EC State aid law applicable to fisheries:
http://ec.europa.eu/fisheries/legislation/state_aid_en.htm (Maritime Affairs and Fisheries)

EC State aid law applicable to transport and coal:
http://ec.europa.eu/dgs/energy_transport/state_aid/index_en.htm (Energy and Transport)

EC law in general and The Official Journal of the European Union:
http://www.eur-lex.eu
This web page should be consulted in order to check if the law has been amended or repealed.

Case law of The European Court of Justice and Court of First Instance:
http://curia.europa.eu

Annual Reports on Competition Policy:
http://ec.europa.eu/comm/competition/annual_reports/

Competition Policy Newsletter:
http://ec.europa.eu/comm/competition/publications/cpn/

CHAPTER 1

THE EU'S BASIC RULES ON STATE AID

THE PROHIBITION OF STATE AID IN ART.87(1) OF THE EC TREATY

The Treaty establishing the European Community (EC Treaty) has three arti-   **1–001**
cles dealing with State aid in general. These are arts 87, 88 and 89. Other provisions in the EC Treaty deal with aid in specific sectors, such as transport and
agriculture. The Treaty establishing the European Coal and Steel Community
(ECSC Treaty) expired in July 2002, and since then all sectors of commerce
have been covered by the State aid rules of the EC Treaty.

Article 87 constitutes the basic rules on State aid in the EC Treaty and it
contains a general prohibition of State aid. Article 88 contains provisions for
the notification and approval of aid. Article 89 deals with the adoption of
more detailed provisions on State aid in the form of secondary legislation.

Article 87(1) states as follows:

> "Save as otherwise provided in this Treaty, any aid granted by a Member
> State or through State resources in any form whatsoever which distorts
> or threatens to distort competition by favouring certain undertakings or
> the production of certain goods shall, in so far as it affects trade between
> Member States, be incompatible with the common market."

The prohibition of State aid in art.87(1) is not directly applicable, in other   **1–002**
words a citizen cannot rely on the prohibition before a national court in
attempting to persuade the national court to recognise that some particular aid
measure is incompatible with Community law. On the other hand, art.88(3),
on unlawfully granted, non-notified aid is directly applicable; see Chs 2 and 8.
To the extent that art.87(1) results in general legislation (cf. the block exemption regulations), or specific State aid decisions by the Commission based on
art.88(2)[1], the prohibition in art.87(1) can also be directly applicable and can
therefore be relied upon before national courts, as a failure to comply with provisions in a block exemption regulation or the failure to comply with specific
decisions on State aid will be equivalent to new aid which is covered by the
stand-still provision in art.88(3).

---

[1] Case 78/76, *Steinike & Weinlig*, [1977] E.C.R. 595, para.10.

The exceptions referred to in art.87(1) are those set out in art.87(2) and (3), as well as those found in other provisions of the EC Treaty, such as those concerning the agriculture and transport sectors.

Article 87(2) contains exceptions to the prohibition of State aid which are expressly stated as being compatible with the common market. These concern:

"(a) aid having a social character, granted to individual consumers, provided that such aid is granted without discrimination related to the origin of the products concerned;

(b) aid to make good the damage caused by natural disasters or exceptional occurrences;

(c) aid granted to the economy of certain areas of the Federal Republic of Germany affected by the division of Germany, in so far as such aid is required in order to compensate for the economic disadvantages caused by that division."[2]

These exceptions will be considered in more detail below in paras 1–047– 1–050.

1–003 Article 87(3) contains a number of exceptions in the form of State aid measures which *can* be considered compatible with the common market. These exceptions are as follows:

"(a) aid to promote the economic development of areas where the standard of living is abnormally low or where there is serious underemployment;

(b) aid to promote the execution of an important project of common European interest or to remedy a serious disturbance in the economy of a Member State;

(c) aid to facilitate the development of certain economic activities or of certain economic areas, where such aid does not adversely affect trading conditions to an extent contrary to the common interest;

(d) aid to promote culture and heritage conservation where such aid does not affect trading conditions and competition in the Community to an extent that is contrary to the common interest;

---

[2] Following the reunification of Germany in 1990 the basis for the exception has largely lapsed. In the years prior to reunification, aid was provided to the areas affected by the split in accordance with the principles for the granting of aid under the provisions in art.87 on regional aid. Following reunification, the Commission has reviewed the aid measures in question together with the Federal Republic. However, it is notable that art.87(2)(c) has been retained following both the Maastricht Treaty and the Amsterdam Treaty, and has been used by the Commission in individual cases since reunification; see Commission Decision 92/465/EEC of April 14, 1992 concerning aid granted by the Land of Berlin to Daimler-Benz AG Germany; and the Decision of April 13, 1994 concerning aid to producers of glass containers and porcelain established in Tettau. However the decision of the Court of First Instance (CFI), in Joined Cases T-132/96 and T-143/96, *Freistaat Sachsen and Volkswagen v Commission*, [1999] E.C.R. II-3663, shows that the scope for applying art.87(2)(c) is very limited. See also s.1.4.c.

(e) such other categories of aid as may be specified by decision of the Council acting by a qualified majority on a proposal from the Commission."

The exceptions in art.87(3) can be called discretionary, in contrast to the exceptions in art.87(2), as the Commission has wide discretion in administering these exceptions with regard to what it will accept; see also the decisions of the European Court of Justice (ECJ).[3]

The exceptions in art.87(3) will be considered in more detail below in paras 1–051–1–061.

As stated, the EC Treaty also contains other specific exceptions to the pro-   **1–004** hibition of State aid in art.87. These exceptions primarily concern transport (arts 73 and 76), agriculture (art.36), and art.86(2) on undertakings entrusted with the operation of services of general economic interest. These are discussed in Chs 4 and 5. Moreover, the Council can adopt measures giving other exemptions than those directly referred to in the EC Treaty by virtue of its powers under art.89; see paras 1–065–1–066.

DIFFERENT KINDS OF AID

In everyday language, the terms used for aid include: environmental aid,   **1–005** operating aid, production aid, investment aid, agricultural support, transport support, compensation, educational support, employment aid, research and development aid, aid for recovery and reconstruction, export aid and aid for small and medium sized enterprises (SMEs).

The purposes for which aid is given can be:

- to promote exports of a Member State's goods and services,
- to hinder imports,
- to promote the use of national raw materials and semi-finished products,
- to promote research and the development of new products,
- to promote regional development in economically disadvantaged areas,
- to promote the use of particular technologies, for example for environmental protection or energy saving,
- to support industry and commerce which is no longer competitive,
- to support structural changes in industry and commerce,
- to support industries which are of national strategic importance, for example, steel and shipbuilding,
- to secure employment,
- to secure incomes for certain sectors of the population, for example, consumers or agriculture,

---

[3] See, e.g. Case T-149/95, *Ducros*, [1997] E.C.R. II-2031, para.63.

- to improve the working environment and ensure good working conditions,
- to ensure the provision of goods and service of general economic interest, and
- to ensure high standards in relation to health, environmental protection and consumer protection.

Operating and investment aid

1–006   In assessing different forms of aid it is important to bear in mind that a distinction must be made between operating aid (also called production aid) and investment aid. The distinction is especially important when assessing the approval of aid in relation to art.87(3)(c), in other words, aid to facilitate the development of certain economic activities etc. Operating aid is normally regarded as being particularly problematic in relation to art.87, as it is by definition protective and, unlike investment aid, is not aimed at economic development. However, operating aid can be approved on a temporary basis in connection with attempts to rescue a threatened undertaking which will be followed by attempts at restructuring as part of a restructuring plan or, for example, under certain conditions as part of regional aid. When, exceptionally, operating aid is approved (mainly as part of regional aid), it must be temporary and regressive (i.e. progressively reduced), but these requirements for the aid to be temporary and regressive can be eased in the case of regional aid and environmental aid.[4]

Employment aid

1–007   Employment aid is also problematic in principle, since it is also of a protective nature. Just as with production or operating aid, employment aid (for example in the form of wage support) is a form of aid which can often be used to protect against competition from foreign undertakings, which is clearly contrary to the aims of the EU; see art.3(1) of the EC Treaty, especially paras (c) and (g), which concern the abolition of obstacles to free movement and ensuring that competition in the internal market is not distorted.

Sectoral aid v horizontal aid

1–008   A distinction is made between sectoral aid (for example for shipbuilding) and horizontal aid (for example for environmental protection), as well as between aid schemes and individual aid, and aid paid as individual aid within the framework of an aid programme, and between general aid (such as a general

---

[4] See the Commission's Report on Competition Policy 1994, annex II E, p. 605.

tax relief or an improvement of the depreciation rules for undertakings, which is permitted and does not constitute aid under art.87(1)) and selective aid which is, in principle, prohibited under art.87(1).

Aid in the form of a grant etc.

Aid can consist of direct or indirect financial support, and can consist of a loan provided by a public body at a specially favourable interest rate or under advantageous terms, guarantees, direct financial grants in the form investments in equity capital or working capital, or release from a debt (for example a tax debt), or taxation benefits.[5]   1–009

Wage supports for individual employees

Aid can also consist of wage supports paid to individual employees. Such aid is considered to be State aid for the undertaking in which such people are employed.   1–010

The provision of premises, consultancy services etc.   1–011

Making available premises or building plots etc. without charge or at very low cost, consultancy advice, release from obligations and giving benefits when allocating contracts can also constitute State aid.

Favouritism when tendering   1–012

Depending on the circumstances, the favouring of an undertaking when offering public contracts can also involve the provision of State aid.[6]

---

[5] However, the EU's VAT rules can justify certain exemptions not being regarded as State aid. See *Schön*: "Taxation and State Aid Law in the European Union", CML. Rev. Vol.36, No.5, September 1999 pp.911–936, which gives a detailed treatment of the problems of taxation and State aid. In this connection see also the *Ferring* case referred to below in para.1–018, which concerned an exemption from a special turnover tax on medicine. See also Case C-387/92, *Banco Exterior de Espana*, [1994] E.C.R. I-877, para.13; and Case T-106/95, FF*SA v Commission*, [1997] E.C.R., II-229.

[6] The ECJ has held that the fact that an undertaking which submits a tender receives subsidies does not in itself exclude the undertaking from submitting a tender in connection with a tender procedure under the EU's public procurement rules; see the judgment in Case C-94/99, *ARGE Gewässerschutz*, [2000] E.C.R. I-11037. On the other hand, an offer can be excluded if is abnormally low as a result of the tenderer obtaining State aid; see art.57 of Directive 2004/17/EC coordinating the procurement procedures of entities operating in the water, energy, transport and postal services sectors (OJ 2004 L 134/1). However, where the contracting entity rejects a tender in these circumstances, it must first consult the tenderer and give that party the possibility of showing that the State aid is approved by the Commission. If it is, then in principle the

1–013 Aid by means of cross subsidisation

Aid can also take the form of cross-subsidisation, among other things by the transfer of funds from the monopoly activities of a public undertaking to the activities which the same undertaking carries on in competition with private undertakings.[7]

In relation to public funding and cross-subsidisation, it is important to note that the Commission bases its assessment of whether State aid exists within the meaning of the EC Treaty on whether the transfer of the economic resources in question would have been made by a private investor on the basis of sound considerations of the market economy (the market economy investor principle).[8] The market economy investor principle is used in general to assess whether there is State aid within the meaning of the EC Treaty.

In connection with cross-subsidisation, according to the *UFEX* cases (which concerned a public undertaking's—La Poste's—provision of logistical and commercial support to a private law subsidiary whose activities were open to competition), in the absence of any possibility of comparing the situation of La Poste with that of a private group of undertakings not operating in a reserved sector, "normal market conditions" (which are necessarily hypothetical) must be assessed by reference to the objective and verifiable elements which are available, which in the case in question were the costs borne by La Poste for the provision of logistical and commercial assistance to its subsidiary. This was because the postal network which was used to provide the services in question was not established and maintained on the basis of a purely commercial approach. On this basis the Court stated that the subsidiary company would not have been found to have received State aid if it had been established (1) that the price charged properly covered all the additional, variable costs incurred in providing the logistical and commercial assistance, an appropriate contribution to the fixed costs arising from use of the postal network and an adequate return on the capital invested, and (2) if there was nothing to suggest that those elements had been underestimated or fixed in an arbitrary fashion.[9]

---

tender cannot be rejected because of the State aid. See also Case T-14/96, *Bretagne Angleterre Irlande (BAI) v Commission*, [1999] E.C.R. II-139, from which it appears that the allocation of contracts can constitute an infringement of art.87(1).

[7] Case T-613/97, *UFEX v Commission*, [2000] E.C.R. II-4055; Joined Cases C-83/01 P, C-93/01 P and C-94/01 P, *Cronopost and others v Commission*, [2003] E.C.R. I-6993; and Case T-613/97, *UFEX v Commission*, [2006] E.C.R. II-1531, which was appealed to the ECJ as Case C-342/06 P. By judgment of July 1, 2008 the ECJ set aside the judgment of the CFI in so far as that judgment annulled the decision of the Commission and dismissed the application of UFEX and others for annulment of the contested decision.

[8] The perspective is that of a medium term investment by a public concern; see paras 6–004 to 6–010.

[9] Case T-613/97, *UFEX v Commission*, [2000] E.C.R. II-4055; Joined Cases C-83/01 P, C-93/01 P and C-94/01 P, *Cronopost and others v Commission*, [2003] E.C.R. I-6993; and Case T-613/97, *UFEX v Commission*, [2006] E.C.R. II-1531, which was appealed to the ECJ as Case C-342/06 P. The ECJ set aside the judgment of the CFI in so far as that judgment had annulled the

Parafiscal charges

Aid can also be given in connection with *parafiscal charges*, which are charges **1–014**
imposed on undertakings in a given commercial sector where the revenue from
the charge is used to support undertakings which are subject to the charge in
question.[10] These charges will normally be assessed in accordance with art.25
or art.90 of the EC Treaty, as discussed in paras 5–025 and 5–026. However,
the use of the revenue from parafiscal charges for the benefit of domestic
goods can constitute State aid if the conditions of art.87(1) of the Treaty
are otherwise fulfilled.[11] However, such aid can be approved if, for example,
it is used for environmental protection purposes, research and development,
or a general sales promotion.[12] For example, aid financed through parafiscal
charges is directly referred to in para.4.6. of the Commission's guidelines for
the examination of State aid to fisheries and aquaculture (OJ C 84, April 3,
2008, p.10); this is discussed further in Ch.4. According to these guidelines, aid
schemes funded by parafiscal charges imposed on certain products irrespective
of their origin, and which benefit both domestic and imported products, are
not for this reason incompatible with the common market.

State aid to undertakings in other countries

State aid may also be found to exist where one Member State provides aid to **1–015**
undertakings in another country, and such undertakings then provide benefits
to undertakings in the first Member State.

Aid provided by the setting of tariffs

Unlawful State aid can be given by means of the setting of the tariffs of public **1–016**
undertakings, for example for gas or electricity, which can benefit certain
undertakings or products. There can be preferential tariffs for some sectors,
for example market gardening or agriculture. However, according to the case

Commission decision that no state aid in the form of cross-subsidisation from la Poste to its
subsidiary had occurred.
[10] As an example of the ECJ's attitude to such charges, see Case C-266/91, *Celulose Beira
Industrial*, [1993] E.C.R. I-4337, where the ECJ held that the use of the revenue from a
parafiscal charge exclusively for the benefit of domestic products may constitute a State aid;
however, such a determination is a matter for the Commission and may be made only after
the procedure provided for in art.93 [now 88] of the Treaty. See also Joined Cases C-34/01 to
C-38/01, *Enirisorse v Ministero delle finanze*, [2003] E.C.R. I-4243, paras 43–45.
[11] Case C-72/92, *firma Herbert Scharbatke v Germany*, [1993] E.C.R. I-5509; and Joined Cases
C-34/01 to C-38/01, *Enirisorse v Ministero delle finanze*, [2003] E.C.R. I-4243.
[12] Thus, in the 1990s the Commission approved such an arrangement as part of the Danish meas-
ures for the reduction of CO_2 emissions. See the Commission's XXII Report on Competition
Policy 1992; and *Madeleine Infeldt*: "Eco-tax reliefs for companies in Denmark, Finland and
Sweden after the Court ruling in *Adria-Wien Pipeline GmbH* case", in *Competition Policy
Newsletter*, No.1, Spring 2003 p.103.

law of the ECJ, a preferential tariff system does not constitute State aid in so far as the tariff is justified by the need to withstand competition from imports from non-member countries in order to retain important existing customers.[13] Preferential tariffs and art.87(1) EC is discussed further in paras 6–019 to 6–020.

Minimum and maximum prices

1–017   Laying down minimum or maximum prices will not normally constitute State aid. This is because State funds are not normally involved. The ECJ has previously considered such questions, for example, in Case 82/77, *van Tiggele*, [1978] E.C.R. 25, concerning a State's setting of a minimum price for spirits. In this case the ECJ ruled that the fixing by a public authority of minimum retail prices for a product did not constitute State aid within the meaning of art.87(1) of the Treaty.

In cases concerning maximum prices, the situation can arise where complying with a maximum price can lead to a loss, for example for suppliers of fuels. If compensation is given for such loss, this will not be considered State aid.[14]

Compensation for providing public services

1–018   Compensation paid by the State to undertakings for the provision of public services has given rise to certain problems in relation to the question of when such payments should be categorised as notifiable State aid.[15] To some extent the problem must be accepted as having been clarified by the ECJ's decision in the *Altmark* case[16] and the initiatives adopted by the Commission in this connection; see further in paras 4–144 and 4–145. Thus, it was stated in the *Altmark* judgment that such compensation did not constitute State aid as long as a number of conditions were fulfilled, including that the compensation must not exceed what is necessary to cover the costs incurred and a reasonable profit for discharging the obligations. Following the judgment the Commission issued guidelines for the assessment of cases of compensation which must be

---

13   Case C-56/93, *Belgium v Commission*, [1996] E.C.R. I-723.
14   Case T-95/94, *Sytraval*, [1995] E.C.R. II-2651, where the CFI considered a complaint that the fuel supplied to Sécuripost's vehicles was paid for with petrol vouchers provided by the French post office, which was its parent company.
15   In its judgment in Case C-53/00, *Ferring*, [2001] E.C.R. I-9067 para.29, given by a bench of five judges, the ECJ found that such compensation does not constitute State aid; see art.86(2) of the Treaty. Conversely, the compensation which was considered by the CFI in Case T-106/95, FFSA, [1997] E.C.R. II-229, was considered to be notifiable State aid. The CFI's judgment was upheld by the ECJ (Case C-174/97 P, [1998] ECR I-1303). The Commission had previously expressed the view given in the ruling in the *Ferring* case; See also *Bartosch* in CML. R., Vol.3, No.3, June 2002 on this problem.
16   Case C-280/00, *Altmark Trans and Regierungspräsidium Magdeburg v Nahverkehrsgesellschaft Altmark*, [2003] E.C.R. I-7747.

notified, and a decision stating when notification is not required. See paras 4–130–4–140 on services of general economic interest.

Export aid

Export aid in the form of subsidies etc. can constitute State aid within the meaning of the EC Treaty, and as an overwhelming rule they will be prohibited and not able to be approved.[17] However, there are limited possibilities for approving aid when it is given solely in connection with trade fairs etc; see below in paras 3–007 to 3–027 on support for small and medium sized enterprises. Subsidies for exports to countries outside the EU/EEA will infringe the prohibition of State aid in art.87(1) if it leads to distortion of competition within the EU,[18] which it will usually be assumed to do. For a more detailed discussion of export subsidies, see paras 4–045–4–048.

1–019

Article 87 in more detail

According to the practice of the courts, all the conditions of art.87(1) of the EC Treaty must be fulfilled before State aid will be found to exist. The provision lays down four conditions. first, there must be aid granted by a Member State or through State resources. Secondly, this aid must affect trade between Member States. Thirdly, it must give an advantage to the recipients. And fourth, it must distort or threaten to distort competition.[19]

1–020

The concept of State aid

The prohibition of State aid is neither unconditional nor absolute. According to arts 87 and 88 the Commission has certain discretionary powers,[20] and it is up to the Commission to decide whether some particular form of aid is compatible with art.87(1). This also means that the prohibition in art.87(1) is not directly applicable, in other words it cannot be relied upon by citizens,

1–021

---

[17] For information on export subsidies see Dagmar Heinisch: "EU-rules on State aid do not allow for export aid", in *Competition Policy Newsletter*, No.2, Summer 2003 p.81.

[18] Under the OECD and WTO regimes there are special rules on the right to provide export subsidies in trade between the member countries; see e.g. the "Gentlemen's agreement" within the OECD.

[19] See Case C-345/02, *Pearle and Others v Hoofdbedrijfschap Ambachten*, [2004] E.C.R. I-7139, in which references are made to further cases. See also *Ronald Feltkamp*: "Some reflections on the structure of the state aid rules in the Treaty of Rome", in *Competition Policy Newsletter*, No.1, Spring 2003 p.29.

[20] Case C-39/94, *SFEI and Others v La Poste*, [1996] E.C.R. I-3547 para.36. However, according to para.49 of the judgment, a national court may have to interpret the concept of aid contained in art.92 of the Treaty (now 87(1)) in order to determine whether a State measure ought to have been notified.

undertakings or trade organisations in proceedings before national courts. This is only possible if art.87(1) has resulted in the adoption of general laws or concrete decisions on the basis of a procedure under art.88(2).

In the *UFEX* case,[21] the CFI, which summarised the well-established case law in the area, stated that the aim of art.87(1) of the Treaty is to prevent trade between Member States from being affected by advantages granted by public authorities which, in various forms, distort or threaten to distort competition by favouring certain undertakings or certain products. The concept of aid thus encompasses not only positive benefits, such as subsidies, but also interventions which, in various forms, mitigate the charges which are normally included in the budget of an undertaking and which, without therefore being subsidies in the strict sense of the word, are of the same character and have the same effect.[22] Thus, for example, a tax exemption which does not in itself involve a transfer of State funds but which gives certain exempted undertakings more advantageous economic conditions than others which are subject to the tax, can constitute State aid.[23] Likewise, a tax reduction for the benefit of certain undertakings or a postponement of payment of tax due can constitute State aid.[24] Article 87(1) thus covers all economic means which the public sector can use to support undertakings, regardless of whether these means are permanently part of the public sector's means. In particular, regard must be had to the effects of the aid on the undertakings or producers which benefit, and not to the situation of the institutions which allocate or administrate the aid.

1–022　　The concept of aid is therefore an objective concept, and its definition is only significant if a public measure gives an advantage to one or more undertakings. According to the case law, it is clear that the capacity of aid to strengthen the beneficiary's competitive position is assessed by reference to the advantage given to the beneficiary, and it is unnecessary to take account of the operating results of its competitors.[25]

In the *SFEI* case[26] the ECJ considered the concept of State aid in the circumstances of the case, and held that a public undertaking's provision of logistical and commercial support to a subsidiary subject to private law, which carried on activities which were open to competition, can constitute State aid within the meaning of art.87(1) if the payment for the support is less than would be expected under normal market conditions.

It follows from the above that, in order to assess whether the measures concerned can constitute State aid, it is necessary to undertake a review of the

---

[21] Case T-613/97, *UFEX v Commission*, [2000] E.C.R. II-4055.
[22] Case C-172/03, *Wolfgang Heiser v finanzamt Innsbruck*, [2005] E.C.R. I-1627; Case C-222/04, *Ministero dell'Economia e delle finanze v Cassa di Risparmio di firenze and Others*, [2006] E.C.R. I-289; and Case C-237/04, *Enirisorse v Sotacarbo*, [2006] E.C.R. I-2843.
[23] Case C-222/04, *Ministero dell'Economia e delle finanze v Cassa di Risparmio di firenze and Others*, [2006] E.C.R. I-289.
[24] *Ministero dell' Economia e delle finaanze v Cassa di Risparmio di Ferenze and Others*, [2006] E.C.R. I-289.
[25] Case T-14/96, *BAI v Commission*, [1999] E.C.R. II-139.
[26] Case C-39/94, *SFEI and Others v La Poste*, [1996] E.C.R. I-3547.

situation with regard to the undertaking to which the measures are addressed, and it must be decided whether that undertaking has received the relevant logistical and commercial support at a price which it would not have obtained under normal market conditions.

In the *SFEI* case the ECJ also stated that this assessment presupposes that an economic analysis is made, taking into account all the factors which an undertaking acting under normal market conditions should have taken into account when fixing the remuneration for the services provided.

The definition of aid

It can be stated with a reasonable degree of certainty that State aid is a **1–023** measure which is taken by some public body and which, by means of State (i.e. public) resources, directly or indirectly gives a beneficiary undertaking an economic or financial advantage which it would not have had under normal circumstances, and which relieves the beneficiary undertaking of a burden to which its finances would otherwise normally be subject.[27]

State aid includes aid from other public authorities and bodies than the State

The term "State aid" is very broad and covers both direct and indirect aid **1–024** from the State, as well as aid from other public authorities and bodies, such as regional and local government bodies. The aid can be given by law or under the authority of law, or by general administrative practice. For example, depending on the circumstances, the decisions of the tax assessment authorities with respect to tax deductions and other tax questions can lead to a breach of the prohibition of State aid under art.87 of the Treaty.

State aid includes aid provided by bodies appointed by or set up by the State

Aid which is given due to decisions taken by bodies which have been appointed **1–025** by the State or other public authorities to carry out specific tasks—such as the approval of prices, etc.—is also covered by the concept of State aid.[28] According to the case law of the ECJ, the fact that art.87(1) distinguishes between aid granted by a Member State and aid granted through State resources merely has the aim of making it clear that the concept of State aid includes aid granted by a public or private body designated or established by

---

[27] Case C-39/94, *SFEI and Others v La Poste*, [1996] E.C.R. I-3547 para.58.
[28] Case 31/87, *Beentjes*, [1988] E.C.R. 4635; and Joined Cases 67, 68 and 70/8, *van der Kooy and Others v Commission*, [1988] E.C.R. 219.

the State.[29] However, in relation to private bodies, there is a requirement that the State must be able to control the use of the resources; see Case C-83/98 P, *Ladbroke Racing*, [2000] E.C.R. I-3271 para.50.

As for resources used by independent bodies designated or established by the State, according to para.50 of the *Ladbroke Racing* case, which itself refers to the judgment in Case T-358/94, *Air France v Commission*, [1996] E.C.R. II-2109, irrespective of whether the means are permanent assets of the public sector, the financial means by which the public sector actually supports undertakings can constitute State aid. What matters is whether the means are in fact used to provide aid.

State aid includes aid to private as well as to public undertakings

1–026   The State aid provisions apply to aid given both to private and to public undertakings; on the latter, see art.86(1) of the Treaty, subject to the provisions in art.86(2).

The effect, not the purpose, is decisive

1–027   It is the intention or effect of a given measure of a public body which determines whether State aid is given.[30]

The State aid concept is in principle an objective concept

1–028   As stated above in paras 1–021 and 1–022, the concept of aid is an objective concept, and the Commission does not normally have wide discretion in assessing whether State aid exists. However, there can be cases which are of such a complex economic or socio-economic character that the exercise of discretion must necessarily be part of the assessment, as the ECJ has acknowledged.

Selectivity

1–029   The concept of *selectivity* is important in assessing whether there is State aid. Entirely general measures such as taxation, tax deductions, aid which is provided to all undertakings or productions on the basis of uniform and objective criteria will not constitute State aid within the meaning of the EC Treaty. However, there can be situations where seemingly general measures are

---

[29] Joined Cases C-52/97, C-53/97 and C-54/97, *Viscido and Others*, [1998] E.C.R. I-2629.
[30] Case C-241/94, *France v Commission* (*Kimberly Clark*), [1996] E.C.R. I-4551, paras 19 and 20.

in reality measures which are only intended to benefit certain undertakings or certain productions. In this case State aid will be found to exist (covert aid).[31]

However, the fact that general measures can have unequal effects because of differences between undertakings does not mean that a measure will be regarded as being State aid. For example, certain depreciation allowances will affect capital intensive and non-capital intensive undertakings differently.

Technical reasons can also mean that in some cases it will be necessary to use different methods to achieve a certain effect. For example, this can be the case with taxes which are sometimes related to the turnover of undertakings, sometimes to profits and sometimes to other criteria.

The fact that aid, for example in the form of a subsidy, is initially given to some undertakings or productions, but is later intended to be extended to the whole economy means that the arrangement is not compatible with art.87(1), but will be regarded as being selective.[32]   **1–030**

If only some undertakings choose to take advantage of an arrangement which is based on subsidies, for example to undertakings which employ the long-term unemployed, this does not make the arrangement selective, as long as the possibility of obtaining subsidies covers all sectors and all undertakings which employ the long-term unemployed.[33]

Depending on the circumstances, exemptions from general laws can be such that they are not considered to be selective, but general. This can be the case, for example, if small undertakings are not covered by general laws on the protection of employees, for example, which would be especially burdensome for them in comparison to medium-sized and large undertakings. This will not be considered to be State aid within the meaning of the EC Treaty.

When the Commission or the ECJ decides on a question of selectivity, it is decisive whether an exemption given to certain undertakings or productions is a logical consequence of the structure and purpose of the system in question. It is obvious that undertakings which do not make any CO_2 emissions will be exempted from paying any carbon emissions taxes without such an exemption being in breach of art.87(1).[34] In determining whether there is selectivity, it will also be decisive whether the undertakings which benefit from an exemption from a general arrangement are in the same factual situation as those that do not.

Taxes or charges that are used selectively, and only affect certain groups of   **1–031**

---

[31] Cases where a general measure is administered in such a way that, in the administration of the measure, the authorities can use discretion with regard to the conditions for the payment and amount of aid can turn a measure which is otherwise a general measure into a State aid measure; see the *Kimberly Clark* judgment referred to in the preceding footnote, paras 23 and 24. Relief from energy taxes which is only granted to undertakings which manufacture goods is regarded by the ECJ as selective, and thus constitutes State aid; see Case C-143/99, *Adria-Wien Pipeline*, [2001] E.C.R. I-8365. The judgment illustrates the problem of selectivity.

[32] Case C-75/97, *Belgium v Commission*, [1999] E.C.R. I-3671 para.41.

[33] See the Commission's XXVIII Report on competition policy, 1998.

[34] Case C-353/95 P, *Tiercé Ladbroke v Commission*, [1997] E.C.R. I-7007 paras 33–35; Case C-53/00, *Ferring*, [2001] E.C.R. I-9067 para.17; and Case C-75/97, *Belgium v Commission*, [1999] E.C.R. I-3671 paras 32–34.

undertakings while others go free, can very well lead to a finding that there is State aid within the meaning of the EC Treaty. Selective exemptions from taxes or charges cannot be justified by reference to the fact undertakings in other Member States are subject to other rules on taxes and charges.[35]

Selectivity can also be expressed in the way in which a State aid measure, for example a basic allowance in relation to purely national environmental taxes, only applies to existing undertakings but not for an expansion of production in existing undertakings or for newly established undertakings. Such arrangements may be permissible from an environmental point of view; see para.158(a) in the new 2008 Community guidelines on State aid for environmental protection which are discussed in paras 3–089 to 3–115. In relation to these, a given tax reduction must be allowable in the same way to the undertakings which find themselves in the same factual circumstances. This opens the possibility for different treatment of existing undertakings and new undertakings, and between existing production and expanded production. It must be assumed that such a difference in treatment, which can fulfil the intentions behind the tax measure, may not go further than is necessary for the fulfilment of the intentions. This means that there can be differentiation of a tax relief instead of only applying it to existing undertakings. A balance must be struck between, on the one hand, concern for the environment and the avoidance of distortion of competition which puts new undertakings in a worse position than existing undertakings, and on the other hand, the fact that new undertakings will find it easier than existing undertakings to take account of the environmental taxes, as the newer undertakings will find it easier to take advantage of newer more environmentally friendly technology etc. to reduce the environmental taxes concerned.

Where tax differentials are combined with an arrangement for the gratis allocation of transferable pollution permits (pollution quotas) to large undertakings, perhaps with the possibility that newly established undertakings will also be granted such gratis quotas, it becomes even more difficult to assess whether a system of environmental taxes, which is based on such clearly different treatment in the form of tax reductions for certain categories of undertakings, can be regarded as being compatible with art.87 of the Treaty. It is clear that in such a situation it is particularly difficult to evaluate the environmental advantages against the risk of a distortion of competition which alters trading conditions to an extent which is contrary to the common interest; see art.87(3)(c).

In para.68 of the new Community guidelines on State aid for environmental protection, which is discussed in more detail in paras 3–028 to 3–062, the Commission states that it still does not have sufficient experience in assessing the compatibility of reductions of environmental taxes combined with participation in tradable permit schemes to provide general guidance thereon. Instead, to the extent that such schemes constitute State aid within the

---

[35] Case 173/73, *Italy v Commission*, [1974] E.C.R. 709.

meaning of art.87(1) of the EC Treaty, the assessment of such cases will be made on the basis of art.87(3)(c) of the Treaty.

Selectivity in relation to art.87(1) is also discussed in paras 1–041 to 1–043.

State resources

One of the conditions for implementing the prohibition in art.87(1) is that   **1–032**
the aid must be granted by a Member State or through State resources. According to the case law on this condition, there is no reason to distinguish between cases where aid is provided directly by the State, and cases where the aid is provided via public or private bodies designated or established by the State. However, for the advantages to be capable of being categorised as aid within the meaning of art.87(1) of the Treaty, they must, first, be granted directly or indirectly through State resources and, second, be imputable to the State.[36]

Aid which is provided from other resources but, on the basis of legislation, at the prompting of or under pressure from the State, cannot in principle constitute State aid which is in breach of the Treaty.[37] However, it can be difficult to draw the line so that, for example, resources from certain sectoral funds to which the State requires obligatory contributions to be made, will be regarded as State aid even if the resources are administered by institutions which are not the responsibility of a public authority; see Case 173/73, *Italy v Commission*, [1974] E.C.R. 709 paras 33–35.

It is clear that direct financial subsidies or, for example, selective tax reliefs given by the State will constitute State aid within the meaning of art.87(1). The same applies to aid provided by regional or local government authorities or public undertakings.[38]

The words in art.87(1) referring to aid "through State resources in any form whatsoever" are aimed at aid from public or private bodies that are designated or established by the State.[39]

---

[36] Case T-136/05, *EARL Salvat père & fils and Others v Commission*, (not yet reported in the E.C.R.); and Case C-345/02, *Pearle and Others v Hoofdbedrijfschap Ambachten*, [2004] E.C.R. I-7139. See also Case C-126/01, *Ministre de l'économie, des finances et de l'industrie v GEMO*, [2003] E.C.R. I-13769. This case is discussed, in relation to its clarification of the relationship between State resources and imputability by *Alain Alexis*: "La Cour de justice précise les notions de ressources d'État et d'imputabilité à l'État: l'affaire Pearle BV", in *Competition Policy Newsletter*, No.3, Autumn 2004 p. 24.

[37] Case C-379/98, *PreussenElektra*, [2001] E.C.R. I-2099; Case 82/77, *van Tiggele*, [1978] E.C.R. 25 paras 24 and 25; and Joined Cases C-72 and 73 /91, *Sloman Neptun*, [1993] E.C.R. I-887 para.19. In the *Preussen Elektra* case according to German legislation private electricity companies were obliged to buy electricity from undertakings producing electricity based on renewable energy sources at a minimum price set by the authorities.

[38] Case 284/84, *Germany v Commission*, [1987] E.C.R. 4013 para.17, which states that the words in art.87(1) that "any aid granted by a Member State or through State resources in any form whatsoever" are directed at all aid financed from public resources.

[39] See Joined Cases C-52/97, C-53/97 and C-54/97, *Viscido and Others*, [1998] E.C.R. I-2629 para.13, where it is stated that the distinction between "aid granted by a Member State" and

1–033   Exemption from general non-tax legislation does not amount to State aid since it does not lead to a transfer of State resources and does not therefore impose a burden on the State. An example of this is an arrangement whereby certain employees are exempted from a State's general legislation on employment and payment terms, even though this may have consequences for social welfare contributions and tax revenues.[40] On the other hand special tax treatment of specific commercial sectors or productions will constitute State aid.

If private bodies provide aid which is not derived from State resources and without the involvement of the State or a public body, this will not be State aid.[41]

What has been decisive for the application of art.87(1) concerning aid provided "through State resources in any form whatsoever" has been that it has thereby been possible to avoid Member States using structures whereby legislation imposes an obligation (perhaps only on certain undertakings or a specific sector[42]) to pay a charge to a separate fund, with the fund's resources thereafter being distributed by a public or private body in support of certain undertakings.

1–034   In all such cases, where resources are derived from the State in a broad sense and the conditions in art.87(1) are fulfilled, it will be found that State aid is involved. The provision is aimed at the decisions of the Member States where, with a view to fulfilling their own social and economic goals, they unilaterally and independently make financial means available for undertakings or citizens, or give them advantages which are intended to help the realisation of the social and economic goals. It must be possible to impute these advantages to the State before they will be characterised as State aid. Aid provided by means of State resources by public bodies or by private bodies designated or established by the State must be imputed to the State, i.e. the aid has been brought about by the State.[43] The purpose of the organ in question does not affect whether State aid exists, as long as the conditions in art.87(1) are fulfilled, including not least that there is provision of aid using State resources. If such a special body has independently decided to provide aid, then this will not be State aid

---

aid granted "through State resources" is intended to include not only advantages which are granted directly by the State, but also those granted by a public or private body designated or established by the State.

[40] Joined Cases C-72 and 73 /91, *Sloman Neptun*, [1993] E.C.R. I-887.

[41] Case 173/73, *Italy v Commission*, [1974] E.C.R. 709.

[42] See for example the fur breeders fund which provided aid to Danish fur breeders; Commission Decision (OJ 1994 C 50/2).

[43] Case T-351/02, *Deutsche Bahn v Commission*, [2006] E.C.R. II-1047. See also Joined Cases 67, 68 and 70/85, *van der Kooy*, [1988] E.C.R. 219 paras 32–38, which concerned the approval of a preferential tariff provided by the Dutch company Gasunie. The company was 50% publicly owned, but in the judgment the emphasis was on the fact that the State controlled the gas price, and that the aid was not commercially based and apparently not based (or not so much based) on the ownership circumstances. In addition, to a certain extent there was in fact State aid through State resources, since the State owned 50% of Gasunie. The judgment is not absolutely clear. See also Case C-305/89, *Italy v Commission* (Alfa Romeo), [1991] E.C.R. I-1603 paras 11–16.

within the meaning of the Treaty.[44] In his Opinion in Case C-482/99, *France v Commission* (the *Stardust Marine* case), Advocate General Jacobs emphasised that it is not easy to decide whether some aid can be imputed to a State, but he provides four tests which can be used in this connection, namely:

- evidence that the measure was taken at the instigation of the State;
- the scale and nature of the measure (including reference to what a private investor/creditor would have done);
- the degree of control of the State over the public undertaking in question; and
- the existence of a general practice under which the State uses the undertaking in question for other than commercial ends or whether in practice the State influences its decisions.

The Advocate General emphasised that a restrictive approach should be used in this respect; in other words, the authorities should not make too great demands for evidence of the existence of State aid, having regard for the difficulties in obtaining evidence and the risks of evasion.

In the *Stardust Marine* case, basing itself on points of view like those of the Advocate General, the ECJ stated that it is not sufficient for imputing a measure to the State that a measure has been adopted by a public undertaking. The fact that a public undertaking is subject to State control is not in itself sufficient to impute to the State the measures taken, such as financial support. It is also necessary to investigate whether the public authorities are involved in one way or another in the adoption of the measure in question. According to the ECJ, it is also necessary to examine the circumstances of the case as a whole, and the context in which the decision has been taken. The assessment of this will include whether the public undertaking is integrated into the structures of the public administration, the nature of its activities and the exercise of the latter on the market in normal conditions of competition with private operators, the legal status of the undertaking (whether subject to public law or private law), the intensity of the supervision exercised by the public authorities over the management of the undertaking, or any other indicator showing an involvement by the public authorities in the adoption of a measure or the probability of their being involved, having regard also to the compass of the measure, its content or the conditions which it contains.[45]

Thus it is not possible to get round the rules on State aid by arranging for aid to be given via a public undertaking, a trust or, for example, by requiring

1–035

---

[44] Case C-305/89, *Italy v Commission* (*Alfa Romeo*), [1991] E.C.R. I-1603 paras 11–16. Both Commission and the ECJ found that the aid could be imputed to the State. See also the judgment in Case T-358/94, *Air France v Commission*, [1996] E.C.R. II-2109; and Case C-83/98 P, *Ladbroke Racing*, [2000] E.C.R. I-3271.

[45] See Case C-482/99, *France v Commission* (the *Stardust Marine* case), [2002] E.C.R. I-4397; as well as Joined Cases 67, 68 and 70/8, *van der Kooy and Others v Commission*, [1988] E.C.R. 219; Case C-303/88, *Italy v Commission*, [1991] E.C.R. I-1433; and Case C-305/89, *Italy v Commission*, [1991] E.C.R. I-1603.

a public undertaking to invest in activities which are untenable from a normal market-based perspective.[46]

State resources is a term which covers all the financial means by which the public sector may actually support undertakings, irrespective of whether or not those means are permanent assets of the public sector.[47] It is not necessary for the financial means to belong to the State treasury, as it is sufficient for regarding them as State resources that they constantly remain under public control, and are therefore available to the competent national authorities.[48]

Furthermore, as stated above, aid which is financed by parafiscal charges imposed on categories of undertakings which receive aid via the revenue from the charges constitutes State aid. If such charges are also levied on imports, there can also be an infringement of the prohibition of measures having an equivalent effect to a quantitative restriction on imports (see art.28 of the EC Treaty), if the aid is only paid to domestic undertakings; see Ch.5 for a more detailed discussion of this.

Tax rebates for certain undertakings will also constitute State aid; see Commission notice on the application of the State aid rules to measures relating to direct business taxation (OJ 1998 C 384/3), where loss of tax revenue is considered as equivalent to the use of State resources.

1–036   Special provisions for the administration of (large) insolvent undertakings constitute State aid in so far as there is a use of State resources and there is selectivity; see Case C-200/97, *Ecotrade*, [1998] E.C.R. I-7907 paras 40 and 41.

According to the practice of the ECJ, see Case C-379/98 *PreussenElektra v Schleswag*, and the subsequent practice of the Community courts it seems no longer possible to maintain that aid provided by means of differentiated tariffs on, for example, prices for gas and electricity will constitute State aid which is in breach of the Treaty, as such aid cannot be said to involve State resources. The opposite had previously been the view of the ECJ and the Commission: see Joined Cases 67, 68 and 70/8, *van der Kooy and Others v Commission*, [1988] E.C.R. 219; Case 290/83, *Commission v France*, [1985] E.C.R. 439; and Case 57/86, *Greece v Commission*, [1988] E.C.R. 2855.[49] If, however, a preferential

---

[46] Case T-358/94, *Air France v Commission*, [1996] E.C.R. II-2109, para.62, where it is stated that "Community law cannot permit the rules on State aid to be circumvented merely through the creation of autonomous institutions charged with allocating aid." See also Case C-482/99, *France v Commission* (the *Stardust Marine* case), [2002] E.C.R. I-4397.

[47] Case T-358/94, *Air France v Commission*, [1996] E.C.R. II-2109 para.67.

[48] Case C-482/99, *France v Commission* (the *Stardust Marine* case), [2002] E.C.R. I-4397. See also Case T-358/94, *Air France v Commission*, [1996] E.C.R. II-2109. In this latter case the court held that State resources were involved, even if the finances in question were derived from private investors who could withdraw their investments. However, the fund established by the legislation was free to apportion the surplus as if the investments were financed by means of taxes and compulsory contributions. In Case T-67/94, *Ladbroke Racing v Commission*, [1998] E.C.R. II-1, the CFI found that the uncollected winnings from betting constitute State resources since such amounts were payable to the State treasury.

[49] In connection with an amendment to the Danish Law on electricity supply, the Commission found that the Law's provisions for accounting for the losses from the electricity companies' subordinate commercial activities (e.g. tomato cultivation, fish farming) in the price of electricity by means of cross-subsidisation constituted State aid, even though the rules applied

tariff, i.e. a gas tariff that discriminates between various groups of purchasers is introduced by a State owned or controlled company, and a normal market investor in a similar situation would not apply such a tariff, but the tariff seeks to help certain enterprises to avoid eceonomic difficulties such a tariff would constitute incompatible State aid.

Even though most of the judgments since 1988 have applied the narrow definition applied in the *Sloman Neptun* case, in the legal literature it has been pointed out that there are difficulties with regard to the definition of State aid, among other things as a consequence of the judgment in Case C-83/98 P, *Ladbroke Racing*, [2000] E.C.R. I-3271, and examples have been given of how, by considering it decisive that State aid must involve the use of State resources, the ECJ has made evasion possible.[50]

It is possible, nevertheless, to conclude that, in the light of the development of the law since the judgment in the *PreussenElektra* case for State aid to be found there must be aid, meaning the conferring of an advantage, that is provided directly or indirectly through State resources, or which constitutes a supplementary burden for the State or for bodies designated or established by the State for that purpose.

to the whole of the electricity sector and not merely to publicly owned electricity companies. The Commission's view was clearly based on the idea that favouring a company via public authority approval of electricity prices could constitute State aid, regardless of whether State resources are involved. After the *PreussenElektra* case and subsequent rulings of the courts it no longer seems possible to maintain such a view. As for parafiscal funds, i.e. funds financed by means of charges imposed on a group of undertakings which, under certain circumstances, can obtain aid via an aid arrangement which is financed by the fund, the question of whether such funds must be regarded as being covered by the ruling in the *PreussenElektra* case depends on whether the resources in funds controlled by the State constitute permanent assets of the State. If they do, then State aid will be found to exist, in contrast to a situation such as that in the *PreussenElektra* case where the resources were transferred directly from a private undertaking to the recipient. In general in relation to this question, see the judgment in Case 290/83, *Commission v France*, [1985] E.C.R. 439, concerning aid from a publicly controlled fund for the benefit of French farmers, where it was considered sufficient to constitute State aid that the aid, which was provided private means, was controlled by the State. This result would seem not to be possible following the *PreussenElektra* case.

[50] See the instructive commentary on the judgment in the *PreussenElektra* case by *Ann Goossens & Sam Emmerechts* in CML. Rev., Vol.38, August 2001 pp. 991–1010. Among other things, it is pointed out that both broad and narrow definitions of the concept of State aid cover advantages financed by public funds at the disposal of the public authorities, but they differ in that a broad definition of the concept of State aid would also cover advantages financed by private resources The authors in question are of the view that it can be difficult to distinguish between cases covered by one or the other of the definitions, as it is possible to adopt a more or less broad definition of the term "public funds" and the term "at the disposal of the public authorities". See, e.g., fn.17 of the CML. Rev. commentary referred to, at p.1001. See also *Leigh Hancher* in CML. Rev. Vol.39, No.4, August 2002, where among other things there is a discussion of whether the ruling in Case 83/98 P, *France v Ladbroke Racing and Commission* (cf. the appeal of the CFI's judgment in Case T-67/94, *Ladbroke Racing*, [1998] E.C.R. II-1) constitutes an alternative to the ruling in the *PreussenElektra* case. *Hancher* finds that this is not so, emphasising that the *PreussenElektra* case concerned the first element in art.87(1), namely State aid, while the *Ladbroke Racing* case concerned the second element, namely aid granted through State resources in any form whatsoever. *Hancher* concludes that there is a need for a clear definition and limitation of the concept of State aid in art.87(1). See the same author in Leigh Hancher, Tom Ottervanger & Piet Jan Slot in *EC State Aids*, 3rd edition, Sweet & Maxwell, 2006.

In Joined Cases 213 to 215/81, *Norddeutsches Vieh- und fleischkontor*, the ECJ held that a Member State's incorrect granting of a quota fell outside the scope of art.87, as the levy which was waived constituted Community resources, and not State resources.[51]

The form of the aid is not decisive

1-037   The form of the aid is not decisive; see art.87(1) which refers to aid granted through State resources in any form whatsoever. If the form were decisive, the prohibition of State aid could easily be avoided. Obviously, true subsidies will be covered by the prohibition in art.87(1). However, aid can come in different guises, such as interest free loans, loans at below market interest rates, loans with interest credit, guarantees on favourable terms, selective tax rebates or similar measures, the provision of goods or services on advantageous terms and capital investments on terms that would not be acceptable to private market investors etc. Even if the form of these examples may vary, they will all give some advantage to the favoured undertaking which can have negative effects on trade and competition. It is for this reason that the form of the aid is not decisive for whether a measure is covered by the prohibition in art.87(1). The same applies if the State provides aid via bodies designated or established by the State. Nor is it decisive for the purposes of art.87(1) whether it is the State itself (or administrative bodies of the State) that actually provides the aid, or whether the State establishes a special body for the purposes of allocating the State aid.

According to the judgment in Case C-21/88, *Du Pont de Nemours*, [1990] E.C.R. I-889 para.20, the fact that a national measure might be regarded as aid within the meaning of art.92 (now 87) is not a sufficient reason to exempt it from the prohibition contained in art.30 (now 28).[52] The ECJ rules that in no circumstances could art.92 [now 87] serve as a basis for the suspension of the Treaty provisions on the free movement of goods.[53]

Compensation and payment

1-038   Compensation (damages) paid by the State is not regarded as being State aid. Thus, the ECJ has held that damages paid by the State for losses resulting from acts of the State which incur liability do not constitute State aid; see Joined Cases 106 to 120/87, *Asteris and Others v Greece and the EEC*, [1988] E.C.R.

---

[51] [1982] E.C.R. 3583.
[52] The case concerned a requirement for Italian authorities to make 30% of their purchases from undertakings in Southern Italy.
[53] Case 103/84, *Commission v Italy*, [1986] E.C.R. 1759, concerning an Italian measure granting a 20% subsidy for the purchase of vehicles, provided the undertakings concerned acquired vehicles manufactured in Italy. According to the ECJ this constituted a measure having an equivalent effect to a quantitative restriction on imports; para.19 of the judgment repeated para.20 from the judgment in the *Du Pont de Nemours* case.

5515. On the other hand this would constitute State aid if the damages were paid to compensate for loss of economic advantages or rights which would in themselves constitute State aid. Compensation paid in connection with compulsory purchase will not normally be considered State aid.

Repayment of overpaid tax or of charges which are incompatible with national law or EU law is obviously not State aid; see Case 61/79 *Denkavit*, [1979] E.C.R. 1205.

The same applies to fees paid by the State, to undertakings which provide some service, for example the collection of environmentally harmful substances etc., but this naturally presumes that the fee paid for the service is reasonable and commercially justifiable in relation to the service provided. It can be that an undertaking provides some service in return for a service which the State provides to the undertaking. It must be possible to categorise such service provision as a market transaction, otherwise if, for example, an undertaking pays a lower interest rate for a loan, it may be said to have received an advantage which may constitute State aid.

Distorts or threatens to distort competition

In contrast to art.81 of the EC Treaty, which contains a prohibition of agreements which have as their object or effect the prevention, restriction or distortion of competition, art.87(1) only refers to aid which distorts or threatens to distort competition by favouring certain undertakings or the production of certain goods, so that these are given advantages over their competitors.   **1–039**

Thus, it is not a requirement under the prohibition in art.87 that it should be the object of the aid that it should distort competition. There can very well be an unintended infringement of art.87(1). Under art.87 it is not even a condition that the aid must have the consequence of distorting competition. It is sufficient that the aid measures should threaten to do so. See also paras 1–044 to 1–047.

Favouring

Article 87(1) expresses that it is a condition for State aid to be found to exist that the measures in question should favour certain undertakings or the production of certain goods. It is not just any advantage which can be found to constitute State aid within the meaning of art.87(1); see for example the judgment in Case C-353/95 P, *Tiercé Ladbroke*, [1997] E.C.R. I-7007 (at p.7021). There must be an abnormal or unfair element in the provision of the advantage for the condition of favouring to be regarded as fulfilled.[54] The ECJ has stated that the concept of State aid can encompass not only positive benefits such   **1–040**

---

[54] See Ross, CML. Rev., April 2000, Vol.37, p.411, who points to the problem of finding the right *comparator* (undertaking to compare with), when assessing the scope of the advantage. See, e.g., Case C-342/96, *Spain v Commission*, [1999] E.C.R. I-2459.

as subsidies, loans or direct investment in the capital of enterprises, but also interventions which, in various forms such as the supply of goods or services on preferential terms, mitigate the charges which are normally included in the budget of an undertaking and which therefore, without being subsidies in the strict sense of the word, are of the same character and have the same effect.[55]

An assessment of a given financing measure in the light of the market economy investor principle, which is discussed in more detail in paras 6–004 to 6–010, could be a useful method for evaluating whether there is favouring which constitutes aid within the meaning of the Treaty.

Certain undertakings or the production of certain goods

1–041   Article 87(1) of the EC Treaty prohibits aid that favours certain undertakings or the production of certain goods, i.e. selective aid. According to the case law, there is a requirement for a determination of whether a State measure which is part of a specific legal measure can favour "certain undertakings or the production of certain goods" in relation to other undertakings which, with regard to the aim of the measure in question, find themselves in a corresponding actual or legal situation. If this found to be the case, then the measure will be found to be selective.[56]

According to the established practice, the term "undertaking" covers any entity which carries on some economic activity, regardless of the entity's legal status or method of financing.[57] In this connection it does not matter whether an undertaking is carried on for profit. The ownership of shares in another undertaking, including controlling shares, does not mean that there is an undertaking for the purposes of art.87(1), if the ownership of shares is only the basis for the exercise of the rights normally associated with being a shareholder and the receipt of dividends. On the other hand, an entity which owns a controlling share of a company and does in fact exercise this control by direct or indirect intervention in the running of the company is regarded as a participant in the commercial undertaking which is carried on by the controlled company and it is therefore also an undertaking for the purposes of art.87(1).[58] The concept of an undertaking does not include bodies that are responsible for the administration of certain legally required social security arrangements that are based on the principle of social solidarity.[59]

---

[55] Case C-126/01, *Ministère de l'Économie, des finances et de l'Industrie v GEMO*, [2003] E.C.R. I-13769.

[56] Case C-172/03, *Wolfgang Heiser v finanzamt Innsbruck*, [2005] E.C.R. I-01627; and Case C-88/03, *Portugal v Commission*, [2006] E.C.R. I-7115.

[57] Joined Cases C-180/98 to C-184/98, *Pavel Pavlov and Others v Stichting Pensioenfonds Medische Specialisten*, [2000] E.C.R. I-6451, which considers the status of a pension fund as an undertaking.

[58] Case C-222/04, *Ministero dell'Economia e delle finanze v Cassa di Risparmio di firenze and Others*, [2006] E.C.R. I-289.

[59] Joined Cases C-180/98 to C-184/98, *Pavel Pavlov and Others v Stichting Pensioenfonds Medische Specialisten*, [2000] E.C.R. I-6451.

Aid to certain undertakings refers not only to aid to certain identifiable or even named individual undertakings, but also to groups of undertakings or different categories of undertakings. For example, State aid can be directed to IT undertakings, to exporting undertakings, or to undertakings which fulfil certain goals with regard to the avoidance of pollution or the provision of a healthy work environment. Aid can be given in the form of energy subsidies to certain groups, or specially low energy tariffs, for example to market gardeners or farmers if the preferential tariffs are given by publicly owned energy companies.

Aid for the production of certain goods can consist, for example, of aid for the manufacture of furniture. If, for example, a public body provides for the manufacture of bricks in order to support the construction industry and raise living conditions or the possibility of getting a home, such aid will be unlawful aid in breach of art.87(1), but on the other hand it would be legally possible to give aid in the form of help for individual citizens to acquire a home (for example, in the form of housing benefits; see art.87(2)(a)). **1–042**

As stated, art.87(1) only comes into play if the condition of selectivity is fulfilled. Thus, general arrangements for taxation, charges, tax deduction measures which can be regarded as general tax or economic policy measures fall outside the scope of art.87(1).[60]

Aid can be selective, even if it covers the whole of an economic sector.[61]

However, an aid measure which constitutes a benefit for the recipient (for the whole of an economic sector) will not be considered selective if it is justified by the nature or structure of the measure of which it forms part.[62]

General aid arrangements, such as aid for consultancy advice for undertakings, will not be selective if they are based on objective criteria and apply to all undertakings in a Member State. However, if such aid is only provided to small and medium sized enterprises this could be a selective measure which may fall within the category of forms of aid which can be given in accordance with specific provisions adopted by the Commission.[63] The question of selection **1–043**

---

[60] Case C-148/04, *Unicredito Italiano v Agenzia delle Entrate Ufficio Genova 1*, [2005] E.C.R. I-11137. See also Case C-66/02, *Italy v Commission*, [2005] E.C.R. I-10901; and Case C-222/04, *Ministero dell'Economia e delle finanze v Cassa di Risparmio di firenze and Others*, [2006] E.C.R. I-289. Case C-88/03, *Portugal v Commission*, [2006] E.C.R. I-7115 is also highly illustrative in relation to tax reductions and selectivity. On the problem of selectivity in relation to taxation, see also *Rados Horacek*: "Commission's negative decision on Gibraltar corporation tax reform: findings on regional and material selectivity", in *Competition Policy Newsletter*, No.2, Summer 2004 p. 97.

[61] Case C-148/04, *Unicredito Italiano v Agenzia delle Entrate Ufficio Genova 1*, [2005] E.C.R. I-11137, which includes references to other cases on the question. See also Case C-172/03, *Wolfgang Heiser v finanzamt Innsbruck*, [2005] E.C.R. I-01627.

[62] Case C-172/03, *Wolfgang Heiser v finanzamt Innsbruck*, [2005] E.C.R. I-01627, with references to the cases on this question. See also Case 308/01, *GIL Insurance and Others v Commissioners of Customs & Excise*, [2004] E.C.R. I-4777.

[63] One should beware of general aid to which all undertakings have a right in principle, if administrative authorities are given some discretion with regard to the intensity of the aid and its payment; see Case C-241/94, *France v Commission (Kimberly Clark)*, [1996] E.C.R. I-4551, paras 23 and 24.

can arise in a special form where, for example, a regional or local authority decides on tax reductions which only apply within the area of that authority in the Member State in question. Such a measure, which only grants a benefit in that part of the national territory is not selective for this reason alone. On this question the ECJ has stated that it is possible that an infra-State body may enjoy a legal and factual status which makes it sufficiently autonomous in relation to the central government of a Member State, so that it is that body and not the central government which plays a fundamental role in the definition of the political and economic environment in which undertakings operate. In such a case it is the area in which the infra-State body responsible for the measure exercises its powers, and not the country as a whole, that constitutes the relevant context for assessing whether a measure adopted by such a body favours certain undertakings in comparison with others in a comparable legal and factual situation, having regard to the objective pursued by the measure or the legal system concerned.[64] However, the question is when such a body has a sufficient measure of autonomy. In this connection the ECJ has stated that the national constitution must give the regional or local authority political and economic status which differs from that of the central government. In addition to this, the decision on the measure in question must be taken without the central government being able to intervene in its content. Finally, the economic consequences of the measure—for example reduced tax rates which apply to undertakings situated in the region—cannot be made up for by contributions from other regions or the central government. Thus, sufficient autonomy requires that the infra-State body has the authority to take decisions within its geographic area independently of any considerations connected with the conduct of the central government, and the body is responsible for the political and economic consequences of a decision, for example, to reduce tax rates. If these conditions are not fulfilled, the aid measure will presumably usually be selective. In this case however, as mentioned above, it will be the selective element, in the form of a tax reduction in a limited area in the Member State which may be justified by the nature or overall structure of the tax system. In this case, the Member State in question may show that that measure results directly from the basic or guiding principles of its tax system.[65]

Sometimes attempts can be made to disguise State aid. This can be the case if an arrangement which is formally speaking a general arrangement in fact only means that an individual group or individual groups of undertakings benefit. This was the situation in a case concerning payroll contributions, where there was a provision that undertakings that employed women should in general pay lower contributions. The Commission considered that this was State aid because in fact it amounted to aid for the textile industry in Italy where the overwhelming majority of those employed were women. The

---

[64] Case C-88/03, *Portugal v Commission*, [2006] E.C.R. I-7115. The case is discussed in the Commission's Report on Competition Policy 2006, p.142.
[65] Case C-88/03, *Portugal v Commission*, [2006] E.C.R. I-7115 para.81.

Commission found that a reduction for women employees was not justified on the basis of the nature and overall structure of the contribution system.[66]

General arrangements (often relating to support for employment), which involve administrative discretion with regard to who shall receive aid and how much, will also constitute the provision of State in breach of art.87(1) of the Treaty.[67] [68]

The effect on trade between Member States and the distortion of competition

Article 87(1) prohibits aid that affects trade between Member States and   **1–044**
distorts or threatens to distort competition. According to the case law of the ECJ, in assessing these two conditions the Commission does not have to show that the aid does in fact affect trade between Member States and in fact distorts competition.[69] The Commission need only examine whether the aid *can* affect trade and *can* distort competition.[70] This means that aid will be incompatible with the common market if it has or can have an effect on trade between Member States and distorts or can distort competition in this trade.[71]

Normally it does not take much for the Commission to consider that aid which distorts or threatens to distort competition is aid which actually or potentially affects trade.[72]

According to the ECJ, when an advantage which is granted by a Member State strengthens the position of an undertaking in relation to other undertakings with which it competes in trade within the common market, it must be assumed that the trade will be affected by this advantage.[73] The fact that the aid given is relatively insignificant, or that the beneficiary undertaking is only small does not immediately mean that trade between Member States cannot be affected. Other factors can play a decisive role in assessing what effect an aid measure has upon trade, including especially whether the aid is cumula-

---

[66] On the question of payroll contributions, see the Commission Decision of September 15, 1980, OJ 1980 L 264/28; and Case 203/82, *Italy v Commission*, [1983] E.C.R. 2525.
[67] Case C-241/94, *France v Commission*, [1996] E.C.R. I-4551.
[68] Case C-200/97, *Ecotrade*, [1998] E.C.R. I-7907 para.40.
[69] Case C-148/04, *Unicredito Italiano v Agenzia delle Entrate Ufficio Genova 1*, [2005] E.C.R. I-11137.
[70] *Unicredito Italiano v Agenzia delle Entrate Ufficio Genova 1*, [2005] E.C.R. I-11137.
[71] *Unicredito Italiano v Agenzia delle Entrate Ufficio Genova 1*, [2005] E.C.R. I-11137.
[72] Joined Cases T-298/97 and Others, *Alzetta Mauro and Others v Commission*, [2000] E.C.R. II-2319 para.73 gives a good insight into the circumstance where the aid in question operates solely at local, regional and national levels etc. The case was appealed to the ECJ, which rejected the appeal; see Case C-298/00 P, *Italy v Commission*, [2004] E.C.R. I-4087. See also *Melvin Könings*: "State aid and the effect on trade criterion. The Netherlands: measures in favour of non-profit harbours for recreational crafts", in *Competition Policy Newsletter*, No.1, Spring 2004 p.86.
[73] Case C-53/00, *Ferring*, [2001] E.C.R. I-9067. See also Case 730/79, *Philip Morris v Commission*, [1980] E.C.R. 2671 para.11.

tive and whether the recipient undertakings operate within a sector which is particularly subject to competition.[74] Even relatively modest aid can affect competition and trade between Member States when there is keen competition in the sector in which the beneficiary undertakings are active.[75] Aid to an undertaking which only operates at a regional or local level can also affect trade between Member States.[76] The ECJ has also stated that the fact that an economic sector has been liberalised at Community level is an element which may serve to determine that the aid has a real or potential effect on competition and on trade between Member States.[77]

It is not necessary to show that the favoured undertaking is involved in importing or exporting.[78] If a Member State gives aid to an undertaking, its domestic activities may be maintained or strengthened, and this will thereby weaken the opportunities of undertakings in other Member States to become established on that Member State's market. Conversely, the strengthening of an undertaking which has not hitherto participated in trade between Member States could enable it to become established on the market of another Member State.[79]

1–045   The fact that other undertakings may receive aid (even unlawful aid) will not normally[80] justify the favouring of an undertaking in some way in order to even out other distortions of competition.[81] The fact that a Member State seeks, by instituting unilateral measures, to approximate the conditions for competition within a specific sector of the economy to the conditions which apply in the other Member States does not mean that such measures lose the character of aid, and does not mean that such measures do not distort or threaten to distort competition.[82] In principle there will be a distortion of competition as soon as aid is given which relieves an undertaking from costs which it would normally have borne for its normal running and customary activities.[83] Other competitive advantages can of course also be sufficient.[84]

The Community courts have adopted the view that there are reasons for keeping separate the terms *distortion of competition* and *affecting trade*, even though giving a modest benefit to an undertaking would not appear to have

---

[74] Case C-113/00, *Spain v Commission*, [2002] E.C.R. I-7601.
[75] Case C-298/00 P, *Italy v Commission*, [2004] E.C.R. I-4087. See also Case T-217/02, *Ter Lembeek International v Commission*, [2006] E.C.R. II-04483. The case has been appealed to the ECJ; see Case C-28/07 P, but has later been withdrawn.
[76] Case C-280/00, *Altmark Trans and Regierungspräsidium Magdeburg v Nahverkehrsgesellschaft Altmark*, [2003] E.C.R. I-7747.
[77] Case C-148/04, *Unicredito Italiano v Agenzia delle Entrate Ufficio Genova 1*, [2005] E.C.R. I-11137.
[78] *Unicredito Italiano v Agenzia delle Entrate Ufficio Genova 1*, [2005] E.C.R. I-11137.
[79] *Unicredito Italiano v Agenzia delle Entrate Ufficio Genova 1*, [2005] E.C.R. I-11137.
[80] However, see Case C-56/93, *Belgium v Commission*, [1996] E.C.R. 723, on a preferential gas tariff and consideration for competition from abroad, where the ECJ accepted that competition from abroad could be taken into consideration.
[81] Cf. Ross, CML. Rev. vol.37, April 2000 p.415.
[82] Case C-172/03, *Wolfgang Heiser v finanzamt Innsbruck*, [2005] E.C.R. I-1627.
[83] Case C-172/03, *Wolfgang Heiser v finanzamt Innsbruck*, [2005] E.C.R. I-1627.
[84] Case C-66/02, *Italy v Commission*, [2005] E.C.R. I-10901.

any, or any notable, effect on trade between Member States.[85] However, these two conditions normally go hand-in-hand.[86]

With regard to the condition that there must be some effect, there is no requirement for an investigation or detailed analysis of the product market and the geographic market, as is required with the application of the EU's competition rules in relation to agreements that restrict competition or the abuse of a dominant position on the market.[87] Another difference from the competition rules just referred to is that with State aid it is sufficient to show that an aid measure threatens to distort competition.

However, according to the case law, in its dealing with State aid cases   **1–046** the Commission must always examine the effect of the aid on the market affected.[88]

The Commission has a duty to examine what effect an actual aid measure could have on competitive conditions and future trade, even if, when the aid is paid, there is no trade between the Member State concerned and the other Member States with regard to the products which the aid concerns.[89]

EXCEPTIONS IN ART.87(2)

The forms of aid referred to in art.87(2), i.e. aid having a social character   **1–047** granted to individual consumers, aid to make good the damage caused by natural disasters, and aid granted to the economy of certain areas of the Federal Republic of Germany affected by the division of Germany, are automatically compatible with the common market; there is a legal right to provide such aid, but such aid must be notified to the Commission.[90] The Commission must approve such aid if it finds that the stated conditions as well as the principle of proportionality are complied with.

(a) Consumer support

According to art.87(2)(a), aid having a social character granted to individual   **1–048** consumers must be compatible with the common market, as long as it is

---

[85] Case T-214/95, *Vlaams Gewest*, [1998] E.C.R. II-717.

[86] Joined Cases T-298/97 and others, *Alzetta Mauro and Others v Commission*, [2000] E.C.R. II-2319. The case was appealed to the ECJ, which rejected the appeal; see Case C-298/00 P, *Italy v Commission*, [2004] E.C.R. I-4087.

[87] However, see paras 69–73 in Case C-105/99, *Conseil des communes et régions d'Europe (CCRE) v Commission*, (see Joined Cases C-15/98 and C-105/99, [2000] E.C.R. I-8855), where the ECJ did not find the Commission's explanation of its decision with regard to the effect on sailings to Sardinia was sufficient to satisfy the requirement in art.253 of the EC Treaty for a statement of reasons.

[88] Case 284/84, *Germany v Commission*, [1987] E.C.R. 4013, para.21; and Joined Cases 296 and 318/82, *Netherlands and Leeuwarder Papierwarenfabriek v Commission*, [1985] E.C.R. 809 para.24.

[89] Joined Cases T-447/93, T-448/93 and T-449/93, *Associazione Italiana Tecnico Economica del Cemento (AITEC) v Commission*, [1995] E.C.R. II-1971.

[90] Leigh Hancher, *EC State Aids*, 3rd ed., Sweet & Maxwell 2006. Hancher questions whether aid having a social character granted to individual consumers must be notified.

granted without discrimination related to the origin of the products concerned. The use of the formulation "shall be compatible" shows that the Commission does not have discretion to approve such aid. It must be approved in principle, as long as the criteria for the exception are fulfilled.

The aim in this respect is to give aid to one or more specific social groups, for example for the purchase of certain kinds of goods such as foods. As long as the aid in question is given without regard for whether the foods come from the Member State giving the aid, this will be compatible with the common market. The same may apply with regard to services, even though this term is not explicitly included in the Treaty text. Here the term *consumers* refers to end users and not to traders.[91]

In general, social benefits paid to all consumers or citizens fall outside the scope of art.87(2)(a) as such support does not fulfil the conditions regarding selectivity in art.87(1). What art.87(2)(a) concerns is aid which in one way or another can promote certain undertakings or products but which will nevertheless be permitted because of its purpose.

1–049   In its XXIV Report on competition policy (para.354) the Commission states that the discrimination referred to in art.87(2)(a) concerning the origin of goods refers to the geographic origin of the goods or services or their suppliers and not to the aid for consumers' acquisition of different types of products (for example, aid for the purchase of electricity rather than gas or oil).

(b) Aid in the event of natural disasters or other exceptional occurrences

Article 87(2)(b) states that "aid to make good the damage caused by natural disasters or exceptional occurrences" shall be compatible with the common market.

While it will not be difficult to establish with a reasonable degree of certainty when there is a natural disaster, and therefore a right to provide aid, there is less certainty about what is covered by the term "exceptional occurrences". Presumably it refers to events such as war, as well as terrorist actions, widespread epidemics, nuclear accidents and suchlike.

The approval of State aid to airlines for losses associated with the closing of airspace between September 11 and 14, 2001 and for the increase in insurance premiums after the terrorist attack on the World Trade Centre in New York are typical examples of the application of art.87(2)(b); see for example Decision IP/02/395.

The provision is an exception to the prohibition of State aid in art.87(1) and it must therefore be given a narrow interpretation. The scope of application for art.87(2)(b) is limited to damage which is directly caused by natural disasters or other exceptional occurrences. There must therefore be a direct connection between the damage which is caused by the exceptional occurrence and the aid, and it is necessary to give as precise a valuation as possible of the

---

[91] For an illustration of the application of art.87(2)(a) see Joined Cases C-442/03 P and C-471/03 P, *P & O European Ferries (Vizcaya) v Commission*, [2006] E.C.R. I-4845. See also the discussion of this case in the Commission's Report on Competition Policy 2003, at p.143.

damage which the intended recipient of the aid has suffered.[92] The aid must in fact correspond to the damage which the recipient has suffered as a result of the natural disaster or exceptional occurrence.[93]

In connection with serious flooding in Germany and Austria in the summer of 2005, the Commission applied art.87(2)(b) to approve State aid for the damage caused by the floods. In this connection the Commission stated as follows in its Report on Competition Policy 2005:

> "The Commission decided in all notified cases not to raise objections and to approve the aid on the basis of Article 87(2)(b). The Commission based its assessment on the following 'guiding principles': in order to avoid a situation where an enterprise would be better off after receiving aid for a natural disaster, overcompensation had to be strictly ruled out, therefore only material damage caused directly by the natural disaster was considered eligible and the maximum compensation of 100% of these costs was not exceeded in any of the cases. To verify that overcompensation was effectively ruled out, a centralised and institutionalised surveillance mechanism needed to be in place to determine to what extent the damage might have been covered by insurance and to guarantee that the maximum possible support was not exceeded. In all cases the concept of damage was based on refinancing costs and/or replacement value. Incurred losses and foregone profits associated with temporary interruptions in the production process and with the loss of orders, customers or markets were not considered to be eligible."

(c) Aid granted to the economy of certain areas of the Federal Republic of Germany affected by the division of Germany

This is no longer so relevant following the reunification of Germany.[94] **1–050**
However, as stated above in paras 1–002 and 1–003, the provision has been used a couple of times since reunification. Aid to the areas in question will now be dealt with on the basis of art.87(3).

However, it can be pointed out that the ECJ has ruled that the words "division of Germany" refer historically to the establishment of the border between the two occupation zones in 1948, and that "the economic disadvantages caused by that division" therefore only covers the economic disadvantages which, in certain German regions, were caused by the isolation that followed from the establishment of this physical border, such as the exclusion from hinterland areas, or the loss of natural sales opportunities following the disturbance of

---

[92] Joined Cases C-346/03 and C-529/03, *Giuseppe Atzeni and Others v Regione autonoma della Sardegna*. See also Case T-171/02, *Regione autonoma della Sardegna v Commission*, [2005] E.C.R. II-2123.

[93] Case C-278/00, *Greece v Commission*, [2004] E.C.R. I-3997; and Case C-73/03, *Spain v Commission*, Judgment of November 11, 2004. The case has been dismissed.

[94] Case C-156/98, *Germany v Commission*, [2000] E.C.R. I-6857.

trading connections between the two areas of Germany. Thus, it is the view of the ECJ that art.87(2)(c) cannot be interpreted so as to cover situations which have not arisen as a direct consequence of the previous existence of an internal border in Germany, but which are to a large degree the concrete result of the economic policies followed by the German Democratic Republic.[95]

EXCEPTIONS IN ART.87(3)

1–051   As usual with regard to the interpretation of exceptions under Community law, the exceptions in art.87(3) of the EC Treaty must be interpreted narrowly. According to the Commission, it is a condition for aid which is approved on the basis of art.87(3) that: the aid must promote development in the EU as a whole, the aid must be necessary for the promotion of the development in question, and the aid given must be reasonable in relation to its purpose, having regard to its duration, intensity and the risk of moving a problem from one Member State to another, as well as the degree of distortion of competition etc.[96]

It has also been established that aid of the kind referred to in art.87(3) only contributes to the fulfilment of the goals laid down in art.87(3) if it can be shown that the favoured undertakings would not be able to achieve the goals in question under normal market conditions.[97]

This provision deals with aid which the Commission may consider to be compatible with the common market, despite the prohibition of State aid in art.87(1). According to the established case law of the Community courts, the Commission has a wide degree of discretion[98] with regard to the approval of such aid; see the use of the wording "*may* consider to be compatible", while the wording of art.87(2) refers to exceptions which *shall* be found compatible with the common market.

1–052   The Commission's discretion with regard to the evaluation of the relevant complex economic and socio-economic circumstances means that the ECJ's review of whether this discretion is exercised correctly cannot be a substitute for the discretion of the competent authorities (i.e. the Commission) with its own discretion. The ECJ's judicial review is therefore limited to judging whether the discretion is clearly wrong, or whether it amounts to an abuse of power.[99]

The exceptions in art.87(3) relate to regional aid, projects of common European interest, remedying serious disturbances in the economy of a Member State, facilitating the development of certain economic activities or of certain economic areas, and aid to promote culture and heritage conservation.

---

[95] Case C-301/96, *Germany v Commission*, [2003] E.C.R. I-9919.
[96] The Commission's XXI Report on Competition Policy, 1991. Case 730/79, *Philip Morris v Commission*, [1980] E.C.R. 2671.
[97] Case 730/79, *Philip Morris v Commission*, [1980] E.C.R. 2671, paras 16 and 17.
[98] Case T-149/95, *Ducros v Commission*, [1997] E.C.R. II-2031 para.63.
[99] Case C-148/04, *Unicredito Italiano v Agenzia delle Entrate Ufficio Genova 1*, [2005] E.C.R. I-11137.

(a) Regional aid

Article 87(3)(a) states that "aid to promote the economic development of   **1–053**
areas where the standard of living is abnormally low or where there is serious
underemployment" may be considered compatible with the common market.

It is well established that the standard of living is to be compared to that
which applies in the EU as a whole.[100]

In this connection reference can be made to the Commission's guidelines
on regional aid and to this exception in general which are discussed in paras
3–120–3–140.

In contrast to what applies under art.87(3)(a), the national regional aid that   **1–054**
can be justified under the exception in art.87(3)(c) concerns aid to "certain
economic areas" which do not fall within the scope the category of areas
where the standard of living is abnormally low under subs.(a), but which are
areas which are disadvantaged compared with other areas in the Member
State in question.

In cases concerning regional aid, including aid which is covered by art.87(3)
(a) (and not merely under subs.(c)), before giving approval, the Commission
has a duty to evaluate the sectoral effects of the planned regional aid, even
where regions likely to fall within art.87(3)(a) are concerned, in order to
avoid a situation in which, as a result of an aid measure, a sectoral problem
is created at Community level which is more serious than the initial regional
problem.[101]

In the case of aid projects which are intended to promote the economic
development of a region which falls under art.87(3)(a), the regional considerations carry greater weight in relation to sectoral or individual considerations
in such areas than in regions covered by subs.(c), just as supplements for aid
under horizontal or sectoral aid measures in the areas covered by subs.(a) are
higher than is the case for areas covered by art.87(3)(c).[102]

(b) Projects of common European interest and serious disturbance in the economy of a Member State

Article 87(3)(b) states that "aid to promote the execution of an important   **1–055**
project of common European interest or to remedy a serious disturbance in
the economy of a Member State" may be considered to be compatible with
the common market.[103]

Aid for projects of common European interest can, for example, concern
projects of common European environmental interest, the manufacture of
aircraft or aircraft parts, energy conservation and research and development
projects which are both quantitatively and qualitatively significant, of a

---

[100] Case 730/79, *Philip Morris v Commission*, [1980] E.C.R. 2671, paras 25 and 26.
[101] Case T-380/94, *AIUFFASS and AKY v Commission*, [1996] E.C.R. II-2169 para.54.
[102] *AIUFFASS and AKY v Commission*, [1996] E.C.R. II-2169 para.55.
[103] See the article by Brice Allibert in *Competition Policy Newsletter*, 2002 p. 67, on a French case
involving aid for research and development in the field of microtechnology. The Commission
approved the aid measure on the basis of art.87(3)(b).

transnational character, and which can enable the Community's industry to take advantage of all the benefits of the internal market.

In the *Glaverbel* case[104] the ECJ agreed with the view of the Commission that a project may not be described as being of common European interest unless it forms part of a transnational European programme supported jointly by a number of Member States, or arises from concerted action by a number of Member States to combat a common threat such as environmental pollution.

1–056   A national law to reduce taxation on certain transactions in the banking sector, the main purpose of which is to improve the competitiveness of commercial undertakings based in the Member State in question, even though only intended to strengthen their competitive position on the domestic market, will not be compatible with the common market, given that the law was a measure in the national privatisation of the sector in question and that, as a consequence, it did not constitute an important project of common European interest; see art.87(3)(b).[105]

In relation to aid given to remedy a serious disturbance in the economy of a Member State, reference can be made to the application of art.92(3)(b) (now art.87(3)(b)) by the Commission in approving aid in the form of the financial reorganisation of companies in the public sector in Greece when it found that the crisis in the Greek economy was spread across more than any one sector of the economy.[106] A disturbance within the meaning of art.87(3)(b) must affect the economy of a Member State, and not merely one of the Member State's regions or part of its territory. In this event, art.87(3)(c) is in principle the relevant provision.[107]

(c) The development of certain economic activities or of certain economic areas

1–057   Article 87(3)(c) states that "aid to facilitate the development of certain economic activities or of certain economic areas, where such aid does not adversely affect trading conditions to an extent contrary to the common interest" may be considered to be compatible with the common market.[108]

As stated above, aid to "certain economic areas" concerns aid to areas of a Member State that are not regions which fall under the provisions in art.87(3)(a), where the standard of living is abnormally low in relation to the EU as a whole, but areas which are disadvantaged in relation to other areas in the Member State in question.

---

[104] Joined Cases 62/87 and 72/87, *Exécutif régional wallon and Glaverbel v Commission*, [1988] E.C.R. 1573, para.23 in particular.

[105] Case C-148/04, *Unicredito Italiano v Agenzia delle Entrate Ufficio Genova 1*, [2005] E.C.R. I-11137.

[106] See the Commission's XVII Report on competition policy, paras 185–187.

[107] Case C-301/96, *Germany v Commission*, [2003] E.C.R. I-9919.

[108] On this provision and the conversion to digital TV, see Christof Schoser & Sandro Santamato, "The Commission's state aid policy on the digital switchover", in *Competition Policy Newsletter*, No.1, Spring 2006 p. 23.

Aid to facilitate the development of certain economic activities must be interpreted not as referring to the development of whole commercial sectors, but it can refer to aid to individual undertakings, for example, with a view to rescuing them by means of giving temporary assistance until a restructuring plan can be implemented, enabling the undertaking to survive in the longer term. In relation to this form of emergency support, a number of framework provisions for rescue and restructuring aid are referred to in paras 3–089 –3–119.

The replacement of equipment, even though it may involve the installation of new technology, is not sufficient to fulfil the conditions of art.87(3)(c). What is required is that the aid measures must be part of a package to rationalise and restructure an undertaking which is in difficulties. The same applies to help for failing undertakings in a period of recession.[109] Such aid does not fulfil the conditions for approval under art.87(3)(c).

Aid that is given under the exception in art.87(3)(c) must ensure that there is an improvement in the way in which the activity in question is carried on, such as by rationalisation or restructuring.[110]   **1–058**

The evaluation must involve the whole of the sector in question and not just a few undertakings.[111] However, there can be cases where this is not necessary, because the individual undertaking is so big that its restructuring would lead to the development of the whole of the sector in question.[112]

Aid can only be given under art.87(3)(c) to beneficiaries which are at least potentially competitive.[113]

Aid for operating costs is not appropriate for the development of economic activities, and according to the case law of the European courts in principle aid for operating costs is not permissible on the basis of the exceptions in art.87(3) (c); see Case T-469/93, *Siemens v Commission*, [1995] E.C.R. II-1675. Tax reliefs, with the aim of strengthening the competitiveness of national undertakings in the banking sector are not compatible with the common market on the basis of art.87(3)(c).[114]

In general, it is a condition for approval under art. 87(3)(c) that the aid may not be contrary to the common interest. This means that regard must be had to whether there is overcapacity in the sector concerned, to the   **1–059**

---

[109] Bellamy & Child, *Common Market Law of Competition*, 4th edn p. 924.
[110] Case C-75/97, *Belgium v Commission (Maribel)*, [1999] E.C.R. I-3671 para.57.
[111] Case C-75/97, *Belgium v Commission (Maribel)*, [1999] E.C.R. I-3671 para.37–58.
[112] Joined Cases T-371/94 and T-394/94, *British Airways and Others v Commission*, [1998] E.C.R. II-2405, where it was stated that the Commission was entitled to form the view that genuine restructuring of one of the three largest European airline companies, which was the recipient of State aid, would have the effect of facilitating the economic development of the European civil aviation sector. This wide-ranging judgment emphasised, among other things, that aid for restructuring can only be approved if it can be assumed that it will promote the development of the commercial sector in question, and there must be genuine restructuring. In general, the Commission requires the prior presentation of a restructuring plan; see the judgment.
[113] Case C-301/87, *France v Commission (Boussac)*, [1990] E.C.R. I-307.
[114] Case C-148/04, *Unicredito Italiano v Agenzia delle Entrate Ufficio Genova 1*, [2005] E.C.R. I-11137.

intensity of the aid, the method of financing the aid, and whether a monopolistic or narrow oligopolistic situation will be created, or whether there will be advantages in the form of strengthening small and medium-sized enterprises. The Commission normally considers the strengthening of small and medium-sized enterprises as less problematic than the strengthening of large enterprises.

The Commission has the burden of proof for showing that some aid is not against the common interest, but the Member States have the burden of proof for establishing the actual circumstances.[115]

Aid for rescue and restructuring is not normally regarded as being in the common interest.[116]

The Commission normally takes a negative approach to measures for general investment aid that is not based on sectoral or regional considerations.[117]

In relation to sectoral aid, for example for specific types of undertaking such as shipbuilders, in its VII Report on competition policy the Commission stated that it would base its evaluation of aid on the following criteria:

1–060
1. the sectoral aid should be limited to cases where it is justified by the circumstances of the industry concerned;
2. the aid should lead to the re-establishment of profitability in the long term by resolving problems sooner rather than later, rather than maintaining the status quo and delaying taking decisions and making changes that are inevitable;
3. nevertheless, since it takes time for changes to take effect, under certain circumstances and subject to strict conditions, a limited use of resources is permissible in connection with the reduction of social and economic costs in connection with the implementation of changes;
4. unless it is provided over a short period, the aid must be reduced progressively, and be clearly linked to the restructuring of the sector concerned;
5. the intensity of the aid must be proportional to the problem it is intended to solve, so that distortion of competition is reduced to a minimum; and
6 industrial problems and unemployment may not be transferred from one Member State to another.[118]

The guidelines, etc. for sectoral aid in different sectors are discussed in more detail in Ch.4.

The guidelines and framework provisions issued by the Commission, for example in connection with environmental aid and regional aid, indicate how

---

[115] cf. *Groeben-Thiesing-Ehlermann*, op. cit., B II, p. 1886.
[116] cf. Groeben-Thiesing-Ehlermann, op. cit., B II, p.1886. See also Case T-171/02, *Regione autonoma della Sardegna v Commission*, [2005] E.C.R. II-2123.
[117] Bellamy & Child, *Common Market Law of Competition*, 5th edn, Ch.19–038.
[118] The Commission's VII Report on competition policy 1978.

the Commission intends to apply the exceptions referred to in art.87(3)(c). The conditions must naturally be compatible with the EC Treaty and are binding on the Commission since, if it departed from them, it would risk breaching the principle of equality of treatment, so that a decision of the Commission could be annulled on that basis. However, the Commission can depart from its discretionary provisions, as long as there are objective and proper reasons for doing so.[119]

The various framework provisions etc. have the advantage of making it possible for the Member States to get a good idea in advance of what aid measures the Commission will be inclined to approve. At the same time they enable others (for example interested parties) to assess whether aid which is approved should in fact have been approved.

The reader is also referred to paras 3–120–3–140 on art.87(3)(c) in relation to regional aid.

(d) Cultural aid

Article 87(3)(d) states that "aid to promote culture and heritage conserva-   **1–061**
tion where such aid does not affect trading conditions and competition in the Community to an extent that is contrary to the common interest" may be considered to be compatible with the common market.

The choice of words in subs.(d) differs somewhat from subs.(c). In contrast to subs.(c), subs.(d) refers not only to trading conditions, but also to the conditions of competition. Furthermore subs.(c) refers to aid which "does not adversely affect trading conditions", while subs.(d) refers to aid which "does not affect trading conditions". It is submitted, however, that these differences in wording are not of legal significance.

Prior to the inclusion of subs.(d) in the EC Treaty, in the practice of the Commission culture benefited from the exception in subs.(c), so it is questionable whether the addition of subs.(d) has made any real difference. Among other things the exception has been used to approve aid given to the film industry in France and the Netherlands (where aid is limited to 50 per cent of the production costs), and it has also been used as the basis for a decision by the Commission on aid for the export of French books.[120]

According to art.151 of the EC Treaty, the Community will contribute to the flowering of the cultures of the Member States, while respecting their national and regional diversity and at the same time bringing the common cultural heritage to the fore, and the Community will take cultural aspects into account in its action under other provisions of the Treaty, in particular in order to respect and to promote the diversity of its cultures.[121]

---

[119] Case T-149/95 *Ducros* [1997] E.C.R. II-2031.
[120] Case T-49/93, *Societé internationale de diffusion et d'edition (SIDE) v Commission*, [1995] E.C.R. II-2501; and Case T-155/98, *Societé internationale de diffusion et d edition (SIDE) v Commission*, [2002] E.C.R. II-1179.
[121] See also communication from the Commission to the Council, the European Parliament, the Economic and Social Committee and the Committee of the Regions on certain legal aspects relating to cinematographic and other audiovisual works, COM(2001) 534 final (OJ C 43,

THE COMMISSION'S EXERCISE OF ITS POWERS UNDER ART.87

1–062   The first task for the Commission is to decide whether, in connection with a specific aid measure, there is in fact aid within the meaning of art.87(1)

In principle, "State aid" is an objective term, but as discussed in paras 1–020 to 1–047 it is often difficult to determine whether an actual measure in fact constitutes aid. However, in principle the Commission does not have any discretionary powers with regard to such a decision. The use of the market economy investor principle as a basis for determining whether aid exists is often connected with a complex economic assessment, so that the ECJ is reluctant to apply its own assessment of whether aid exists in place of the Commission's assessment; see for example para.105 of the judgment in Case T-296/97, *Alitalia v Commission*, [2000] E.C.R. II-3871.

When the Commission has decided whether aid exists which is in principle contrary to art.87, it will then consider whether, depending on the circumstances, it involves a form of aid (individual aid or an aid scheme) which can be found compatible with the common market under art.87(2) or (3). In relation to the de jure exceptions in art.87(2) (aid to consumers, aid in connection with natural disasters etc.), the task is not usually so difficult, since the compatibility of the aid with the circumstances in question will be relatively easy to establish. A natural disaster is sufficiently unusual and of such a character that it can immediately be classified as such, though the Commission must always assess whether the aid measures involved are causally linked to the disaster, and whether they go beyond what is necessary.

The situation is more complex with regard to the exceptions in art.87(3) (a), (b) and (c), in other words concerning (a) regional aid, (b) important projects of common European interest or to remedy a serious disturbance in the economy of a Member State, and (c) the development of certain economic activities or economic areas.

1–063   In these situations, especially in relation to subpara.(c), it can be necessary to consider complex economic, socio-economic or technical matters. According to the case law of the ECJ, the Commission has wide but not unlimited discretion.[122]

This also means that undertakings and others who may bring an action

---

16.2.2002, p.6). The criteria laid down in the communication are to remain in force until at least December 31, 2009, according to the notice in OJ C 134, 16.6.2007, p.5. See also communication from the Commission on the application of State aid rules to public service broadcasting (OJ C 320, 15.11.2001, p.5). finally, see also Jérôme Broche, Obhi Chatterjee, Irina Orssich & Nóra Tosics, "State aid for films—a policy in motion?", in *Competition Policy Newsletter*, No.1, Spring 2007 p.44.

[122]   In the exercise of its discretion the Commission can apply the criteria which it finds best suited for examining whether an aid measure can be considered to be compatible with the common market; see Case T-214/95, *Vlaams Gewest*, [1998] E.C.R. II-717 para.89. Thus, it can lay down the criteria it wishes to apply in guidelines which are in accordance with the EC Treaty. The adoption of such guidelines is part of its discretionary powers, and this means that, in order

for the annulment of a decision of the Commission, for example to approve some specific aid measure in accordance with art.87(3)(c), must primarily base their criticism of the Commission's decision on a procedural point (for example, that a decision to approve aid lacks a proper basis), or, if relevant, seek to prove that the factual circumstances on which the decision is based are wrong, or show that the Commission has made a manifest error of assessment[123] (Case T-149/95 *Ducros* [1997] E.C.R. II-2031 para.63) with regard to the factual circumstances, or that there is a misuse of powers.[124] With regard to the economic circumstances, the CFI cannot substitute its own discretion for the Commission's.[125]

The ECJ will not normally use independent expert witnesses when considering cases of State aid, but it has happened (Case C-169/84, *Société CdF Chimie azote et fertilisants v Commission*, [1990] E.C.R. I-3083). However, subject to the reservations referred to above, the ECJ will not examine the Commission's exercise of its discretion in cases decided on the basis of art.87(3)(c).

The Commission has stated that, when it examines whether a given aid measure can be approved, it takes the following into account:

1-064

a) Whether the aid promotes a development which is in the interests of the whole Community; the promotion of purely national interests is not sufficient;
b) Whether the aid is necessary to bring about the development in question; in other words, whether the recipient of the aid would not be able to achieve the desired result under normal market conditions; and
c) Whether the conditions of the aid, i.e. its intensity, duration, the risk of transferring the problems from one Member State to another, the degree of distortion of competition etc., are reasonable in relation to its aim.[126]

In this connection it will also be relevant to consider whether the Commission has followed its own framework provisions and guidelines (which provide the norms for the Commission's discretion), which have the aim of ensuring the uniform application of the State aid rules to similar cases, or whether it has departed from them. In the latter case, if the departure from the rules cannot be objectively justified, this will give rise to doubt about compliance with the principle of equal treatment. If the rules have not been complied with, this in itself can lead to the Commission's decision being overturned by the European courts.[127]

---

to comply with the principle of equal treatment, the Commission limits itself to evaluating aid in accordance with its own guidelines.

[123] Case T-296/97, *Alitalia v Commission*, [2000] E.C.R. II-3871 para.169.

[124] Case C-56/93, *Belgium v Commission*, [1996] E.C.R. I-723 para.11 and the other cases referred to here.

[125] Case T-380/94, *AIUFFASS and AKY v Commission*, [1996] E.C.R. II-2169 para.56.

[126] The Commission's XII Report on competition policy, para.160.

[127] Joined Cases C-278/92, C-279/92 and C-280/92, *Spain v Commission (Hytasa)*, [1994] E.C.R. I-4103 paras 54–58.

The issuing by the Commission of framework provisions and guide-lines, together with the principle of equal treatment, also has the effect that the Member States have a justified expectation that the Commission will apply arts 87 and 88 in the manner set out in the Commission's statements.

THE POSSIBILITY FOR EXCEPTIONS TO THE PROHIBITIONS OF STATE AID IN ART.87(1) ADOPTED BY THE COUNCIL

1–065   According to art.87(3)(e) of the EC Treaty, categories of aid, other than those listed in art.87(3)(a) to (d), may be considered compatible with the common market, where specified by a decision of the Council acting by a qualified majority on a proposal from the Commission.

In accordance with art.87(3)(e), the Council has adopted rules on aid to the shipbuilding industry and for the production of coal and steel; see Ch.4.

Moreover, under art.88(2), third paragraph, on application by a Member State, the Council, acting unanimously, may decide that aid which that State grants or intends to grant is to be considered as being compatible with the common market, in derogation from the provisions of art.87 and art.89, if such a decision is justified by exceptional circumstances.

If the Commission has initiated the procedure referred to in the first para-graph of art.88(2), such a request by a Member State to the Council has the effect of suspending the proceedings until the Council has decided on the question.

1–066   However, the Commission can give its decision on the case if the Council has not made its decision known within three months of the application being made.

The Council has seldom used its powers in art.88(2), third paragraph, except in a few cases on agriculture. The Commission has some years ago brought a case against the Council for the abuse of these powers in relation to the Portuguese pig sector.

In this case the ECJ has interpreted the Council's powers so that if a request is not submitted to the Council by a Member State on the basis of art.88(2), third paragraph, before the Commission has declared the aid in question to be incompatible with the common market, and thus concluded the procedure under art.88(2), first paragraph, the Council no longer has powers to exercise powers under art.88(2), third paragraph, which means that the Council cannot then declare the aid to be compatible with the common market. Nor can the Council thwart the effectiveness of such a decision by declaring compatible with the common market, on the basis of art.88(2), third paragraph, aid designed to compensate the beneficiaries of unlawful aid declared incompat-ible with the common market for the repayments they are required to make pursuant to that decision.[128] If this were not the case, the Council could avoid the restriction on its application of art.88(2), third paragraph.

THE COUNCIL'S POWERS UNDER ART.89 TO MAKE APPROPRIATE REGULATIONS FOR THE APPLICATION OF ARTS 87 AND 88

Article 89 of the EC Treaty states as follows: "The Council, acting by a quali-   **1–067**
fied majority on a proposal from the Commission and after consulting the European Parliament, may make any appropriate regulations for the applica-tion of Articles 87 and 88 and may in particular determine the conditions in which Article 88(3) shall apply and the categories of aid exempted from this procedure" (in other words, exempted from the obligation to notify in art.88(3)).

This competence has been used by the Council in a couple of cases. Thus it has issued Council Regulation (EC) No 994/98 of May 7, 1998 on the appli-cation of arts 92 and 93 of the Treaty establishing the European Community to certain categories of horizontal State aid (OJ L 142, May 14, 1998, p.1), which gives the Commission powers to issue block exemption regulations on State aid, and Council Regulation (EC) No.659/1999 of March 22, 1999 laying down detailed rules for the application of art.93 of the EC Treaty (OJ L 83, March 27, 1999, p.1).[129]

THE SCOPE OF APPLICATION OF THE STATE AID RULES

The EC Treaty rules on State aid apply to the EU, but art.62(d) of the   **1–068**
EEA Treaty (the treaty establishing the European Economic Area) contains provisions corresponding to those in art.87 of the EC Treaty. The EEA rules are administered by the Commission in the case of the EU Member States and by the EEA Surveillance Authority in the case of the three EFTA countries, Norway, Iceland and Liechtenstein that together with the EU constitute the EEA.

---

[128] Case C-110/02, *Commission v Council*, [2004] E.C.R. I-6333. This case is discussed by Koen Van de Casteele, "The European Court of Justice clarifies the powers of the Council in State aid cases", in *Competition Policy Newsletter*, No.3, Autumn 2004 p.21. See also Case C-399/03, *Commission v Council*, [2006] E.C.R. I-5629.

[129] Sinnaeve, "Block exemptions for state aid: More scope for state aid control by member states and competitors", in CML. Rev., Vol.38, No.6, December 2001 p.1479 gives a review of the background to the origin of the three block exemption regulations concerning State aid, as well as a description of the content of the regulations on de minimis aid, aid to small and medium sized enterprises, and aid for educational purposes, as well as considering the future roles of the Member States, competitors, the national courts and the Commission, following the block exemption regulations from 2001. The block exemptions on SME-aid and on aid for educational purposes have now been replaced by provisions in the General Block Exemption that entered into force on 29.08.08. See also Case C-110/03, *Belgium v Commission*, [2005] E.C.R. I-2801.

The EEA Surveillance Authority works on the basis of a set of rules that are very similar to the provisions that apply within the EU.[130] In reality the EU rules extend to the EFTA countries that are members of the EEA.

The Commission works closely with the Surveillance Authority in each their own area, and there are regular meetings between the two authorities with a view to mutual orientation on developments in the area of State aid, so that there is a basis for uniform development of the law.

The agreements entered into between the EU and the countries in Central and Eastern Europe that have become members of the EU since 2004 contain State aid rules corresponding to the EU's. The same applies to the association agreement with Turkey.[131]

1–069   The World Trade Organization (WTO) also has rules on State aid, and its Members, including the EU, have to submit annual reports on the State aid they give. The EU submits these reports on behalf of the Member States. WTO Members (now including China and Taiwan) can notify certain kinds of aid, namely aid for research and development, regional aid and environmental aid, to the WTO with the effect that such aid measures thereafter are not considered as breaches of the rules. Such measures therefore do not justify the imposition of countervailing measures, nor can they be challenged under the WTO rules.

The WTO allows anti-dumping measures to be taken against forms of State aid which are not compatible with the WTO's rules. In the case of the EU, anti-dumping measures can take the form of countervailing duties, in order to counteract aid given by other states.[132] Such measures cannot be taken as between EU Member States, but they can be taken against EFTA countries and other third countries—including those seeking admission to the EU.[133]

The OECD has rules on export credits; see the "gentlemen's agreement" (Guidelines for Officially Supported Export Credits) which excludes aid to exports between the countries which are members of the OECD.

The prohibition of State aid applies both in relation to the EC Treaty and the Euratom Treaty.

1–070   The European Coal and Steel Community Treaty (ECSC Treaty) which entered into force in 1952 expired on July 22, 2002. From the very start this

---

[130] For the State aid rules applicable to the EEA, see the website of the EEA Surveillance Authority *www.eftasurv.int/fieldsofwork/fieldstateaid/*

[131] Schütterle, P. (2002), "State Aid Control: An Accession Criterion", CML. Rev., Vol.39, No.3 pp. 577–590.

[132] Countermeasures can be taken against imports if the imports are: 1) subsidised, 2) cause damage or threaten to cause damage, and 3) there is a direct link between the subsidy and the damage. Damage can only be found to exist where the total aid exceeds 5% of the value of the goods, and if the imports exceed 5% market share. Thus, only subsidies which affect international trade are covered. A countermeasure will typically be a countervailing duty.

[133] On this, see the case between the then candidate country, Austria, and the EU concerning unlawful aid given to Opel Austria, which was finally decided by the ECJ on January 22, 1997 in Case T-115/94.

Treaty was furnished with its own provisions on State aid. Thus art.4 of the ECSC Treaty stated that:

"The following are recognized as incompatible with the common market for coal and steel and shall accordingly be abolished and prohibited within the Community, as provided in this Treaty ... (c) subsidies or aids granted by States, or special charges imposed by States, in any form whatsoever".[134]

In other words, the ECSC Treaty introduced an absolute prohibition of State aid, but in the light of crises in the two sectors in the 1970s and 1980s the Commission had to introduce rules on aid to the coal and steel industries (in 1976 and 1980 respectively).

Following the expiry of the ECSC Treaty, the State aid rules in the EC Treaty are applicable to those sectors which were previously covered by the State aid rules in the ECSC Treaty.

The prohibition of State aid in art.87(1) of the EC Treaty applies to all sectors of commerce except trade in arms, and agriculture is only partly covered by the State aid rules in arts 87 and 88. Agricultural products are considered below in paras 4–090–4–129.

---

[134] Article 4 of the ECSC Treaty was supplemented by art.67 of the ECSC Treaty. On the relationship between the two articles see Case 30/59, *De Gezamenlijke Steenkolenmijnen in Limburg v High Authority of the ECSC*, [1961] E.C.R. 3; and Joined Cases 27–58, 28–58 and 29–58, *Compagnie des hauts fourneaux et fonderies de Givors and others v High Authority of the ECSC*, [1960] E.C.R. 503.

CHAPTER 2

THE ADMINISTRATIVE PROCEDURE IN STATE AID CASES

NOTIFICATION AND PROCEDURE

The basic rules on notification of State aid and on procedure are found in   **2–001**
art.88 of the EC Treaty and in Council Regulation (EC) No.659/1999 of
March 22, 1999 laying down detailed rules for the application of art.93 (now
art.88) of the EC Treaty. These are described in paras 2–002 to 2–060.

ARTICLE 88 OF THE EC TREATY ON NOTIFICATION

Article 88 of the EC Treaty deals with the basic procedure which must be fol-   **2–002**
lowed when dealing with cases of State aid. It is complemented by Regulation
(EC) No.659/1999, containing procedural rules, which was adopted by
the Council under the authority of art.89 of the Treaty. The Regulation is
described in paras 2–007 to 2–060.

Article 88 of the Treaty states as follows:

"1. The Commission shall, in cooperation with Member States, keep under
    constant review all systems of aid existing in those States. It shall propose
    to the latter any appropriate measures required by the progressive devel-
    opment or by the functioning of the common market.
2. If, after giving notice to the parties concerned to submit their comments,
    the Commission finds that aid granted by a State or through State
    resources is not compatible with the common market having regard to
    Article 87, or that such aid is being misused, it shall decide that the State
    concerned shall abolish or alter such aid within a period of time to be
    determined by the Commission.

    If the State concerned does not comply with this decision within the
    prescribed time, the Commission or any other interested State may, in
    derogation from the provisions of Articles 226 and 227, refer the matter
    to the Court of Justice direct.

    On application by a Member State, the Council may, acting unani-
    mously, decide that aid which that State is granting or intends to grant

shall be considered to be compatible with the common market, in derogation from the provisions of Article 87 or from the regulations provided
for in Article 89, if such a decision is justified by exceptional circumstances. If, as regards the aid in question, the Commission has already
initiated the procedure provided for in the first subparagraph of this
paragraph, the fact that the State concerned has made its application to
the Council shall have the effect of suspending that procedure until the
Council has made its attitude known.

　　If, however, the Council has not made its attitude known within three
months of the said application being made, the Commission shall give
its decision on the case.

3. The Commission shall be informed, in sufficient time to enable it to submit
its comments, of any plans to grant or alter aid. If it considers that any
such plan is not compatible with the common market having regard to
Article 87, it shall without delay initiate the procedure provided for in
paragraph 2. The Member State concerned shall not put its proposed
measures into effect until this procedure has resulted in a final decision."

2–003　　Article 88 makes the Commission the authority for granting consent in cases
of State aid. Thus it has sole competence both with regard to the approval of
individual aid measures, existing aid measures and new aid measures.[1] This
status can be seen as expressing the belief of the founders of the Community
that the Commission was more suitable than the Council for deciding on the
compatibility with the EC Treaty of a State aid measure. If this task had been
given to the Council, one could imagine that the Council might have indulged
in some "horse trading", resulting in the mutual approval of each other's
State aid.[2]

　　In cases concerning State aid, the Commission has a more direct and therefore more rapid right to bring a Member State before the European Court of
Justice (ECJ) than in the more usual cases of breaches of the Treaty brought
on the basis of art.226, where it is necessary to make a written submission
with a reasoned statement, with intervening deadlines for the Member State
to react, before the case can be brought before the ECJ. By using the most
common grounds for the postponement of deadlines, the administrative procedure for cases of breach of the Treaty can often take half a year or more to
bring. It is clear that the State aid procedure is quicker and more effective.

　　Article 88 constitutes the basis for the control which the Commission exercises over the Member States' compliance with the prohibition of State aid in
art.87. Article 88 contains an obligation to give notice and creates the basis
for making a procedural distinction between notified and non-notified State
aid. In principle, non-notified State aid is unlawful. Unlawful aid is not ipso

---

[1] For the definition of existing and new aid measures, see para.2–012.
[2] The same thought processes can be seen in the fact that it is also the Commission which has
decision-making powers in relation to the application of the provisions in art.86(3) of the EC
Treaty.

facto aid that is incompatible with the common market. This is decided by the Commission under a State aid procedure.[3] The unlawfulness of State aid can be claimed directly before national courts by individuals or undertakings. In other words, art.88(3) has direct effect.

In principle, all forms of new aid or changes to existing aid must be notified, **2–004** unless special rules apply to notification in the sector in question. The obligation to notify also applies to forms of horizontal aid that are covered by the various framework provisions, for example aid for research, development and innovation, and environmental aid. However, in some cases the frameworks contain special rules on notification, or a special rapid procedure.

The reader is referred to Chs 3 and 4 for a discussion of the special areas and special sectors. However, even at this juncture it should be emphasised that aid given in conjunction with one of the block exemption regulations need not be notified. For example, aid of less than €200,000 over a three-year period (de minimis aid) need not normally be notified.

When a general aid scheme has been notified and approved, individual grants of aid which comply with the conditions for the approval of the aid scheme in question need not be notified (subject to individual exceptions concerning large grants of aid etc.). In connection with an aid scheme the Commission can restrict itself to examining the content of the scheme, without being required to examine every single application of the scheme with a view to assessing whether the individual grant in question contains elements of aid.[4]

With regard to aid to public undertakings or undertakings that have been entrusted with carrying out certain services of general economic interest, see art.86(2) of the Treaty, the question of notification has been clarified by the ECJ's judgment in the *Altmark* case and by the Commission's legislative initiatives which followed that case. The reader is referred to the discussion of this in paras 4–141 to 4–151. Export aid must also be notified; see art.132 of the Treaty.[5]

Aid concerning which a Member State is in doubt about its compatibility **2–005** with the prohibition of State aid in the Treaty must also be notified; see Case C-301/87, *France v Commission* (*Boussac*), [1990] E.C.R. I-307 para.13.

As already stated, the first sentence in art.88(3) has direct effect. In order to determine whether a State measure has been introduced in breach of art.88(3), it can be necessary for a national court to interpret the State aid concept in art.87(1). According to art.87(1), the following conditions must be fulfilled for a measure to be regarded as constituting State aid. First, there must be aid granted by a Member State or through State resources. Second, this aid must affect trade between Member States. Third, it must favour certain undertakings. Fourth, it must distort or threaten to distort the

---

[3] Case C-301/87, *France v Commission* (*Boussac*), [1990] E.C.R. I-307.
[4] Case C-66/02, *Italy v Commission*, [2005] E.C.R. I-10901; and Joined Cases C-182/03 and C-217/03, *Belgium and Forum 187 ABSL v Commission*, [2006] E.C.R. I-5479.
[5] Case C-142/87, *Belgium v Commission*, [1990] E.C.R. I-959, according to which art.132 does not hinder the application of arts 87–89.

conditions of competition.[6] The national court must examine whether the measure in question gives an advantage and whether it is selective; in other words, whether it favours certain undertakings or the production of certain goods within the meaning of art.87(1).[7] Only State aid which falls within the meaning of art.87(1) is subject to the notification procedure in art.88(3). Article 87(1) of the Treaty provides that, in order for it to be found that State aid exists, a measure must affect trade between Member States.[8]

In principle, the national government authorities which are subject to the obligation to notify must make the same evaluation.

On the other hand, national courts cannot give direct effect to the prohibition of State aid in art.87(1) of the Treaty. It can be necessary for them to assess whether aid exists or could be thought to exist, and therefore whether there is an obligation to notify it (Case 78/86, *Steinike & Weinlig v Germany*, [1977] E.C.R. 595 para.14), and in this connection in cases of doubt they can address a question to the Commission,[9] but the Commission has sole competence to decide whether or not a given State aid measure is compatible with the common market.[10]

2–006   The role of the national courts in cases concerning State aid is looked at in Ch.8.

It is for the Commission to decide, on the one hand, whether the prohibition in art.87(1) should be regarded as having been infringed, and on the other hand, whether in this case the aid in question is compatible with the Treaty. According to the case law, the assessment of whether State aid exists is an objective question.[11] The Commission's decisions in respect of the exception contained in art.87(2) (the de jure exceptions) are also not discretionary, but according to the case law the Commission has wide discretion to decide with regard to the exceptions in art.87(3).

National courts can also refer questions to the ECJ for preliminary rulings (under art.234 of the EC Treaty) on the interpretation of the State aid rules. As an overwhelming rule, national courts must refer questions of interpretation of Community law to the ECJ.

Article 88(2) gives the Commission authority to decide that State aid is not compatible with the common market. Before making such a decision the Commission must give the interested parties the opportunity to put their views forward. If, for example, the Commission decides that some State aid is not compatible, an undertaking which is an intended recipient of the aid can bring a case before the Court of First Instance (CFI) for annulment of the decision in accordance with art.230 of the Treaty. The lawfulness of a Community legal

---

[6] Case C-172/03, *Wolfgang Heiser v finanzamt Innsbruck*, [2005] E.C.R. I-1627.
[7] Case C-368/04, *Transalpine Ölleitung in Österreich GmbH and Others v finanzlandesdirektion für Tirol and Others*, [2006] E.C.R. I-9957.
[8] Case C-71/04, *Administración del Estado v Xunta de Galicia*, [2005] E.C.R. I-7419.
[9] See the Commission's notice on cooperation between national courts and the Commission. The Commission has promised to give quick replies.
[10] Case 78/86, *Steinike & Weinlig v Germany*, [1977] E.C.R. 595 paras 9 and 10.
[11] See e.g. Case T-67/94, *Ladbroke Racing*, [1998] E.C.R. II-1, para 52.

act, for example a decision by the Commission in accordance with art.88(2), must be judged according to the factual and legal circumstances that existed at the time when the act was taken, and the Commission's assessment may only be assessed on the basis of the information which the Commission had available to it at the time when it took its decision. A plaintiff, for example an undertaking, cannot therefore dispute the lawfulness of a decision by reference to circumstances of which the Commission did not have knowledge during the administrative procedure. The same applies if the plaintiff did not participate in the administrative proceedings, even though in the proceedings the undertaking was referred to as a recipient of the aid in question and the Commission had invited participation. If the Commission has made it possible for the interested parties, including the undertaking in question, to make their views known, it cannot be criticised for not having taken into account factual circumstances that could have been laid before it under the administrative proceedings, but which have not been, since the Commission is not obliged of its own initiative to investigate and imagine about circumstances which might have been laid before it—but were not.[12]

It is thus important for undertakings to be aware of their opportunities during the Commission's processing of cases on State aid, see the section below and Ch.8.

REGULATION (EC) NO.659/1999 ON PROCEDURAL RULES[13]

Council Regulation (EC) No.659/1999 of March 22, 1999 laying down detailed rules for the application of art.93 (now art.88) of the EC Treaty was adopted by the Council under the authority of art.89 of the Treaty. It creates greater clarity about the procedure that is to be followed when dealing with cases of State aid.[14] The Regulation is also intended to strengthen control over the

2–007

---

[12] Case T-17/03, *Schmitz-Gotha Fahrzeugwerke v Commission*, [2006] E.C.R. II-1139.

[13] Council Regulation (EC) No. 659/1999 of March 22, 1999 laying down detailed rules for the application of art.93 of the EC Treaty (OJ L 83, 27.3.1999, p.1). Regulation (EC) No.659/1999 has been amended a number of times. Article 1(b)(i) was amended on the accession of the Czech Republic, Cyprus, Estonia, Hungary, Latvia, Lithuania, Malta, Poland, Slovakia and Slovenia; annex II, 5(6), (OJ C 227E, 23.9.2003), and again on the accession of Bulgaria and Romania; see Council Regulation (EC) No.1791/2006 of November 20, 2006 (OJ L 363, 20.12.2006, p.1).

[14] Regulation (EC) No.659/1999 is supplemented by Commission Regulation (EC) No.794/2004 of April 21, 2004 implementing Council Regulation (EC) No.659/1999 laying down detailed rules for the application of art.93 [now art.88] of the EC Treaty (OJ L 140, 30.4.2004, p.1). This regulation has been amended by Commission Regulation (EC) No.1935/2006 of December 20, 2006 amending Regulation (EC) No.794/2004 implementing Council Regulation (EC) No.659/1999 laying down detailed rules for the application of art.93 [now art.88] of the EC Treaty (OJ L 407, 30.12.2006, p.1) and by Commission Regulation (EC) No.271/2008 of January 30, 2008 amending Regulation (EC) No.794/2004 implementing Council Regulation (EC) No.659/1999 laying down detailed rules for the application of art.93 [now 88] of the EC Treaty, (OJ L 82, 25.03.2008, p.1). The Commission has also published details of arrangements for the electronic transmission of State aid notifications including addresses together with the arrangements for the protection of confidential information (OJ C 237, 27.9.2005, p.3).

provision of State aid. The Regulation contains four different procedures for State aid: (1) on notified aid; (2) on unlawful aid (i.e. non-notified aid); (3) on the misuse of aid; and (4) on existing aid schemes. It also contains provisions on complaints and monitoring.

The procedures are specific for each category, but they do overlap and there are cross-references between them. The main procedure is that which applies to notified aid which is based on a two-phase procedure (preliminary examination and formal investigation). The procedure for unlawful aid only lays down provisions where they vary from the provisions on notified aid, and they include cross-references to the relevant provisions in the chapter on notified aid. The chapter on misuse of aid only consists of one article, as it is essentially based on the chapter on unlawful aid. finally, the chapter on existing aid schemes largely codifies the provisions in art.88(1) of the EC Treaty together with the long-term practice followed by the Commission.

The topics covered by the Regulation

2–008
- Notification of new aid
- Preliminary procedure
- Formal procedure
- Obligation of Member States to provide information
- Deadlines (among other things for the Commission's decision on the preliminary examination—two months)
- On the scope for interested parties (for example other Member States or undertakings) to submit comments
- The closure of the Commission's investigation procedure (by a decision)
- Revocation of a decision based on incorrect information
- Complaints concerning unlawful aid
- Standstill (i.e. a Member State's postponement of implementation of aid)
- The Commission's right to implement interim measures including orders relating to information, suspension and recovery of aid
- The Commission's right to have direct and rapid access to the Court of Justice
- Recovery of aid in general
- The period of limitation for the recovery of unlawfully paid aid (ten years)
- The procedure regarding the misuse of aid (including the question of repayment in such cases)
- On the rights of third parties to protect their interests in cases of State aid
- Ongoing examinations etc. and appropriate measures in relation to existing aid schemes

- Reporting obligations with regard to existing aid schemes
- On-site monitoring etc.
- Publication to the general public and to interested parties
- The Commission's duty of confidentiality
- The setting up of an advisory committee on State aid, which must be consulted before the Commission issues provisions under Regulation (EC) No.659/1999.

In relation to cases which are notified, the procedure is split into a pre- **2–009** liminary examination and a formal investigation. The preliminary examination is intended to eliminate quickly those measures which do not constitute aid and those measures where the Commission decides not to raise an objection.

Where notification has not been made, for example in cases where a complaint has been made, the case is dealt with under special provisions in the Regulation.

The Regulation distinguishes between notified and non-notified (unlawful) aid, and contains special provisions for dealing with complaints.

Unlawful aid

Unlawful aid is aid which is granted in breach of art.88(3) (previously **2–010** art.93(3)) of the Treaty, in other words non-notified aid.

Aid schemes and individual aid

Regulation (EC) No.659/1999 also distinguishes between *aid schemes* and *individual aid*.

According to art.1(d) of the Regulation, an *aid scheme* is **2–011**

- any act on the basis of which, without further implementing measures being required, individual aid awards may be made to undertakings defined within the act in a general and abstract manner, and
- any act on the basis of which aid which is not linked to a specific project may be awarded to one or several undertakings for an indefinite period of time and/or for an indefinite amount.

The second part of this definition of an aid scheme covers cases of aid which contain elements that could relate both to individual aid and an aid scheme.

According to art.1(d) of the Regulation, *individual aid* is aid that is not awarded on the basis of an aid scheme and notifiable awards of aid on the basis of an aid scheme (for example, amounts of aid above a certain size given on the basis of a measure for aid to small and medium sized undertakings).

The Regulation also distinguishes between new aid and existing aid.[15]

Existing aid and new aid

2–012   According to art.1(b)(i) of Regulation (EC) No.659/1999, existing aid is aid which existed prior to the entry into force of the EC Treaty in the Member State in question, i.e. aid schemes and individual aid which were in force before, and are still in force after, the entry into force of the EC Treaty.

Existing aid can also be:

- authorised aid, i.e. aid schemes and individual aid which have been authorised by the Commission or by the Council;
- aid which is deemed to have been authorised pursuant to art.4(6) of the Regulation or prior to the Regulation but in accordance with this procedure (i.e. notified aid in respect of which the Commission has not taken a decision and which, after the expiry of the two month deadline, the Member State has implemented after having notified the Commission);
- aid which is deemed to be existing aid pursuant to art.15 of the Regulation (i.e. aid the recovery of which has not been required within the period of limitation of ten years);
- aid which, at the time it was put into effect, did not constitute aid and subsequently became aid due to the evolution of the common market.[16]

According to art.1(c) of the Regulation, *new aid* means all aid schemes and individual aid, which is not existing aid, including alterations to existing aid; in other words it refers to the introduction of aid and to substantial changes to existing aid schemes. Joined Cases T-195/01 and T-207/01, *Gibraltar v Commission*, [2002] E.C.R. II-02309 paras 105-116, gives a useful indication of when a change to an existing aid scheme will be found to constitute new aid.[17]

Subject to the exception of special procedural rules in specific sectors, the provisions on procedural rules in Regulation (EC) No.659/1999 apply to aid in all sectors.

---

[15] For an example of the assessment of the distinction between new and existing aid, see Case T-288/97, *Regione autonoma Friuli-Venezia Giulia v Commission*, [1999] E.C.R. II-1871.

[16] When certain measures become aid as a result of the liberalisation of a sector under Community law, such measures are not regarded as existing aid after the date laid down in the liberalising measures; see art.1 of Regulation (EC) No.659/1999.

[17] The distinction between new and existing aid is discussed by Davide Grespan: "An example of the application of State aid rules in the utilities sector in Italy", in *Competition Policy Newsletter*, No.3, October 2002 p.17. See also Georg Roebling: "Existing aid and enlargement", in *Competition Policy Newsletter*, No.1, Spring 2003, p.33.

Commission decision: terminology

Regulation (EC) No.659/1999 gives the Commission authority to take a   **2–013**
number of different decisions in the course of a State aid proceeding. Where,
after a preliminary examination, the Commission finds that a measure constitutes State aid within the meaning of art.87(1) of the EC Treaty, but that
no doubts are raised as to the compatibility with the common market of a
notified measure, it should adopt a "decision not to raise objections" (art.4(3)
of the Regulation). If, on the other hand the Commission finds that doubts
are raised as to the compatibility with the common market of a notified
measure, it should adopt a "decision to initiate the formal investigation
procedure" (art.4(4) of the Regulation), in other words a decision to initiate
the procedure referred to in art.88(2) of the EC Treaty. Among other things
this means that interested parties have a right to submit their comments on
the aid.

Where, after the formal investigation procedure, the Commission finds
that there is no doubt as to the compatibility of the notified measure with
the common market, it should adopt a "positive decision" (art.7(3) of the
Regulation). The Commission may attach conditions to a positive decision,
subject to which aid may be considered compatible with the common market,
and it may also lay down obligations to enable compliance with the decision
to be monitored. Such a decision is referred to as a "conditional decision"
(art.7(4)). If, on the other hand, the Commission finds that the notified aid is
not compatible with the common market, it should adopt a "negative decision"
(art.7(5)).

In relation to allegedly unlawful aid measures, Regulation (EC) No.659/1999   **2–014**
gives the Commission authority to request information from the Member
State concerned with a view to examining the situation with regard to the
rules on State aid. This request for information is to be made in the form
of an "information injunction" (art.10(3)). In addition to this, after giving
the Member State concerned the opportunity to submit its comments, the
Commission may adopt a decision requiring the Member State to suspend
any unlawful aid until the Commission has taken a decision on the compatibility of the aid with the common market. This is referred to as a "suspension injunction" (art.11(1)). Moreover, under certain further conditions, the
Commission may adopt a decision requiring the Member State to recover
any unlawful aid until the Commission has taken a decision on the compatibility of the aid with the common market. This is referred to as a "recovery
injunction" (art.11(2)).

In the event of making a negative decision, the Commission must, in principle, decide that the Member State concerned shall take all necessary measures
to recover the aid from the beneficiary, referred to as a "recovery decision"
(art.14(1)).

The obligation to notify

2–015   The cornerstone of the control system on which Regulation (EC) No.659/1999 is based is laid down in art.88 of the EC Treaty, and it consists of the obligation of the Member States to notify aid and their obligation not to put into effect aid measures before the Commission has taken a decision regarding them; see arts 2 and 3 of the Regulation.

The obligation to notify aid only covers aid that fulfils all the criteria in art.87(1) of the EC Treaty; in other words, it must also fulfil the criteria with regard to its effect. The Regulation confirms that the concept of State aid in art.87(1) and in art.88(3) is the same. However, this should be seen in the context of the risk that non-notified State aid can be brought before the national courts and repayment of the aid may be required. The only way a Member State can guard against this is, if there is the slightest doubt about the compatibility of the aid with the common market, to notify the aid and await the Commission's decision.

After notification, the Commission immediately informs the Member State concerned of the receipt of a notification. The obligation to give a rapid response is due to consideration for the strict deadlines which apply to the handling of cases; i.e. two months for the Commission's preliminary examination and 18 months in all.

The obligation to notify also applies to aid for transport, even though aid for transport is otherwise regulated under art.73 of the EC Treaty. Regardless of the provisions in art.73, art.87 also applies to the transport sector. One can say that the situation is that art.87 applies to aid for transport, but that special rules apply under art.73.

2–016   Depending on the circumstances, the obligation to notify also applies to aid that is provided to undertakings that have taken on the provision of services of general economic interest or have the character of a revenue-producing monopoly; see art.86(2) of the EC Treaty, and see paras 4–141 to 4–151.

Notification must contain all the information necessary to enable the Commission to decide, as part of its preliminary examination, whether the case requires a more thorough formal investigation, or whether the procedure can be closed on the basis that it does not find any reason to raise objections.

An aid scheme may be financed by a charge which is payable on both domestic and imported goods. Such charges may be in breach of art.25 or art.90 of the EC Treaty. If this is the case, the Commission may not declare an aid scheme of which the charge is a part to be compatible with the common market. The Commission's examination of an aid scheme must necessarily include the way in which the aid is financed, if it is an integral part of the measure. In such cases the notification of the aid scheme under art.88(3) of the EC Treaty must also include information about its financing, so that the Commission can make its decision on the basis of full information.[18]

---

[18] Joined Cases C-261/01 and C-262/01, *Belgium v Eugène van Calster and Others*, [2003] E.C.R. I-12249. This case is referred to further in paras 5–025 and 5–026.

In this connection the ECJ has also stated that an aid measure which is   **2–017**
unlawful, because it has not been notified in accordance with art.88(3), i.e.
prior to its implementation, cannot subsequently be made lawful by the
Commission's decision that it is compatible with the common market. The
opposite conclusion would deprive art.88(3) of its effect.[19] Its financing constitutes an integral part of an aid scheme if there is a necessary connection
between the charge made and the aid given under the relevant national law, so
that the revenue from the charge must be used for financing the aid.[20] Such a
connection means that the revenue has a direct effect on the amount of the aid,
and thus on the assessment of the compatibility of the aid with the common
market.[21]

If under national law an undertaking has an obligation to pay a charge
which is an integral part of an aid scheme, this is sufficient for that undertaking to acquire rights under art.88(3). The undertaking may thus challenge the
charge by reference to art.88(3), even if the undertaking is not affected by the
distortion of competition that is a consequence of the aid scheme.[22]

Only aid that falls within the scope of art.87(1) of the Treaty must be
notified. There is thus consistency between the concept of aid under art.87(1)
and the measures which must be notified under art.88(3) and Regulation (EC)
No.659/1999. This means that the Member States are not obliged to give
notification of all kinds of measures which could possibly be considered as
constituting aid.

There are a number of Community provisions containing rules for de
minimis aid, aid to small and medium sized enterprises, aid for education
and employment, as well as aid for research and development and environmental aid, which means that in a number of cases notification of individual
grants of aid of the kind in question need not be notified, but only the
general aid schemes. The particular provisions are described individually in
Ch.3.

As for measures about which there can be cause to doubt whether they   **2–018**
constitute State aid within the meaning of the Treaty, the Commission
assumes that there is a duty to notify; see Case C-301/87, *France v Commission*
(*Boussac*), [1990] E.C.R. I-307 para.13. In any case, it can be sensible to notify
aid about which there can be doubt about its compatibility with the prohibition of State aid in art.87(1), particularly since there can be a requirement to
recover aid if the case comes to the Commission's notice by some other means
than by notification.

In favour of the assumption that the obligation to notify under art.88(3)

[19] Joined Cases C-261/01 and C-262/01, *Belgium v Eugène van Calster and Others*, [2003] E.C.R.
I-12249 paras 63 and 64.
[20] Case C-526/04, *Laboratoires Boiron v Union de recouvrement des cotisations de sécurité sociale
et d'allocations familiales (Urssaf) de Lyon*, [2006] E.C.R. I-7529 para.44 et seq.
[21] Case C-175/02, *Pape v Minister van Landbouw*, [2005] E.C.R. I-127; and Case C-174/02,
Streekgewest Westelijk Noord-Brabant v Staatssecretaris van financiën, [2005] E.C.R. I-85.
[22] Case C-175/02, *Pape v Minister van Landbouw*, [2005] E.C.R. I-127; and Case C-174/02,
Streekgewest Westelijk Noord-Brabant v Staatssecretaris van financiën, [2005] E.C.R. I-85.

does not cover all measures which could possibly be thought to contain an element of State aid, speaks the fact that the obligation of national courts according to the ECJ's case law to give direct effect to art.88(3) and to treat non-notified aid as unlawful—and where appropriate to order the suspension or repayment of aid, or to take other interim measures—can have quite unexpectedly far-reaching consequences in relation to the intention of the Treaty, which is to prevent public measures which infringe the State aid rules and thereby distort competition.

A Member State cannot simply refrain from notifying because it is of the view that a measure is compatible with art.87(1) and does not constitute State aid. This would undermine the possibility of exercising effective control over compliance with the rules on State aid.[23]

2–019   A measure such as capital investments which a Member State may not believe constitute State aid, since it may be justifiable on commercial grounds as being in accordance with the market economy investor principle, should be notified if there can be the doubt about whether the market economy investor principle is complied with. As for financial payments etc., to public undertakings, see the Transparency Directive.

According to the Transparency Directive,[24] the Member States have an obligation to inform the Commission, upon request, about financial transactions between them and public undertakings. In relation to all public manufacturing undertakings with a turnover of more than €250 million, Member States must submit an annual report giving an account of all financial transactions between them and the undertakings in question.

Chapter II of Commission Regulation (EC) No.794/2004 of April 21, 2004 implementing Council Regulation (EC) No.659/1999 laying down detailed rules for the application of art.93 [now art.88] of the EC Treaty contains supplementary rules on the reporting of State aid cases.[25]

According to art.2(1) in Regulation (EC) No.659/1999, new aid must be notified using the form printed in Annex I to Regulation (EC) No.794/2004.[26] Supplementary information which is necessary for evaluating a measure

---

[23] Case C-332/98, *France v Commission*, [2000] E.C.R. I-4833 para.31.

[24] Commission Directive 2006/111/EC of November 16, 2006 on the transparency of financial relations between Member States and public undertakings as well as on financial transparency within certain undertakings (OJ L 318, 17.11.2006, p.17) – the "Transparency Directive".

[25] There is a commentary on this Regulation in Annette Matthias-Werner, "Reform of procedural rules for state aid cases", in *Competition Policy Newsletter*, No.2, Summer 2004.

[26] Annex I was amended by Commission Regulation (EC) No.1627/2006 of October 24, 2006 amending Regulation (EC) No.794/2004 as regards the standard forms for notification of aid (following the adoption by the Commission of new guidelines on national regional aid for 2007 to 2013) (OJ L 302, 1.11.2006, p.10); and by Commission Regulation (EC) No.1935/2006 of December 20, 2006 amending Regulation (EC) No.794/2004 implementing Council Regulation (EC) No.659/1999 laying down detailed rules for the application of art.93 [now art.88] of the EC Treaty (following the adoption by the Commission of the Community guidelines for State aid in the agricultural and forestry sector 2007 to 2013) (OJ L 407, 30.12.2006, p.1), and by Commission Regulation (EC) No.271/2008 of January 30, 2008 amending Regulation (EC) No.794/2004 implementing Council Regulation (EC) No 659/1999 laying down detailed rules for the application of art.93 [now art.88] of the EC Treaty (OJ L 82, 25.3.2008, p.1).

in accordance with the regulations, guidelines etc. on State aid must be submitted using the supplementary information forms which are set out in annex I.

The practical requirements for submitting notification are described in art.3 **2–020** of Regulation (EC) No.794/2004.[27] From this it appears that correspondence between a Member State sending information and the Commission must in principle be sent via the Member State's permanent representation, and the correspondence should be via electronic means. In this connection the Commission has laid down more detailed provisions on the electronic submission of notices on State aid, including addresses and any provisions which may be necessary for the protection of confidential information. These more detailed provisions have been published in OJ C 237, September 27, 2005, p.3.

Article 4 of Regulation (EC) No.794/2004 contains rules for a simplified notification procedure for certain amendments to existing aid schemes.

Article 1(c) of Regulation (EC) No.659/1999 states that all *new aid* means all aid schemes and individual aid, which is not existing aid, including alterations to existing aid. Article 4(1) of Regulation (EC) No.794/2004 lays down that, for the purposes of art.1(c) of Regulation (EC) No.659/1999, an alteration to existing aid means any change, other than modifications of a purely formal or administrative nature which cannot affect the evaluation of the compatibility of the aid measure with the common market. An increase in the original budget of an existing aid scheme by up to 20 per cent is not considered an alteration to existing aid.

According to art.4(2) of Regulation (EC) No.794/2004, the following alterations to existing aid must be notified using the simplified notification form set out in Annex II:

1) Increases in the budget of an authorised aid scheme exceeding 20 per cent;
2) Prolongation of an existing authorised aid scheme by up to six years, with or without an increase in the budget; and
3) Tightening of the criteria for the application of an authorised aid scheme, a reduction of aid intensity or a reduction of eligible expenses.

The Commission will use its best endeavours to decide on any aid notified **2–021** on the simplified notification form within a period of one month, as the simplified notification procedure is not used to notify alterations to aid schemes in respect of which Member States have not submitted annual reports (on this, see paras 2–053 to 2–054), unless the annual reports are submitted at the same time as the notification.

Article 9 in Directive 2003/87/EC of the European Parliament and of the Council of October 13, 2003 establishing a scheme for greenhouse gas

---

[27] After an amendment to art.3 in Regulation (EC) No.794/2004 with amendments it is obligatory to use certain specific IT systems for submitting notices and correspondence to the Commission on this.

emission allowance trading within the Community and amending Council Directive 96/61/EC contains an arrangement under which the Member States are to draw up a national allocation plan (NAP) for the allocation of quotas. This plan must be made public and submitted to the Commission. The Commission has three months from its submission to evaluate whether the NAP is in accordance with the Directive. In connection with this, the Commission can reject the NAP in whole or in part.

The question of the relationship between submission in accordance with art.9 of the Directive, and notification in accordance with art.88(3) of the Treaty has been referred to the CFI.[28]

The CFI approached the case on the basis that two different areas of the law were concerned, but the CFI emphasised that on the one hand the Commission must have regard for the compatibility of an NAP with the rules on State aid, and that on the other hand it was not impossible that the submission of an NAP could, under certain circumstances, also consti-tute a notification as referred to in art.88(3) of the Treaty. In extension of this the CFI held that those aspects of a submitted NAP which could be in breach of art.87 of the Treaty must be subject to a preliminary examination by the Commission, which can lead to the institution of parallel procedures under the rules in Regulation (EC) No.659/1999. As stated, depending on the circumstances, the submission of an NAP can also constitute a full notification for the purposes of art.88(3). In this case, the Commission will have three months to deal with the NAP and two months to decide on the notification; see art.4(5) and (6) of Regulation (EC) No.659/1999. If the Commission does not decide on the notified State aid within the deadline of two months, this is tantamount to an approval; see art.4(6) of Regulation (EC) No.659/1999.

Standstill clause

2–022   According to both art.3 of Regulation (EC) No.659/1999 and art.88(3) of the Treaty, as long as the Commission has not given approval for notified aid, the Member State may not implement it. The standstill clause naturally applies for the duration of the preliminary procedure, but it expires if the Commission does not take a decision under the preliminary procedure.

However, a Member State may not implement aid in such cases until it has given prior notice to the Commission, after which, under art.4(6), the Commission has 15 days in which to react. If the Commission does not react, the Member State can implement the aid. If the Commission adopts a negative decision, the standstill clause is terminated, and is replaced by the prohibition in the decision. The standstill obligation ends if the Commission closes the formal procedure with a positive decision.

[28] Case T-387/04, *EnBW Energie Baden-Württemberg v Commission*, [2007] E.C.R. II-1195.

Member States' information obligation in connection with notification

As stated above, in connection with notification a Member State must give the **2–023** Commission all the information necessary to enable the Commission to take a decision on the basis of full notification as part of the preliminary examination of a case.

If the Commission finds that the information submitted is incomplete, it can request further information. Where a Member State responds to such a request, the Commission will inform the Member State of the receipt of the response. If a Member State does not provide the information requested, the Commission will send a reminder, allowing an appropriate additional period within which the information must be provided (art.5(2) of Regulation (EC) No.659/1999).

If a Member State fails to provide the information requested before the expiry of the relevant deadline or deadlines, the notification is deemed to have been withdrawn. However, this does not apply if, before the expiry of the relevant deadline, a Member State informs the Commission that the information requested is not available or has already been given and that the Member State therefore considers the notification to be complete. In this case, the two month period for the Commission's preliminary examination of the case begins to run from the date on which the Member State has declared that it considers the notification to be complete (art.5(3) of Regulation (EC) No.659/1999).

If a notification is deemed to have been withdrawn, as referred to, as in cases where there has been no notification at all, the Member State is put in the awkward position that, under art.13(2) of Regulation (EC) No.659/1999 the Commission is not bound by the time-limit set out in arts 4(5), 7(6) and 7(7), and a negative decision can be taken on the basis of the available information, either because the Member State has not complied with an information injunction or because the information provided is insufficient to establish that the aid is compatible with the common market.

Preliminary examination

The preliminary examination of new State aid constitutes the first of two **2–024** phases in such cases.[29] The preliminary examination is dealt with in art.4 of Regulation (EC) No.659/1999 which, among other things, sets out what forms of decisions the Commission can take. The Commission can decide: (1) that the notified measure does not constitute aid; (2) that no doubts are raised as to the compatibility with the common market of a notified measure (a "decision not to raise objections"); or that (3) doubts are raised as to the compatibility

---

[29] The term "preliminary" is not such a happy choice, as the procedure will often also be the final procedure. In relation to preliminary examination under art.4 of Regulation (EC) No. 659/1999, see Case T-357/02, *Freistaat Sachsen v Commission*, [2007] E.C.R. II-1565. The case has been appealed in order to have the judgment of the CFI overturned; see Case C-334/07.

with the common market of a notified measure (a "decision to initiate the formal investigation procedure").[30]

Under the preliminary examination the Commission can also decide that an aid measure is incompatible with art.87(1) of the EC Treaty. It is only on the basis of the formal procedure laid down in art.88(2) and in art.6 of Regulation (EC) No.659/1999 that interested parties can make their views known. On several occasions the Community courts have annulled a decision where the Commission has found that there was not State aid without initiating the formal procedure, but the courts have even more frequently rejected Commission decisions to the effect that there was aid which was compatible with the common market, without initiating the formal procedure.

When the Commission has to determine whether State aid is compatible with the common market, in principle it uses the substantive rules which applied to the case at the time when the aid was provided; see Commission notice on the determination of the applicable rules for the assessment of unlawful State aid (OJ C 119, May 22, 2002, p.22).[31]

The preliminary examination has three characteristics: (1) it is not transparent; (2) it is normally conducted in the form of a direct dialogue between the Commission and the Member State concerned; and (3) it is quick.[32] It does not involve "interested parties". The Commission has no obligation to involve third parties (interested parties) in the preliminary phase.[33]

2–025   According to the case law of the ECJ, interested parties may bring a case before the CFI against a decision of the Commission not to initiate the procedure under art.88(2) of the EC Treaty.[34]

The Commission is not required to make public notices of planned aid received from the Member States.[35]

The decisions referred to as part of the preliminary examination must be taken within two months from the date on which the Commission receives full information.

---

[30] In Case T-475/04, *Bouygues v Commission*, not yet reported, the CFI explained the difference between the preliminary examination and the formal investigation. The judgment has been appealed to the ECJ on other points; see Case C-431/07 P.

[31] Case T-357/02, *Freistaat Sachsen v Commission*, [2007] E.C.R. II-1565, gives a good description of the factors which are relevant in connection with the establishment of the substantive rules on the basis of which a notification is assessed, particularly when the Commission wishes to apply rules which have been issued after notification is made. The judgment has been appealed to the ECJ on other points; see Case C-334/07.

[32] Case C-367/95 P, *Commission v Sytraval*, [1998] E.C.R. I-1719 and Case T-266/94, *Skibsværftsforeningen v Commission*, [1996] E.C.R. II-1399.

[33] According to the case law, see Case 323/82, *Intermills v Commission*, [1984] E.C.R. 3809, para.16, concerned or interested parties are persons, undertakings or associations whose interests might be affected by the grant of the aid. This has now been codified in art.1(h) of Regulation (EC) No.659/1999 according to which such interested parties may in particular be the aid recipient, competing undertakings or trade associations. The reader is also referred to paras 8–023 to 8–026 on the right to bring a case for annulment against a decision of the Commission.

[34] Case C-198/91, *Cook v Commission*, [1993] E.C.R. I-2487.

[35] Joined Cases 91/83 and 127/83, *Heineken v Inspecteur der Vennootschapsbelasting*, [1984] E.C.R. 3455.

If the Commission has not taken a decision within two months, the aid measure is regarded as having been approved.[36] After that, the Member State can implement the aid, having first given the Commission notice of this, unless within 15 days of receiving the notice from the Member State the Commission adopts a decision on the aid. This arrangement can be seen as a safety valve which makes it possible to avoid the consequences of misunderstandings between the Commission and the Member States or of maladministration. According to the decision in Case T-187/99, *Agrana Zucker v Commission*, [2001] E.C.R. II-1587, in such a case the aid is regarded as being existing aid.

Case C-398/00, *Spain v Commission*, [2002] E.C.R. I-5643, deals with problems in relation to the date from which the deadline of 15 days begins to run. In accordance with art.88(3) of the Treaty, Spain had given notice to the Commission of some planned projects involving State aid which had not been implemented. At the time when notice was given there was thus new aid in accordance with art.2 of Regulation (EC) No.659/1999. The Commission considered the notification to be incomplete and therefore asked for further information. This information was sent to the Commission on May 24, 2000. The Commission did not react to this, so that the notification could be considered as having been completed on July 25, 2000. Thereafter, in accordance with art.4(6) of Regulation (EC) No.659/1999 Spain sent a notice to the Commission stating that the notified aid measures would be implemented. This notice was sent both by telefax, which arrived at the Commission on July 28, 2000 at 17.49, and by post which was delivered to the Commission on August 1, 2000. Spain believed that the deadline of 15 working days within which the Commission had to take a decision began to run on July 31, 2000. The Commission argued that the deadline first began to run on August 1, 2000.[37] The Commission argued that the telefax should be disregarded. The ECJ held that, given the factual circumstances of the case, the telefax was a notice for the purposes of art.4(6) of Regulation (EC) No.659/1999. The deadline of 15 working days therefore began to run from July 31, 2000, and expired on August 21, 2000. What is interesting in the case is that the Commission took a decision on August 17, 2000 (within the deadline) which was communicated to the Spanish authorities on August 23, (after the deadline). According to art.4(6) of Regulation (EC) No.659/1999, the Commission has a period of 15 working days in which to take a decision. On the other hand art.254(3) of the EC Treaty provides that decisions must be notified to those to whom they are addressed and take effect upon such notification. The ECJ concluded that in this context the deadline had been exceeded, as the decision did not take effect before August 23, 2000, and at the same time it noted that,

2–026

---

[36] On this point Regulation (EC) No.659/1999 codifies the decision in Case 120/73, *Lorenz v Germany*, [1973] E.C.R. 1471.

[37] According to art.2(2) of Regulation (EEC, Euratom) No.1182/71 of the Council of June 3, 1971 determining the rules applicable to periods, dates and time limits (OJ L 124, 8.6.1971, p.1), "working days" means all days other than public holidays, Sundays and Saturdays. According to art.3(1) of the Regulation, where a period is expressed in days, the day during which an event occurs is not be considered as falling within the period in question.

under art.25 of Regulation (EC) No.659/1999, the Commission should have notified Spain without delay. The deadline expired on August 21, 2000, and from that date the aid had the character of existing aid. As a consequence, the Commission could not base its decision on art.88(3) of the EC Treaty (which only applies to new aid), in order to prevent aid projects which have been initiated. The decision was thus legally at fault and it was annulled.

The principle introduced in art.4(6) of Regulation (EC) No.659/1999, and illustrated above, can only be relied on in connection with aid that has been notified in accordance with the procedure under art.88(3) of the Treaty. It does not apply in the context of a procedure which the Commission has introduced in connection with non-notified aid.[38]

2–027   The preliminary examination can take considerably longer than two months, as the deadline runs again from the beginning each time there is a request for information from the Member State and an answer to such request. This could be used both by the Commission and by a Member State to draw out the process.[39]

If a response is not received to a question from the Commission in due time, it can choose to regard the notification as not having been made; see art.5(3) of Regulation (EC) No.659/1999. However, the Commission may instead choose to extend the deadline for a response, and the Member State can now also ask the Commission to take a decision if it finds that the information requested is not available or has already been given to the Commission. A Member State can thereby make the processing of the preliminary examination shorter, but there is also a risk of misuse by a Member State. If the Commission finds this to be the case, it can initiate the formal investigation procedure.

The Commission presumably cannot make a decision conditional if it is taken under the preliminary examination, as it can with the formal examination.[40]

It is important that there should be no doubt about the decision of the Commission, since approved State aid can have far-reaching consequences for competitors and it cannot be recovered, and any procedural failings can make the Commission liable to pay damages.

It is not possible to go before the CFI with a claim that a State aid measure is lawful as long as the Commission has not made a final decision.

Formal investigation procedure

2–028   Article 6 of Regulation (EC) No.659/1999 states that a decision to initiate the formal investigation procedure (i.e. the procedure referred to in art.88(2)

---

[38] Joined Cases T-116/01 and T-118/01, *P & O European Ferries (Vizcaya) v Commission*, [2003] E.C.R. II-2957 para.217. The case was appealed to the ECJ, which rejected the appeal; Joined Cases C-442/03 P and C-471/03 P, *P & O European Ferries (Vizcaya) v Commission*, [2006] E.C.R. I-4845.

[39] The Commission can also ask questions during the formal investigation, but these do not have suspensive effect with regard to the deadline for the Commission's adoption of a decision.

[40] Case T-167/04, *Asklepios Kliniken v Commission*, not yet reported.

of the Treaty) must summarise the relevant issues of fact and law, include a preliminary assessment of the Commission as to the aid character of the proposed measure, and set out any doubts as to its compatibility with the common market. The decision must be sufficiently precise to enable interested parties to participate effectively in the formal investigation procedure, including being able to submit arguments in accordance with art.20(1) of the Regulation.[41] The decision must also contain a invitation to the the Member State concerned and other interested parties to submit comments with a certain time limit that should not, normally, exceed one month, but the Commission can prolong the time limit.

If the Member State and interested parties believe that the facts given in a decision to initiate a formal investigation are incorrect, they must draw this to the attention of the Commission in an administrative procedure, as they will not otherwise be able to dispute the facts in litigation.[42] The obligation for a Member State not to implement planned measures continues until the Commission has taken its final decision in the case, on closing the formal investigation.

The formal procedure does not involve third parties as part of an adversary procedure to which they are parties. The Commission has consistently considered it to be a bilateral procedure between it and the Member State concerned, and this has been confirmed by Regulation (EC) No.659/1999. Interested parties are not informed about the observations of Member States or other interested parties.

It is only on the basis of the formal procedure that the Commission can decide that an aid measure is not compatible with the common market.

The formal procedure is adversarial, which means that the Member State **2–029** concerned must be given the opportunity to express its views on the arguments on which the Commission intends to base its decision. If the Member State has not had such an opportunity, the Commission cannot use such arguments as a basis for its decision in the case.[43]

However, such a situation can lead to an annulment if, without the defect referred to, the procedure would have led to a different decision. It is the established case law that the formal procedure must be used if the Commission encounters serious problems in its investigation of whether some aid is compatible with the common market. The CFI's examination of this is more wide-ranging than a mere examination of whether an investigation has made a manifestly wrong assessment; see Case T-73/98, *Prayon-Rupel v Commission*, [2001] E.C.R. II-867.

In the decision to initiate the formal investigation procedure, the Member

---

[41] Joined Cases T-111/01 and T-133/01, *Saxonia Edelmetalle and Others v Commission*, [2005] E.C.R. II-1579.

[42] Case T-318/00, *Freistaat Thüringen v Commission*, [2005] E.C.R. II-4179.

[43] Case C-288/96, *Germany v Commission*, [2000] E.C.R. I-8237 para.100. See also Case C-288/96, *Belgium v Commission*, [1986] E.C.R. 2263; and Case C-301/87, *France v Commission*, [1990] E.C.R. I-307, para.31.

State concerned and other interested parties (whether Member States, undertakings or individuals) are invited to submit their comments by a deadline which is normally a maximum of one month. It would be contrary to art.6(1) of the Regulation to fail to name the recipient of the aid in the decision, or to name the wrong recipient.[44]

If the Commission makes a mistake of this kind, and becomes aware of it, it is possible to correct the mistake by extending the deadline for the submission of comments.[45]

2–030   The Commission cannot always disregard observations which are received after the deadline. The Commission is required to carry out a thorough and impartial investigation, and important information should be included in this, even if it is received by the Commission after the deadline.[46]

The comments received are forwarded to the Member State (anonymously, if the interested party so requests). The Member State can respond to the comments within a deadline laid down, which can be extended by the Commission. In contrast, interested parties cannot comment on the comments put forward by Member States, other interested parties or possible aid recipients; see Case C-367/95 P, *Commission v Sytraval*, [1998] E.C.R. I–1719 para.53.

Naturally, the reason for consulting interested parties is to get as much information about the case as possible before the Commission makes its final decision.

Conclusion of the formal investigation procedure

2–031 The conclusion of the formal investigation procedure (i.e. the procedure in accordance with art.88(2) of the Treaty—see art.7 of Regulation (EC) No.659/1999) takes place by the adoption of a decision as referred to in paras 2–024 to 2–028. Such decisions must be taken as soon as any doubt about the compatibility of an aid measure with the common market has been removed.[47]

The Commission must notify the decision to the interested parties who have submitted observations during the administrative procedure. The same applies to any beneficiary of individual aid; see art.20(1) of Regulation (EC) No.659/1999. In its reasoning, the Commission must take account of the most significant complaints which have been made during the administrative procedure by the interested parties whose views have not been accepted. Other interested parties can ask to be sent a copy of the decision.

---

[44] Case T-34/02, *EURL Le Levant 001 v Commission*, [2006] E.C.R. II-267.
[45] *EURL Le Levant 001 v Commission*, [2006] E.C.R. II-267.
[46] Case T-366/00, *Scott v Commission*, [2003] E.C.R. II-1763. This case was appealed to the ECJ, which rejected the appeal; see Case C-276/03 P, *Scott v Commission*, [2005] E.C.R. I-8437.
[47] For the sake of good order, it should be noted that State aid decisions must be adopted by the college of Commissioners; Case T-442/93, *Association des Amidonneries de Céréales de la CEE and Others v Commission*, [1995] E.C.R. II-1329.

A final decision can either grant approval, refuse approval, or it may find that, in order for the measure in question to obtain approval, it must be amended or approval may be granted subject to certain conditions. For example, a condition may be that the amount of the aid must be reduced, or certain restructuring measures must be implemented. There can also be a condition that aid may only be paid out if there is a recovery of previously paid aid which is unlawful and incompatible with the common market.[48] It can also be a condition that aid must be paid in instalments. Failure to comply with a condition relating to aid that must be paid in instalments can mean that subsequent instalments can be presumed to be incompatible with the common market, and can only be paid out if the Commission approves in a new decision.[49]

As emphasised in Case C-367/95 P, *Commission v Sytraval*, [1998] E.C.R. I-1719, a reference must be made to an exception under art.87 of the EC Treaty if it has been the basis for a positive decision, i.e. a decision to approve an aid measure.

As far as possible the final decision must be taken within 18 months from   **2–032**
the start of the State aid procedure.[50] The deadline can be extended by agreement with the Member State concerned.

If the deadline has finally expired without a decision being taken as part of the formal investigation procedure, and if the Member State so requests, the Commission will take a decision within two months on the basis of the information it has.

The right to request a decision to be made within two months after the end of the normal deadline of 18 months (i.e. without taking account of any extension of it), means that the formal procedure can easily last for up to two years. This is open to criticism, and one may question the necessity of an aid measure for which the implementation can be delayed for nearly two years after notification.

If the information given is insufficient to establish that the aid is compatible with the common market, the Commission can make a negative decision, i.e. reject the compatibility of the aid with the common market.

However, in contrast to what applies under the preliminary procedure, the   **2–033**
Commission's failure to take a decision by the deadline under the formal procedure does not mean that the aid can be regarded as having been approved.

Competing undertakings can bring an action for the annulment of a

---

[48] Joined Cases T-244 and 486/93, *Textilwerke Deggendorf*, [1995] E.C.R. II-2265.
[49] Case T-140/95, *Ryanair v Commission*, [1998] E.C.R. II-3327.
[50] The period of 18 months in art.7(6) of the Regulation is a goal, but not a binding deadline; Case T-190/00, *Regione Siciliana v Commission*, [2003] E.C.R. II-5015. According to the judgment in this case, good administrative practice requires the Commission to act within a reasonable period when taking administrative decisions concerning competition policy. The assessment must be made from case to case whether the length of the administrative procedure can be regarded as reasonable, taking into account the context of the cases, the various stages of the administrative procedure, the complexity of the case, and its importance for the parties involved. See also Case T-171/02, *Regione autonoma della Sardegna v Commission*, [2005] E.C.R. II-2123, where the Commission was not criticised for dealing with a case unreasonably slowly, as the Member State had also been responsible for drawing out the case.

positive decision, but they must be able to demonstrate that their position on the market will be significantly affected by the decision. Participation in an administrative procedure is an element which suggests that an undertaking can be regarded as being directly and individually concerned (as referred to in art.230 of the EC Treaty), but it will not automatically be sufficient, just as it is not enough to constitute an interested party.[51]

Within two months, which is the deadline in art.230, the Member State concerned can bring judicial proceedings against the Commission's decision. If such action is not taken, in the event of proceedings by the Commission because of the Member State's failure to comply with its decision, the Member State can only object on the basis that it is absolutely impossible to implement the Commission's decision correctly (for example, with regard to the recovery of aid). This requirement is interpreted very strictly; see Case C-280/99, *Italy v Commission*, [1998] E.C.R. I-259.

Depending on the circumstances, industrial organisations can have competence to bring an action.[52]

It is difficult to be regarded as individually concerned in relation to a general aid measure for which a decision has been made approving it.[53]

Procedure on unlawful aid

2–034   Unlawful aid is non-notified aid, aid which has been notified but which has then been implemented before the Commission has given approval, aid which is given in breach of conditions for its approval, aid amounts which exceed the approved amounts, or aid to a large undertaking even though the aid measure only applies to small and medium sized undertakings.

According to art.1(g) of Regulation (EC) No.659/1999, *misuse of aid* means aid used by the beneficiary in contravention of a decision approving the aid.

If a Member State infringes the provisions on prior notification and the standstill obligation, the State aid procedure will be largely the same as that which applies to notified aid, but there are several additional provisions.

---

[51] See Case C-367/95 P, *Commission v Sytraval*, [1998] I-1719, Case T-266/94, *Skibsværftsforeningen v Commission*, [1996] II-1399, Case 169/84, *Cofaz e.a. v Commission*, [1986] E.C.R. 391, Case T-435/93, *ASPEC e.a. v Commission* [1995] II-1281, and Case T-189/97 [1998] II-335, *CDE de la Société francaise de production*, as upheld in Case C-106/ 98 P, E.C.R. [2000] I-3659. Non-participation in the administrative procedure does not preclude the ability to stand in an annulment case under art.230, see Case T-266/94 quoted above. According to Regulation (EC) No.659/1999, the final decision must be published in the Official Journal. In Case T-14/96, *BAI v Commission*, [1999] E.C.R. II-139 the CFI held that the deadline for third parties to bring an action first begins to run from the date of publication of a Commission decision in the Official Journal, even though the third party may have obtained knowledge of the decision from a press release from the Commission.
[52] Case T-122/96, *Federolio v Commission*, [1997] E.C.R. II-1559, which refers to situations where industrial organisations have been regarded as being individually concerned.
[53] Case T-86/96, *Arbeitsgemeinschaft Deutscher Luftfahrt-Unternehmen and Others v Commission*, [1999] E.C.R. II-179 (rejected).

For example with regard to unlawful, non-notified aid, if the Commission becomes aware of this by way of a complaint, under art.13 of Regulation (EC) No.659/1999, as part of the preliminary procedure laid down in art.4(2) the Commission may decide that the measure does not constitute State aid. Also, under art.4(3), the Commission can decide not to raise an objection, because it finds the aid to be compatible with the common market, and if relevant it must refer to which of the exceptions in the EC Treaty it relies on in making such a decision. Finally, under art.4(4), the Commission can decide to initiate the formal investigation procedure, if it finds that there is doubt about the compatibility of the aid with the common market.

Under art.10 of Regulation (EC) No.659/1999, if the Commission obtains **2–035** information about alleged unlawful aid, it must examine that information. This is the case regardless of the source of the information, and the basis for this can thus be a complaint, or reports in the press, or an annual report forwarded to the Commission on the basis of the Transparency Directive (2006/111/EC), see paras 2–060 to 2–065.

There is no deadline for the Commission's handling of cases regarding non-notified aid. No special consideration is due to the Member State which has failed to notify the aid, or to the recipient of the aid who has benefited from the aid. However, in these cases the Commission tries to take a decision as quickly as possible out of consideration for the interested parties (for example, competitors). This applies especially if the case is initiated on the basis of a complaint.[54]

According to art.10(1) of Regulation (EC) No.659/1999, the Commission must investigate complaints without delay, and if necessary the Commission can request information from the Member State concerned. If, despite reminders, the Member State does not provide the information requested within a deadline set by the Commission, or if the information is incomplete, the Commission can issue an *information injunction*; see art.10(3). The decision must state what information is required[55] and lay down a suitable deadline for the provision of the information.

If a Member State does not provide the information required, or if it is **2–036** incomplete, the Commission can take a final decision on the basis of the information available to it; see art.13(1) of the Regulation. This possibility is an effective means of applying pressure to get information from an uncooperative Member State. However, when applying such pressure the

---

[54] See the judgment in Case T-95/96, *Gestevision Telecinco v Commission*, [1998] E.C.R. II-3407, where the CFI stated that, where there is a complaint, the Commission must respect reasonable deadlines, and added that, also out of consideration to the recipient of aid, a deadline should be used which does not vary materially from the deadline (two months) which applies to notified aid. On this problem see also Case T-395/04, *Air One v Commission*, [2006] E.C.R. II-1343.

[55] The Commission must specify the information required, e.g. a formulation such as "documents, information and useful data in order to allow the Commission to examine the compatibility with art.87 of the measures" is insufficiently precise; see Case T-366/00, *Scott v Commission*, [2003] E.C.R. II-1763, which case was appealed to the ECJ, which rejected the appeal; see Case C-276/03 P, *Scott v Commission*, [2005] E.C.R. I-8437; this can have consequences for the legal force of the Commission's decision if it then applies the provision in art.13(1), third sentence.

provisions of arts 5(2), 10(3) and 13(1) of the Regulation must be complied with.[56]

When the Commission, acting pursuant to art.10(3), issues an information injunction pursuant to art.13(1) where a Member State does not provide the information requested, the Commission may adopt a decision to close the investigation procedure on the basis of the information available. It is not released from its obligation to state sufficiently the reasons which have led it to consider that the information provided by a Member State, in response to the information injunction, cannot be relied on in the final decision which it intends to adopt.[57] This is not the same as a situation where a Member State fails to provide any information to the Commission in response to an injunction issued pursuant to art.10(3). In this case the reasons may be limited to merely stating that the Member State has failed to respond to the injunction.[58] However, if the Commission does not use its powers to obtain information from a Member State, it cannot base its decision on the grounds that the information available to it was incomplete.[59]

2–037   In the event of unlawful, i.e. non-notified aid, the Commission can use interim measures to minimise the risk of any harmful effects from the unlawful aid. Thus, after giving the Member State concerned the opportunity to submit its comments, the Commission may adopt a decision requiring the Member State to suspend the unlawful aid. If such a suspension injunction is not complied with, then according to the case law and art.12 of Regulation (EC) No.659/1999, the Commission may refer the matter directly to the ECJ.[60]

A suspension injunction will typically be issued at the same time as the initiation of or during the formal investigation procedure, i.e. the procedure referred to in art.88(2) of the Treaty.

As previously referred to, the Commission cannot require aid paid as unlawful aid to be recovered, unless it has established that the aid in question is incompatible with the common market.[61] Under art.11 of the Regulation the Commission can, after giving the Member State concerned the opportunity to submit its comments, adopt a decision requiring the Member State provisionally to recover any unlawful aid in order to counteract the harmful effects of the aid. However, the following criteria must be fulfilled: (a) according to an established practice there must be no doubts about the aid character of the measure concerned, (b) there must be an urgent need to act, and (c) there must be a serious risk of substantial and irreparable damage to a competitor.

2–038   In such cases the Commission must then comply with the deadlines that

---

[56] Case T-196/02, *MTU Friedrichshafen v Commission*, [2007] E.C.R. II-2889. An appeal has been brought against this decision, see C-520/07 P.
[57] Joined Cases T-111/01 and T-133/01, *Saxonia Edelmetalle and Others v Commission*, [2005] E.C.R. II-1579 para.145.
[58] *Saxonia Edelmetalle and Others v Commission*, [2005] E.C.R. II-1579 para.145.
[59] Case T-274/01, *Valmont v Commission*, [2004] E.C.R. II-3145.
[60] Case C-301/87, *France v Commission (Boussac)*, [1990] E.C.R. I-307 para.23.
[61] Case C-354/90, *Fédération Nationale du Commerce Extérieur des Produits Alimentaires v France*, [1991] E.C.R. I-5505, paras 13 and 14.

apply to notified aid. The Commission can approve the payment of rescue aid to an undertaking which suffers financial difficulties as a result of being required to make such repayment on an interim basis.

The procedure for dealing with cases of non-notified aid is the same as the procedure for dealing with notified aid – in two phases; see art.13 of Regulation (EC) No.659/1999.

According to the case law, good administrative practice requires the Commission to resolve the situation when a case is referred to it on the basis of a complaint. Depending on the circumstances, this can mean that it has a duty to conduct a diligent and impartial examination of the complaint, which may make it necessary for it to examine matters not expressly raised by the complainant.[62]

As for the right of complainants to bring an action for annulment, see paras 8–001 to 8–022 on the courts' powers.

Injunction to suspend or provisionally recover aid—final recovery decision

After giving a Member State the opportunity to submit its comments, the Commission may adopt a decision requiring the Member State to suspend any unlawful aid until the Commission has taken a decision on the compatibility of the aid with the common market (art.11(1) of Regulation (EC) No.659/1999). This decision is called a *suspension injunction*. Under the same conditions, under art.11(2) the Commission may adopt a decision called a *recovery injunction*. As stated in paras 2–034 to 2–038, the issue of a recovery injunction requires the following three conditions to have been fulfilled:

2–039

- according to an established practice there must be no doubts about the aid character of the measure concerned;
- there must be an urgent need to act; and
- there must be a serious risk of substantial and irreparable damage to a competitor.

The last named, referring to the serious risk of substantial and irreparable damage, is very similar to the conditions which generally apply to the right of the Commission and the ECJ to use interim measures in general in relation to infringements of EU law. As regards State aid, it is unlikely that the circumstances will often be such as to require such suspension.

Only in respect of unlawful aid paid out after the entry into force of Regulation (EC) No.659/1999 can the Commission authorise a Member State to link the recovery of such aid with the payment of rescue aid to an undertaking that has received aid.

---

[62] Case C-367/95 P, *Commission v Sytraval*, [1998] E.C.R. I-1719 para.62.

Under art.12 of the regulation, if a Member State fails to comply with a suspension injunction or a recovery injunction, the Commission can refer the matter to the CFI.

2–040   The decisions which the Commission can take with regard to unlawful aid are the same as those discussed above, with reference to art.4(2), (3) or (4) of the Regulation, or in cases where the formal investigation is used, a decision as referred to in art.7 of the Regulation, as discussed in paras 2–031 to 2–033.

Under art.14 of the Regulation, where a negative decision is taken, i.e. a decision to refuse approval of aid, the Commission must decide that the Member State concerned must recover the aid from the beneficiary (*recovery decision*). The aid recovered must include interest payable from the date on which the unlawful aid was at the disposal of the beneficiary until the date of its recovery; see Ch.7.

Recovery of aid must be carried out without delay and in accordance with the procedures under the national laws of the Member State concerned, provided that they allow the immediate and effective execution of the Commission's decision; see art.14(3) of the Regulation. Long experience shows that in about 10 per cent of the cases where recovery has been ordered recovery of aid has not been carried out as much as after ten years later; see Ch.7.[63]

2–041   Regulation (EC) No.659/1999 laid down that the Commission has a duty to require the recovery of unlawful aid. Such a clear duty was not clearly expressed in Community legislation prior to the Regulation, but the Commission's right to require recovery was approved by the ECJ . However, the Commission must not require recovery of aid if this would be contrary to a general principle of Community law; see art.14(1) of the Regulation and, for example, Commission Decision 2001/212/EC of May 16, 2000 on the aid scheme implemented by Italy to assist large firms in difficulty (OJ L 79, March 17, 2001, p.29).

The Commission may not require recovery of aid merely because it is non-notified or aid implemented in breach of art.88(3) of the Treaty (standstill provision). The aid must also be incompatible with the common market. It is only national courts which have a right to order repayment on the grounds of aid being non-notified or because of an infringement of the standstill provision.

Limitation period for recovery

2–042   According to art.15 of the Regulation, the Commission cannot require the recovery of aid after a limitation period of ten years. The limitation period

---

[63] Only the final decision to initiate proceedings under art.88(2) of the Treaty or to approve aid is made public. Under art.4(6) of Regulation (EC) No.659/1999 the Commission must make public a notice of any aid deemed to have been approved in cases where the Commission does not react to a Member State's notification of aid within the two months deadline. Something similar applies to cases concerning the repayment of unlawfully collected taxes in Member States; see Case 199/82, *Amministrazione delle finanze dello Stato v San Giorgio*, [1983] E.C.R. 3595.

begins to run on the day on which the unlawful aid is awarded to the benefici-ary either as individual aid or as aid under an aid scheme. The limitation starts to run afresh after any action taken with regard to the unlawful aid by the Commission or by a Member State acting at the request of the Commission. It is sufficient to interrupt the limitation period if the Commission sends a letter to the relevant national authorities with a request for supplementary information.[64] Furthermore, it is not a condition for the interruption of the period of limitation that the beneficiary of the aid should be informed about the measures.[65] This is consistent with the fact that the beneficiary of aid does not have the status of a party to proceedings under art.88(2). Beneficiaries of aid only have rights which enable them to give information to the Commission and to submit comments.

The limitation period is suspended while a decision of the Commission is the subject of proceedings before the ECJ.

A limitation period of 10 years seems reasonable, as the Commission can easily interrupt it, and because the most important cases of State aid which cause serious distortion of competition could hardly be kept hidden for as long as ten years.

Procedure regarding misuse of aid

In Regulation (EC) No.659/1999 *misuse of aid* is defined as aid used by a benefi-ciary in contravention of a decision taken pursuant to art.4(3) or art.7(3) or (4) of the Regulation; in other words in cases where the Commission decides not to raise objections (art.4(3)), or has given a positive decision, with or without conditions (art.7(3) and (4)).[66]   **2–043**

The procedure for misuse of aid largely follows the procedure applicable to unlawful aid. The most important difference is that in cases of misuse of aid by a beneficiary of aid, the Commission cannot take a decision without initiating formal proceedings; see art.88(2) of the Treaty. Another difference is that a recovery injunction cannot be used.

In the event of misuse of aid which has already been approved, accord-ing to art.16 of the Regulation the Commission can initiate the preliminary examination procedure in art.4(4), subject to a number of the other provisions in the Regulation.

[64] Case T-366/00, *Scott v Commission*, [2003] E.C.R. II-1763. This case was appealed to the ECJ, which rejected the appeal; see Case C-276/03 P, *Scott v Commission*, [2005] E.C.R. I-8437; and Case T-369/00, *Département du Loiret v Commission*, [2003]E.C.R. II-1789, which has been appealed to the ECJ, see Case C-295/07 P. These cases also concern the problems of limitation which can arise in relation to the application of Regulation (EC) No.659/1999 to a case where aid has been given before the entry into force of the Regulation, but where the Commission has taken a decision after the entry into force of the Regulation.
[65] *Scott v Commission*, [2003] E.C.R. II-1763, *Scott v Commission*, [2005] E.C.R. I-8437 and *Département du Loriet v Commission*, [2003] E.C.R. II-1789.
[66] For an illustration of art.7(4), see *Sabine Crome*: "Conditional decisions and EC State aid law: The MobilCom case", in *Competition Policy Newsletter*, No.3, Autumn 2004. p.55.

2-044   Misuse of aid can occur, for example, if a Member State grants individual aid under an approved scheme without complying with the conditions attached to the approval of the aid, or for example if a Member State grants aid which could lawfully be given as investment aid but which is used by the beneficiary as aid for operating costs.[67] Misuse can thus concern both the granting and the use of aid in contravention of approved aid, whereby the beneficiary of the aid obtains the aid in breach of the Commission's conditions. In such cases the Commission must require the aid to be recovered.

In principle it is up to the Commission to show that aid or part of some aid that has been approved in a previous decision has been misused by a beneficiary. If the Commission is unable to substantiate this, the aid must be regarded as being covered by the approval. However, should a Member State not comply with a request for information, in art.16 of the Regulation, a reference to art.13 does enable the Commission to take a decision to conclude the formal investigation procedure on the basis of the available information. Therefore, if a Member State does not give sufficiently clear and precise information about the use of some aid, about which on the basis of available information the Commission has raised doubts as to compliance with the conditions for its approval, the Commission is empowered to establish that there is misuse of the aid concerned, even if it is not in a position to prove the actual use of the aid in question.[68]

Procedure regarding existing aid schemes

2-045   This procedure only applies to aid schemes, and not to individual grants of aid, and *appropriate measures*, as referred to in art.18 of Regulation (EC) No.659/1999, cannot be proposed and applied with regard to individual aid.[69]

With regard to existing aid schemes, the definition of which is discussed in para.2–012, as stated in art.88(1) of the Treaty, the procedure is based on cooperation between the Commission and the Member States, which lays down obligations both for the Commission and for the Member States; see Case C-135/93, *Spain v Commission*, [1995] E.C.R. I-1651 para.24; however, it is the Commission which must take the initiative in taking action. The

---

[67] Case T-140/95, *Ryanair v Commission*, [1998] E.C.R. II-3327, according to which the failure to comply with a condition laid down in the approval, that the aid should be paid in instalments, had the effect that the subsequent instalments were assumed not to be compatible with the common market. Thus, according to the judgment they could not be paid unless the Commission took a new decision giving formal dispensation from compliance with the condition in question.

[68] Joined Cases T-111/01 and T-133/01, *Saxonia Edelmetalle and Others v Commission*, [2005] E.C.R. II-1579.

[69] If the Commission finds that an existing aid scheme is not—or is no longer—compatible with the common market, then under art.18, it must issue a recommendation proposing appropriate measures to the Member State concerned; these can relate to making substantive amendments to the aid scheme, or introducing procedural requirements, or revoking the aid scheme.

Member States do not have an obligation to notify with respect to existing aid.[70]

Article 17 of the Regulation on the procedure for existing aid lays down that the Commission must obtain from the Member State concerned all necessary information for the review (this concerns the first phase in the handling of a case), in cooperation with the Member State, pursuant to art.88(1) of the Treaty. There is presumably an obligation for Member States to comply with such a request; see the duty of loyalty in art.10 of the Treaty.

If, in the second phase of the investigation, the Commission finds that there   **2–046** is no reason to take the matter further, it can close the case and inform the Member State concerned accordingly.

The decision about whether a case concerns new aid or existing aid must not be taken by the Commission on a subjective basis; Case C-295/97, *Piaggio v International Factors Italia and Others*, [1999] E.C.R. I-3735 paras 45-48. This concerns an objective concept.

If the Commission is in doubt, it can request that the Member State provide further information. If the Member State does not give it, the Commission can require the payment of the aid to be suspended, and it can decide on the compatibility of the aid with the common market on the basis of the Treaty, as if it concerns new aid.[71]

On the other hand, if in the second phase the Commission finds on the basis of its preliminary examination of a case that the existing aid either is not or is no longer compatible with the common market, it informs the Member State accordingly, and gives the Member State one month in which to submit comments. This deadline can be extended. Existing aid can be aid which has originally been lawful, but which has since become unlawful, for example because it is in a country which has subsequently acceded to the EU, or because the sector in question has since been liberalised (for example telecommunications), so that the State is no longer entitled to provide aid.[72]

If thereafter, as part of a third phase of dealing with a case, the Commission   **2–047** still finds that the existing aid is incompatible with the common market, it can address a proposal to the Member State on appropriate measures. These can involve amending the content of a scheme, introducing procedural require-

---

[70] On existing aid, see Case T-288/97, *Regione Friuli Venezia Giulia v Commission*, [1999] E.C.R. II-1871. See also Case C-99/98, *Austria v Commission*, [2001] E.C.R. I-1101.

[71] Case C-47/91, *Italy v Commission*, [1994] E.C.R. I-4635 para.35. According to the judgment in Case C-295/97, *Piaggio v International Factors Italia and Others*, [1999] E.C.R. I-3735, the question whether aid should be regarded as existing or new should be considered without regard for the time that has elapsed since the implementation of the measure. Delay in the Commission's handling of a case does not in itself make a measure existing aid.

[72] An example of existing aid which was not regarded as aid when the Treaty was originally signed, but which has since become so as a result of the development of the market is the Commission's decision on tax exemptions for certain French insurance undertakings (Bulletin Quotidien Europe, 16.11.2001, p.15). Among other things the Commission found that when the Third Insurance Directive entered into force and was made applicable to mutual companies, the insurance market in Europe became more and more competitive, which made such aid incompatible with the common market.

ments, or terminating the arrangement.[73] If the Member State accepts the Commission's proposal, it must then implement the appropriate measures; see art.19(1) of the Regulation. If the Member State does not accept the Commission's proposal, the Commission must follow the procedure referred to in art.88(2) of the Treaty and make a formal decision; see art.19(2) of the Regulation. This means that the relevant articles (arts 6 and 7 of the Regulation) apply mutatis mutandis, and that all the procedural rules with regard to new aid are applicable, with the exception of the standstill clause; see art.19(2).

The rules on unlawful aid are not applicable to the procedure for existing aid, so that orders or decisions concerning recovery of aid cannot be used. Only if the Commission adopts a negative decision on the conclusion of a formal investigation procedure does an existing aid scheme become unlawful, and such a decision only relates to the future, if the aid scheme continues to be in breach of a decision to amend or terminate it.[74]

Article 19 in Regulation (EC) No.659/1999 sets out what means are at the disposal of the Commission if a Member State does not accept its proposed measures. For example the Commission can order the Member State to annul an aid measure by a given deadline.[75]

Interested parties and rights of third parties

2–048   All interested parties can, according to art.6 of Regulation 659/99, submit comments after the Commission has initiated the formal procedure. Interested

[73] According to art.7(4) of Regulation (EC) No.659/1999, the Commission may attach conditions to a positive decision. For an example of conditions approved by the European courts, see Joined Cases T-244 and 486/93, *Textilwerke Deggendorf*, [1995] E.C.R. II-2265 para.55, upheld by the ECJ in Case C-355/95 P, [1997] E.C.R. I-2549. The Commission had suspended Germany's right to pay an aid which had otherwise been approved, as long as the beneficiary undertaking had not repaid a previous non-notified and incompatible aid.

[74] See Joined Cases C-182/03 and C-217/03, *Belgium and Forum 187 ABSL v Commission*, [2006] E.C.R. I-5479, concerning among other things a successful attempt to claim the protection of a legitimate expectation that a decision of the Commission should contain transitional provisions. In this case the principle of equal treatment was relied upon with success.

[75] When the Commission has to decide on cases of individual aid, it must first examine whether the aid in fact falls within the scope of the approved aid scheme. If it does so, it must be considered as being approved, i.e. existing aid; see Case C-47/91, *Italy v Commission*, [1994] E.C.R. I-4635. As long as aid is compatible with an aid scheme approved by the Commission, the Commission will not be able to require suspension of payment of the aid, since under art.87(3) of the EC Treaty it only has powers to do so in relation to new aid; see para.25. A negative decision on a general aid scheme, previously approved by the Commission, does not have retrospective effect, and aid which has already been paid out will not be subject to a recovery order under a subsequent Commission decision to reject the scheme. As for an existing scheme, previously approved by the Commission, which the Commission may want, for example, to re-evaluate in connection with an actual aid case, as long as the Commission has not taken a decision in accordance with art.88(2) of the EC Treaty, a Member State may implement the aid scheme; see Case 47/91, *Italy v Commission*, [1994] E.C.R. I-4635 paras 24 and 25, where it was stated that the court must first examine whether the aid is covered by the general scheme and satisfies the conditions laid down in the decision approving it. If following the examination the Commission finds that the individual aid is in conformity with its decision approving the scheme it must be regarded as authorised aid, and thus as existing aid.

parties who have submitted comments on aid or on an aid scheme, as well as beneficiaries of individual aid, are sent a copy of the decision which the Commission takes in accordance with art.7 of Regulation (EC) No.659/1999 on the decision to close the formal investigation procedure, in other words, approval, conditional approval or rejection.

All interested parties can inform the Commission about alleged unlawful aid. If, because it finds an insufficient basis for doing so, the Commission decides not to take action on receipt of a complaint, it notifies the interested party accordingly, who will also receive notice of any decisions the Commission may take in the case.

As stated above, third parties only have limited rights in the administrative procedure. This can be unfortunate, as it can lead to approval being given without a sufficiently broad view being taken of the case because the Commission only relies on the explanations given by the Member State which is responsible for the aid. This can result in cases being brought before the CFI when this could be avoided.

The limited right to be involved in the State aid procedure does not apply in practice to the potential beneficiaries of aid. According to the practice of the Commission they are allowed to be involved during the whole of the formal investigation procedure, and it must be assumed that the Commission is obliged, at least upon request, to give aid beneficiaries the possibility of commenting on the observations which the Commission receives from the interested parties; see art.88(2) of the Treaty. It is uncertain whether the potential beneficiaries of aid have a direct "right of reply" to the observations of third parties, but the State which, as potential provider of aid does have such a right, will normally consult the potential aid beneficiaries before replying to the Commission. **2–049**

In Case 730/79, *Philip Morris Holland v Commission*, [1980] E.C.R. 2671, it was established that a beneficiary of aid can bring an action to annul a negative decision of the Commission against proposed aid.

Even though Regulation (EC) No.659/1999 does not oblige the Commission to involve a complainant or other interested parties in the preliminary procedure, in the interests of sound administration the Commission is required to conduct a "diligent and impartial examination" of the complaint (see Case C-367/95 P, *Commission v Sytraval*, [1998] E.C.R. I-1719 para.62), which may make it necessary for it to examine matters not expressly raised by the complainant.[76]

Naturally, the Commission's decisions on State aid must be stated clearly, **2–050**

---

[76] In so far as a complainant, e.g. a competing undertaking, falls under the heading of an "interested party", as discussed in paras 2–024–2–030, the complainant must be permitted to bring an action for annulment. Thus, when on the basis of art.88(3) the Commission without opening the formal procedure under art.88(2) finds that State aid is compatible with the common market, persons, undertakings or associations whose interests may be affected by the granting of an aid, in particular competing undertakings or trade associations, who are intended, as parties concerned, to benefit from the procedural guaranties where the procedure in Article 88(2) is implemented, must be permitted to bring an action for annulment as provided for in art.230 of the EC Treaty, see Case C-397/95 P, *Commission v. Sytraval*, [1998] E.C.R. I-1719, paras 40 and 41.

as required by art.253 of the EC Treaty, so that interested parties can assess the basis on which they are made, and the Community's courts can exercise judicial review.

A refusal by the Commission to accept a complaint must also provide the complainant with an adequate explanation of the reasons why the Commission finds that the complaint does not lead to a finding that art.87 of the Treaty has been infringed.[77]

If the Commission initiates proceedings under art.88(2) of the Treaty it must give interested parties the opportunity to submit their comments on the notified aid scheme. A breach of this requirement by the Commission would constitute an infringement of an essential procedural requirement, see art.230 of the EC Treaty, and could lead to the annulment of the decision. Conversely, the right in art.20(1) of the Regulation for interested parties to submit comments does not amount to an obligation on the Commission to enter into a form of adversarial proceeding with interested parties.[78] Interested parties have an important role as a source of information for the Commission in the procedure under art.88(2).[79]

2–051   According to art.20(1) of the Regulation, the Commission must send a copy of its final decision to any interested parties who have submitted comments during an administrative procedure and to any beneficiary of individual aid. Such persons thereby have a basis for considering whether there are grounds for challenging the decision through an action for annulment. Under the second sentence of art.20(1) the Commission must send a copy of its decision after the conclusion of the formal investigation procedure notification to the Member State concerned. The legality of a legal act is assessed on the basis of the actual legal circumstances which existed on the date of the adoption of the act. Since the legality of a measure must be assessed by reference to the facts and legal factors prevailing at the time of its adoption, infringement of the requirement under art.20(1) cannot lead to a finding that the contested decision is unlawful and, therefore, to its annulment.[80]

Article 20(2) of the Regulation gives an interested party a right to inform the Commission of any alleged unlawful aid and any alleged misuse of aid. The Commission is assumed to have an obligation to inform the interested party about what it will do about the case. The Commission can decide to take a decision on the case, or it can find that, on the basis of the information available to it, there are insufficient grounds for deciding on the case.

The Commission is also assumed to have limited scope for refraining from taking a decision on such cases. Only in cases where it is clear that measures

---

[77] Case C-367/95 P, *Commission v Sytraval*, [1998] E.C.R. I-1719.
[78] Case C-232/02 P(R), *Commission v Technische Glaswerke Ilmenau*, [2002] E.C.R. I-8977.
[79] Case T-366/00, *Scott v Commission*, [2003] E.C.R. II-1763. This case was appealed to the ECJ, which rejected the appeal; see Case C-276/03 P, *Scott v Commission*, [2005] E.C.R. I-8437; and Case T-369/00, *Département du Loiret v Commission*, [2003] II-1789, para.84.
[80] Case T-198/01, *Technische Glaswerke Ilmenau v Commission* , [2004] E.C.R. II-2717. The case was appealed to the ECJ, which rejected the appeal; see Case C-404/04 P, *Technische Glaswerke Ilmenau v Commission*, [2005] E.C.R. I-3539.

do not constitute State aid will it be justified in not talking a decision. In less obvious cases a refusal will constitute a decision which can be referred to the CFI; see art.13(1). The Commission's scope for refraining from taking action is reinforced by the fact that art.87(1) of the Treaty does not have direct effect, and this is only partly countered by the fact that art.88(3) gives the national courts the right to intervene against non-notified aid.

The Community courts have compensated for the lack of the right of third   **2–052**
parties to participate in the preliminary examination procedure by recognising that within the meaning of art.88(2) interested parties have a right to bring an action before the CFI against a decision of the Commission not to initiate the formal procedure, i.e. the art.88(2) procedure. Under this procedure interested parties have certain procedural guarantees.[81]

Under art.230 of the EC Treaty, the limitation period for bringing an action for annulment must be assumed to run from the date on which an interested party has received a copy of the Commission's decision, and not from the date of the publication of the decision.

Under art.232 of the EC Treaty it is possible for a third party to bring an action against the Commission for its failure to act upon receipt of a complaint.[82]

Monitoring and control

Article 21 of Regulation (EC) No.659/1999 requires the Member States to   **2–053**
submit annual reports to the Commission on all existing aid schemes in respect of which no specific reporting obligations have been imposed in a conditional decision pursuant to art.7 of the Regulation. If the condition is not complied with, the Commission can require the Member State either to amend an aid scheme or to terminate it; see art.18 of the Regulation.

The more detailed rules for such reporting, including standard forms, are set out in Ch.III of Commission Regulation (EC) No.794/2004 of April 21, 2004 implementing Council Regulation (EC) No.659/1999 and its annexes. Among other things, the reports are used for preparing the table of results which the Commission publishes annually and which contains a summary of the contents of the reports. The reports do not constitute notification for the purposes of art.88(3) of the Treaty, nor do the reports anticipate the result of an examination of alleged unlawful State aid under Ch.III of Regulation (EC) No.659/1999.

According to art.22 of the Regulation, where the Commission has serious doubts as to whether decisions not to raise objections, positive decisions or

---

[81] Case C-367/95 P, *Commission v Sytraval*, [1998] E.C.R. I-1719 paras 40 and 41; Case C-198/91, *Cook v Commission*, [1993] E.C.R. I-2487; and Case C-225/91, *Matra v Commission*, [1993] E.C.R. I-3203. Such an action may only be an examination of whether the Commission has failed in its obligation to initiate the formal investigation procedure (the art.88(2) procedure).

[82] Case T-351/02, *Deutsche Bahn v Commission*, [2006] E.C.R. II-1047.

conditional decisions on individual aid are being complied with, after having been given the opportunity to submit its comments the Member State concerned must allow the Commission to undertake on-site monitoring visits. The Commission may be assisted if necessary by independent experts. More detailed provisions regarding the powers to ask for explanations and examine books, etc. and on the requirements for the officials of the Commission and the experts authorised to carry out the on-site monitoring to produce an authorisation in writing from the Commission, are laid down in Article 22 (2) and (3).

2–054   Article 23 of Regulation (EC) No.659/1999 lays down that, if a Member State does not comply with a conditional or negative decision, in particular in cases concerning the recovery of aid under art.14, the Commission may refer the matter to the ECJ directly, in accordance with art.88(2) of the Treaty.

If the Commission considers that the Member State concerned has not complied with a judgment of the ECJ, it may pursue the matter in accordance with art.171 (now art.228) of the EC Treaty, which means that a Member State may be fined a lump sum or penalty payment, in other words an amount which depends on the time taken to comply with the judgment of the ECJ.

Confidentiality

2–055   According to art.24 of Regulation (EC) No.659/1999, the Commission and the Member States, their officials and other servants, including independent experts appointed by the Commission, must not disclose information which they have acquired through the application of the Regulation and which is covered by the obligation of professional secrecy; see also art.25. The duty of confidentiality also applies in connection with making public the Commission's decisions on State aid cases; see the following section.

Publication of decisions

2–056   The Commission's decision on cases of State aid must be published in accordance with art.26 of Regulation (EC) No.659/1999. The Commission's decisions—in some cases in summary or in short form—must be published in the Official Journal of the European Union. There are three forms of publication: (1) a summary notice of the decisions which the Commission makes without initiating the formal investigation procedure; (2) on the initiation of the formal procedure, a full disclosure in the original language, as well as a meaningful summary in the other Community languages; and (3) full publication in all Community languages of a final decision on the conclusion of the formal investigation procedure.

The Member States can request the Commission not to make public certain information in the decision, on the grounds that such disclosure would be contrary to the Commission's duty of confidentiality. On the one hand, both under the provisions of Regulation (EC) No.659/1999 and art.287 of the EC Treaty, the Commission has a duty not to disclose confidential information, including commercial secrets. On the other hand, the Commission's decisions must be reasonable and transparent. The Commission seeks to reconcile these two opposing requirements in the Commission communication of December 1, 2003 on professional secrecy in State aid decisions (OJ C 297, December 9, 2003, p.6). The communication lays down rules for as to what information (commercial information and other confidential information) in a Commission decision should not be made public, and the procedure to be followed in this respect.

Implementing provisions, Advisory Committee, notification and time-limits

The provisions in arts 27–29 of Regulation (EC) No.659/1999 lay down that **2–057** the Commission may adopt implementing provisions concerning the form, content and other details of notifications, and of annual reports, details of time-limits and the calculation of time-limits, and on the interest rates applicable in recovery proceedings, in a procedure which involves an Advisory Committee consisting of representatives of the Member States and chaired by the Commission (arts 28 and 29). The Advisory Committee does not get involved in individual cases of State aid. These implementing provisions are laid down in Commission Regulation (EC) No.794/2004 of April 21, 2004 implementing Council Regulation (EC) No.659/1999 laying down detailed rules for the application of art.93 [now 88] of the EC Treaty.

Regulation (EC) No.794/2004 has been amended by Commission Regulation (EC) No.271/2008 of January 30, 2008 amending Regulation (EC) No.794/2004 implementing Council Regulation (EC) No.659/1999 laying down detailed rules for the application of art.93 [now 88] of the Treaty (OJ L 82, March 25, 2008, p.1). This amendment makes it mandatory—unless otherwise agreed— (from July 1, 2008) for Member States to submit notifications via the web application State Aid Notification Interactive (SANI). All correspondence in connection with a notification shall be transmitted electronically via a secured e-mail system called Public Key Infrastructure (PKI). Regulation (EC) No.794/2004 provides furthermore for forms to be used for the practical notification of State aid.

Chapter IV of Commission Regulation (EC) No.794/2004, as amended, lays down rules for the calculation of the time-limits which are laid down in Regulation (EC) No.659/1999, or by the Commission in accordance with art.88. Regulation (EC) No.794/2004 refers to Regulation (EEC, Euratom) No.1182/71 of the Council of June 3, 1971 determining the rules applicable to periods, dates and time limits (OJ L 124, June 8, 1971, p.1), and Regulation (EC) No.794/2004 applies in the event of conflict between the two sets of rules.

2–058   According to Regulation (EC) No.794/2004, time limits must be specified in months or in working days. Article 2(2) of Regulation(EEC, Euratom) No.1182/71 states that all days are to be considered working days, except public holidays, Sundays and Saturdays, which are however included in time-limits unless they are expressly excluded or unless a time-limit is expressed as being calculated in working days. The Commission has published, both in the Official Journal and on its website, a list of which days are public holidays, both in the individual Member States and for the Commission.

Article 3 of Regulation(EEC, Euratom) No.1182/71 continues that where a period expressed in days, weeks, months or years is to be calculated from the moment at which a relevant event occurs or an action takes place, the day during which that event occurs or that action takes place is not considered as falling within the period in question.

Regulation (EC) No.794/2004 states that, for determining when time limits for action by the Commission begin to run, *the receipt* of the notification or subsequent correspondence is the relevant event.

2–059   For determining when time-limits for action by Member States begin to run, the receipt of the relevant notification or correspondence from the Commission, in principle by the Member State's permanent representative to the EU, is the relevant event.

With regard to the time-limit for the submission of comments by any third parties or Member States which are not directly involved in the action, following initiation of the formal investigation procedure, the publication of the notice of initiation in the Official Journal is the relevant event.

If during the proceedings a Member State needs to request an extension of a time limit, the request must be duly substantiated, and be submitted in writing to Commission at least two working days before expiry; see art.8(6) of Regulation (EC) No.794/2004.

THE TRANSPARENCY DIRECTIVE

2–060   The current Transparency Directive is descended from Commission Directive 80/723/EEC of June 25, 1980 on the transparency of financial relations between Member States and public undertakings.[83] For the purposes of clarity and rationalisation, the Directive has now been codified by Commission Directive 2006/111/EC of November 16, 2006 on the transparency of financial relations between Member States and public undertakings as well as

---

[83] In its most recent form it is Commission Directive 2005/81/EC of November 28, 2005 amending Directive 80/723/EEC on the transparency of financial relations between Member States and public undertakings as well as on financial transparency within certain undertakings (OJ L 312, 29.11.2005, p. 47)—see OJ L 229, 28.8.1985, p.20; OJ L 254, 12.10.1993, p.16; and OJ L 193, 29.7.2000, p.75. In Joined Cases 188 to 190/80, *France, Italy and the United Kingdom v Commission*, [1982] E.C.R. 2545, the ECJ recognised the legality of the transparency obligations which the Commission had imposed on public undertakings.

of financial transparency within certain undertakings (OJ L 318, November 17, 2006, p.17).

The Directive refers to the Commission's duty to ensure that the Member States do not provide aid either to public or private undertakings which is incompatible with the common market.

The Directive emphasises that relations between Member States and public undertakings can be so complex as to make it difficult for the Commission to control State aid, that the State aid rules in the EC Treaty can only be applied fairly if such relations are transparent, and that the transparency should make it possible to distinguish between the State as public authority and the State as owner of an undertaking. Following an amendment of the Directive in 2000, it now contains rules on the keeping of separate accounts for certain undertakings which have special or exclusive rights, or which have been entrusted with the operation of a service of general economic interest; see art.86 of the Treaty.

According to the preamble to the Directive, it ought to be possible to **2–061** achieve transparency, irrespective of the manner in which such public funds are made available; and it ought to be possible to ensure that adequate information is made available as regards the reasons for such provision of public funds and their actual use. Moreover, specific funds can be provided as compensation for the provision of specific services (for example, the provision of transport services), and there ought also to be clarity about such use of public funds.

Due to their nature or turnover, some undertakings or sectors are exempted from the provisions laid down by the Directive.

Article 1(1) of the Directive states that the Member States must ensure that financial relations between public authorities and public undertakings are transparent, as provided in this Directive, so that the following emerge clearly:

a) which public funds are made available directly by public authorities to the public undertakings concerned;

b) which public funds are made available by public authorities through the intermediary of public undertakings or financial institutions; and

c) the use to which these public funds are actually put.

Article 1(2) of the Directive lays down that the Member States must ensure that the financial and organisational structure of any undertaking required to maintain separate accounts is correctly reflected in the separate accounts, so that the following emerge clearly:

a) the costs and revenues associated with different activities; and

b) full details of the methods by which costs and revenues are assigned or allocated to different activities.

2–062   In art.2, the term *public authorities* is defined as meaning all public authorities, including the State, regional, local and all other territorial authorities; and the term *public undertakings* is defined as meaning any undertaking over which the public authorities may exercise directly or indirectly a dominant influence by virtue of their ownership of it, their financial participation therein, or the rules which govern it.

Also according to art.2, a *dominant influence* on the part of the public authorities is presumed to exist when, directly or indirectly in relation to an undertaking, a public authority:

a) holds the major part of the undertaking's subscribed capital; or
b) controls the majority of the votes attaching to shares issued by the undertakings; or
c) can appoint more than half of the members of the undertaking's administrative, managerial or supervisory body.

The term *public undertakings operating in the manufacturing sector* is also defined in art.2. It is defined as: all undertakings whose principal area of activity, defined as being at least 50 per cent of total annual turnover, is in manufacturing.[84]

Article 2 also states which *undertakings are required to maintain separate accounts*. These include any undertaking that enjoys a special or exclusive right granted by a Member State pursuant to art.86(1) of the Treaty or is entrusted with the operation of a service of general economic interest pursuant to art.86(2) of the Treaty, that receives public service compensation in any form whatsoever in relation to such service and that carries on other activities.

Furthermore, art.2 contains other definitions, such as *exclusive rights* and *special rights*.

2–063   Article 3 of the Directive provides that financial relations between public authorities and public undertakings applies, among other things, to: the setting-off of operating losses; the provision of capital; non-refundable grants, or loans on privileged terms; the granting of financial advantages by forgoing profits or the recovery of sums due; the forgoing of a normal return on public funds used; and compensation for financial burdens imposed by the public authorities.

Article 4 lays down that transparency requires the Member States to take the measures necessary to ensure that for any undertaking required to maintain separate accounts:

---

[84] Undertakings in the manufacturing sector are undertakings whose main activity falls under s.D—Manufacturing being subs.DA up to and including subs.DN and the NACE (Rev.1.1) classification. NACE is to be found in the Annex to Commission Regulation (EC) No.29/2002 of December 19, 2001 amending Council Regulation (EEC) No.3037/90 on the statistical classification of economic activities in the European Community (OJ L 6, 10.1.2002, p.3). Manufacturing includes the manufacture of foods, textiles, clothing, leather goods, timber, paper, petroleum products, chemical products, rubber, glass, iron and steel, machines and so on.

a) the internal accounts corresponding to different activities[85] are kept separate;

b) all costs and revenues are correctly assigned or allocated on the basis of consistently applied and objectively justifiable cost accounting principles; and

c) the cost accounting principles according to which separate accounts are maintained are clearly established.

Article 5 provides that the transparency referred to in art.1(1) of the Directive does not apply to financial relations between the public authorities and public undertakings, as regards services the supply of which is not liable to affect trade between Member States to an appreciable extent. Also, it does not apply to central banks, public credit institutions (as regards deposits of public funds placed with them by public authorities on normal commercial terms) or public undertakings whose total annual net turnover is below a certain threshold (undertakings whose annual net turnover over the period of the two financial years preceding the date when the public funds are made available or used has been less than €40 million. However, for public credit institutions the corresponding threshold is a balance sheet total of €800 million).

Article 5 also states that the transparency referred to in art.1(2) of the   **2–064**
Directive does not apply to: (a) undertakings, as regards services the supply of which is not liable to affect trade between Member States to an appreciable extent; (b) undertakings whose total annual net turnover is less than a certain threshold (€40 million in a single year in the two financial years preceding any year in which it enjoys a special or exclusive right or in which it is entrusted with the operation of a service of general economic interest by a Member State pursuant to art.86 of the Treaty). However, for public credit institutions the corresponding threshold is a balance sheet total of €800 million.

Also, undertakings which have been entrusted with the operation of services of general economic interest are exempt if the compensation they receive is fixed for an appropriate period following an open, transparent and non-discriminatory tendering procedure.

Article 6 of the Directive provides that Member States must ensure that information concerning the financial relations referred to is kept available to the Commission for five years from the end of the financial year in which the public funds were made available to the public undertakings concerned. If the Commission requests the information, it must be provided. Correspondingly, information concerning the financial and organisational structure of undertakings referred to in art.1(2) must be kept at the disposal of the Commission for five years.

Article 8 lays down an obligation for undertakings operating in the manu-   **2–065**

---

[85] Different activities cover, on the one hand, products and services for which an undertaking is granted special or exclusive rights, or services of general economic interest which have been entrusted to an undertaking to provide and, on the other hand, all the other products or services which are included in an undertaking's business activites.

facturing sector (more than 50 per cent of their turnover must come from manufacturing, as defined in art.2 of the Directive), to give the Commission the information referred to in art.8(2) and (3) annually. The information must be provided within 15 working days of the date of publication of the annual report of the public undertaking concerned or, for undertakings which do not publish an annual report, not later than nine months following the end of the undertaking's financial year. Among other things this includes: the annual accounts and annual report as defined by the Fourth Council Directive 78/660/ EEC of July 25, 1978, with amendments, based on art.54(3)(g) of the Treaty on the annual accounts of certain types of companies;[86] the provision of any share capital or quasi-capital funds similar in nature to equity, specifying the terms of its or their provision; non-refundable grants, or grants which are only refundable in certain circumstances; loans, including overdrafts and advances on capital injections, with a specification of interest rates and the terms of the loan and its security, if any, given to the lender by the enterprise receiving the loan; guarantees given to the enterprise by public authorities in respect of loan finance, specifying terms and any charges paid by enterprises for these guarantees; dividends paid out and profits retained; and any other forms of State intervention, in particular, the forgoing of sums due to the State by a public undertaking, or of the payment of corporate or social taxes or any similar charges. The obligation to provide information covers all public undertakings whose turnover for the most recent financial year was more than €250 million. As regards the form in which such information is to be provided, see art.8(4) second and third paragraphs.

According to art.8(6), the Member States must send the Commission a list of the undertakings covered by art.8.

COMMISSION COMMUNICATION ON THE APPLICATION OF ARTS 87 AND 88 OF THE EC TREATY AND OF ART.5 OF THE TRANSPARENCY DIRECTIVE TO PUBLIC UNDERTAKINGS IN THE MANUFACTURING SECTOR

2–066   The Commission's communication contains a lot of detailed information.[87] Among other things these include the principles which must form the basis of a decision on whether State aid exists, on increased transparency, and on the application of the market economy investor principle (see paras 6–004 to 6–010, on the compatibility of aid with the common market and on different forms of State intervention, such as capital investment, loan guarantees, loan financing and the dividends on investments).

The communication can be seen as being an appendix to the Transparency

---

[86] OJ L 222, 14.8.1978, p.11.
[87] Commission communication to the Member States—Application of arts 92 and 93 of the EEC Treaty and of art.5 of Commission Directive 80/723/EEC to public undertakings in the manufacturing sector (OJ L 307, 13.11.1993 p.3).

Directive, and it focuses in particular on it. Even though it expressly states that it is aimed at undertakings in the manufacturing sector, the communication states that it is possible that the Commission will adopt the same approach to other sectors, depending on the circumstances and adapted to different circumstances, as may be necessary.

The communication is characterised by containing a number of comments concerning and explanations about the market economy investor principle. Among other things there is a reference to the distinction made by the ECJ in Case C-305/89, *Italy v Commission* (*Alfa-Fiat and Lanerossi*), [1999] E.C.R. I-1603 and Case C-303/88, *Italy v Commission*, [1991] E.C.R. I-1433, between a private investor, whose time horizon is short, and may even be of a speculative nature, and a private holding company with a more long-term perspective. The communication also emphasises that the ECJ stated that it is necessary to focus on the fact even if the private investor, with whose conduct the intervention of the public investor is to be compared, may not necessarily be an ordinary investor who invests with a more or less short-term view to gaining profit, it must at least be a private holding company or a private undertaking that pursues a structured global or sectoral policy, and whose decisions must be determined by the aim of making a profit in the long term.

The communication also emphasises that, in this context, a private investor   **2–067**
could very well think about investing new capital in an undertaking which may be in temporary difficulties in order for it to survive and, perhaps after restructuring, become profitable again; and it is also possible that a parent company may carry the loss of a subsidiary for a limited period, in order to make it possible to withdraw from the sector under the most favourable conditions, and that such decisions can be motivated not only by the possibility of obtaining a direct profit, but by other considerations such as the maintenance of the reputation of the whole corporate group, or changing its activities. The ECJ also stated that if the investment of new capital is made without regard for profit even in the long term, such investment must be regarded as aid.

It is notable that in s.v, the communication deals with the Commission's approach to notifications in cases where a public authority must decide whether a capital investment or similar constitutes aid. In this respect the communication emphasises that it is only in cases where there is no objectively reasonable expectation that an investment will give a reasonable return which could be acceptable to a private investor in a corresponding private undertaking which operates under normal market conditions that there will be considered to be State aid, even when the financing is made in whole or in part using public means.[88]

---

[88] In the communication of the Commission concerning public undertakings in the manufacturing sector, the Commission emphasises that it will have regard for the nature of the capital interests of public authorities when assessing their conduct in relation to the criteria which apply for a private investor who acts under the conditions of a market economy. This also applies

THE REGULATION ON HORIZONTAL STATE AID

2–068   Regulation (EC) No.994/98—the so-called enabling regulation—on the application of arts 92 and 93 (now arts 87 and 88) of the EC Treaty to certain
categories of horizontal State aid was adopted by the Council in 1998.[89] It
empowers the Commission to adopt regulations laying down certain categories
of aid which, subject to certain conditions, are not subject to the notification
requirements of art.89(3) of the EC Treaty. This refers to the block exemption
regulations corresponding to the kind of block exemption regulations which
are used to exempt certain categories of agreements between undertakings
from the prohibition in art.81 of the Treaty on agreements which restrict
competition. In contrast to art.87(1), these regulations are directly applicable; in other words, aid in an area which is covered by such a block exemptin
regulation is in principle exempted from the notification requirement and is
regarded as lawful. However, if the courts find that an aid measure does not
comply with the conditions in such a block exemption regulation, the aid is
treated as being new aid which must be notified and which is therefore subject
to the direct effect of art.88(3). Cases of non-notified aid constitute unlawful
aid and this can, for example, lead to a national court suspending the aid by
virtue of the direct effect.

Until the adoption of Regulation (EC) No.994/98 the Commission had
used notices as the usual means of informing the general public and in particular the Member States about how the Commission intended to apply the
State aid rules in arts 87–89 of the EC Treaty.

The advantage of using regulations, i.e. legally binding rules, is not least
that it creates greater legal certainty and clarity about the enforcement of the
State aid rules in the EC Treaty. The regulations are directly applicable by
national courts.

The areas covered by block exemption regulations

2–069   According to art.1(1) of Regulation (EC) No.994/98, block exemption regulations can be issued in respect of:

with regard to the assessment of requests to invest extra funds which are necessary to finance
specific projects. The latter can be particularly important in relation to public undertakings
which have been deliberately under-capitalised due to non-commercial considerations, such as
public budget restrictions. It is also worth noting that minority shareholders, who do not have
inside information about the undertaking concerned, will typically have stricter requirements
for make additional capital investments than a controlling owner who will naturally have
access to more detailed information about the financial circumstances of the undertaking.
[89] Council Regulation (EC) No.994/98 of May 7, 1998 on the application of arts 92 and 93 [now
87 88] of the Treaty establishing the European Community to certain categories of horizontal
State aid (OJ L 142, 14.5.1998, p.1).

a) aid in favour of:

    (i) small and medium-sized enterprises;
    (ii) research and development;
    (iii) environmental protection; and
    (iv) employment and training;

(b) aid that complies with the map approved by the Commission for each Member State for the grant of regional aid.

Conditions 2–070

Article 1(2) of the Regulation provides that for each category of aid the following must be specified:

(a) the purpose of the aid;
(b) the categories of beneficiaries;
(c) thresholds expressed either in terms of aid intensities (see paras 6–016 to 6–018 for a discussion of this concept) in relation to a set of eligible costs or in terms of maximum aid amounts;
(d) the conditions governing the cumulation of aid (i.e. the permissible use of several types of aid in respect of the same area); and
(e) the conditions of monitoring.

In addition, according to art.1(3), block exemption regulations may, among other things:

(a) set thresholds or other conditions for the notification of awards of individual aid;
(b) exclude certain sectors from their scope; and
(c) attach further conditions for the compatibility of aid exempted under such regulations.

As stated immediately above, to the extent that a block exemption regulation is adopted, the national courts will be able to apply art.87(1) of the EC Treaty directly which they cannot otherwise do according to the case law of the ECJ. Outside the scope of adopted block exemption regulations, the Commission retains its sole right to assess whether specific cases of State aid either comply with one or more of the exceptions in art.87(2) or may be considered to comply with one or more of the exceptions in art.87(3).

De minimis aid

2–071   Article 2 of Regulation (EC) No.994/98 states that the Commission may, by means of a regulation adopted in accordance with the procedure laid down in the Regulation, decide that, provided that aid granted to the same undertaking over a given period does not exceed a certain fixed amount, it need not be notified. This option has been used by the Commission to issue a general regulation on de minimis State aid and regulations on de minimis State aid in the sectors of agriculture and fisheries, see further Chs 3 and 4.

Reporting requirements

2–072   Article 3 of Regulation (EC) No.994/98 lays down the reporting and information obligations of Member States in relation to the application of block exemption regulations.

As soon as an aid scheme which is permitted by virtue of a block exemption regulation is initiated, as well as cases of individual aid which are granted outside a scheme and which is exempted from notification by virtue of such a regulation, the Member State must send the Commission a summary of the measures concerned with a view to their publication in the Official Journal.

Member States must record and compile all information regarding the application of the block exemptions, and if the Commission has doubt about whether an exemption regulation is being applied properly, the Member States must forward to it any information it considers necessary.

An Advisory Committee, consisting of representatives of the Member States, is consulted by the Commission in the preparation of block exemption regulations.

CHAPTER 3

HORIZONTAL AID

THE DE MINIMIS REGULATION

As stated in Ch.2, in connection with the discussion of art.2 in the Enabling   **3–001**
Regulation (Regulation (EC) No.994/98), de minimis State aid, i.e. certain
forms of more modest aid, need not be notified. This refers to State aid
which is below a certain value threshold. The rules of this are in Commission
Regulation (EC) No.1998/2006 of December 15, 2006 on the application of
arts 87 and 88 of the Treaty to de minimis aid.[1]

The Member States will typically use limited grants of aid to small and
medium-sized enterprises (SMEs), but the de minimis rule also applies to large
undertakings which can receive such aid without notification.

According to the preamble to the De minimis Regulation it is in effect an
exemption to art.87(1) of the EC Treaty, and not just a procedural exception
relating to notification, as the basis for it is that aid of such a modest extent
does not really affect trade between the Member States and/or it does not
distort or threaten to distort competition.

Scope of application

The scope of the Regulation is set out in art.1. Here it is stated that in principle   **3–002**
the Regulation applies to all sectors, so that de minimis aid can be granted in
all sectors. However, there are a number of exceptions to this. Thus, export aid
and aid which is granted on condition that domestic products are used, rather
than imported products, are not covered by the Regulation. Aid towards the
cost of participating in trade fairs, or for research or consultancy services for
the launch of new products or existing products on a new market does not
normally constitute export aid.[2] Export aid is characterised by being directly

---

[1] OJ L 379, 28.12.2006, p. 5. The previous Commission Regulation (EC) No.69/2001 of January
12, 2001 on the application of arts 87 and 88 of the EC Treaty to de minimis aid (OJ L 10,
13.1.2001, p.30) expired on December 31, 2006. Before that, the de minimis rules were based
on the Commission notice on the de minimis rule for State aid (OJ C 68, 6.3.1996, p.9).
[2] Such aid may in the case of SMEs be covered by provisions in the General Block Exemption,
see s.2.

related to the volume of exports, or for establishing and running a distribution network, or for the running costs connected with export business.

In addition to this, aid to undertakings which operate in the fishery and aquaculture sectors[3] or undertakings active in the coal sector[4] is also not covered by the Regulation. The same applies to aid granted to undertakings in difficulty.[5] The transport sector is in principle covered by the Regulation, since transport activities have been liberalised. However, undertakings in the road haulage and personal transport sectors are small on average, and there is a certain overcapacity in the area and a general desire not to promote an increase in traffic. For this reason the Regulation does not apply to aid for the acquisition of road freight transport vehicles granted to undertakings providing road freight transport for hire or reward, and in cases where the Regulation applies to the transport sector there is a lower threshold of €100,000 for de minimis aid.

The primary production of agricultural products[6] is not covered by the Regulation. On the other hand, aid for undertakings engaged in the processing[7] and marketing[8] agricultural products is covered, except in the following two situations: (1) when the amount of the aid is fixed on the basis of the price or quantity of such products purchased from primary producers or put on the market by the undertakings concerned, and (2) when the aid is conditional on being partly or entirely passed on to primary producers.

De minimis aid and associated conditions

3–003   The criteria for the granting of de minimis aid are set out in art.2 of the regulation. If all these criteria are met then the aid will not be regarded as fulfilling the criteria in art.87(1) of the EC Treaty, in other words there will not be State aid within the meaning of the Treaty and the aid will thus not be caught by the duty to notify in art.88(3).

The starting point is that the total of de minimis aid granted to any one undertaking may not exceed € 200,000 over any period of three fiscal years (meaning the accounting period used by the undertaking for tax purposes).

---

[3] As covered by Council Regulation (EC) No.104/2000. On aid to this sector, see Ch.4.
[4] Undertakings as defined in Regulation (EC) No.1407/2002. On aid to this sector, see Ch.4.
[5] In this area the framework provisions for State aid for the rescue and restructuring of undertakings in difficulties apply. This is discussed later in this chapter.
[6] This refers to agricultural products listed in Annex I to the EC Treaty, with the exception of fishery products. On aid to this, see Ch.4.
[7] "Processing of agricultural products" means any operation on an agricultural product resulting in a product which is also an agricultural product, except farm activities necessary for preparing an animal or plant product for the first sale; see art.1(2)(b) of the Regulation.
[8] "Marketing of agricultural products" means holding or display with a view to sale, offering for sale, delivery or any other manner of placing on the market, except the first sale by a primary producer to resellers or processors and any activity preparing a product for such first sale. A sale by a primary producer to final consumers is considered as marketing if it takes place in separate premises reserved for that purpose; see art.1(2)(c) of the Regulation.

For undertakings in the road transport sector the ceiling is €100,000. The three year period is rolling, so that each time new de minimis aid is granted, the total de minimis aid granted in the current year and the two preceding years is added together. The de minimis aid is regarded as being granted on the date when an undertaking is granted a right to receive the aid. The ceiling of € 200,000 applies regardless of the purpose or form of the aid, and regardless of whether it is financed in whole or in part by Community funds.

If the total amount of aid exceeds the ceiling referred to, then the possibility of granting de minimis aid under the Regulation lapses. This applies even for that part of the aid granted which is below the ceiling; see art.2(2) of the Regulation. This strict rule should be seen in the context of the duty of loyalty in art.10 of the EC Treaty, under which the Member States must facilitate the achievement of the Commission's enforcement of the State aid rules; this is discussed in more detail below.

The ceiling of € 200,000 is expressed as being equivalent to a cash grant. If **3–004** the aid is given in some form other than a cash grant, then the amount of the aid must be calculated as the gross grant equivalent of the aid. This is consistent with the fact that the Regulation only applies to transparent aid, meaning aid whose gross grant equivalent can be calculated precisely, without the need to undertake a risk assessment; see art.2(4). If, for example, the aid is paid in instalments it must be discounted to its value at the date it is granted, i.e. the date when the right to receive the aid accrued. For this purpose the reference rate at the date of grant of the aid (which is considered as the market interest rate) is regularly published both in the Official Journal of the European Union and on the Commission's website.

In addition to cash grants and aid paid in instalments, low interest rates and limited tax exemptions are also considered to be transparent aid. In addition to this, according to art.2(4) the following forms of State aid are also considered to be transparent:

1. Aid comprised in loans when the gross grant equivalent has been calculated on the basis of market interest rates prevailing at the time of the grant.
2. Aid comprised in capital injections if the total amount of the public injection does not exceed the de minimis ceiling.
3. Aid comprised in risk capital measures if the risk capital provided is kept below the de minimis ceiling (see also below on the EC guidelines on State aid for risk capital investments in SMEs).
4. Individual aid provided under a guarantee scheme to undertakings which are not undertakings in difficulty is treated as transparent de minimis aid when the guaranteed part of the underlying loan provided under such a scheme does not exceed € 1.5 million per undertaking. For undertakings in the road transport sector a ceiling of € 750,000 per undertaking applies. This amount is calculated on the basis of a maximum rate (net insolvency rate) of 13 per cent which represents the

most pessimistic scenario for guarantee schemes. If the guaranteed part of the underlying loan only accounts for a proportion of this ceiling, the gross grant equivalent of that guarantee is deemed to correspond to the same proportion of the applicable ceiling, i.e. €200,000, or € 100,000 for undertakings in the road transport sector. The guarantee may not exceed 80 per cent of the underlying loan. Guarantee schemes are also considered to be transparent if: (i) before the implementation of the scheme, the methodology for calculating the gross grant equivalent of guarantees has been accepted following notification of this methodology to the Commission under another Regulation adopted by the Commission in the State aid area (for example, in connection with regional investment aid), and (ii) the approved methodology explicitly addresses the type of guarantees and the type of underlying transactions at stake in the context of the application of the Regulation.

As for cumulation, art.2(5) of the Regulation states that de minimis aid may not be cumulated with State aid in respect of the same eligible costs if such cumulation would result in an aid intensity which exceeds that laid down in other rules.

Member State control

3–005 In principle it is the responsibility of the Commission to ensure that the State aid rules are complied with. However, this does not relieve the Member States of the responsibility for helping the Commission in this task. Under their obligations under art.10 of the EC Treaty the Member States must help ensure that the State aid rules are complied with, including in respect of the de minimis provisions. On this basis art.3 of the Regulation requires the Member States to carry out a number of monitoring tasks.

The Member States are thus not entitled to grant de minimis aid without ensuring that the aid will not mean that the ceiling of € 200,000 (and € 100,000 for road transport undertakings) over three fiscal years is exceeded.

The Member States must gather and record all information on the application of the Regulation. Such records must include all information which is necessary for establishing whether the conditions laid down in the Regulation have been met. This information must be made available to the Commission on request, and must be kept for ten years.

The Member States also have a number of administrative obligations, which depend on whether the Member State has set up a central register of de minimis aid containing complete information on all de minimis aid granted by any authority within that Member State; see art 3(1) and (2). If a Member State grants aid under a guarantee scheme which is financed by the European Investment Fund, special provisions apply, as set out in art.3(2).

Period of validity of the Regulation and transitional provisions

The Regulation applies from January 1, 2007 until December 31, 2013, see **3–006** art.6, but it also applies to aid granted before the date of its entry into force (i.e. December 29, 2006) to undertakings in the transport sector and undertakings which process and market agricultural products; see art.5. Naturally, this is provided that the aid fulfils the conditions in arts 1 and 2.

Individual de minimis aid granted up to June 30, 2007 which fulfils the conditions of the previous de minimis Regulation is not covered by art.87(1) of the EC Treaty and is therefore not caught by the notification requirement in art.88(3) of the Treaty. At the end of the period of validity of the regulation (i.e. December 31, 2013), there is a supplementary period of six months during which de minimis aid can be granted on the conditions laid down in the Regulation.

INTRODUCTION TO THE GENERAL BLOCK EXEMPTION REGULATION (GBER)

Characteristics and objectives of the GBER

The GBER Commission Regulation (EC) No.800/2008 of August 6, 2008 **3–007** declaring certain categories of aid compatible with the common market in application of arts 87 and 88 of the Treaty (General Block Exemption Regulation) (OJ L 214, August 9, 2008, p.3) has been issued according to Council Regulation (EC) No.994/98 of May 7, 1998 on the application of art 92 and 93 (now art 87 and 88) of the Treaty establishing the European Community to certain categories of horizontal State aid (OJ 142, May 14 1998, p.1) ("the Enabling Regulation"). This regulation gives (in its art.1) the Commission the powers to declare that certain categories of State aid are compatible with the common market and *therefore not subject to the notification requirement of art.88(3) of the Treaty provided a set of specified conditions are met.* These conditions are given in Commission regulations issued on the basis Regulation (EC) No.994/98. Such regulations are called block exemption regulations. Consequently, State aid measures which fulfil the conditions laid down in the GBER are considered to be compatible with state aid rules, i.e. compatible with the common market, without prior notification to the Commission and hence without a positive Commission decision to that end. Notification of state aid to the Commission would otherwise normally be a requirement cf. art.88 (3) EC. The practical consequence of a State aid measure fulfilling the conditions in the GBER on the part of Member States is that they may implement the state aid without having to notify the aid to the Commission and await a positive Commission decision on the compatibility with the common market.

It should be noted, however, that the Commission has adopted, and can be expected to adopt in the future, various guidelines, frameworks, and notices that also deal with the types of aid dealt with in the GBER as well as in other block exemption regulations. To the extent that an aid, or an aid scheme, does not fulfil the conditions laid down in a block exemption regulation and, as a consequence, must be notified to the Commission the guidelines, frameworks, and notices adopted by the Commission serve to provide information to Member States as to the points of view that will guide the Commission with regard to its assessment of such aid.

One of the main objectives of the GBER is to create a simple, user-friendly and coherent set of legislative rules—within the boundaries of the Enabling Regulation—applicable to certain categories of State aid which can be considered to fulfil the conditions of compatibility in art.87 (3) EC. One way of achieving simplification is to adopt a block exemption regulation. According to art.249 EC a regulation shall have general application and it shall be binding in its entirety and directly applicable in all Member States. This naturally also applies to a block exemption regulation. This implies that the GBER will be applied directly by national administrations in all Member States and in cases before national judges. On this background another objective of the GBER has been to impose conditions as straightforward as possible in order to ensure the uniform and correct application of the GBER throughout the EU.

3–008   The GBER has a wider objective than merely lifting off some of the work-load of the national administrations and the Commission. It should be seen in the context of recent Commission commitments to regulate in a better and simpler way and to reduce aid while targeting it where it promotes EU interests like job creation. SMEs are the main driving force of the economy and a major source of job creation. This is recognized throughout EC State aid policy and other EU policies and in the GBER which is quite advantageous to SMEs as SMEs are eligible to benefit from all the State aid categories (26) covered by the GBER. Based on the EU's Lisbon objectives[9] and in line with the Commission's proposal to adopt a Small Business Act, the GBER facilitates the access of the Member States to grant subsidies with clear horizontal objectives such as environmental protection, promotion of research and development, aid to employees working on new investments in SMEs or in assisted regions and entrepreneurship.

As mentioned, SMEs are important to the growth in EU. However, SMEs often face specific difficulties, e.g. problems with access to finance, which the markets themselves cannot overcome. For that reason, the GBER allows different types of State aid in order to help SMEs overcome market failures. Such types of aid are e.g. aid for setting up new enterprises, aid for investments in machines or for hiring additional workers, aid in the form of risk capital,

---

[9] The Lisbon Strategy seeks to promote sustainable development, i.e. economic growth and job creation, together with competitiveness and security of energy supplies. Sustainable development is based, amongst others, on a high level of protection and improvement of the quality of the environment.

innovation aid, aid contributing to intellectual property rights costs, aid for adapting to new environmental Community standards or aid for environmental studies.

Another interesting aspect of the GBER is *social State* aid. According to the GBER, State aid that—on the one hand—helps disabled or otherwise disadvantaged workers to find mainstream jobs and —— on the other hand— allows for compensating additional costs on the part of the enterprises hiring the said workers, may be compatible with the common market. Such additional costs could stem from setting up facilities in favour of employees with wheelchairs or using IT for visually impaired workers. The GBER also brings costs to child care, parent care and parental leave within it scope of application.

The ideas behind *regional State aid* are described in s.6. It follows that   **3–009** regional State aid is important from political considerations concerning, e.g. growth and cohesion. The GBER acknowledges the importance of regional State aid and allows for up to €37 million of regional investment in the form of State aid in order to promote large scale new industrial establishments in the most disadvantaged regions and for State aid to small scale start-ups in assisted areas which is aimed at promoting local entrepreneurship.

Also State aid measures aimed at tackling *environmental and climate change* issues are governed by the GBER. The measures include, e.g. investment in energy savings, renewable energy sources and tax reductions with a positive environmental effect.

It is a current wish of the EU to become a more knowledge-based economy. This is reflected e.g. in the substantially increased amount of means available under the 7th Framework Programme of the European Community for research, technological development and demonstration activities compared to the means available under the previous frameworks.[10] This is important in a globalised economy where knowledge is an important resource and a major competitive parameter. Therefore, the GBER includes within its ambit State aid for *research and development projects* and the realization of technical feasibility studies. The GBER also promotes SMEs to protect their rights stemming from research and development by allowing State aid to cover costs connected with obtaining intellectual property rights, e.g. patents. Research and development often go hand in hand with innovation and the GBER naturally also deals with certain categories of State aid in favour of innovation activities. Consequently, the GBER allows State aid in favour of young innovative enterprises, State aid covering costs for innovation advisory and support services and hiring of highly qualified personnel.

---

[10] *http://ec.europa.eu/research/fp7/*

The relationship between the GBER and the existing block exemption regulations and guidelines etc.

3–010   The Commission has previously issued block exemption regulations regarding training aid,[11] SME aid,[12] employment aid,[13] and regional aid.[14] The GBER repeals those regulations and incorporates them into a single text. The relationship between these regulations and the GBER will be discussed below. The de minimis regulation is not affected by the GBER.

The substantive conditions of the GBER regarding eligible beneficiaries, maximum aid intensities and eligible expenses often correspond to conditions in Community frameworks and guidelines on the same issues. This is the case with respect to certain categories of State aid in the newly adopted (since 2006) guidelines on State aid for environmental protection, the Community guidelines on state aid to promote risk capital investments in small and medium-sized enterprises and the Community Framework for State aid for Research and Development and Innovation. Those corresponding conditions is a result of the experience gained by the Commission when assessing the compatibility of certain State aid categories with the common market cf. art.87 (3) EC.

Despite the corresponding conditions, a state aid measure which does not fall within the scope of application of the GBER may nevertheless be compatible with the common market as a result of an application of the relevant guidelines, etc. However, this requires a notification of the aid to the Commission according to art.88 (3) EC and a subsequent positive Commissions decision on the compatibility with the common market *before* the aid is implemented.

---

[11] See Commission Regulation No.68/2001 of January 12, 2001 on the application of arts 87 and 88 of the EC Treaty to training aid (OJ L 10, 13.1 2001, p.20) amended by Commission Regulation No.363/2004 of February 25, 2004 amending Regulation (EC) No.68/2001 on the application of arts 87 and 88 of the EC Treaty to training aid (OJ L 63, 28.2.2004, p.20).

[12] See Commission RegulationNo.70/2001 of January 12, 2001 on the application of arts 87 and 88 of the EC Treaty to State aid to small and medium-sized enterprises (OJ L 10, 13.1.2001, p.33), Commission Regulation No.364/2004 of February 25, 2004 amending Regulation (EC) No.70/2001 as regards the extension of its scope to include aid for research and development (OJ L 63, 28.02.2004, p.22), and Commission Regulation (EC) No.1857/2006 of December 15, 2006 on the application of arts 87 and 88 of the Treaty to State aid to small and medium-sized enterprises active in the production of agricultural products and amending Regulation (EC) No.70/2001 (OJ L 358, December 16, 2006, p.3).

[13] See Commission Regulation No.2204/2002 of December 12, 2002 on the application of arts 87 and 88 of the EC Treaty to State aid for employment (OJ L 337, 13.12.2002, p.3) and Corrigendum to Commission Regulation No.2204/2002 of December 12, 2002 on the application of arts 87 and 88 of the EC Treaty to State aid for employment (OJ L 349, December 24, 2002, p.126).

[14] See Commission Regulation (EC) No.1628/2006 of October 24, 2006 on the application of arts 87 and 88 of the Treaty to national regional investment aid (OJ L 302 of 1.11.2006, p.29)

Major substantive differences and similarities between the existing block exemption Regulations and the GBER

Commission Regulation No.1628/2006 on *regional aid* has been—to a large   **3–011**
extent —integrated fully in the GBER. The differences between the two regulations are essentially the new condition concerning incentive effect and the
inclusion of child care and parent care cost as eligible costs under the GBER.
The GBER furthermore exempts—in line with the regional aid guidelines—
aid for newly created small enterprises in assisted regions.

Also the Commission Regulation No.68/2001 on *training aid* has mainly
been incorporated into the GBER with, however, an increase from 50 per cent
to 60 per cent regarding basic aid intensity for general training for employees.
Under the previous block exemption Member States were allowed to grant
up to €1 million without having to observe the notification requirement. The
notification ceiling is now €2 million.

With respect to investment and employment aid for *SMEs* (cf. Commission   **3–012**
Regulation No.70/2001 on state aid to SMEs with amendments) the basic
aid intensities have been increased by a third. The GBER provides for aid
intensities up to 20 per cent for small enterprises and 10 per cent for medium-
sized enterprises. Furthermore, the notification ceiling is now increased
allowing Member States to grant State aid up to €7.5 million without having
to observe the notification duty in art.88 (3) EC. Finally the GBER simplifies
the definition of "undertakings in difficulty" and the condition of "incentive
effect".

Rules on *employment aid* (cf. Commission Regulation No.2204/2002) are
now contained in the GBER. The aid intensity for disabled workers is now 75
per cent instead of the previous 60 per cent. Severely disadvantaged workers
may under the GBER benefit from a subsidised salary for an increased
period of two years. The GBER provides furthermore for an increased notification threshold of up to €10 million per year (previously €5 million per
year).

Entry into force, repeal and transitional provisions

The GBER entered into force on August 29, 2008 and repealed at the same   **3–013**
time the previous block exemption regulations cf. art.44. Any references to the
repealed regulations shall hereinafter be construed as references to the GBER.
The GBER applies until December 31, 2013 cf. art.45.

The GBER also applies to individual State aid (both ad hoc aid and aid
granted according to an aid scheme) granted before the date of entry into
force of the GBER provided the said aid fulfils all the conditions in the GBER
except from art.9 in the GBER concerning certain duties Member States have
to comply with *before* they avail themselves of the opportunity of granting aid
according to the GBER cf. art.44.

Situations may arise where State aid granted according to one of the previous block exemption regulations does not fulfil the conditions in the GBER. The GBER contains in art.44 (2) a provision which takes those situations into account. According to that provision, State aid granted before December 31, 2008 according to the previous block exemption regulations will remain compatible with the common marked and exempted from the notification duty in art.88 (3) EC.

State aid schemes which fulfil the conditions in the GBER remain exempted from the duty of notification for an adjustment period of six months after the expiry of the GBER. However, regional State aid schemes expire at the same time as the approved regional State aid maps. Schemes adopted by the Member States according to Regulation No.1628/2006 on regional State aid before the entry into force of the GBER are allowed to be implemented unaffected of the GBER until 2013.

Scope of application of the GBER

Sectors

3–014 The starting point of the GBER is that it applies to state aid in all sectors. This is, however, subject to a number of exceptions. Essentially, the exceptions concern certain forms of aid within certain sectors of the economy. The exceptions to the starting point are listed in art.1(3). Accordingly, the following situations are excluded from the scope of application of the GBER:

- Regional aid favouring activities in the sectors of *steel, shipbuilding* and *synthetic fibres;*[15]
- State aid favouring activities in the *coal* sector (apart from training aid, research, development and innovation aid and environmental aid);[16]
- State aid favouring activities in the *processing and marketing of agricultural products*[17] in case one of the following two situations: (1) the amount of is fixed on the basis of the price or quantity of such products purchased from primary producers or marketed by the undertakings concerned, *or* (2) when the aid is conditional on being partly or fully passed on to the primary producers;
- State aid favouring activities in the *primary production of agricultural products* except for training aid, aid in the form of risk capital, aid for

---

[15] The steel sector is defined in art.2, litra 29 and the synthetic fibres sector is defined in art.2, litra 30.

[16] The coal sector is regulated by Regulation No.1407/2002 of July 23, 2002 with amendments.

[17] "Agricultural product" is defined in art.2, litra 22 and "processing" and "marketing" of agricultural products are defined in art.2, litra 23 and 24.

research and development, environmental aid, and aid for disadvantaged[18] and disabled[19] workers;[20]

- State aid favouring activities in the *fishery and aquaculture sectors* apart from training aid, aid in the form of risk capital, aid for research and development and innovation and aid for disadvantaged and disabled workers;[21]
- A more general exception is given in art.1(4). According to that provision the GBER does not apply to *regional aid schemes* which are targeted at specific sectors of economic activity within manufacturing or services. The argument behind this exception is that the objective and likely effects of such regional aid schemes may be sectorial rather than horizontal. The *tourism sector*[22] is not covered by this exception due to do its positive effect on regional development and important role in national economies.
- State aid to undertakings in difficulty cf. art.1 (6).[23]

Forms of State aid

According to art.1 (1) the GBER applies only to the following forms of aid[24]:   **3–015**

- regional aid,
- SME investment and employment aid,
- aid for the creation of enterprises by female entrepreneurs,
- aid for environmental protection,
- aid for consultancy in favour of SMEs and SME participation in fairs,
- aid in the form of risk capital,
- aid for research, development and innovation,
- training aid, and
- aid for disadvantaged or disabled workers.

---

[18] "Disadvantaged" is defined in art.2, litra 18.

[19] "Disabled" is defined in art.2.

[20] This applies in so far the mentioned categories of aid are not covered by Commission Regulation (EC) No.1857/2006 of December 15, 2006 on the application of arts 87 and 88 of the Treaty to State aid to small and medium-sized enterprises active in the production of agricultural products and amending Regulation (EC) No.70/2001.

[21] This applies to activities in the fishery and aquaculture sectors as covered by Council Regulation (EC) No.104/2000 of December 17, 1999 on the common organisation of the markets in fishery and aquaculture products.

[22] The definition of "tourism" is given in art.2, litra 25.

[23] According to art.1(7) "undertakings in difficulty" means (regarding SMEs): limited companies where more than ½ of its registered capital has disappeared and more than ¼ of that capital has been lost over the preceding 12 months, *or* companies with at least some members subject to unlimited liability for the debt of the company when more than ½ of its capital as shown in the company accounts has disappeared and more than ¼ of that capital has been lost over the preceding 12 months, *or* when the company—irrespective of its type—fulfils the criteria under domestic law for being subject to collective insolvency proceedings. SMEs not older than three years are not to be regarded as in difficulty unless they fulfil the criteria for being subject to collective insolvency proceedings.

[24] Relevant definitions for the purpose of applying art.1(1) are given in art.2.

GENERAL CONDITIONS (CHAPTER I OF THE GBER)

Modus operandi, transparency and monitoring

3–016   Within its scope of application (sectors and forms of State aid), the GBER lists a number of additional general conditions together with special conditions which have to be met. If these conditions are observed the aid shall be compatible with the common market within the meaning of art.87(3) EC and exempted from the duty of notification entailed in art.88(3) EC. These general conditions apply to all those categories of State aid which fall within the scope of application of the GBER and, as a consequence, the general conditions have horizontal application.

    Thus, the GBER exempts—according to art.3—from the notification duty in art.88(3) EC aid schemes[25] and individual aid[26] granted under such schemes together with ad hoc aid[27] provided *that* such aid fulfil all the conditions in the GBER and provided *that* the scheme, the individual aid granted under a scheme and the ad hoc aid all contain an express reference to the GBER together with a citation of its title and publication reference in the Official Journal of the European Union (the OJ). Individual aid granted under a scheme and ad hoc aid must furthermore contain express references to the relevant (special) provisions of the GBER. In this way, and under the observance of arts 9 (transparency) and 10 (monitoring), cf. below, the need to ensure transparency as well as the need to monitor aid is observed. These conditions (contained in arts 3, 9 and 10) may seem formalistic. They are, however, express conditions for exemption.

    Transparency is an important pillar of the GBER because the GBER essentially allows the Member States to grant State aid to undertakings without involving the Commission. Articles 9 and 10 of the GBER contain provisions to that end.

3–017   Article 9 concerns *transparency*. It applies horizontally and to State aid which has been exempted pursuant to the GBER. According to that provision the Member State concerned and the Commission have to observe a number of requirements in order to ensure transparency. With respect to *State aid schemes and the awarding of ad hoc aid* the Member State is obliged to forward a summary of information regarding such measures within 20 working days, cf. art.9(1). For that purpose the Member State must make use of a special form (attached to the GBER as annex III). The completed form must be submitted

---

[25] "aid" means any measure fulfilling all the criteria laid down in art.87(1) EC. "aid scheme" means any act on the basis of which, without further implementing measures being required, individual aid awards may be made to undertakings defined within the act in a general and abstract manner and any act on the basis of which aid which is not linked to a specific project may be awarded to one or several undertakings for an indefinite period of time and/or for an indefinite amount.

[26] "individual aid" means ad hoc aid and notifiable awards of aid on the basis of an aid scheme.

[27] "Ad hoc aid" means individual aid not awarded on the basis an aid secheme.

to the Commission electronically. This summary will be published in the OJ and on the Commission's website. The Member State is furthermore under a duty to publish on the internet the full text of the measures concerned including—in cases of State aid schemes—the conditions laid down in national law which ensure compliance with the GBER. These texts must be accessible on the internet as long as the State aid measure in question is in force. The State aid granting act regarding *individual aid* shall include an explicit reference to: (1) the relevant special provisions (cf. Ch.II of the GBER), and (2) the national law ensuring compliance with the GBER and to the internet address where the Member State has published the full text of the measure. Article 9(4) sets out special transparency requirements with respect to individual aid exceeding €3 million for research and development projects and individual regional investment aid granted on the basis of an existing aid scheme for large investment projects.

Article 9 is supplemented by art.10 on *monitoring*. That provision places the Commission under a duty to monitor on a regular basis aid measures of which it has been informed pursuant to art.9. Member States must for that purpose keep detailed records of all information necessary to establish whether the conditions of the GBER have been complied with. For this purpose the Commission has the right to request—in writing—the necessary information. Non-compliance on the part of a Member State with the duty to submit requested information may ultimately lead to a suspension of the Member State's application of the GBER.

Transparency of aid

Article 9 deals with transparency in the concrete application of the GBER.   **3–018**
Another form of transparency is prescribed in art.5. That provision deals with transparency of the actual aid measure and requires an aid to be transparent in order to be exempted under the GBER. Transparency in this connection means aid in respect of which it is possible to calculate precisely the *gross equivalent*[28] ex ante (i.e. prior to the implementation of a State aid measure) without need to undertake a risk assessment cf. art.2, litra 6. By introducing such a requirement, the Commission aims at respecting principles like equal treatment and effective monitoring and at the same time minimizing the risk of a non-uniform application of the GBER throughout the EU.

According to art.5 the following categories of aid are *considered* transparent respectively non-transparent:

---

[28] Regarding the notion "grant equivalent" see also Ch.6.

Transparent State aid	Non-transparent State aid
Grants	Capital injections
Interest rate subsidies	Risk capital measures (see s.6 of the GBER)
Loans[29]	
Guarantee schemes[30]	
fiscal measures[31]	
Repayable advances[32]	

Incentive effect

3–019   One of the cornerstones of the State aid reform was to have less and better targeted State aid. In order inter alia to meet these objectives it is stressed in recent EC State aid policy that State aid should only be awarded in so far it tackles problems which the markets themselves are not capable of overcoming and promotes EU interests as, e.g. innovation.[33] The GBER only applies to State aid which has an incentive effect, cf. art.8. State aid to activities which the beneficiary would nevertheless have engaged in under normal market conditions without the aid, does not have an incentive effect. Aid has an incentive effect if it promotes the development of further activities or projects (in the Community interest).

Within the scope of application of the GBER, cf. art.8 (2), State aid to *SMEs* is considered to have an incentive effect provided the SME concerned submits an application to the authorities of the Member State in question *before* the activities relating to the implementation of the aided project or

[29]   If the gross grant equivalent has been calculated on the basis of the reference rate at the time of the grant, see Communication from the Commission on the revision of the method for setting the reference and discount rates (OJ C 14, 19.1.2008, p.2).

[30]   Aid comprised in guarantee schemes is considered transparent according to the GBER in two situations. The first situation covers cases where the method to calculate the gross grant equivalent has been subject to prior notification and acceptance by the Commission in the context of *either* the application of the GBER *or* Regulation (EC) No.1628/2006 on the application of arts 87 and 88 of the Treaty to national regional aid according to which an arrangement on regional investment aid which includes a State guarantee is only considered to be transparent if the method for calculating the aid intensity of the guarantee prior to its implementation has been notified to and approved by the Commission after October 24, 2006. The approved methodology must explicitly address the type of guarantee and the type of underlying transaction at stake. The second situation covers cases where the beneficiary is a SME and the gross grant equivalent on the basis of the safe-harbour premiums laid down in ss.3.3 and 3.5 of the Commission Notice on the application of arts 87 and 88 of the EC Treaty to State aid in the form of guarantees, see s.8 below.

[31]   Provided the fiscal measure in question contains a cap ensuring that the applicable notification threshold cannot be exceeded. No cap is necessary in case of environmental tax reductions, cf. art.25, because such aid must fulfill the conditions of Directive 2003/96/EC.

[32]   Provided the total amount does not exceed the applicable thresholds stated in the GBER. "Repayable advance" is defined in art.2, litra 26: a loan for a project which is paid in one or more installments and the conditions for the reimbursement of which depend on the outcome of the research and development an innovation project.

[33]   See "STATE AID ACTION PLAN — Less and better targeted state aid: a roadmap for state aid reform 2005–2009" (COM(2005) 107 final).

activities are initiated. On this point the GBER is quite easily applied in the case of SMEs.

The definitions of SME's (micro, small and medium-sized enterprises) are given in annex I to the GBER cf. art.2 in annex I. In this context, an enterprise is considered to be any entity engaged in an economic activity, irrespective of its legal form. The definitions are summarised in the box below:

	Number of employees	Annual turnover and/or balance sheet (in € million)
Micro	<10	≤2
Small	<50	≤10
Medium	<250	≤50 (turnover)/43 (balance sheet)

Aid to *large enterprises* (i.e. undertakings not fulfilling the criteria in the box above) is considered to have an incentive effect, if the following conditions, cf. art.8 (3), are met: **3–020**

- An application is submitted before work on the project/activity has started, and
- at least one of the following criteria is satisfied:

  - a material increase in size *or* scope of the project/activity due to the aid; or
  - a material increase in the total amount spent by the beneficiary on the project/activity due to the aid; or

- a material increase in the speed of completion of the project/activity concerned; or
- alternatively, as regards regional investment aid the project would not have been carried out as such in the assisted region concerned in the absence of the aid.

In principle, the conditions concerning incentive effect are also applicable in case of *fiscal measures*. However, such measures, may also be considered to have an incentive effect if the conditions in art.8 (4) are satisfied, i.e.: (1) the fiscal measure has been adopted prior to the beginning of work on the aided project/activity, *and* (2) it established a legal right to aid based on objective criteria leaving the Member State no discretion when granting the aid.

It should be noted that art.8(5) contains special provisions with respect to State aid to additional costs of employing disabled workers, the recruitment of disadvantaged workers, in the form of environmental tax reductions and risk capital.

Aid intensities and eligible costs

3–021   The horizontally applicable art.4 contains provisions on how to calculate aid intensity and requirements as to the documentation of the eligible costs which shall be clear and itemised. "Aid intensity" is defined as the *aid amount* expressed as a percentage of the eligible costs. These aid intensities, given in the GBER, are fixed on the basis of the experience gained by the Commission as to striking the right balance between minimising distortion of competition and at the same time tackling the market failure or cohesion issue concerned to which end the State aid is deemed necessary.

The figures forming the basis for calculating aid intensity is before any deduction of tax or other charges. Apart from State aid in the form of grants, the *aid amount* shall be the *grant equivalent* of the aid. State aid payable in *several instalments* must therefore be discounted on the basis of the reference rate at the time of the granting of the aid whereby the aid amount is established. In cases of tax exemptions or reductions on future taxes due, the discounting of aid tranches should take place on the applicable reference rate at the points in time when the tax advantages become effective. The precise calculation in such cases could be impossible because the reference rate and the exact amount of the tranches may not be known in advance. This problem may be solved by means of applying a cap on the discounted value of the aid respecting the applicable aid intensity. Then, when the aid amount of the aid tranche in a given year becomes known, discounting takes place at that time (when the tax advantage becomes effective) by applying the applicable reference rate. On that basis the discounted value of each aid tranche can be calculated. This value is then deducted from the aforementioned cap.

The reference rate is calculated by the Commission on the basis of "Communication from the Commission on the revision of the method for setting the reference and discount rates" (OJ C 14, January 1, 2008, p.2). The applicable reference/discount rates from August 1, 1997 till now are published on the Commission's webpage.[34]

The eligible costs which may be aided under the various aid categories are specified in Ch.II of the GBER. Also the maximum aid intensities applicable to the various aid categories are found in Ch.II. Article 12 of the GBER contains specific conditions on eligible costs applicable to investment aid which need to be met in order to be considered eligible costs for the purposes of the GBER.

Individual notification threshold and cumulation

3–022   According to art.6 the possibility for Member States to grant State aid without observing the notification requirement in art.88 (3) EC only comes into play if

---

[34]   See *http://ec.europa.eu/comm/competition/state_aid/legislation/reference_rates.html*

the thresholds in the box below are complied with. Regional investment aid in favour of large investment projects is subject to the provision in art.6 (2).

Aid regarding	Threshold in grant equivalent (million €/undertaking/project or study or year)
SME investment and employment	7.5
Investment aid for environmental protection	7.5
Consultancy in favour of SMEs	2
SME participation in fairs	2
Research and development projects and feasibility studies[35] regarding predominantly[36]: 1) fundamental research 2) industrial research 3) all other projects not covered by 1) and 2).	 20 10 7.5
Industrial property rights costs for SMEs	5
Training	2
Recruitment of disadvantaged workers	5
Employment of disabled workers (wage costs)	10
Compensating for additional expenses of employing disabled workers	10

When determining whether the notification thresholds in art.6 are com-   **3–023**
plied with, art.7 regarding *cumulation* provides the necessary provisions to that end.[37] It should be noted that art.7 also applies when determining if the maximum aid intensities laid down in Ch.II of the GBER (special provisions) are respected.

It follows from art.7(1) that the total amount of public support meas-ures for the aided activity or project shall be taken into account, regard-less of whether that support is financed from local, regional, national or Community sources when determining if the above mentioned thresholds (and the aid intensities limits in Ch.II) are respected. Article 7(2) allows State aid exempted by the GBER to be cumulated with any other aid exempted under the GBER provided those aid measures concern *different identifiable* costs. Cumulation with respect to the same—partly or fully overlapping—eligible costs is subject to the provision in art.7(3). According to that provi-sion State aid exempted by the GBER shall not be cumulated with any other aid exempted under the GBER *or* de minimis aid *or* with other Community aid if such cumulation would result in the highest aid intensity or aid amount

---

[35] In case of EUREKA projects the thresholds may be doubled. For further information on EUREKA see *http://www.eureka.be*

[36] "Predominantly" means more than 50% of the eligible costs are incurred through either fun-damental or industrial research. If the predominantly character cannot be established, the 7.5 threshold applies.

[37] Cumulation is elaborated upon in Ch.6.

(applicable in case of risk capital) applicable to the aid at hand under the GBER being exceeded.[38]

Example

3–024   As an example art.27 of the GBER allows for State aid for SME participation in fairs. According to that provision, the eligible costs are the costs incurred for renting, setting up and running the stand for the first participation of an undertaking in any particular fair or exhibition. The related aid intensity is also specified in art.27 and it is set to maximum 50 per cent (i.e. up to 50 per cent of the costs may be covered by State aid, e.g. through a grant whereby the requirement of the aid being transparent is satisfied cf. above and the aid amount is easily established without having to discount the aid cf. on aid intensity above). This means that the undertaking concerned must finance the remaining minimum 50 per cent of the eligible and same costs with non-public means (due to the provisions on cumulation, cf. above). However, if this calculation results in the SME concerned receiving more than €2 million, the individual threshold, cf. the box above, has been exceeded and the aid must be notified to the Commission according to art.88(3) EC. Given that the beneficiary is a SME, the requirement that the aid must have an incentive effect is satisfied by the SME submitting an application for State aid to the appropriate authorities *before* work on the participation in the fair has begun. The Member State concerned must remember to meet the requirements on transparency and monitoring, cf. arts 9 and 10, because non-compliance with respect to those provisions renders the GBER inapplicable and thereby makes art.88(3) relevant.

Outstanding recovery orders (Deggendorf case law)

3–025   It should be noted that in continuation of the Deggendorf[39] case law the GBER is inapplicable to individual State aid under a State aid scheme and ad hoc State aid in favour of undertakings which are subject to an outstanding recovery order following a previous Commission decision declaring an aid illegal and incompatible with the common market cf. art.1(6). Consequently, a national State aid scheme must explicitly exclude from its ambit such undertakings in order to benefit from the GBER.

---

[38] An exception to art.7(3) is given in art.7(4) regarding State aid in favour disabled workers (see arts 41 and 42 of the GBER). This exception allows within its ambit cumulation of the same eligible costs. This cumulation may lead to the highest threshold under the GBER being exceeded but the cumulation must not result in the aid intensity exceeding 100% of the relevant costs during the disabled workers employment. Furthermore, art.7(5) provides special cumulation rules on risk capital measures and on State aid in favour of young, innovative enterprises.

[39] Case C-355/95 P, *Textilwerke Deggendorf GmbH (TWD) v Commission of the European Communities and Federal Republic of Germany*, [1997] E.C.R. I-2549.

Export and discriminatory State aid

The previous block exemptions did not cover State aid to export related   **3–026**
activities and State aid which discriminates in favour of domestic products over
imported products. Export aid is characterised by being directly related to the
volume of exports, or for establishing and running a distribution network, or for
the running costs connected with export business. The GBER also eliminates
export and discriminatory State aid from its scope of application cf. art.1(6).

Specific conditions (Ch.II of the GBER)

Chapter II of the GBER lists 26 categories of State aid which are compatible   **3–027**
with the common market within the meaning of art.87(3) of the EC Treaty and
therefore exempted from the notification requirement of art.88 (3) of the EC
Treaty. This is, however, only the case if the general conditions (cf. above and
Ch.I of the GBER) and the specific conditions (cf. Ch.II of the GBER) are
met. These special conditions vary from each category of aid to another but in
general they concern eligible costs, maximum aid intensities, and requirements
as to the beneficiary and—in some cases—additional conditions applicable to
the individual category of State aid. Applying those special conditions follow
in principle the same modus operandi as applied in the example above.

The 26 aid categories are listed in the box below with a reference to the
relevant article in the GBER were the special conditions are found.

Regional aid	Aid for consultancy in favour of SMEs and SME participation in fairs
Article 13: Regional investment and employment aid	Article 26: Aid for consultancy in favour of SMEs
Article 14: Aid for newly created small enterprises	Article 27: Aid for SME participation in fairs
Aid for research, development and innovation	**Aid for environmental protection**
Article 31: Aid for research and development projects	Article 18: Investment aid enabling undertakings to go beyond Community standards for environmental protection or increase the level of environmental protection in the absence of Community standards
Article 32: Aid for technical feasibility studies	
Article 33: Aid for industrial property rights costs for SMEs	Article 19: Aid for the acquisition of transport vehicles which go beyond Community standards or which increase the level of environmental protection in the absence of Community standards

Aid for research, development and innovation	Aid for environmental protection
Article 34: Aid for research and development in the agricultural and fisheries sectors Article 35: Aid to young innovative enterprises Article 36: Aid for innovation advisory services and for innovation support services Article 37: Aid for the loan of highly qualified personnel	Article 20: Aid for early adaptation to future Community standards for SMEs Article 21: Environmental aid for investment in energy saving measures Article 22: Environmental investment aid for high-efficiency cogeneration Article 23: Environmental investment aid for the promotion of energy from renewable energy sources Article 24: Aid for environmental studies Article 25: Environmental aid in the form of tax reductions
Aid for female entrepreneurship Article 16: Aid for small enterprises newly created by female entrepreneurs	**SME investment and employment aid** Article 15: SME Investment and employment Aid
Aid for disadvantaged and disabled workers Article 40: Aid for the recruitment of disadvantaged workers in the form of wage subsidies Article 41: Aid for the employment of disabled workers in the form of wage subsidies Article 42: Aid for compensating the additional costs of employing disabled workers	**Training aid** Article 39: Training aid **1. Aid in the form of risk capital** Article 29: Aid in the form of risk capital

ENVIRONMENTAL AID

General guidelines on environmental aid

In January 2008 the Commission published a communication concerning the   **3–028**
extension of the validity of Community guidelines on State aid for environmental protection, which contains guidelines for when the Commission will
consider aid for environmental protection purposes as being compatible with
art.87 of the EC Treaty. The new provisions take effect from the date following their publication in the Official Journal of the European Union. They
have been published on April 1, 2008 (OJ C 82, April 1, 2008, p.1).The former
guidelines expired on April 30, 2008 (OJ C 316, December 28, 2007, p.58). The
new guidelines will have to be taken into account by the Member States with
regard to existing environmental aid arrangements as well as in the planning
and notification to the Commission of future aid schemes and individual
grants of aid for environmental purposes.

With regard to the duty to notify State aid measures to the Commission, see
art.88(3), the General Block Exemption (the GBER); see paras 3–007–3–027
specifies which aid measures of an environmental character can be adopted
by Member States without notification to the Commission provided they fulfil
the conditions laid down in the GBER, see s.2.

Environmental protection is a key policy area for the EU, and consideration   **3–029**
for the environment must be an integrated part of all its policies; see art.6 of
the EC Treaty which states that environmental protection requirements must be
integrated into the definition and implementation of the Community policies
and activities, in particular with a view to promoting sustainable development.

In the guidelines the Commission establishes that the aim of control of
State aid in the area of the environment is to ensure that State aid measures
result in a higher level of environmental protection than that which would
apply without the aid, and to ensure that the positive effects of the aid outweigh their negative effects on competition, at the same time having regard for
the principle that the polluter pays.

The new provisions include a balancing test which consists of three steps,
of which the first two include an assessment of the positive effects of the aid
concerned, and the third looks at the negative effects, followed by a balancing
of the positive against the negative effects. In relation to the environment there
is an examination of whether the aid is suitable for achieving the stated aim,
whether the aid prompts undertakings to change their behaviour, and whether
the aid is reasonable in relation to the goal (in other words, whether the desirable change of behaviour could have been achieved with less aid), and finally
how far the distortion of competition and the effect on trade is limited so that
the overall effect can be regarded as positive.

Under both art.2 and art.6 of the EC Treaty, environmental protection is an   **3–030**
important goal which is of common interest. According to the guidelines, an
aid measure must be aimed at protecting the environment, and the aid must

address a market failure. In the area of the environment, market failure often consists of organising production in the interests of the producer, and without regard for the total social costs of the production. Undertakings therefore have a tendency to generate too much pollution or to use inadequate measures to protect the environment. These market failures could, in principle, be corrected by consistent application of the principle that the polluter pays; see art.174 of the EC Treaty. However, it is the view of the Commission that this principle is not used to a sufficient degree. Furthermore, the polluter-pays principle has a negative effect on the economic activities of undertakings. For this reason, in addition to regulation, the Member States are entitled to use State aid as a positive incentive for achieving a higher level of environmental protection. This can be done both by giving individual aid to undertakings to change their behaviour, so that the undertaking's pollution is reduced, and by compensating undertakings for the additional costs imposed by national standards which are stricter than the EU's standards or requirements.

Under the EC Treaty, the polluter-pays principle is the main rule in connection with environmental protection. However, as stated, it is difficult to apply the principle consistently. For example, it is not always easy to establish the exact cost of pollution when taking account of differences between industries. In addition to this the environmental policies pursued differ between the different Member States. Further, a sudden increase in the prices of a number of industrial products will cause disturbances in the economy. This can give the public authorities an incentive to move slowly in imposing the full cost of pollution caused by the production processes of certain industries. State aid can thus supplement the principle that the polluter pays and play an important role in increasing environmental protection. The idea is that State aid can create positive incentives for undertakings to carry out activities or make investments which are not obligatory and which would not be carried out by undertakings which focus purely on profit. Against this background, State aid can be regarded as a suitable instrument.

As stated above, the State aid must have an incentive effect. This means that State aid for environmental protection must lead to the recipients of the aid changing their behaviour so that the level of environmental protection will be higher than it would otherwise be. This incentive effect can be demonstrated by means of a counterfactual analysis, establishing that the undertaking would not implement the environmental protection measure involved unless it received the State aid.

3–031   In addition to this the aid must be proportionate. This will be the case if the same result could not be achieved with less aid; in other words, the aid granted must be limited to that which is strictly necessary for achieving the environmental protection desired. Because of the special circumstances applying to SMEs, in some cases these can be granted a higher level of aid (bonus).

Finally, the negative effects of the environmental aid (distortion of competition) must be limited as far as possible, so that the resulting balance is in favour of the proposed aid. If the balance is negative, the aid will not be compatible with the common market. The negative effects of aid will often be very limited if the aid is targeted so that it only covers the additional costs associated with the higher level of environmental protection.

In Ch.3 of the Community guidelines on State aid for environmental protection, a number of measures are identified which it is assumed will either correct for market failures which prevent environmental protection or improve the level of environmental protection. In this context there are a number of conditions (concerning aid intensity and costs eligible for aid) which ensure that the measures do in fact have an incentive effect, are proportionate and have a limited negative effect on competition and trade. If these conditions are fulfilled the measures are compatible with the common market in accordance with art.87(3)(c) of the EC Treaty. The measures referred to are:

1. investment aid for undertakings which go beyond Community standards or which increase the level of environmental protection in the absence of Community standards;
2. investment aid for SMEs for early adaptation to future Community standards;
3. investment and/or operating aid enabling undertakings to achieve energy savings;
4. investment and/or operating aid for the promotion of energy from renewable sources;
5. investment and/or operating aid for cogeneration;
6. investment and/or operating aid for energy-efficient district heating installations;
7. investment aid for the management of waste of other undertakings, including activities of re-utilisation, recycling and recovery;
8. aid for the remediation of contaminated sites, if the polluter cannot be identified or be made liable in accordance with the polluter-pays principle;
9. investment aid for relocation of undertakings to new sites for environmental protection reasons where required by an administrative or judicial decision;
10. aid in the form of reductions of or exemptions from environmental taxes; and
11. Aid involved in tradable permit schemes.

3–032

Chapter 5 of the Community guidelines contains further criteria which are applicable in connection with evaluating whether the measures which are to be subject to a detailed assessment are compatible with the common market on the basis of art.87(3)(c). These measures include both those that must be notified to the Commission under block exemption provisions, and a number of measures which exceed the stated thresholds, such as those relating to amounts of money, production or energy consumption.

The provisions of the guidelines operate with two forms of assessment; a *standard assessment* for measures involving aid under a certain threshold and a *detailed assessment* for measures involving aid above that threshold or aid granted for new installations for the production of renewable energy, where the amount of aid is calculated on the basis of the environmental damage which is avoided as a result of the aid.

3–033   The Community guidelines define *environmental protection* as any action designed to remedy or prevent damage to physical surroundings or natural resources by a beneficiary's own activities, to reduce the risk of such damage or to lead to more efficient use of natural resources, including energy-saving measures and the use of renewable sources of energy. Thus the Commission finds that energy-saving measures and measures promoting the use of renewable sources of energy are also environmental protection measures.

The *internalisation of costs* means the principle that all costs associated with the protection of the environment should be included in a polluting undertaking's production costs. According to the guidelines, the true costs include the external costs connected with negative environmental effects from the production of the goods or services and these should be included in the price of the product.

On the face of it, the polluter-pays principle and the requirement that undertakings should internalise the costs of environmental protection would seem to argue against the allocation of environmental aid to the undertakings. However, the guidelines allow for the possibility of aid in two situations. These are as follows:

- under certain specific circumstances where it is not yet possible to internalise fully the costs of environmental protection, so that the aid can encourage undertakings to adjust to environmental requirements and thus constitute an interim "next best" solution; and
- aid can also act as an incentive to undertakings to go further than the applicable requirements or to make further investments to make their installations less polluting.

According to the guidelines it will no longer be possible to give aid to undertakings to comply with existing or new EU technical standards.[40]

3–034   The Community guidelines recognise that aid which has the aim of attaining a higher level of protection than required under Community standards can be appropriate. This can be in connection with the adoption of national environmental requirements which are higher than the Community standards. It can also be appropriate to grant aid when, as a result of a purely national requirement, an undertaking has to invest in environmental protection in a situation where this is not established by a Community standard in the area.

---

[40] "Community standard" means a mandatory Community standard setting the levels to be attained in environmental terms, as well the obligation to use the best available techniques without taking on disproportionately high costs; see para.2(2) of the guidelines.

The Community guidelines also deal with environmental taxes. The principal rule is that tax reliefs which certain categories of undertakings may be granted, which amounts to State aid within the meaning of art.87 of the EC Treaty, can be approved by the Commission under certain circumstances and for a limited period. This can be up to 10 years. Thereafter the tax measure in question must be re-notified to the Commission for a new assessment. State aid for renewable energy can also be accepted under certain conditions.

Scope of application

The Commission guidelines apply to all sectors covered by the EC Treaty.   **3–035**
They also apply to all sectors that are subject to special Community provisions on aid (steel production, shipbuilding, cars, synthetic fibres, transport, coal, agriculture and fisheries), unless such special rules determine otherwise. The provisions do not cover aid for the design and production of environmentally friendly products, machines or means of transport with a view to the use of fewer resources, or measures taken in factories or production units with a view to improving safety or hygiene.

For agriculture and fisheries, the guidelines apply to aid for environmental protection given to undertakings active in the processing and marketing of agricultural or fisheries products. The guidelines contain more detailed provisions on agricultural and fisheries products in para.61.

The financing of environmental protection in relation to infrastructure for air, road and railway transport, as well as inland waterways and maritime transport, including Community projects subject to Community guidelines for the development of a trans-European network, are not covered by the guidelines. Aid for research, development and innovation in the environmental area is covered by special rules on research, development and innovation, see paras 3–063 to 3–088, while eco-innovation[41] is covered by the guidelines.

Training for environmental purposes is covered by the General Block Exemption, see s.2. The same goes for aid for SMEs for consultancy services for environmental purposes.

Investment aid for environmental purposes

Aid for the purpose of environmental protection is compatible with the   **3–036**
common market as long as, according to a balancing test, it leads to increased environmental protection without affecting trading conditions to an extent that is contrary to the common interest; see art.87(3)(c) of the EC Treaty.

---

[41] The term "eco-innovation" refers to any measure which promotes or is intended to promote significant use of new processes, methods etc.

Such environmental aid can be provided within reasonable time limits, as according to the guidelines a Member State can re-notify a measure after the time limit set by a Commission decision has passed. The Member States may support notifications of aid measures by rigorous evaluations of similar past aid measures demonstrating the incentive effect of the aid. The guidelines provide for both investment aid and operating aid for environmental purposes.

Aid for undertakings which go beyond Community standards or which increase the level of environmental protection in the absence of Community standards

3–037   Investment aid can be given to enable undertakings to go beyond Community standards or increase the level of environmental protection in the absence of Community standards. The aid intensity permitted is 50 per cent, but it can be increased to 60 per cent for medium-sized enterprises and 70 per cent for small enterprises.

For eco-innovative projects the aid intensity can be increased to 60 per cent, 70 per cent and 80 per cent respectively. Aid for eco-innovation can be provided for the acquisition of eco-innovative assets or projects which involve a clear degree of risk in technological, market or financial terms, which is higher than the risk generally associated with comparable non-innovative assets or projects.

According to point 80 of the guidelines eligible costs must be limited to the extra investment costs necessary to achieve a higher level of environmental protection than required by the Community standards and will be calculated in two steps. First, the cost of the investment directly related to environmental protection will be established by reference to the counterfactual situation, where appropriate. Second, operating benefits will be deducted and operating costs will be added.

3–038   Point 81 states that where the cost of investing in environmental protection can be easily identified in the total investment cost, that precise environmental protection-related cost constitutes the eligible costs. In all other cases the extra investment costs must be established by comparing the investment with the counterfactual situation in absence of the State aid. The correct counterfactual situation is the cost of a technically comparable investment that provides a lower degree of environmental protection (corresponding to mandatory Community standards, if they exist) and that would credibly be realised without the aid ("reference investment"). Technically comparable investment means an investment with the same production capacity and all other technical characteristics (except those directly related to the extra investment for environmental protection). In addition such a reference investment must be a credible alternative to the extra investment under assessment.

As regards the problem of identifying operation benefits/costs, the following applies according to point 82 of the guidelines: the eligible investment costs must, unless otherwise provided for in Ch.3 of the guidelines, be calculated net of any operating benefits and operating costs related to the extra investment and arising during the first five years of the life of the investment concerned. That means that such operating benefits must be deducted and such operating costs must be added to the extra investment costs.

According to point 83 of the guidelines the eligible investment may take the form of investment in tangible and/or in intangible assets.

With regard to investments aiming at a level of environmental protection higher than the Community standards point 84 of the guidelines state that the counterfactual should be chosen as follows: **3–039**

a) Where the undertaking is adapting to national standards adopted in the absence of Community standards, the eligible costs consist of the additional investment necessary to achieve the level of environmental protection required by the national standards;

b) Where the undertaking is adapting to, or going beyond, national standards which are more stringent than the relevant Community standards, the eligible costs consist of of the additional investment costs necessary to achieve a level of environmental protection higher than the level required by the Community standards. The costs of investments needed to reach the level of protection required by the Community standards is not eligible.

c) Where no standards exist, eligible costs consist of the investment costs necessary to achieve a higher level of environmental protection than that which the undertaking in question would achieve in the absence of any environmental aid.

The guidelines refer to a form of competitive bidding process whereby investment aid can be granted on the basis of clear, transparent and non-discriminatory criteria that effectively ensure that the aid is limited to the minimum necessary for achieving the desired environmental advantages. In such cases the aid intensity may amount to up to 100 per cent of the eligible investment costs. This procedure can only be used if a sufficient number of undertakings participate and aid may not be given to them all.

Transport equipment

Exceptionally, aid can also be given for the acquisition of new transport vehicles which go beyond Community standards or which increase the level of environmental protection in the absence of Community standards. Such aid can also be given where the acquisition takes place before the entry into force of new Community requirements, and such new requirements cannot apply   **3–040** with retrospective effect with regard to means of transport already acquired in the fields of air, sea, road or rail transport or inland waterways etc. As in the preceding paragraph, the aid intensity in this case is also 50 per cent, 60 per cent and 70 per cent, or 60 per cent, 70 per cent and 80 per cent in the case of eco-innovative measures.

For retrofitting operations with an environmental protection objective in the transport sector the elegible costs are the total extra net costs involved according to the methodology of calculating eligible costs mentioned above under paras 3–037 to 3–040 (i.e. points 80–84 of the guidelines) if the existing means of transport are upgraded to environmental standards that were not yet in force at the date of entry into operation of those means of transport or if the means of transport are not subject to any environmental standards.

Aid for early adaptation to future Community standards

3–041   Investment aid can be given for early adaptation to future Community standards, as long as the requirements have been adopted and the investment is carried out at least one year before the new requirements enter into force. The aid intensity is 25 per cent, 20 per cent and 15 per cent for small, medium and large enterprises respectively, as long as the implementation and finalisation take place more than three years before the mandatory date of transposition or date of entry into force, and 20 per cent, 15 per cent and 10 per cent if it is between one and three years before the relevant dates.

Eligible costs must be limited to the extra investment costs necessary to achieve the level of environmental protection required by the Community standard compared to the existing level of environmental protection required prior to the entry into force of that standard. The eligible cost must be calculated net of any operating benefits and operational costs related to the extra investment and arising during the first five years of the life of the investment in question, as set out under points 81, 82 and 83 of the guidelines and described above under paras 3–037 to 3–040.

Aid for environmental studies

3–042   Aid can be given for studies in relation to investments made with the aim of improving the environment by meeting certain environmental requirements, achieving energy savings or producing renewable energy. The aid intensity is a maximum of 50 per cent. A bonus of 10 extra percentage points can be given for medium-sized enterprises and 20 extra percentage points for small enterprises.

Aid for energy saving

i) Investment aid

Aid can be given for energy saving measures either in the form of investment   **3–043**
aid or operating aid. Aid for investment in energy saving installations can be
up to 60 per cent for large, 70 per cent for medium-sized, and 80 per cent for
small enterprises. In the same way as referred to in para.3–039, a competitive bidding process can be used for selecting undertakings which can receive
100 per cent aid.

Where the investment aid is granted in a genuinely competitive bidding
process on the basis of clear, transparent and non-discriminatory criteria the
aid intensity may amount to 100 per cent of the eligible investment as defined
in point 98 of the guidelines which refer to points 80–84 of the guidelines
described above under paras 3–037 to 3–039. A sufficient number of undertakings must participate and the budget must be a binding constraint in the
sense that not all participants can receive such aid. Aid must be granted on
the basis of the first bid, so that no subsequent negotiations can be made. The
eligible costs must be limited to the extra investment costs necessary to achieve
energy savings beyond the level of the Community standards. The calculation
of extra costs must in so far as the identification of the part of the investment
directly related to energy saving is concerned follow the rules described above
with regard to points 81–83 of the guidelines. The calculation of the extra cost
with regard to reaching a level of energy saving higher than the Community
standards must be identified as laid down in point 84 of the guidelines, see
above under paras 3–037 to 3–039.

The method of identifying benefits/costs follows the same principles as
described above in paras 3–037 to 3–039 but point 98 of the guidelines state
that as far as SMEs are concerned only the benefits/costs during the first
three years of the life of the investment will be taken into account, the first
four years with regard to large enterprises that are not part of the EU CO 2
Emission Trading System and five years for large enterprises that are part of
that system. For large undertakings that period can be reduced to the first
three years where the depreciation time of the investment can be demonstrated
not to exceed three years.

ii) Operating aid

Operating aid for energy saving may be granted as long as the aid is limited   **3–044**
to compensating for net extra production costs resulting from the investment.
The operating aid can be given for a maximum of five years and any investment aid granted to the undertaking in question in respect of the new plant
must be deducted from the production costs. In the case of regressive aid,
the aid intensity must not exceed 100 per cent in the first year, and must fall
to zero in a straight line by the end of the fifth year. If aid does not decrease
gradually, the aid intensity must not exceed 50 per cent of the eligible extra
costs.

Aid for renewable energy sources

i) Investment aid

3–045 Aid can be given for promoting the use of renewable energy sources either in the form of investment aid or operating aid. State aid may be justified if there is no mandatory Community standard for the share of energy from renewable sources for individual undertakings. Aid for the production of biofuels is only allowed for sustainable biofuels. The maximum permitted aid is 60 per cent, 70 per cent and 80 per cent for large, medium-sized and small enterprises respectively. Also in relation to this type of aid a competitive bidding process can be used for selecting undertakings which can receive 100 per cent aid, see point 104 of the guidelines. The costs which are eligible for aid are established on the basis of a comparison between the extra costs of the investment which the recipient of the aid makes, and the costs of a conventional power plant or with a conventional heating system with the same capacity, and the costs must be calculated net of any operating benefits and costs related to the extra investment during the first five years of the life of the investment.

Eligible costs for renewable energy must be limited to the extra investment cost borne by the beneficiary compared with a conventional power plant or with a conventional heating system with the same capacity in terms of effective production of energy.

ii) Operating aid

3–046 Operating aid can be given for the production of renewable energy in order to cover the difference between the cost of producing energy from renewable energy sources and the market price of the form of energy concerned. Any investment aid granted to the undertaking in question for the new plant must be deducted from production costs. Aid can be granted for the production of renewable energy for sale as well as for the undertaking's own consumption.

Operating aid for renewable energy sources may be granted in three ways:

a) Aid can be given to compensate for the difference between the cost of producing energy from renewable sources, including depreciation of extra investments for environmental protection, and the market price. Operating aid may be granted until the plant has been fully depreciated according to normal accounting rules, allowing for a normal return on capital, but it cannot cover energy produced after the plant has been fully depreciated.

b) Member States may also grant aid for renewable energy sources by using market mechanisms such as green certificates or tenders; see para.110 of the guidelines.

c) Member States may grant operating aid in accordance with the provisions set out in para.100 of the guidelines, i.e. regressive aid over five years, starting with 100 per cent and falling in a straight line to zero by the end of the fifth year or, if aid does not decrease gradually, the aid intensity must not exceed 50 per cent of the eligible extra costs over a period of five years.

With regard to operating aid connected with biofuels where, in comparison with most other forms of renewable energy generation there are relatively low investment costs but higher operating costs, the Commission may allow operating aid for the production of renewable energy from biomass which exceeds the amount of the investment where a Member State can show that the total costs for the beneficiary of the aid, after depreciation of the plant, is still higher than the market price for energy.

Aid for cogeneration of electricity and heat

Aid can be given for investment in cogeneration of electricity and heat if a new   **3–047**
cogeneration unit will make energy savings compared to separate production as defined by Directive 2004/8/EC and Decision 2007/74/EC.[42] Such aid can also be given for the improvement of an existing cogeneration unit or conversion of an existing power generation unit into a cogeneration unit in order to achieve energy savings compared to the original situation.

The permitted aid intensity is 60 per cent, 70 per cent and 80 per cent for large, medium-sized and small enterprises respectively. As with a number of other forms of aid, a competitive bidding process can be used for selecting undertakings which can receive 100 per cent aid. For operating aid for cogeneration of electricity and heat, aid can be granted in accordance with the same rules as apply to renewable energy.

Eligible costs must be limited to the extra investment costs necessary to   **3–048**
realise a high-efficiency cogeneration plant as compared to a reference investment and must be calculated net of any operating benefits and operating costs related to the extra investment and arising during the first five years of the life of the investment as set out in points 81 to 83 of the guidelines, see paras 3–037 to 3–039, above.

Operating aid may be granted in accordance with the rules for operating aid for renewable described above at paras 3–045 and 3–046. In cases where: (a) the costs of producing high-efficiency cogeneration electric power or heat exceeds its market price or (b) where for the industrial use of the combined production of electric power and heat it can be shown that the cost of producing one unit of energy using that technique exceeds the

---

[42] Directive 2004/8/EC on the promotion of cogeneration based on a useful heat demand in the internal energy market and amending Directive 92/42/EEC (OJ L 52, 21.2.2004, p.50) and Commission Decision of December 21, 2006 establishing harmonised efficiency reference values for separate production of electricity and heat in application of Directive 2004/8/EC (OJ L 32, 6.2.2007, p.183).

market price of one unit of conventional energy. The production costs may include the plant's normal return on capital, but any gains by the under-taking in terms of heat production must be deducted from the production costs.

Aid for energy-efficient district heating.

3–049   Such aid will be compatible with the common market within the meaning of art.87(3)(c) of the EC Treaty provided that it leads to primary energy savings and provided that the beneficiary district heating installation satisfies the defi-nition of energy-efficient district heating set out in point 70 of the guidelines, and that:

   a) the combined operation of the generation of heat (as well as electricity in the case of cogeneration) and the distribution of heat will result in primary energy savings; or
   b) the investment is meant for the use and distribution of waste heat for district heating purposes.

3–050   The aid intensity must not exceed 50 per cent of the eligible investment costs. If the aid is intended solely for the generation part of a district heating installation, energy-efficient district heating installations using renewable sources of energy or cogeneration will be covered by the rules set out in s.3.1.6. and 3.1.7. of the guidelines respectively on aid for the use of renew-able energy and aid for the use of cogeneration, see above at paras 3–045 to 3–048. Aid intensity may be increased where the aid is to be given to SMEs. The increase can be 10 percentage points for medium-sized enterprises and 20 for small enterprises. As a consequence aid intensity for small enterprises can be 70 per cent, for medium-sized 60 per cent and for large enterprises 50 per cent.

   Also in this case it is possible to apply a competitive bidding process according to the lines set out above at paras 3–037 to 3–039 and cover 100 per cent of the eligible costs as defined in points 124 and 125 of the guide-lines.

   Eligible costs are limited to the extra investment costs necessary to realise an investment leading to energy-efficient district heat as compared with a ref-erence investment and must be calculated as set out in points 81 and 83, see above at para.3–039.

Aid for waste management

3–051   Aid for waste management for others than the recipient of the aid can be given, provided that the investment is aimed at reducing pollution generated by other undertakings and does not extend to pollution generated by the beneficiary of the aid, and that the aid does not indirectly relieve the polluters from a burden that should be borne by them under Community law, or from a burden that should be considered a normal company cost for the polluters. The aid must be given for measures or installations that go beyond the state-of-the-art or which use conventional technologies in an innovative manner, and it is a condition that the materials treated would otherwise be disposed of, or be treated in a less environmentally friendly manner. Finally, the investment must not merely increase demand for the materials to be recycled without increasing collection of those materials. The permitted aid intensity is 50 per cent, 60 per cent and 70 per cent for large, medium-sized and small enterprises respectively.

The eligible costs must be limited to the extra investment costs necessary to realise an investment leading to waste management and borne by the beneficiary compared to the reference investment, i.e. a conventional production not involving waste management with the same capacity. The cost of such a reference investment must be deducted from the eligible costs. Costs must be calculated net of any operating benefits and operating costs related to the extra investment arising during the first five years of the life of the investment.

Aid for the remediation of contaminated sites

Aid can be granted for the remediation of contaminated sites. Where the **3–052** poluter can be identified, that person must finance the remediation, and no State aid may be granted. Where the polluter cannot be identified, the person responsible for the work may receive aid. Aid can be granted up to but not beyond 100 per cent. The eligible costs are equal to the cost of the remediation work less the increase in the value of the land.[43]

Aid for the relocation of undertakings

Investment aid can be given for relocation of undertakings to new sites for **3–053** environmental protection reasons where the change of location is ordered by an administrative authority, or by judicial decision or is agreed between the undertaking and a competent public authority. The undertaking must comply with the strictest environmental standards in the new region where it is located. The beneficiary can be an undertaking established in an urban area or in a special conservation area designated under Natura 2000,[44] which

---

[43] See Saskia Dirkzwager-De Rijk, "Two Dutch cases on State aid and soil rehabilitation", in *Competition Policy Newsletter*, No.1, Spring 2007 p.130.

[44] Natura is an ecological network within the EU that supplements EU legislation aiming at protecting the most threatened habitats and species across Europe.

lawfully carries out an activity that creates major pollution and must, on account of that location, move from its current location to a more suitable area. The beneficiary can also be an establishment or installation falling within the scope of the Seveso II Directive.[45] The permitted aid intensity is 50 per cent, 60 per cent and 70 per cent for large, medium-sized and small enterprises respectively.

The amount of costs eligible for aid is calculated on the basis of the yield from the sale or renting of the plant or land abandoned, the compensation paid in the event of compulsory purchase and other forms of financial gains connected with the transfer of the plant, including technological and operating improvements resulting from better use of the plant, with the deduction of the removal costs, costs for the establishment of a plant with the same capacity, and any penalties imposed on the undertaking for having terminated contracts for the renting of land or buildings.

Aid involved in tradable permit schemes

3–054   In certain circumstances the use of tradable permit schemes may involve State aid, for example when permits are granted for less than their market value and such granting is imputable to Member States. The guidelines lay down a number of conditions for the approval of State aid as part of such schemes. Up to the end of 2012 only the following conditions must be fulfilled:

a) the tradeable permit scheme must be set up in such a way as to achieve environmental objectives beyond those intended to be achieved on the basis of Community standards that are mandatory for the undertakings concerned;

b) the allocation must be carried out in a transparent way, based on objective criteria and on data sources of the highest quality available;

c) the total amount of tradable permits granted to each undertaking for a price below their market value must not be higher than its expected needs compared with the situation in the absence of the trading scheme;

d) the allocation methodology must not favour certain undertakings or certain sectors, unless this is justified by the environmental logic of the scheme itself or where such rules are necessary for consistency with other environmental policies;[46] and

---

[45] The Seveso II directive, see Directive 96/82 of 9.12.96 on control of major-hazard accidents involving dangerous substances (OJ L 010, 14.1.97, p.13.)

[46] See case T-233/04, 10.4.2008, not yet reported, in which the CFI annulled a Commission decision according to which a Dutch emission trading scheme for nitrogen oxides was incompatible with the State aid rules. The CFI observed that a measure although constituting an advantage for its beneficiary may be justified by the nature or general scheme of the system of which it is a part and therefore not fulfil the condition of selectivity. The CFI referred to the

e) new entrants must not receive permits on more favourable conditions than existing undertakings operating on the same markets. Granting higher allocations to existing installations compared to new entrants should not result in creating undue barriers to entry.[47]

For the period following 2012, special rules apply to the Commission's evalua-   **3–055**
tion of the appropriateness of State aid in connection with the use of tradable permits; see para.141 of the guidelines.

The choice of beneficiaries must be based on objective and transparent criteria, and the aid must be granted in principle in the same way for all competitors in the same sector/relevant market if they are in a similar situation. Full auctioning must lead to a substantial increase in production costs for each sector or category of individual beneficiaries. The substantial increase in production costs cannot be passed on to customers if it leads to important sales reductions. Aid can only be granted if it is not possible for individual undertakings to reduce emission levels in order to make the price of the certificates bearable. Irreducible consumption may be demonstrated by proving the emission levels derived from the best performing technique in the the European Economic Area (EEA) and using it as a benchmark.

Incentive effect

The guidelines contain a detailed explanation of how incentive effects are to be   **3–056**
assessed. The main rule is that aid cannot be approved for projects that have been started before the application for aid is made. If the aided project has not been started before the aid application, the requirement for an incentive effect is presumed to be automatically met for all categories of aid granted to a small or medium-sized enterprise, except where the aid is subject to a detailed assessment. For all other aided projects, the Commission will require the incentive effect to be demonstrated by the notifying Member State, by means of a counterfactual analysis, and showing that the investment would not be sufficiently profitable without aid, including the value of tradable permits which may become available to the undertaking concerned following the environmentally friendly investment.

Adria-Wien Pipeline case, see case C-143/99 [2001] E.C.R. I-8365.i.a., paras 41 and 42 of that case. Case T-233/04 has been appealed to the ECJ. The Nef lien laws dispute the conclusion by the CFI that the Dutch regime constitutes State aid according to art.(87)1 though the CFI found it to be compatible with art.87(3)(c).

[47] Concerning the State aid assessment of cases where an environmental tax scheme is combined with the grant of tradable permits or quotas, see Ch.1, s.3.8 on selectivity, where it appears that the Commission will deal with such cases on the basis of art.87(3)(c), and finds it too soon to issue general guidelines on such cases; see para.68 of the Community guidelines on State aid for environmental protection.

Aid for environmental projects of common European interest

3–057   Aid given to support the execution of important projects of common European interest which are an environmental priority may be considered compatible with the common market according to art.87(3)(b) of the EC Treaty; see para.147 of the guidelines.

Aid in the form of reductions of or exemptions from environmental taxes

3–058   Aid in the form of reductions of or exemptions from environmental taxes constitutes State aid within the meaning of the EC Treaty,[48] but it can be approved provided that it contributes at least indirectly to an improvement of the level of environmental protection and that the tax reductions and exemptions do not undermine the general objective pursued. The guidelines distinguish between national environmental taxes and EU taxes.

As for harmonised taxes, especially those harmonised on the basis of Directive 2003/96/EC restructuring the Community framework for the taxation of energy products and electricity, the aid must be compatible with the relevant Community legislation. Aid in the form of tax reductions and exemptions from harmonised environmental taxes is considered to be compatible with the common market within the meaning of art.87(3)(c) of the EC Treaty for a period of 10 years, provided the beneficiaries pay at least the minimum tax level set by the relevant applicable Directive.

In respect of other purely national environmental taxes, aid can be regarded as compatible with the common market for a period of 10 years, subject to certain conditions laid down in paras 155–159 of the guidelines. Such aid can give undertakings time to adjust to a new tax regime when a Member State has introduced a new environmental tax. In para.158 of the guidelines it is established that the Commission will regard aid as being necessary if:

a) the choice of beneficiaries is based on objective and transparent criteria, and the aid is granted in principle in the same way for all competitors in the same sector/relevant market if they are in a similar factual situation;

b) the environmental tax without reduction will lead to a substantial increase in production costs for each sector or category of individual beneficiaries; and

---

[48] On the use of reductions of environmental taxes, see Anne Theo Seinen and Céline Guillemaut, "Exemptions from the fuel excise tax for alumina production", in *Competition Policy Newsletter*, No.1, Spring 2006 p.103. See also Johan Lannering and Birgitta Renner-Loquenz: "State aid and eco-taxes: bundling of eco-taxes for State aid assessment", in *Competition Policy Newsletter*, No.3, Autumn 2003 p.75; and Melvin Könings, "Energy taxation and state aid. The Netherlands: energy tax exemption for energy intensive end-users", in *Competition Policy Newsletter*, No.1, Spring 2004 p.84.

c) the substantial increase in production costs cannot be passed on to customers without leading to important sales reductions.

In para.159 of the guidelines it is stated that the Commission will consider a   **3–059**
tax reduction or exemption to be permissible if at least one of three conditions is fulfilled. First, the reductions or exemptions are conditional on the conclusion of agreements between the Member State and the recipient undertakings or associations of undertakings whereby the undertakings or associations of undertakings commit themselves to achieve environmental protection objectives. Such agreements or commitments may relate to a reduction in energy consumption, a reduction in emissions or any other environmental measure. This will be assessed by the Commission on notification of the scheme. The agreements with undertakings or associations of undertakings must stipulate sanctions if the commitments are not met.

Secondly, undertakings can obtain tax relief relating to their environmental performance. Under the scheme undertakings which achieve the best possible performance in the EEA can benefit, at most, from a reduction corresponding to the increase in production costs from the tax which cannot be passed on to customers. Undertakings with a worse environmental performance will benefit from a lower reduction, proportionate to their environmental performance.

Thirdly, a reduction of an environmental tax can be approved if the aid beneficiaries pay at least 20 per cent of the national tax, unless a lower rate can be justified in view of a limited distortion of competition.

Aid subject to a detailed assessment

The guidelines contain a number of detailed provisions for how the   **3–060**
Commission will assess aid that is subject to a detailed assessment. Such aid involves those cases where, in accordance with a block exemption provision, there must be notification of individual aid as laid down in the block exemption provision in question, as well as in a number of cases laid down in the guidelines themselves. As for the latter, these concern: investment aid for environmental purposes where the aid amount exceeds €7.5 million for one undertaking (even if part of an approved aid scheme); operating aid for energy saving where the aid amount exceeds €5 million; operating aid for the production of renewable energy electricity when the aid is granted to renewable electricity installations in sites where the resulting renewable electricity generation capacity exceeds 125 MW; operating aid for the production of biofuel when the resulting production exceeds 150000 tons per year; and operating aid for cogeneration where with the resulting cogeneration electricity capacity exceeds 200 MW.

Paragraphs 165 to 185 of the guidelines describe a number of criteria which the Commission will apply where it must undertake a detailed assessment of aid. These concern provisions relating to: the positive effects of the aid; considerations about market failure; the use of the appropriate aid instrument; the incentive effect, necessity and proportionality of aid; the degree of distortion of competition and the effect on trade; the assessment of dynamic incentives and the risk of crowding out;[49] the keeping of inefficient firms afloat; market power and exclusionary behaviour;[50] effects on trade and on the location of undertakings. Paragraphs 186 to 188 of the guidelines contain provisions on the balancing test and the decision. The criteria referred to are essentially those which the Commission generally uses when assessing State aid cases, but they are expressed in particular detail in paras 165–188 of the guidelines.

Cumulation, reporting and monitoring

3–061   The final provisions of the guidelines contain rules on cumulation, reporting, transparency, monitoring and evaluation.

Implementation of the guidelines

3–062   The guidelines encourage the Member States to adopt the necessary measures to change their existing environmental aid schemes to bring them into line with the guidelines within 18 months of their publication. However, para.200 contains some exceptions to this provision. The guidelines are stated to apply from the first day following their publication in the Official Journal of the European Union i.e. April 2, 2008. They replaced the guidelines on State aid for environmental protection of February 3, 2001. The new guidelines will be applicable until December 31, 2014.

AID FOR RESEARCH, DEVELOPMENT AND INNOVATION

Introduction

3–063   State aid for research, development and innovation is regulated by the Community framework for state aid for research and development and

---

[49]   The term "crowding out" refers to the risk that a Member State will use such significant environmental aid for new innovative technology that undertakings in other Member States will give up the use of corresponding innovative technology so that, ultimately the use of the technology is concentrated in a single Member State.

[50]   The term "exclusionary behaviour" refers to situations where an undertaking with significant market power is granted aid, with the risk that it will become even more powerful, so that competing undertakings may in the end give up competing. However, the Commission will normally regard aid to undertakings with a market share of less than 25 % as unproblematic in this respect.

innovation (OJ C 323, December 30, 2006, p.1).[51] The framework applies from January 1, 2007 until December 21, 2013.

With regard to notification the General Block Exemption Regulation specifies in which cases Member States can implement aid to R&D&I without notification to the Commission provided the aid measures in question fulfil the conditions specified in the GBER, see paras 3–007 to 3–027, above.

From a European economic perspective, investment in research, development and innovation (R&D&I) is very important. This is because such investment can strengthen competitiveness and create growth. According to art.163 of the EC Treaty, the Community has the objective of strengthening the scientific and technological bases of Community industry and encouraging it to become more competitive at international level, while promoting all the research activities deemed necessary (in other words, a goal of common interest). It is against this background that, for example, the 7th Framework Programme for Research and Technological Development 2007–2013 has been initiated.

From a theoretical point of view it is markets themselves which bring about the best results in the form of investment in R&D&I. However, the fact is that, among other things, market failure means that investment in R&D&I is below the desirable level. In other words, the markets do not give the most efficient result. In so far as this lack of efficiency is due to market failure, it can be countered by means of State aid. State aid can thus contribute to the attainment of an appropriate level of investment in R&D&I, and thereby increase growth.   3–064

State aid is compatible with the common market if the aid is expected to lead to an increased investment in R&D&I and the effects of such aid in distorting competition are not regarded as being contrary to the common interest.

In applying the framework, the Commission regards "the common interest" as being equivalent to "economic efficiency". "Economic efficiency" refers to the extent to which total welfare is optimised in a particular market or in the economy at large. Additional R&D&I increases economic efficiency by shifting market demand towards new or improved products, processes or services, which is equivalent to a decrease in the quality adjusted price of these goods. In principle it is markets themselves that must ensure economic efficiency. If this cannot be achieved without intervention there is market failure, and this market failure can be eliminated by State aid (intervention). The aim of the framework is to contribute to the improvement of economic efficiency, and in particular to make it easier for Member States to better target the aid to the relevant market failures.

---

[51] The new rules are discussed by Thibaut Kleiner and Renate Repplinger-Hach, "The new community framework for state aid for research and development and innovation", in *Competition Policy Newsletter*, No.1, Spring 2007 p.3.

Scope of application

3–065   The provisions of the framework apply to State aid for R&D&I for all sectors, unless otherwise provided in sector-specific rules. However the framework does not apply to aid for R&D&I granted to undertakings in difficulty within the meaning of the Community guidelines on State aid for rescue and restructuring undertakings in difficulty. As for agriculture and fisheries, reference is made to the special rules on these in Ch.9 of the framework.

The balancing test

3–066   State aid for R&D&I will be assessed on the basis of a balancing test. This test forms the basis both for the framework provisions themselves and for the Commission's assessment of whether a notified aid scheme for R&D&I is compatible with the common market. This will be the case if all the elements of the balancing test lead to an overall positive assessment of the measure. The test consists of the following three steps:

(1) Does the aid measure have a well-defined objective of common interest (e.g. growth, employment, cohesion, the environment)?
(2) Is the aid well designed to deliver the objective of common interest, i.e. does the proposed aid address the market failure or other objective?

(i)   Is State aid an appropriate policy instrument?
(ii) Is there an incentive effect, i.e. does the aid change the behaviour of undertakings?
(iii) Is the aid measure proportional, i.e. could the same change in behaviour be obtained with less aid?

(3) Are the distortions of competition and effects on trade limited, so that the overall balance is positive?

3–067   In connection with the framework for R&D&I, the relevant aims of common interest are the promotion of R&D&I. The aim is to improve economic efficiency by counteracting well-defined market failures which prevent the EU from achieving optimal levels of R&D&I. First, such market failures can consists of the fact that projects which may benefit society as a whole, by means of knowledge transfer, may not necessarily give an attractive return for a private investor and so may not be carried out. Thus market forces alone will not encourage the realisation of such projects.

Secondly, the exploitation of certain forms of knowledge can be protected by, for example, patents. On the other hand, other forms of knowledge, for example basic research, are usually publicly accessible (public property) and can thus be freely used by people other than the inventor or discoverer. This means that undertakings will tend not to invest in gaining such knowledge and will instead take advantage of publicly available knowledge which has been brought about by others. If there were a higher level of the discovery of publicly available knowledge, this would lead to the general spread of knowledge through the economy to the benefit of the whole of society.

Thirdly, market failure can be caused by there being inadequate or asymmetric information. This refers to the fact that R&D&I has a high risk and uncertainty and because of inadequate and/or asymmetric information private investors can be reluctant to finance valuable projects. Furthermore, highly qualified personnel can lack knowledge of the possibilities for being employed in innovative undertakings. For these reasons both financial and human resources may not be available for R&D&I projects so that such projects are not carried out and the economic growth which such projects would have resulted in will not be realised.

Fourthly, the market failures can be due to lack of coordination and network failures. Such problems may arise because of the inability of undertakings to co-ordinate R&D and find adequate partners.

In accordance with the balancing test the Member States must, in concrete cases, assess whether State aid is the most suitable instrument for countering the market failure in question. This means that the Member States must clearly identify and describe the market failure they intend to target with the aid measure. For example, if regulation or increased investment in universities is more appropriate for dealing with a specific market failure, a Member State should not choose State aid undertakings as the solution. If it is found that State aid is a suitable means, the next element in the balancing test will be to see whether the beneficiary of the aid will change its behaviour so that it increases its level of R&D&I activity, and so that R&D&I projects or activities are initiated which would not otherwise be carried out, or which would be carried out in a more restricted manner (incentive effect). The Commission considers that as a result of State aid, R&D&I activity should be increased in size, scope, amount spent or speed. Member States must clearly demonstrate how they intend to ensure that the incentive effect will be manifested. **3–068**

The last element of the balancing test's assessment of an aid measure's positive effects is the proportionality of the aid. A State aid measure is considered to be proportional if the actual aid in question—neither more nor less—is necessary for achieving the desired end.

The last question of the balancing test requires an assessment to be made of the negative effects of the aid. The negative effects in the form of distortions of competition can be categorised, for example, as inefficient production, exclusionary practices and enhancing market power, etc. Regardless of what the distortion consists of, the negative effects must be limited so that the overall balance is positive. A number of considerations will be relevant in this respect. The negative effects are normally higher for larger aid amounts and for aid granted for products or services which are close to commercial exploitation. Therefore, aid intensities are generally higher for research related activities than for activities linked to development and innovation. In any case, the definition of eligible costs must ensure that costs which arise from routine company activities are not eligible for aid.

Article 87(1) of the EC Treaty and R&D&I

3–069 The balancing test is used to establish whether a State aid measure is or is not compatible with the common market. This means that the test is only applicable if a measure relates to State aid which is covered by art.87(1).

In principle, an assessment must be made of whether in the actual circumstances an undertaking is favoured in a way which fulfils the conditions of art.87(1); see Ch.1 of this book.

However, Ch.3 of the framework contains some guidance for when it will be found that there is State aid in the area of R&D&I within the meaning of art.87(1).

The most immediately relevant question in connection with R&D&I is whether publicly funded research organisations receive State aid, and whether undertakings receive State aid via publicly funded research organisations.

3–070 In relation to research organisations, the question of State aid can be relevant if the organisation can be categorised as an undertaking. This depends on whether the organisation carries on economic activities, such as supplying services to a market, and this applies regardless of how the organisation is funded and of its legal status (public or private structure).[52] Often a research organisation will carry out both economic and non-economic activities. The latter will normally be activities such as training, carrying out independent research and development, and communicating research results. These activities will normally be the main activities of the organisation. If both economic and non-economic activities are carried on, and these are the object of public financing, both activities must be kept separate so that there is no cross-subsidisation.

If the research organisation has economic activities, such as the sale of services to commercial undertakings or research contracts, the public financing of these activities can constitute State aid. However, in such situations there is not State aid to the undertaking with which a research organisation, whose conduct can be ascribed to the State, has entered into a contract if the organisation charges market prices, or alternatively if the charges cover the full costs of the research organisation plus a reasonable profit margin.

There can also be relations between research organisations and undertakings which are not directly based on a contract between them for the provision of agreed services, but rather have the character of cooperation where the parties plan and implement projects together, sharing the risk and the profit. This cooperation must be assessed on a case-by-case basis, but it will not constitute indirect State aid to the commercial party if one of the following conditions is fulfilled:

---

[52] See paras 46 and 47 in Case C-309/99, *Wouters and Others*, [2002] E.C.R. I-1577.

- the participating undertakings pay for all the costs;
- the results can to a great extent be made available to others and any intellectual property rights to which the activities of the research organisation give rise are transferred wholly to the research organization; or
- the research organisation receives payment corresponding to the market price for the intellectual property rights which arise from the research project and which are transferred to the participating undertakings.

The basis for the compatibility of aid with the common market

Aid for R&D&I can in principle be declared compatible with the common market on the basis of art.87(3)(b) or (c) of the EC Treaty.   **3–071**

Article 87(3)(b) gives the Commission authority to declare State aid to promote the execution of an important project of common European interest as being compatible with the common market. The conditions which must be fulfilled in this connection are set out in Ch.4 of the framework. Projects eligible to fall within the scope of application of art.87(3)(b) are characterised—on the one hand—by having clearly defined terms of implementation, list of participants and objectives, and—on the other hand—by contributing in a concrete, clear and identifiable manner to the community interest, for example by enabling significant progress to be made towards achieving specific Community objectives. Under art.87(3)(c) the Commission may declare aid to facilitate the development of certain economic activities or of certain economic areas to be compatible with the common market, where such aid does not adversely affect trading conditions to an extent contrary to the common interest. If the balancing test gives a positive result, the aid measure is compatible with the common market on the basis of art.87(3)(c).

The structure of the framework and the implementation of the balancing text

In Ch.5 of the framework there is a list of measures, with accompanying conditions; see paras 3–074 to 3–085. In Ch.6 the Commission sets out the criteria which must be satisfied if an aid measure is to be considered as having the necessary incentive effect; see para.3–086. Thus, if a measure fulfils the conditions in Ch.5 and there is an incentive effect, it can be declared compatible with the common market. Chapter 7 lists the criteria for the detailed assessment which the Commission is sometimes required to make.   **3–072**

A number of measures can be declared compatible with the common market on the basis of Chs 5 and 6 if: (1) an application concerning the aid is submitted before a specific project is started, and (2) the relevant criteria in Ch.5 are fulfilled. For these measures there is an automatic assumption that they will have an incentive effect if condition (1) is fulfilled. This applies to the following measures:

1) project aid and feasibility studies where the aid beneficiary is an SME and where the aid amount is below €7.5 million per SME for a project (project aid plus aid for feasibility study);
2) aid for industrial property rights costs for SMEs;
3) aid for young innovative enterprises;
4) aid for innovation advisory services and aid for innovation support services; and
5) aid for the loan of highly qualified personnel.

Another group of measures will be subject to the detailed assessment referred to in Ch.7, namely, those for an amount of aid which exceeds the following thresholds:

1. for project aid and feasibility studies:
   - if the project is predominantly fundamental research, €20 million per undertaking, per project/feasibility study;
   - if the project is predominantly industrial research, €10 million per undertaking, per project/feasibility study; and
   - for all other projects, €7.5 million per undertaking, per project/feasibility study.
2. for process or organisational innovation in services activities, €5 million per project per undertaking; and
3. for innovation clusters (per cluster), €5 million.

In addition to these, cases which must be notified to the Commission in accordance with a special provision in one of the block exemption regulations will also be subject to a detailed assessment.

3–073   The above measures are subjected to a detailed examination because they are assessed as being particularly critical in relation to the risk for distortion of competition, contrary to the common interest. The criteria in Chs 5 and 6 also form the basis for the detailed examination, while Ch.7 contains supplementary guidance on which further positive or negative elements the Commission can include in the detailed assessment/balancing test.

For all other measures the Commission will undertake a supplementary examination of the compatibility of the aid with the common market on the basis of the balancing test. The supplementary examination will normally consist of a more thorough and detailed analysis of the factual circumstances of the case, and it includes an evaluation of whether the criteria in Ch.5 are complied with, and whether there is evidence of an incentive effect.

Aid to certain categories of R&D&I

3–074   In principle, State aid for R&D&I is compatible with the common market on the basis of art.87(3)(c) of the Treaty, if it is established by the balancing test that the aid will lead to increased R&D&I, and if it does not adversely affect trading conditions to an extent contrary to the common interest. Chapter 5 of the framework lists the eight measures/categories (with associated conditions), which can be found compatible with the common market on this basis.

Aid for research and development projects

Under this category which is also covered by the GBER aid can be given for fundamental research, industrial research, and/or experimental development.[53] Aid can be given for a certain percentage of a number of eligible costs.   **3–075**

First of all, eligible costs include personnel costs. The costs for instruments and equipment, and costs for buildings and land, to the extent they are used for the research project, are also eligible for aid. If moveable property or buildings and land are not used for the whole of the duration of the research project, only the depreciation costs relating to the research project will be eligible costs. For land, costs of commercial transfer or actually incurred capital costs are eligible. Furthermore, the costs of contractual research, technical knowledge and patent rights bought from outside sources at market prices and on arm's length terms are eligible for aid, as are the costs of consultancy and equivalent services used exclusively for the research activity. Finally, general costs and additional overheads incurred directly as a result of the research project are eligible for aid.

The aid intensity, calculated on the basis of the eligible costs, may not exceed the following rates, though these rates may be raised in special cases to match the aid which is received by competitors outside the EU.

3–076

	Small undertakings	Medium-sized undertakings	Large undertakings
Fundamental research	100%	100%	100%
Industrial research	70%	60%	50%
Industrial research 15% bonus if:	80%	75%	65%
1. There is effective collaboration between at least two undertakings which are independent of each other and no single undertaking bears more than 70% of the eligible costs of the project, and the project involves at least one SME or cross-border collaboration.			

[53] In connection with the categorising of research activities, reference can be made to The Measurement of Scientific and Technological Activities, Proposed Standard Practice for Surveys on Research and Experimental Development, Frascati Manual, OECD, 2002.

| 2. There is effective collaboration between an undertaking and a research organisation, and if the research organisation bears at least 10% of the eligible project costs and has the right to publish the results of the research carried out by it.

3. If the results of the project are widely disseminated.			
Experimental research	45%	35%	25%
Experimental research 15% bonus if:

1. There is effective collaboration between at least two undertakings which are independent of each other and no single undertaking bears more than 70% of the eligible costs of the project, and the project involves at least one SME or cross-border collaboration.

2. There is effective collaboration between an undertaking and a research organisation, and if the research organisation bears at least 10% of the eligible project costs and has the right to publish the results of the research carried out by it. | 60% | 50% | 40% |

Aid for technical feasibility studies

3–077   The costs of technical feasibility studies preparatory to industrial research or experimental development activities are eligible for aid. The eligible costs are the costs of research. The aid intensity is set out in the following table:

	Small undertakings	Medium-sized undertakings	Large undertakings
Studies preparatory to industrial research activities	75%	75%	65%
Studies preparatory to experimental development activities	50%	50%	40%

Aid for technical feasibility studies is also covered by the GBER.

Aid for SMEs' costs for intellectual property rights

The costs of SMEs incurred in obtaining and validating intellectual property   **3–078**
rights, including patents, are eligible for aid. This includes the costs for the
preparation, filing and prosecution of the application in the first place, as well
as the costs incurred in obtaining the grant or validation of the right in other
jurisdictions. The same applies to the costs of enforcing the rights. This aid is
compatible with the common market up to the same level of aid as is permissible for aid for the research and development activities which give rise to the
intellectual property rights; see paras 3–075 and 3–076.

This category is also found in the GBER.

Aid to young innovative enterprises

Small, young and innovative enterprises can receive up to €1 million in aid,   **3–079**
which can be increased to €1.5 million in the areas referred to in art.87(3)
(a), and up to €1.25 million in the areas referred to in art.87(3)(c). This aid
can only be given once, but it can be cumulated with other aid under the
framework provisions, or with aid given in accordance with the guidelines
on risk capital, or aid for SMEs for R&D&I in accordance with the rules
in the General Block Exemption Regulation (GBER). Such an undertaking
may not thereafter receive any other form of aid (other than R&D&I aid and
risk capital aid) for the three years following receipt of aid in its capacity as a
young innovative enterprise.

To what extent an undertaking can be characterised as *small* is decided in
accordance with the criteria given in annex 1 of the GBER. Accordingly, an
undertaking is small if it employs fewer than 50 people and has an annual
turnover or an annual balance sheet total of no more than €10 million.

An undertaking is *young* if it has been in existence for less than six years at
the time when the aid is granted.

According to the framework, there are two possible bases on which an
undertaking can be characterised as being *innovative*. First, an undertaking
can be characterised as innovative if the Member State can demonstrate, by

means of an evaluation carried out by an external expert, that the beneficiary will in the foreseeable future develop products, services or processes which are technologically new or substantially improved compared to the state of the art in its industry in the Community, and which carry a risk of technological or industrial failure. Secondly, an undertaking can be characterised as innovative if its R&D expenses represent at least 15 per cent of its total operating expenses in at least one of the three years preceding the granting of the aid. In the case of a start-up enterprise without any financial history, the basis will be its accounts for the current year.

The GBER also contains provisions on aid to young innovative enterprises.

Aid for process and organisational innovation in services

3–080   According to the framework, aid can be given for process and organisational innovation in services. Process innovation refers to the implementation of new or significantly improved production or marketing methods, such as significant changes of technique, equipment and/or software. Organisational innovation refers to the introduction of new organisational methods in the undertaking's business practices, organisation of the workplace or external relations. However, not all kinds of improvements are entitled to aid. Thus, routine or periodic changes made to products, production lines, manufacturing processes, existing services and other operations in progress do not qualify for State aid.

In order to be eligible, the innovation must be formulated as a project with an identified and qualified project manager, as well as identified project costs, and the result of the aided project must be the development of a standard, of a business model, methodology or concept, which can be systematically reproduced. In addition, the process or organisational innovation must be new or substantially improved compared to the state of the art in its industry in the Community, and the innovation project must entail a clear degree of risk. An organisational innovation must always be related to the use and exploitation of information and communication technologies.

The eligible costs are the same as are permissible for aid for the research and development activities which give rise to intellectual property rights; see paras 3–075 and 3–076.

3–081   On the basis of these eligible costs, aid that is given in accordance with the following aid intensities is compatible with the common market under art.87(3)(c):

	Aid intensity
Small undertakings	35%
Medium-sized undertakings	25%
Large undertakings, provided they collaborate with an SME which bears at least 30% of the eligible costs	15%

Aid for innovation advisory services and for innovation support services

SMEs can receive aid up to €200,000 over a three-year period for the purchase   **3–082**
of innovation advisory services and innovation support services. Such services
must be bought at market price or, if the service provider is a non-for-profit
entity, at a price which reflects its full costs plus a reasonable margin, and the
service provider must be certified. If the service provider is not certified the aid
may not cover more than 75 per cent of the eligible costs.

Eligible costs for innovation advisory services are: management consulting,
technological assistance, technology transfer services, training, consultancy
for acquisition, protection and trade in intellectual property rights and for
licensing agreements, as well as consultancy on the use of standards. For
innovation support services the following costs are eligible: office space, data
banks, technical libraries, market research, use of laboratories, quality label-
ling, testing and certification. If the service provider is a not-for-profit entity,
the aid may be given on the basis of the difference between the price paid and
the market price.

De minimis aid can still be given, but in respect of other eligible costs.

This category is also covered by the GBER.

Aid for the loan of highly qualified personnel

SMEs can receive aid for the loan (secondment) of highly qualified workers   **3–083**
from research institutions or from large undertakings. Highly qualified personnel means researchers, engineers, designers and marketing managers with a
tertiary education degree and at least five years of relevant professional experience, and they must have been employed for at least two years in the lending
research organisation or large undertaking. The seconded personnel must be
employed by the SME in a newly established post, and must be engaged in
R&D&I activities.

The eligible costs in connection with such secondment are all personnel
costs for borrowing and employing the highly qualified personnel, and the
maximum aid intensity is 50 per cent of the eligible costs, for a maximum of
three years per undertaking and per person borrowed.

Aid for the loan of highly qualified personnel may also be granted on the
basis of the GBER.

Aid for innovation clusters

In the framework "innovation clusters" are defined as groupings of inde-   **3–084**
pendent undertakings operating in a particular sector and region, and which
are designed to stimulate innovative activity by promoting intensive interac-
tions, sharing of facilities and exchanging knowledge and expertise, and by

contributing effectively to technology transfer, networking and information dissemination between the undertakings in the cluster.

It is a condition for the granting of aid that a legal entity is set up to operate the innovation cluster, to manage participation and access to the cluster's premises, facilities and activities. There must be unrestricted access to the cluster's premises, facilities and activities, and the fees charged for this should reflect their actual costs. The aid must be granted to the legal entity.

3–085   The framework allows for the possibility both of giving investment aid and, something which is unusual, aid for operating costs.

Investment aid can be given for training facilities and research centres, open-access research infrastructures (laboratories, testing facilities) and for broadband network infrastructures. The eligible costs are those relating to investment in land, buildings, machinery and equipment.

As a starting point the aid intensity is 15 per cent, but this can be increased to 35 per cent for aid to small undertakings and to 25 per cent for aid to medium-sized undertakings. There are also special rates of aid intensity in areas which are eligible for regional aid.

Operating aid may also be granted to the legal entity operating the innovation cluster. The eligible costs include personnel and administrative costs relating to marketing, management of the cluster's open-access facilities, and the organisation of training programmes, workshops and conferences.

The aid intensity may amount to 100 per cent in the first year, falling in a straight line to zero by the end of the fifth year (degressive aid), or a maximum of 50 per cent of the eligible costs for a maximum of five years (non-degressive aid). The five-year period can be extended to 10 years on the basis of convincing evidence provided by the notifying Member State.

The incentive effect and necessity of aid

3–086   As stated above, State aid for R&D&I must have an incentive effect. This means that the aid must result in the beneficiary changing its behaviour so that it increases the level of its R&D&I activity in size, scope, amount spent or speed. This is controlled by requiring Member States, in connection with the notification of individual aid measures, to give a forecast of the increased R&D&I activity. The basis for this is a comparison of a situation in which State aid is not given with a situation in which State aid is given. If by this means a Member State can show that an aid measure will increase the size (costs or number of assigned people), scope, number of expected deliverables from the project, amount spent (e.g. the total R&D&I spending by the aid beneficiary) or speed of a project (faster completion of the project), or an increase in the beneficiary's costs for R&D&I, the Commission will normally conclude that the necessary incentive exists.

If an undertaking seeks aid for R&D&I from the national authorities after it has commenced the R&D&I project for which aid is sought, the Commission will not consider that there is an incentive effect. If State aid is granted to an R&D&I project which has already been started, the condition for there to be an incentive effect is not fulfilled and the aid is therefore incompatible with the common market. Carrying out a feasibility study prior to the application for aid for an R&D&I project does not exclude the possibility of an incentive effect.

The Commission considers that if aid is requested before a project is started, the incentive effect is automatically met for the following aid measures:

- project aid and feasibility studies where the aid beneficiary is an SME and where the aid amount is below €7.5 million for a project per SME;
- aid for the costs connected with intellectual property rights costs for SMEs;
- aid for young innovative enterprises;
- aid for innovation advisory services and innovation support services; and
- aid for the loan of highly qualified personnel.

Cumulation

Where costs are eligible for aid both under the framework and under other rules on State aid, the common portion of eligible costs will be granted aid under the most favourable applicable rules. This limitation does not apply to aid granted in accordance with the Community guidelines on State aid to promote risk capital investments in SMEs. Aid for R&D&I may not be cumulated with de minimis support in respect of the same eligible expenses if this would exceed the maximum aid intensities laid down in the framework.

3–087

Furthermore, regardless of whether the support for the aid is financed entirely from State resources or is partly financed by the Community, the aid ceilings fixed under the framework apply, except under the special conditions established for Community funding under the R&D framework programmes.[54]

Obligations of the Member States

The Member States have some special obligations in connection with aid schemes in the area of R&D&I. Thus, the Member States must publish the full text of their R&D&I aid schemes on the internet, and a Member State may not implement a scheme before this has been done. The reason for this is that such measures increase transparency and thereby give interested parties

3–088

[54] http://cordis.europa.eu/fp7/home_en.html

easy access to information about the aid scheme. The Commission must be informed of the internet address concerned.

Where, a Member State provides aid under an approved aid scheme in excess of €3 million, the Member State must specifically inform the Commission by filling out the form in the annex to the framework and sending it to the Commission within 20 working days after the grant of aid.

The Member States must send annual reports on R&D&I measures to the Commission, in accordance with the rules on this in Regulation (EC) No.659/1999, as amended. These reports must contain information about the beneficiaries' names, the amount of aid per beneficiary, the aid intensity, and the sectors in which aid projects have been initiated. If Member States provide aid to large undertakings under an approved aid scheme, the report must include explanations on how the requirement for an incentive effect has been fulfilled. The Commission publishes these reports on the internet.

Finally, the Member States must keep detailed records of aid to all R&D&I projects, containing the information necessary to be able to decide whether the framework's rules on aid intensity are complied with. The Member States must keep these records for 10 years and make them available to the Commission on request.

AID FOR RESCUING AND RESTRUCTURING FIRMS

The Community guidelines on State aid for rescuing and restructuring firms in difficulty

3–089   The Community guidelines on State aid for rescuing and restructuring firms in difficulty are published in OJ C 244, October 1, 2004, p.2; these are a revision of the 1999 guidelines (OJ C 288, October 9, 1999, p.2).[55] Among other things, the revision was made in the light of the conclusions of the meetings of the European Council in Stockholm (2001) and Barcelona (2002). At these meetings the Member States were encouraged to reduce the amount of State aid and at the same time to target it more horizontally towards goals of common interest, including economic and social cohesion. At a more technical level, the new guidelines make it clear that the principle of one-off aid (one time, last time) means that undertakings must not be given aid for rescue and restructuring more than once in order to keep them alive artificially. In addition, the term "rescue aid" has been made broader, and the principle that the beneficiary must make a real contribution has been laid down unequivocally. The new guidelines are in force from October 10, 2004 until October 9, 2009.

The guidelines include, in Ch.3, conditions for the authorisation of rescue and/or restructuring aid notified individually to the Commission; while Ch.4

---

[55] This revision is discussed by Eva Valle and Koen Van de Casteele, "Revision of the State aid Rescue and restructuring Guidelines", in *Competition Policy Newsletter*, No.3, Autumn 2004 p.58.

deals with aid schemes for SMEs which the Commission can approve, so that under certain conditions individual grants of aid need not be notified.

Even though State aid can distort competition between undertakings and can hinder or delay the process of structural adjustment by giving aid to undertakings which ought either to go out of business or restructure, and even though it can mean that the burden of structural adjustment is passed to other more effective undertakings, there can be circumstances where aid to rescue firms in difficulty to help them restructure can be justified. Among other things, this can be justified on the grounds of social policy or regional policy, from a desire to preserve a competitive market in cases where the closing down of undertakings could lead to the establishment of a monopoly or oligopoly, or out of consideration for the positive role of SMEs for the economy.

However, it is also clear that aid for rescue and restructuring is one of the forms of State aid which most distorts competition. Therefore, the principle that State aid is prohibited must be the main rule, and exceptions to this must be limited as far as possible.

Scope of application

The Commission applies the guidelines to undertakings in all sectors, except those operating in the coal or steel sectors, unless otherwise provided for in specific sectoral rules for undertakings in difficulty. This is e.g. the case with respect to undertakings active in the transport sector. Chapter 5 of the guidelines contains special rules for agriculture. The guidelines also apply to the fisheries and aquaculture sector, with the exception of para.79 concerning SMEs.   **3–090**

The legal basis for the guidelines on State aid for rescuing and restructuring firms

The guidelines are based on art.87(3)(c) of the Treaty, which constitutes an exception to the prohibition of State aid in art.87(1). Thus, the guidelines only come into play if a firm which is in difficulties receives State aid which falls within the scope of art.87(1). Aid which is provided to an undertaking on the normal terms of a market economy does not constitute such State aid; see Ch. 6 on the principle of the market economy investor. If the conditions of the guidelines are fulfilled, it is assumed that the aid will be compatible with the common market in accordance with art.87(3)(c). If the undertaking in question is located in an area which is eligible for regional aid, the Commission will take account of regional considerations on the basis of art.87(3)(a) and (c); see paras 55 and 56 of the guidelines.   **3–091**

Who can provide aid?

3–092   Aid for rescue and restructuring can be provided by any public body at
central, regional or local government level, as well as public undertakings
as defined in the Transparency Directive discussed above in paras 2–060 to
2–065.

A "firm in difficulty"

3–093   The Commission regards an undertaking as being "in difficulty" when it
is unable, whether through its own resources or with the funds it is able to
obtain from its owner/shareholders or creditors, to stem losses which, without
outside intervention by the public authorities, will almost certainly condemn
it to going out of business in the short or medium term.

According to the guidelines, in principle and irrespective of its size, an
undertaking is regarded as being in difficulty for the purposes of the guidelines:

a) in the case of a limited liability company, where more than half of its
   registered capital has disappeared and more than one quarter of that
   capital has been lost over the preceding 12 months;
b) in the case of a company where at least some members have unlimited
   liability for the debt of the company, where more than half of its capital
   as shown in the company accounts has disappeared and more than one
   quarter of that capital has been lost over the preceding 12 months;
   and
c) whatever the type of company concerned, where it fulfils the criteria
   under its domestic law for being the subject of collective insolvency proceedings.

The symptoms of an undertaking in difficulties can include growing stock
inventories, excess capacity, declining cash flow, increasing losses, diminish-
ing turnover, mounting debt, rising interest charges and falling or nil net asset
value. These circumstances can justify an undertaking being regarded as being
in difficulties even if none of the circumstances in points (a) to (c) apply. In
acute cases the firm may already have become insolvent or may be the subject
of collective insolvency proceedings. In the latter case, the guidelines apply to
any aid granted in the context of such proceedings which leads to the undertaking continuing in business. In any event, an undertaking in difficulty is
only eligible for aid where it is shown that it cannot recover through its own
resources or with the funds obtained from its owners/shareholders or from
the market.

Newly created firms

The guidelines do not allow aid to be given to a newly created firm, even if   **3–094**
the firm's financial position is precarious. This also applies where a new firm
emerges from the liquidation of a previous firm or merely takes over such firm's
assets. A firm is considered as newly created for the first three years following
the start of operations. This means that for the first three years an undertaking
will not be considered eligible for rescue and restructuring aid. After three years
the now no longer newly created undertaking can be eligible for aid for rescue
and restructuring on the same terms as other undertakings in difficulties.

Companies that are part of a corporate group

Companies that are part of a corporate group, or are about to become so,   **3–095**
are not in principle entitled to aid for rescue and restructuring unless it can
be shown that the difficulties of the company in question are intrinsic and are
not the result of an arbitrary allocation of costs within the group, and that the
difficulties are too serious to be dealt with by the group itself.

Undertakings that have previously received unlawful State aid

An undertaking can—but should not—receive State aid which is subse-   **3–096**
quently declared by the Commission to be unlawful and incompatible with
the common market, with a requirement for repayment. If subsequently,
before repayment has been made, the undertaking experiences difficulties,
the question arises as to what significance the non-repaid State aid has in the
assessment of whether the undertaking which is now in difficulties should be
granted aid for rescue and restructuring. According to the practice of the ECJ,
such assessment must take account both of the overall effect of the previous
aid, and the new aid for rescue and restructuring, as well as of the fact that
the previous aid has not been repaid.[56]

The nature of rescue and restructuring aid

The guidelines on State aid for rescuing and restructuring firms in difficul-   **3–097**
ties states that rescue aid is by nature temporary and its primary objective is
to make it possible to keep an ailing firm afloat for the time needed to work
out a restructuring or liquidation plan, or for the period necessary for the
Commission to decide on the plan in question.

In other words, rescue aid gives an undertaking some breathing space,

---

[56] Case C-355/95 P, *Textilwerke Deggendorf v Commission and Others*, [1997] E.C.R. I-2549.

normally up to six months, during which the causes of the financial problems can be analysed, so as to make it possible to prepare a plan for how the problems can be overcome.

Rescue aid is limited to the minimum necessary and consists of reversible liquidity support in the form of loan guarantees or loans, with an interest rate at least comparable to market rates for healthy undertakings, and in particular the reference rates adopted by the Commission.

As stated, rescue aid is given so that an undertaking can have time to prepare a plan for what to do with the business. Once a restructuring or liquidation plan has been established and is being implemented, the rescue aid comes to an end. All further aid will be considered as restructuring aid. However, in contrast to the 1999 guidelines, under the 2004 guidelines it is possible to implement irreversible restructuring measures (for example, the immediate cessation of loss-making activities) by using rescue aid; see in further detail below.

The nature of restructuring aid

3–098   Restructuring is an extension of rescuing, and it is based on a feasible, coherent and far-reaching plan to restore a firm's long-term viability. Restructuring usually involves one or more of the following elements: the reorganisation and rationalisation of the firm's activities on a more efficient basis, typically involving the withdrawal from loss-making activities; the restructuring of existing activities that can be made competitive again; and, possibly, diversification into new and viable activities.

The above elements of restructuring are normally accompanied by financial restructuring (capital injections, debt reduction).

The plan must ensure the transition to a new structure which creates security for the profitability of the undertaking in the long term, and makes it capable of sustaining itself out of its own resources without the need for further aid. The restructuring aid must contribute to the realisation of the plan.

Restructuring aid can be given in the form of capital injections, debt reduction, interest rate support, exemptions from tax and social insurance contributions, as well as loan guarantees, and such aid can given by any public body or public undertaking.

On the other hand, restructuring aid may not consist of financial aid to cover previous losses. It must tackle the causes of the losses.

The principle of one-off aid (one time, last time)

3–099   Aid for rescue and restructuring is aimed at helping an undertaking overcome current problems and put it on an even keel so that it can operate under normal market conditions in future. An undertaking that needs aid for rescue and restructuring several times will not usually be a healthy undertaking. Thus the principle is that aid for rescue and restructuring can only be given once within a 10-year period. It is the undertaking which is in focus, and the principle that aid should be one-off is not affected by changes in the ownership of the undertaking after aid has been granted if it is essentially the same business being carried on. The same applies if the undertaking has been subject to some legal or administrative procedure whereby its debts are reduced, old debts wound-up and the undertaking's finances reorganised.

Aid for rescue and aid for restructuring are not linked in a way that means that if the Commission first approves rescue aid, it automatically approves restructuring aid. The two kinds of aid are assessed separately.

When giving notice of rescue or restructuring aid, the Member States must inform the Commission as to whether the undertaking in question has, within the preceding 10 years, received aid for rescue or restructuring. The period of 10 years is calculated from the date when: (1) the rescue aid was granted, (2) the restructuring period came to an end, or (3) implementation of the restructuring plan was halted, whichever is the latest. If 10 years has not elapsed, the undertaking in difficulties may not receive rescue or restructuring aid again. However, there are the following three exceptions to this rule:

1. where restructuring aid follows the granting of rescue aid as part of a single restructuring operation;
2. where rescue aid has been granted in accordance with the conditions in the guidelines (see paras 3–101 and 3–102), and this aid was not followed by a State supported restructuring, provided that the firm could reasonably be believed to be viable in the long-term following the granting of rescue aid, and new rescue or restructuring aid becomes necessary after at least five years due to unforeseeable circumstances for which the company is not responsible; or
3. in exceptional and unforeseeable circumstances for which the company is not responsible.[57]

An undertaking which buys the assets of another undertaking—namely **3–100** an undertaking which has been subject to the procedures referred to or insolvency proceedings, etc.—and which has already received rescue or restructuring aid, is not subject to the rule on one-off aid if the buyer is clearly separate from the previous undertaking and the assets have been acquired at a market price. However, this is subject to the further assumption that there is no evasion of the rule on one-off aid, which may be the case if, for example, the buyer's difficulties were clearly foreseeable when acquiring the previous undertaking.

---

[57] An unforeseeable circumstance is a circumstance which could in no way be anticipated by the company's management when the restructuring plan was drawn up and which is not due to negligence or errors of the company's management or decisions of the group—if the undertaking is part of a group—to which it belongs.

For corporate groups which have received aid for rescue or restructuring, the principle of one-off aid applies, so that further aid cannot normally be given within 10 years (as calculated above), to the group itself or to its member companies. However, where an entity belonging to a corporate group has received rescue or restructuring aid, the group as a whole, as well as the other entities of the group, remain eligible for rescue or restructuring aid, subject to compliance with the other provisions of the guidelines. Member States must ensure that no aid is passed on from the group or other group entities to the earlier beneficiary of the aid, so that the principle of one-off aid is complied with.

Individual rescue aid

3–101 Rescue aid can be expected to be approved by the Commission if these conditions are fulfilled:

   a) the aid must consist of liquidity support in the form of loan guarantees or loans.[58] In both cases the loan must be provided at an interest rate at least comparable to those observed for loans to healthy firms and in particular the reference rates adopted by the Commission;

   b) any loan must be repaid and any loan guarantee must come to an end within six months of the payment of the first instalment to the undertaking;

   c) the aid must be warranted on the grounds of serious social difficulties and have no unduly adverse spill-over effects on other Member States;

   d) on notification the aid must be accompanied by an undertaking given by the Member State concerned to communicate to the Commission, not later than six months after the rescue aid measure has been authorised, a restructuring plan or a liquidation plan or proof that the loan has been reimbursed in full and/or that the guarantee has been terminated;[59]

   e) the aid must be restricted to the amount needed to keep the undertaking in business for the period during which the aid is authorised (such as covering wages and salaries or operational supplies). This may include aid for urgent structural measures; and [60]

   f) the rule on one-off aid must be complied with (see paras 3–099 and 3–100).

---

[58] The guidelines provide for an exception in the case of rescue aid in the banking sector, in order to enable the credit institution in question to continue temporarily carrying on its banking business in accordance with the prudential legislation in force (Directive 2000/12/EC of the European Parliament and of the Council, OJ L 126, 26.5.2000, p.1); see para.25 of the guidelines, and fn.15, which contains a discussion of the possibilities for providing rescue aid other than in the form of a loan or a loan guarantee.

[59] See para.25(c) for special circumstances where the aid is not notified.

[60] In calculating what is needed, the starting point is the formula which is set out in the annex to the guidelines.

If the rescue aid is limited to €10 million,[61] and at least one of the circumstances referred to in para.3–093, (a)–(c) is present, the Commission will try to take a decision within one month.

The first approval of aid is for a six-month period. If before the expiry of six months from the date of approval[62] the Member State in question presents a restructuring plan, the deadline for the repayment of the loan or termination of the guarantee is extended until the Commission has decided on the restructuring plan. However, in specific cases the Commission can decide that an extension is not justified.[63]   **3–102**

If a Member State does not comply with the obligation to submit documentation showing that the loan has been repaid and/or the guarantee has been terminated before the expiry of six months, the Commission will initiate the procedure under art.88(2) of the Treaty, in other words the Commission can decide that the aid is not compatible with the Treaty, and if the Member State does not comply with the decision, it can bring the case before the ECJ, using a special rapid procedure. The same applies if the Member State fails to submit a credible and well-documented restructuring plan or a liquidation plan to the Commission.

Individual restructuring aid

The guidelines lay down the principle that restructuring aid can only be approved where it can be shown that the aid is not contrary to the common interest. This is only possible if strict conditions are fulfilled and if there is certainty that the possible effects of the aid in distorting competition are outweighed by the benefits of keeping the undertaking going (for example if the consequences of the undertaking going under would be the existence of a monopoly or an oligopoly).[64] In addition, it must be considered whether there is sufficient compensation to competitors.   **3–103**

[61] Calculated according to the formula set out in the annex to the guidelines.

[62] In the case of non-notified aid, six months from the implementation of the measure concerned.

[63] See Max Lienemeyer, "Clarification of the procedure for terminating rescue aid where the presentation of a restructuring plan does not justify the prolongation—comment on the decisions in case of rescue aid to CIT and Ottana", in *Competition Policy Newsletter*, No.1, Spring 2007 p.127.

[64] On restructuring aid, see the following recent decisions of the Community courts: Case T-149/95, *Ducros v Commission*, [1997] E.C.R. II-2031; Case T-214/95, *Vlaams Gewest v Commission*, [1998] E.C.R. II-717; Case T-394/94, *British Midland Airways v Commission*, [1998] E.C.R. II-2405; Case T-371/94, *British Airways and Others v Commission*, [1998] E.C.R. II-2405; Case T-140/95, *Ryanair v Commission*, [1998] E.C.R. II-3327; Joined Cases T-126 and 127/96, *Breda Fucine Meridionali v Commission*, [1998] E.C.R. II-3427; Case T-123/97, *Salomon v Commission*, [1999] E.C.R. II-2925; Case T-110/97, *Kneissl Dachstein Sportartikel v Commission*, [1999] E.C.R. II-2881; Case T-72/98, *Astilleros Zamacona v Commission*, [2000] E.C.R. II-1683; Case C-106/98 P, *Comité d'entreprise de la societé francaise de production and Others v Commission*, [2000] II-3659; Joined Cases T-204 & 270/97, *EPAC v Commission*, [2000] E.C.R. II-2267; Case T-73/98, *Prayon-Rupel v Commission*, [2001] E.C.R. II-867; Case C-17/99, *France v Commission*, [2001] E.C.R. I-2481.

It is a condition for the Commission's approval of restructuring aid that the undertaking should be in difficulties; see para. 3–093. Moreover, the following conditions must be fulfilled:

1. The re-establishment of long-term profitability

3–104   The grant of restructuring aid must be in accordance with terms that implement a restructuring plan that has been approved by the Commission. The plan must include a description of the difficulties that have led to the undertaking being in its current difficulties and the measures, including structural measures, which will turn around the development so that after restructuring the undertaking will be able to cover all its costs and achieve a return on its invested capital, and so that the undertaking is competitive. The plan must take account of the current and expected competitive situation, and include good, bad and mid-range scenarios for the undertaking. The plan must also describe the undertaking's strengths and weaknesses.

The plan must cover as short a period as possible and, within a reasonable period and on the basis of a realistic assessment of the undertaking's future operating conditions, it must be able to lead to a healthy and profitable business in the longer term. This means that the Commission must be presented with a realistic and detailed restructuring plan, with which the aid is to be linked, including among other things an analysis of the market.[65]

The improvement of profitability must first and foremost be achieved through internal measures contained in the restructuring plan. Improvements in profitability may only be based on external factors, for example variations in prices or demand, if the stated expectations are generally accepted. A restructuring plan must lead to the cessation of all activities which, even after restructuring, will continue to be loss-making for structural reasons; and if the problems are due to weaknesses of management, these must also be corrected.

These requirements also apply to restructuring plans for SMEs, though such plans are not approved by the Commission but by the Member State concerned, which also controls compliance with the plan. However, the approved plan must be sent to the Commission.

---

[65] For an instructive example of the CFI's approach to restructuring, the requirement for the prior presentation of a restructuring plan, and sustainable prospects for the undertaking, reference can be made to Joined Cases T-126/96 and C-127/96, *Breda Fucine Meridionali v Commission*, [1998] E.C.R. II-3437, especially paras 75, 76, 77 and 98. As an example of a Commission decision where aid for reconstruction was not approved, see Commission Decision 97/765/EC of June 26, 1997 concerning State aid in favour of *SKET Schwermaschinenbau Magdeburg* (OJ L 314, 18.11.1997, p.20). The refusal of aid was due, among other things, to the failure to re-establish profitability and the incomplete preparation of the restructuring plan.

2. Avoidance of undue distortions of competition (compensation to competitors)

Paragraph 38 of the Community guidelines on State aid for rescuing and   **3–105**
restructuring firms in difficulty make it a condition that compensatory measures must be taken to minimise the adverse effects on trading conditions as
much as possible, so that the positive effects pursued outweigh the adverse
ones. Otherwise, the aid will be regarded as "contrary to the common interest", as referred to in art.87(3)(c) of the Treaty.

   This condition often leads to a restriction or reduction of the position
which the undertaking can take in the market after restructuring. The compensation can consist of the disposal of assets, restriction of capacity or the
level of activity in the market, and the removal of hindrances to access to the
markets in question. The writing off or cessation of loss-making activities
does not constitute compensation. These measures are necessary to make the
undertaking viable. On the contrary, the restrictions must be directed at the
market or markets in which, after restructuring, the undertaking will have a
strong position. The extent of compensation must be clearly established on
a case-by-case basis. The decisive guideline is that the measures must be in
proportion to the distorting effects of the aid and, in particular, to the size
and the relative importance of the firm on its market or markets. Thus if, for
example, the undertaking operates in a market with structural overcapacity
in the long term, it can be necessary to restrict its capacity or activity level by
100 per cent. In this case there will not be much of the undertaking left, and
in such cases the Commission will only allow aid to alleviate the social costs
of the restructuring and environmental aid for the remediation of polluted
sites which might otherwise be abandoned. Aid for social measures (such as
retraining) which benefits workers who are laid off from the undertaking is not
included in the assessment of the extent of the necessary compensation.

   If after restructuring the undertaking's position relates to a market which is   **3–106**
not important from an EU/EEA point of view, or if its market share is insignificant, the assessment ought to be that there is not an unreasonable distortion
of competition. This means that the approval of restructuring plans for SMEs
will not normally lead to an unreasonable distortion of competition, unless
the rules on State aid for the area in question state otherwise.

   In other words, if restructuring concerns a small undertaking, the restructuring plan need not necessarily restrict its capacity or production, and the
prospect of it continuing to compete with other undertakings, solely on the
basis of receiving State aid, will not be seen as being contrary to the common
interest, as referred to in art.87(3)(c).

   The restriction or reduction referred to which is often included in a restructuring plan constitutes compensation for competitors.

   It is, therefore, possible to derogate from granting compensation if the
restriction or reduction would risk leading to a worsening of the market
situation, for example by indirectly promoting the creation of a monopoly or

narrow oligopoly. This would not be desirable, and in its assessment of the
need for compensation the Commission must also consider the market structure and competitive situation.

3. Restriction of aid to a minimum—an effective contribution from the undertaking

3–107   The amount of aid and the aid intensity must be restricted to the absolute
minimum necessary for carrying out the restructuring. The aid may not be
used to finance new investments which are not necessary for re-establishing the
profitability of the undertaking. Of course the aid may not be given in a form
or for an amount which gives the undertaking a cash surplus that can be used
for aggressive activities which distort the market but which are not connected
to the restructuring.

Following a revision of the guidelines it has now been made quite clear
that the recipient of aid must itself make a significant contribution to the
restructuring, and this contribution may not include aid. By this means the
markets show that they have confidence in the ability of the undertaking to
return to viability within a relatively short period, and it also ensures that
the restructuring aid and the distortion of competition is limited as much
as possible.

3–108   The contribution must be real. This means that it must be actual, excluding all future expected profits such as cash flow, and must be as high as possible. The contribution must be made from the undertaking's own means or
by external financing obtained on market terms, and it must be as much as
possible.

According to para.44 of the guidelines, the Commission will normally consider the following contributions to be appropriate:

- at least 25 per cent in the case of small enterprises,
- at least 40 per cent, for medium-sized enterprises, and
- at least 50 per cent for large firms.

These rates are not absolute so that they cannot be reduced. However, this will
require the undertaking to be located in an area which is entitled to receive
regional aid, or that the Member State can show that the actual situation is
quite exceptional. If a Member State is able to prove this, the Commission can
accept a reduced contribution from the undertaking.

4. Special conditions for the authorisation of aid

3–109   According to para.46 of the guidelines, the Commission may impose any
conditions and obligations, in addition to compensation, which it considers

necessary to ensure that the aid does not distort competition contrary to the common interest. For example, it may require the Member State:

(i) to take certain measures itself (for example, to open up certain markets directly or indirectly linked to the company's activities to other Community operators),
(ii) to impose certain obligations on the conduct of the recipient firm; and
(iii) not to grant other aid to the recipient firm during the restructuring period.

5. Full implementation of restructuring plan and observance of conditions

According to para.47 of the guidelines, the beneficiary undertaking must fully implement the restructuring plan and must discharge any other obligations laid down in the Commission decision authorising the aid. Otherwise the Commission will consider there to be a misuse of the aid.   **3–110**

Where restructuring is spread over several years and involves substantial amounts of aid, the Commission may require payment of the restructuring aid to be split into instalments, and may make the payment of each instalment subject to the continuing implementation of the restructuring plan, as approved. Also, as part of its control of the implementation of the restructuring plan, the Commission can require prior approval of the payment of each instalment.

6. Monitoring and annual report

According to paras 49–50 of the guidelines, there must be monitoring of the proper implementation of the restructuring plan through detailed annual reports.   **3–111**

In the case of aid to large firms, the first of these reports will normally be submitted to the Commission within six months after approval of the aid. After that reports are submitted annually. The reports must contain all the information the Commission needs in connection with evaluating whether the conditions for the approval of the aid are being complied with, or whether the circumstances have changed.

There are special, less strict requirements with regard to information on restructuring aid for SMEs. Unless the Commission decides otherwise, it will be sufficient to submit the undertaking's balance sheet and profit and loss account each year.

Amendment of the restructuring plan

3–112   It is possible that the conditions on which the restructuring plan and the restructuring aid are based may change after the Commission has given approval. It can therefore be necessary to make changes to the plan or to the amount of aid. According to the guidelines, the Commission can allow such amendments. This requires that the new or amended plan also shows that the undertaking's profitability will be restored within a reasonable period. As stated earlier, the distorting consequences of the aid to competition must be compensated for. If the aid has to be increased, then the compensation must be more comprehensive than initially. On the other hand, if the proposed compensation is less than initially, then the aid must be reduced correspondingly. The compensation must be delivered in accordance with a schedule. If this is prolonged compared with the original schedule, this may not be due to the circumstances of the undertaking itself or of the Member State, and if this is the case, there must be a proportionate reduction in the amount of the aid.

As stated, the Commission can lay down the conditions and obligations which must be fulfilled in order to avoid distorting competition, contrary to the common interest. If such conditions or obligations are imposed, and if there is a request that they should be eased, there must either be a reduction in the amount of the aid, or new conditions must be laid down.

It is important that the Member State does not make any changes to the restructuring plan which the Commission has approved without involving the Commission. The Commission will otherwise initiate proceedings under art.88(2) of the Treaty for misuse of the aid.

Restructuring aid in areas entitled to regional aid

3–113   The starting point is that undertakings which are located in areas which are entitled to regional aid can be granted restructuring aid under the same conditions as apply to all other undertakings. However, a justified need for regional development can mean that there will be less stringent requirements with regard to the payment of compensation and the amount of the undertaking's own contribution; see para.56 of the guidelines.

Aid for restructuring SMEs

3–114   Aid for small enterprises normally affects trading conditions less than aid for medium-sized and large enterprises. However, this does not alter the fact that aid to both small and medium-sized enterprises is in principle subject to the same conditions as apply to all other undertakings. However, the conditions can be applied less strictly to SMEs. Hence small enterprises are not normally required to provide compensation for the receipt of restructuring aid (unless otherwise provided in special sectoral rules), and the requirements for monitoring and reporting are also less strict for SMEs. Furthermore, the restructuring plans of SMEs do not have to be approved by the Commission, but rather by the Member State concerned, which also ensures that such plans are complied with. However, such plans must be forwarded to the Commission. The principle of one-off aid (one time, last time) also applies to restructuring aid for SMEs.

Aid to cover the social costs of restructuring

Part 3.2.6 of the guidelines deals with aid to cover the social costs that arise in   **3–115**
connection with restructuring. As stated, a restructuring plan will often result in a reduction of capacity, and thus typically a reduction of the workforce of the undertaking. Aid for training, counselling and practical help with finding alternative employment, assistance with relocation, and professional training and assistance for employees wishing to start new businesses will typically be part of a restructuring package. The Commission will thus have a positive approach to such aid for an undertaking in difficulties.

The obligations of a company under employment legislation or collective agreements with trade unions, to provide redundancy benefits and/or early retirement pensions are part of the normal running costs of a business which a firm has to meet from its own resources. This being so, any contribution by the State to these costs is counted as aid. The Commission has no objection in principle to such aid when it is granted to firms in difficulty, as it brings economic benefits above and beyond the interests of the firm concerned, facilitating structural change and reducing hardship.

It is particularly important that the forms of aid for social measures which are included in a restructuring plan should be clearly described. Aid measures that are targeted exclusively at redundant employees will be disregarded for the purposes of determining the extent of the compensatory measures.

National rescuing and restructuring schemes for SMEs

Chapter 4 of the guidelines deals with national aid schemes for rescuing and/   **3–116**
or restructuring SMEs.[66] Member States can thus draw up such schemes and expect approval from the Commission, if the schemes fulfil the requirements for the aid for rescue and restructuring to be compatible with the common market, as reviewed above. The advantage for the Member States in having a scheme approved is that aid which is provided under such a scheme is exempted from the requirement for individual notification. However, this

---

[66] These must be SMEs which fall within the definition given in the annex to the General Block Exemption Regulation, see s.2 of this chapter.

requires that the aid is granted to an undertaking which is in difficulties, in other words that at least one of the criteria referred to in para.3–093, subs.(a) to (c) is fulfilled, and that the undertaking does not operate in a market which has structural over-capacity in the long term, or in a sector which has special State aid rules for rescue and restructuring. Furthermore, aid granted as part of a scheme must fall within the terms of the scheme, so that the grant of aid in the specific case is also compatible with the common market.

The granting of aid for rescuing and restructuring SMEs outside an approved aid scheme requires individual notification to the Commission.

The approval of an aid scheme for both rescue and restructuring SMEs requires the scheme to contain a statement of the maximum amount of aid that can be granted to individual undertakings for rescue and/or restructuring, including if there is a change to the plan. Any aid which exceeds the stated maximum must be notified individually to the Commission. The amount may not exceed €10 million, including cumulation with other sources or other schemes. The principle of one-off aid must also be complied with; see paras 3–099 and 3–100.

3–117   The Commission's approval of schemes for rescue aid requires the schemes to fulfil the conditions referred to in paras 3–101 and 3–102, subs.(a) to (f). In other words, the same conditions apply as to individual rescue aid. Furthermore, rescue aid can only be provided for a maximum of six months. This period must be used for analysing the circumstances of the undertaking. The Member State must then either approve a restructuring plan or a liquidation plan, or require the aid to be repaid.

The Commission will only approve schemes for restructuring aid if the aid given under the scheme is conditional on the beneficiary fully carrying out a restructuring plan that has the prior approval of the Member State, and which fulfils the following conditions:

- the restoration of profitability; see paras 3–103 to 3–109, No.1;
- the prohibition of the increase of the capacity of small undertakings by the restructuring; medium-sized enterprises must follow the rules on compensation referred to in paras 3–103 to 3–109, No.2;
- aid must be limited to the minimum necessary; see paras 3–103 to 3–109, No.3; and
- any changes to the restructuring plan must be in accordance with the rules referred to in para.3–110.

According to para.86 of the guidelines, approval of an aid scheme is normally conditional on an annual report being submitted on the implementation of the aid scheme, containing all the information laid down in the Commission's instructions on standard reports,[67] and the reports must

---

[67] See annex III, A and B (Standardised reporting format for existing state aid) of Commission Regulation (EC) No.794/2004 of April 21, 2004 implementing Council Regulation (EC)

contain an overview of all beneficiary undertakings, giving for each of them: the company name; the company's sectoral code, using the NACE sectoral classification codes;[68] the number of employees; annual turnover and balance sheet value; the amount of aid granted; the amount and form of the beneficiary's contribution; the form and degree of any compensatory measures; any restructuring aid or similar support which it has received in the past; and a statement of whether the beneficiary company has been wound-up or has been subject to insolvency proceedings during the restructuring period.

Restructuring aid in the agricultural sector

Chapter 5 of the guidelines for rescuing and restructuring undertakings in difficulties contains detailed provisions on restructuring aid for the agricultural sector. Only the primary production of agricultural products listed in annex I to the Treaty is covered by Ch.5.   **3–118**

In principle, in contrast to what applies to SMEs, in this sector the Commission normally imposes some conditions, in accordance with the principles referred to in paras 3–103 to 3–109, No.2, for all recipients of restructuring aid, i.e. reduction of capacity.

If there is a structural surplus of production capacity there will be a requirement for an irreversible reduction or removal of capacity.

The Commission defines "structural overcapacity" on a case-by-case basis, having regard to the extent of and the growth or decline of the relevant product sector in the previous three years, market stabilisation measures, special export restrictions and buy-backs, price developments on the world market and sector-specific restrictions.

Agricultural areas that are subject to reductions in capacity must remain unused for 15 years, after which they can be put to use again.

If the aid measure is targeted at specific products or producers, the reduction in capacity must constitute at least 10 per cent of the capacity for which the restructuring aid is provided. If the aid is less specifically targeted, the requirement is for a reduction of at least 5 per cent.[69]   **3–119**

However, the requirement for an irreversible reduction of production capacity can be satisfied at market level. In other words, the reductions need

---

No.659/1999 laying down detailed rules for the application of art.93 [now 88] of the EC Treaty (OJ L 140, 30.4.2004, p.1) with amendments.

[68] The general classification for economic activities in the EU, published by the Statistical Office of the European Communities. NACE is found in the Annex to Commission Regulation (EC) No.29/2002 of December 19, 2001 amending Council Regulation (EEC) No.3037/90 on the statistical classification of economic activities in the European Community (OJ L 6, 10.1.2002, p.3).

[69] The requirements for reductions referred to are reduced by two percentage points if the restructuring aid is given in disadvantaged areas. If decisions on granting restructuring aid concern undertakings in a given sector over a continuous period of 12 months do not involve altogether more than 1% of the production capacity in that sector in the Member State in question, the Commission will derogate from the requirement for a reduction in capacity.

not necessarily be made by the undertaking which receives the aid, but can be made at other levels of the relevant market. If the Member State chooses to make reductions at market level, steps must be taken to achieve this within one year of the grant of the aid. When the reductions have in fact been made, the Member State in question may not grant State aid for an increase in capacity in the sector in question during the following five-year period.

The principle that aid can only be given once ("one time, last time") also applies in the agricultural sector, but only for five years.

The general rules on monitoring and reporting also apply in the agricultural sector (though not the requirements laid down in para.86 of the guidelines on State aid for rescuing and restructuring firms in difficulty, as discussed in paras 3–114 and 3–115). The report must contain information about the production capacity which has been taken account of by the restructuring aid, and about the reduction in capacity which has been carried out.

REGIONAL AID

Introduction

3–120   Some regions in the EU suffer from certain disadvantages, such as not being able to attract investment and workers. Undertakings will be reluctant to set themselves up in such areas where there is an insufficient or insufficiently qualified work force, and workers themselves will not move to areas where there is no work. This vicious circle can be broken by regional aid. The idea behind regional aid is, among other things, to support development in the worst off areas by promoting investment and job-creation. In such areas State aid is aimed at promoting the expansion, rationalisation and modernisation of undertakings, and the diversification of their economic activities, especially by encouraging undertakings to make new start-ups in these areas. However, it is absolutely vital that regional aid should only be given to activities that are viable. In general it is not helpful to aid undertakings by merely covering some of their operating costs. On the contrary, regional aid must create true incentives and encourage investments which would otherwise not be made in the areas which are eligible for regional aid, and they must act as an incentive for new activities. Regional aid not only has positive effects, it can also distort competition. For this reason the benefits of aid for promoting development in disadvantaged regions must outweigh the distortions of competition which can be caused by the aid.[70] The Commission can declare regional aid to be compatible with the common market in accordance with art.87(3)(a) of the EC Treaty, which refers to areas where the standard of living is abnormally low or where there is serious underemployment. In addition, the Commission

---

[70] Case 730/79, *Philip Morris*, [1980] E.C.R. 2671; and Case C-169/95, *Spain v Commission*, [1997] E.C.R. I-135.

can also declare that regional aid is compatible with the common market under art.87(3)(c) of the Treaty if it facilitates the development of certain economic areas, where such aid does not adversely affect trading conditions to an extent contrary to the common interest. When assessing the aid against its effects which may distort competition, there must be regard for whether the aid is provided in an art.87(3)(a) region or an art.87(3)(c) region. Greater distortions of competition are accepted in art.87(3)(a) regions than in art.87(3) (c) regions.[71]

This balancing between the positive effects of regional aid and its effects in distorting competition are expressed in the Commission's application of the rules of the Treaty and of the legal acts which the Commission has issued on regional aid. In 2006 the Commission issued new rules on regional aid which are in force for the period 2007–2013. They are now included in the General Block Exemption Regulation, see s.2, above, and in a set of guidelines for State aid with regional aims. The guidelines are discussed below. Before that there must be a brief discussion of the distinction between art.87(3)(a) regions and art.87(3)(c) regions.

With regard to the need to notify measures on regional aid to the Commission, see art.88(3) discussed in Ch.2 and the General Block Exemption Regulation discussed in paras 3–007–3–027.

Definition of regions

Regions covered by Article 87(3)(a)

As stated, according to art.87(3)(a) of the EC Treaty, the Commission can declare aid to areas where the standard of living is abnormally low or where there is serious underemployment to be compatible with the common market. This only refers to those areas where the economic situation is abnormally low compared to the EU as a whole.[72] This condition will be fulfilled if the region[73] has a gross national product (GNP) per head of population measured in Purchasing Power Standard (PPS) of less than 75 per cent of the EU average. The GNP of the region and of the EU is calculated by Eurostat. Some regions exceed the 75 per cent threshold solely on the basis of the statistical effect of the expansion of the EU. These are called "statistical effect regions", and they retain their status as art.87(3)(a) regions until December 31, 2010. If the GNP of these regions again falls below the 75 per cent threshold, they retain

3–121

---

[71] Case T-380/94, *AIUFFASS and AKT v Commission*, [1996] E.C.R. II-2169.
[72] Case 248/84, *Germany v Commission*, [1987] E.C.R. 4013.
[73] This corresponds to a geographic unit at NUTS II level, i.e. an average population of between 800,000 and 3 million; cf. Regulation (EC) No.1059/2003 of the European Parliament and of the Council of May 26, 2003 on the establishment of a common classification of territorial units for statistics (NUTS) (OJ L 154, 21.6.2003, p.1). The NUTS nomenclature is used by Eurostat for the collection, processing and issuing of harmonised regional statistics in the EU, and for socio-economic analyses of the regions.

their status as an art.87(3)(a) region. If not, they become art.87(3)(c) regions. Regardless of the standards relating to GNP, the EU's outermost regions are classified as art.87(3)(a) regions; cf. art.299(23) of the EC Treaty.[74]

Regions covered by Article 87(3)(c)

3–122   Article 87(3)(c) gives authority for the promotion of development in certain economic areas without the economic conditions referred to in art.87(3) (a) being present, but aid to promote development in such areas must not adversely affect trading conditions to an extent contrary to the common interest.[75] These "certain areas" where economic development may be promoted are areas where the economic situation is worse than the national average. However, State aid is still prohibited in principle, and the general rule applies that exceptions must be interpreted restrictively. This also applies to the exception in art.87(3)(c). The geographic scope and the permitted intensity are strictly limited. Thus normally only a small part of a Member State's territory will be covered by the exception. A Member State's selection of the regions which are covered by art.87(3)(c) is made in two stages. First, the Commission decides the maximum population that may be covered by this form of aid in each of the Member States.[76] Next, there is the selection of the regions which are eligible for aid. It is the Member States which select these regions. However, this selection must follow the principles for selection laid down by the Commission.[77] For example, a Member State may choose a thinly populated region, islands and other regions that are characterised by similar geographic isolation, regions with a low population, and a low GNP per capita and high unemployment.[78]

Regional aid map

3–123   On the basis of the rules laid down in the guidelines, Member States must decide whether they wish to give investment aid and if so up to what level, provided that the limits laid down in the guidelines are not exceeded.[79] Briefly, the limits in art.87(3)(a) regions are:

[74] Azores, Madeira, the Canary Islands, Guadaloupe, Martinique, Réunion and French Guyana.
[75] Case 248/84, *Germany v Commission*, [1987] E.C.R. 4013.
[76] More detailed rules on this and on the calculation method are given in paras 3–121–3–124 and annex IV of the guidelines on national regional aid for 2007–2013 (OJ C 54, 4.3.2006, p.13).
[77] See s.3.4.2 of the guidelines.
[78] See para.30 of the guidelines, which lists the characteristics of regions that can be covered by art.87(3)(c).
[79] The Commission previously used the net grant equivalent, but has given up using this as a result of the decision in Joined Cases T-298/97 and others, *Alzetta Mauro and Others v Commission*, [2000] E.C.R. II-2319. It now uses the gross grant equivalent which, in cases of notified aid is calculated at the date of notification by means of the Commission's reference rates. The case was appealed to the ECJ, which rejected the appeal; cf. Case C-298/00 P, *Italy v Commission*, [2004] E.C.R. I-4087.

The region's GNP in relation to the per capita GNP in the EU-25	Maximum aid intensity as gross grant equivalent for large enterprises	Maximum aid intensity as gross grant equivalent for small(+20%)/medium-sized (+10%) enterprises (this SME bonus is not given in the transport sector)
Under 75%	30%	50%/40%
Under 60%	40%	60%/50%
Under 45%	50%	70%/60%

In art.87(3)(c) regions, the starting point is that there is a ceiling gross grant equivalent of 15 per cent. This is reduced to 10 per cent in regions where both the GNP per capita is more than 100 per cent of the EU-25 average and unemployment lies under the EU-25 average. The ceiling can be raised by 20 per cent of the gross grant equivalent for small enterprises, and 10 per cent for medium-sized enterprises. Reference is made to s.4.1.2 of the guidelines in relation to outermost regions and "statistical effect regions" among other things, and the Member States' regional aid maps. In addition, the adjusted aid ceiling applies to major investment projects as discussed below.

Member States that wish to grant regional aid must notify the Commission **3-124** of an overall regional aid map covering the whole of the Member State's territory; see art.88(3) of the EC Treaty. The Commission's decision on the notified regional aid map is an integrated part of the guidelines, and is binding if it is accepted by the Member State concerned.[80] Regional aid schemes and ad hoc aid must be compatible with the regional aid map. For this reason the Commission will normally first deal with notifications of aid schemes and ad hoc aid which take effect after January 1, 2007, once the regional aid map for the Member State in question has been adopted. As per mid 2007, all Member States had notified their regional aid maps for the period 2007–2013. The regional aid map is also important in relation to block exemption regulations which exempt regional aid from the obligation to notify in accordance with art.88(3) of the Treaty. This is because the map defines the extent of each block exemption regulation which exempts regional aid from the notification obligation.[81]

A Member State's regional aid map thus constitutes on the one hand a statement of the regions in that Member State which are eligible for regional investment aid in accordance with art.87(3)(a) and (c) of the Treaty, and on the other hand a statement of the ceilings for aid intensity for initial investments that are approved for each individual region. The map also shows the regions

[80] Case C-242/00, *Germany v Commission*, [2002] E.C.R. I-5603.
[81] See art.1(1)(b) of Council Regulation (EC) No.994/98 of May 7, 1998 on the application of arts 92 and 93 of the Treaty establishing the European Community to certain categories of horizontal State aid (OJ L 142, 14.5.1998, p.1).

in which aid can be implemented. Aid for operating costs is not covered by the map.

The regional aid maps of all Member States are shown on the Commission's website.[82]

Guidelines on national regional aid for 2007–2013

3–125   Regional aid measures that are not exempted from the obligation to notify the Commission in accordance with the General Block Exemption Regulation, see s.2, must be notified to the Commission, which will assess whether they are compatible with the common market on the basis of the guidelines on national regional aid for 2007–2013 (OJ C 54, 4.3.2006, p.13).[83]

The Multisectoral framework on regional aid for large investment projects (OJ C 70, 19.3.2002, p.8) has been integrated in the guidelines and ceased to apply after December 31, 2006.

Under the guidelines, on certain conditions regional aid, operating aid and aid to newly established small undertakings can be given.

Scope of application

3–126   The guidelines apply to all sectors with the exception of the fisheries, the coal industry, the steel industry and the synthetic fibres sector. The guidelines do not apply to the production of agricultural products but they do apply to the processing and marketing of such products to the extent laid down in the Community guidelines for State aid in the agriculture sector. Special rules apply in the transport and shipbuilding industries which vary the guidelines to take account of the special conditions in these sectors. The guidelines deal with regional investment aid, operating aid and aid to newly established small undertakings.

The Commission does not favour schemes which are targeted at specific sectors. This is clear from the guidelines which emphasise that regional aid ought in principle to be part of a multi-sectoral scheme which is included in a regional development strategy with clearly defined goals. If, exceptionally, a Member State wishes to depart from this approach, it must demonstrate that the project contributes to a cohesive regional development strategy and does not (by its nature and extent) lead to unacceptable distortions of competition.

---

[82] *http://ec.europa.eu/comm/competition/state_aid/regional_aid/regional_aid.html*
[83] Evi Papantoniou: "New guidelines on national regional aid for 2007–2013", in *Competition Policy Newsletter*, No.1, Spring 2006 p.18.

Regional investment aid

1. Definition and conditions

Regional investment aid can take many forms. For example it can be given in **3–127** the form of a direct subsidy, a low-interest loan, an interest-rate subsidy, State guarantees, buying capital shares or some other form of capital investment on favourable terms, exemptions from or reductions of taxes and obligatory charges. Making land, goods or services available at advantageous prices can also be considered State aid. In relation to the Regional guidelines, what is decisive is whether the conditions in art.87(1) of the Treaty are fulfilled and whether the case concerns regional investment aid.

Regional investment aid is aid awarded for an initial investment project. This means an investment in material and immaterial assets relating to the setting-up of a new establishment, the extension of an existing establishment, diversification of the output of an establishment into new, additional products or a fundamental change in the overall production process of an existing establishment. The acquisition of the assets of an establishment may also be regarded as initial investment, provided they are acquired by an independent investor, and provided the establishment has closed or would have closed had it not been purchased.

Regional investment aid is calculated either on the basis of the material and immaterial investment costs resulting from the initial investment project, or on the estimated wage costs for jobs directly created by the investment project within three years of completion of the investment.

A job is deemed to be directly created by an investment project if it **3–128** concerns the activity to which the investment relates and is created within three years of completion of the investment, including jobs created following an increase in the utilisation rate of the capacity created by the investment. In the case of the acquisition of an establishment, only the costs of buying assets from third parties under market conditions are taken into consideration.

In connection with material or immaterial investment costs, or the costs of acquisition of an undertaking, the beneficiary must provide a financial contribution of at least 25 per cent of the eligible costs. This 25 per cent may not include any public support, not even de minimis aid. The undertaking must thus finance the 25 per cent either through its own resources or by external financing. Among other things, this contribution is to ensure that the investment is viable and profitable.

One of the aims of regional aid schemes is to give an incentive for investing in areas in which investment would not otherwise be made. For this reason aid may only be granted under aid schemes if the beneficiary has submitted an application for aid and the authority responsible for administering the scheme has confirmed in writing that the project in principle meets the conditions of eligibility laid down by the scheme before the start of construction work or the first firm commitment to order equipment for the project. This confirmation may be made subject to detailed verification and to the Commission's approval of the notified aid measure. An express reference to both these conditions must be included in all aid schemes. In the case of ad hoc aid, the competent authority must have issued a letter of intent before work is commenced, subject to Commission approval of the measure. If work is commenced before these conditions are fulfilled, the project as a whole will lose its entitlement to aid.

3–129   Regional investment aid is intended to encourage investment in a region in order to help its development. For this reason the investments must remain in the region. According to the guidelines, the investment must make a real and sustained contribution to regional development. With this in mind, the guidelines require the investment or the jobs to be maintained within the region concerned for a period of five years from the date when the investment is completed or the post is first filled. This can be ensured through conditions linked to the aid or in the way in which the aid is disbursed. It may be that, due to rapid technological change, it becomes necessary to replace plant or equipment which has become outdated within this five-year period. In this case such replacement of obsolete plant or equipment may be made, but the economic activity must be retained in the region for five years. However, for SMEs the Member State can determine that the investment or jobs created must be retained in the region for at least three years.

The same applies to immaterial assets, in that investment in these must be retained in the region. With a view to ensuring this, immaterial assets which are entitled to aid must exclusively be used in the undertaking to which regional aid is granted. The assets must remain in the beneficiary undertaking for a minimum of five years. This limit can be reduced to three years for SMEs. Furthermore, such assets must be purchased from third parties under market conditions, must be regarded as amortisable assets and must be included in the assets of the firm.

2. Aid ceilings and costs eligible for aid

3–130   In relation to *aid ceilings*, the reader is referred to the discussion above and the Member States' regional aid maps. The costs which are a consequence of the initial investment project and which are *eligible for aid* are discussed here.

In principle regional investment aid can be calculated on the basis of material or immaterial investment costs, or on the basis of estimated wage costs for jobs directly created by the investment project.

Costs relating to the purchase of land, buildings and plant/machinery and material assets are eligible for initial investment aid, with the exception of the transport sector where expenditure on the purchase of transport equipment (moveable assets) is not eligible for aid for initial investment. The assets acquired should be new. However, this may be derogated from in the case of SMEs.

This requirement can also be derogated from in the case of the acquisition **3–131** of undertakings, and in such cases only the costs of buying assets from third parties under market conditions are taken into consideration. If aid has been given in respect of the assets before they are bought, the amount of this aid should be deducted.

SMEs have a special entitlement to receive aid for the costs of preparatory studies and consultancy costs linked to investment. Such costs may be taken into account up to an aid intensity of 50 per cent of the actual costs incurred.

Costs for leasing can also be eligible for aid. In relation to assets other than land and buildings, the lease must take the form of financial leasing and contain an obligation to purchase the asset at the expiry of the term of the lease. For the lease of land and buildings, the lease must continue for at least five years after the completion of the investment project for large companies, and three years for SMEs. This period runs from the anticipated date of the completion of the investment project.

For immaterial assets, the full costs of SMEs investments in intangible **3–132** assets by the transfer of technology, through the acquisition of patent rights, licences, know-how or unpatented technical knowledge may be eligible for aid. For large companies, such costs are eligible only up to a limit of 50 per cent of the total eligible investment expenditure for the project.

In calculating aid on the basis of wage costs, what is decisive is whether the initial investment project will result in the creation of jobs. Job creation means a net increase in the number of employees directly employed in a particular establishment compared with the average over the previous 12 months. Any jobs lost during that 12 month period must be deducted from the number of new jobs created during the same period. The amount of aid must not exceed a certain percentage of the wage cost of the person hired, calculated over a period of two years. The percentage is equal to the intensity allowed for investment aid in the area in question, as shown on the regional aid map.

3. Large investment projects

A "large investment project" is an initial investment with an eligible expendi- **3–133** ture above €50 million. This threshold will be reached if either the value of the investment costs or the value of the wage costs exceeds €50 million. A large investment project may not be artificially divided into sub-projects in order to escape the provisions of these guidelines.

Large investment projects are subject to an adjusted regional aid ceiling, as shown in the following table; SME bonuses are not granted in respect of large investment projects.

Expenditure eligible for aid	Adjusted regional aid ceiling
Up to €50 million	100% of the regional aid ceiling
Between €50 – 100 million	50% of the regional aid ceiling
Over €100 million	34% of the regional aid ceiling

This table can be presented in the following formula, which states the permitted aid for large investment projects:

$$R (50 + 0.5 \times B + 0.34 \times C).$$

Where
R = the unadjusted regional aid ceiling
B = the expenditure eligible for aid between €50 and 100 million
C = the expenditure eligible for aid above €100 million

3–134   The Member States must always notify individual ad hoc aid as well as aid for investment projects that is given as *part of an aid scheme* whose accumulated total exceeds the maximum permitted aid for an investment with expenditure eligible for aid of over €100 million. For example, the notification threshold for aid for a large project in a region with a permitted aid intensity of 30 per cent is thus:

Notification threshold = 30 % × (€50 million + 0.5 × €50 million + 0.34 × €0 million) = €22.5 million.

The notification thresholds for the most usual aid intensities can be summarised as follows:

Aid intensity	10%	15%	20%	30%	40%	50%
Notification threshold in millions of euro	7.5	11.25	15	22.5	30	37.5

If aid for a large project is not required to be notified to the Commission, the Member State concerned must send the Commission information by using standard forms, as set out in annex III of the guidelines. The Commission will publish this information on the internet. Member states must keep lists showing all large investment projects having received State aid. The lists must contain the information which is necessary to assess whether the maximum permitted aid intensities have been complied with. The information must be kept for 10 years from the date of the grant of the aid.

3–135   Certain large investment projects can distort competition in such a way that the Commission will only approve these following the opening of the procedure provided for in art.88(2) of the Treaty.

These large investment projects are characterised by the fact that the aid beneficiary accounts for more than 25 per cent of the sales of the product covered by the investment project on the relevant market, or will account for more than 25 per cent after the investment.

Another situation where the art.88(2) procedure may be applicable is where the production capacity created by the project is more than 5 per cent of the market, measured on the basis of the apparent consumption data (production plus imports minus exports) for the product concerned. This is on condition that the average annual growth rate of the apparent consumption over the last five years is above the average annual growth rate of the GDP of the EEA.

If one of these two situations exists, and the total amount of aid from all sources exceeds 75 per cent of the maximum amount of aid which an investment with eligible expenditure of €100 million could receive, applying the approved regional aid map, the Commission will only approve the aid measure following the opening of the procedure provided for in art.88(2) of the Treaty. Approval requires that the aid must be necessary for creating an incentive for the investment and that the advantages of the aid measure outweigh the distortive consequences and the effect on trade.

4. Cumulation

When aid is granted from more than one regional aid scheme or in combination with ad hoc aid, the regional aid intensity ceilings apply to the accumulated aid. This applies even if some of the aid is provided from local funds and some of the aid is provided from national or Community funds.   **3–136**

If the expenditure which is eligible for regional aid is eligible in whole or in part for aid for some other purpose, the common portion will be subject to the most favourable ceiling under the applicable rules. Regional investment aid may not be cumulated with de minimis support in respect of the same eligible expenses in order to circumvent the maximum aid intensities.

Operating aid

Operating aid is aimed at reducing a firm's current expenses. This is normally   **3–137** a form of aid which does not have effects that are in the common interest. Therefore operating aid is normally prohibited. However, such aid may be granted in regions covered by art.87(3)(a) of the Treaty. This requires the operating aid to be justified on the basis of its contribution to regional development and by its nature. Also, the Member State must show that the extent of the operating aid is proportional to the disadvantages it seeks to alleviate.

Operating aid should only be granted in respect of a predefined set of eligible costs, such as replacement investments, transport costs or labour costs, and should be limited to a certain proportion of those costs.

According to the guidelines, operating aid is intended to overcome delays and bottlenecks in regional development. This development is intended to result in a situation where operating aid is no longer necessary. For this reason operating aid should always be temporary and reduced over time, and should be phased out when the problems of the region are solved.

3–138　　The principle that operating aid should be progressively reduced can be subject to certain flexibility if the aid scheme is intended to counter geographic disadvantages in the outermost regions. According to the guidelines, operating aid which is not both progressively reduced and limited in time may only be authorised in the outermost regions to offset the additional costs of the pursuit of economic activities referred to in art.299(2) of the Treaty, and in the least populated regions, in so far as it is intended to prevent or reduce the continuing depopulation of these regions. If, in these regions, compensation is given for part of the additional transport costs, the guidelines lay down a number of conditions. For example, the aid may not develop into export aid, for which operating aid cannot be granted—which applies in all areas.

Operating aid for financial undertakings[84] and intra-group activities[85] is not permitted, unless such aid is granted under general schemes which are open to all sectors and which are designed to offset additional transport or employment costs.

Aid for newly created small enterprises

3–139　　The economic development of assisted regions is hindered, among other things, by the relatively low levels of entrepreneurial activity and the fact that they have lower than average rates of business start-ups. It is clear that these factors are a threat to regional development. The guidelines therefore introduce a new form of aid which is aimed at the establishment of newly created small enterprises and the early stage development of small enterprises in the assisted areas which can be granted in addition to regional investment aid.

As with all other forms of State aid, aid for newly created small enterprises is not without concern from the point of view of competition. Aid for newly created small enterprises must therefore be for limited amounts and must be progressively reduced. In addition, aid schemes which are for the benefit of newly created small enterprises must be administered so that existing small enterprises do not close down with a view to reopening in order to receive such aid.

Small undertakings employ fewer than 50 people and have an annual turnover or an annual balance sheet total not exceeding €10 million. The undertaking may not be more than five years old and must be independent, meaning that another undertaking may not own a majority of the voting

---

[84] As defined in s.J (codes 65, 66 and 67) of the NACE code.
[85] Section K (code 74) of the NACE code.

rights in the undertaking.[86] Aid schemes which benefit newly created small enterprises in regions eligible for aid under art.87(3)(a) may be approved by the Commission provided they do not allow for more than up to €2 million per enterprise. This amount is reduced to €1 million per enterprise for small enterprises in regions eligible for the aid under art.87(3)(c). In both cases the annual amounts of aid awarded may not exceed 33 per cent of the €2 million and €1 million respectively.

The expenses which are eligible for aid in connection with setting up a new **3–140** enterprise are legal, advisory, consultancy and administrative costs. After setting up the enterprise and within the first five years of the creation of the enterprise, the following costs are eligible for aid:

- interests on external finance and a dividend on own capital employed not exceeding the reference rate;
- fees for renting production facilities/equipment;
- energy, water, heating, taxes (other than VAT and corporate taxes on business income) and administrative charges; and
- depreciation, fees for leasing production facilities/equipment as well as wage costs including compulsory social charges may also be included provided that the underlying investments or job creation and recruitment measures have not benefited from other forms of aid.

The aid intensity as a percentage of the eligible costs may not exceed the following limits:

	Art.87(3)(a) regions	Art.87(3)(c) regions
0–3 years after creation	35%	25%
3–5 years after creation	25%	15%

These aid intensities can be raised by 5 per cent:

- in art.87(3)(a) regions with a GNP per capita of less than 60 per cent of the average for the EU-25,
- in regions with a population density of less than 12.5 inhabitants per km², and
- for small islands with a population of less than 5,000 and other communities of the same size which are correspondingly isolated.

Aid for newly created small enterprises may not be cumulated with other public aid, including de minimis aid, so that the maximum aid intensities or amounts referred to above may not be exceeded.

---

[86] For detailed rules on the classification of an undertaking as small, see the annex attached to the General Block Exemption Regulation, see s.2.

RISK CAPITAL INVESTMENTS IN SMALL AND MEDIUM-SIZED ENTERPRISES

Introduction

3–141   The Community guidelines on state aid to promote risk capital investments in small and medium-sized enterprises (OJ C 194, August 18, 2006, p.2) replace the 2001 Communication on State aid and risk capital.[87] The new guidelines should be seen in the context of the State Aid Action Plan—less and better targeted state aid: a roadmap for state aid reform 2005–2009 (COM(2005) 107 final). In its Action Plan the Commission proposed a revision of the Communication on State aid and risk capital. The background to the revision was a desire to counter market failure in the area of the provision of risk capital for new and young, innovative SMEs.

With regard to the need to notify aid measures in the form of risk capital the General Block Exemption Regulation specifies that such aid does not have to be notified to the extent that it fulfils the conditions laid down in the GBER, see above, paras 3–006–3–027.

In principle it is the job of the market to make sufficient risk capital available. However, the Commission has identified an "equity gap", i.e. a lack of equity capital in the risk capital market. This means that there is a continuing imbalance in the capital market which prevents the supply of risk capital which matches the demand at a price which is acceptable to both sides. This imbalance has had a negative effect on the development of SMEs, and this is particularly unfortunate if these undertakings have a good business model and good growth prospects. The reason why the market itself has been unable to overcome these problems is to be found, among other things, in incomplete and asymmetric information. It is very difficult for potential investors to get access to trustworthy information about the business prospects of an SME or a new undertaking, and consequently to monitor and support the development of the undertaking. This is especially so in the case of innovative or risky projects. This also means that the costs of evaluating such investments and other transaction costs can be high in relation to the risk capital involved. Because of the incompleteness or asymmetry of information, investors' risk willingness is reduced.

3–142   State aid which is directed at the provision of risk capital can be one way of dealing with the market failure and for gearing private capital. Conversely, State aid must only be permitted if it brings greater benefit than harm. This means that it is necessary to test the balance between the positive effects of the aid in achieving its goal, which is based on the common interest, and the negative effects of the aid in the form of distortion of competition and trade. This balancing test, which is derived from the Action Plan referred to above, consists of the following stages:

---

[87] The new guidelines are discussed by Bente Tranholm Schwarz, "New Guidelines on State aid promoting risk capital investments in SMEs", in *Competition Policy Newsletter*, No.3, Autumn 2006 p.19.

(1) Is the aid measure aimed at a well-defined objective of common interest, such as growth, employment, cohesion and the environment?

(2) Is the aid well designed to deliver the objective of common interest, i.e. does the proposed aid address the market failure or some other objective?

    (i) Is State aid an appropriate policy instrument?

    (ii) Is there an incentive effect, i.e. does the aid change the behaviour of firms and/or investors?

    (iii) Is the aid measure proportional, i.e. could the same change in behaviour be obtained with less aid?

(3) Are the distortions of competition and effect on trade limited, so that the overall balance is positive?

The guidelines are basically an expression of the result of this balancing test in the area of risk capital investments in SMEs, and as such its application in practice has also been a matter of weighing the positive effects of aid against its negative effects. The guidelines make the balancing test more specific. The Commission does not follow the criteria in the guidelines slavishly when evaluating whether a scheme is compatible with the common market; it makes a more overall assessment of their relative importance.

Scope of application

These guidelines only apply to risk capital *schemes*. In other words they apply   **3–143** to schemes intended to provide or promote aid in the form of risk capital. Thus ad hoc measures, that will make capital available for individual undertakings cannot be declared compatible with the common market on the basis of the guidelines.

"Risk capital" is defined as equity and quasi-equity financing to companies during their early growth stages (seed, start-up and expansion phases). The guidelines are thus targeted at SMEs in the early growth stage.

In principle the guidelines apply to all sectors, with the exception of the shipbuilding, coal and steel industries. Furthermore, the guidelines cannot be used to declare the provision of aid to enterprises in difficulties to be compatible with the common market. Risk capital schemes must specifically exclude aid to such undertakings.

Finally, the guidelines do not apply to aid to export-related activities,[88] as well as aid which is contingent upon the use of domestic in preference to imported goods.

The de minimis rule applies to risk capital investments. However, in risk

---

[88] Namely aid directly linked to the quantities exported, to the establishment and operation of a distribution network or to other current expenditure linked to export activities.

capital measures the application of the de minimis rule is made more complicated, if not impossible, by difficulties in the calculation of the aid so as to ensure the transparency of de minimis aid. Where these difficulties can be overcome, however, the de minimis rule remains applicable.

The application of the State aid concept to risk capital

3–144   "Risk capital measures" are defined in the guidelines as schemes to provide or promote aid in the form of risk capital. This involves a Member State creating incentives for investors to make financing available for another group which, for present purposes, means an SME. The structures which are used for this purpose can be very complex and the investment will often be made in a fund or other investment vehicle which stands between the investors and the enterprises in which the investment is made (SMEs). The guidelines only come into play if it is possible to identify State aid either at the investors, the fund/investment vehicle or the SME. This means that there can be State aid at three levels.

Aid to *investors* can be present where, for example, a state measure allows private investors to make equity or quasi-equity investments in a company or set of companies on terms more favourable than normally possible.

The Commission considers that an *investment fund or an investment vehicle* is an intermediary vehicle for the transfer of aid to investors and/or enterprises in which investment is made, rather than being a beneficiary of aid itself. However, measures such as fiscal measures or other measures involving direct transfers in favour of an investment vehicle or an existing fund with numerous and diverse investors with the character of an independent enterprise may constitute aid.

3–145   It is the Commission's view that there will be *aid to the target enterprises* where aid is present at the level of the investors, the investment vehicle or the investment fund, as in such cases the Commission will normally consider that the aid is at least partly passed on to the target enterprises. In cases where the investment is made on terms which would be acceptable to a private investor in a market economy, there will be an assumption that the target enterprises are not beneficiaries of aid. For this purpose, the Commission will consider whether such investment decisions are exclusively profit-driven and are linked to a reasonable business plan and projections, as well as to a clear and realistic exit strategy.[89]

State aid is provided by the Member States, so it is these that choose the form in which the aid is given. However, this choice is restricted by the way in which the Commission may have laid down certain conditions which must be

---

[89]   i.e. a strategy for the liquidation of holdings by a venture capital or private equity fund according to a plan to achieve maximum return, including trade sale, write-offs, repayment of preference shares/loans, sale to another venture capitalist, sale to a financial institution and sale by public offering.

fulfilled before the Commission will declare an aid scheme to be compatible with the common market. As a result of the balancing test referred to above, among other things the aid scheme must give an incentive to market investors to make risk capital available to the target enterprises and must lead to the investment decisions being taken on a profit-driven basis (commercial basis). In the guidelines the Commission states that the types of measure capable of producing this result include the following:

1. the setting up of investment funds (venture capital funds) in which the State is a partner, investor or participant, even if on less advantageous terms than other investors;
2. guarantees to risk capital investors or to venture capital funds against a proportion of investment losses, or guarantees given in respect of loans to investors/funds for investment in risk capital, provided the public cover for the potential underlying losses does not exceed 50 per cent of the nominal amount of the investment guaranteed;
3. other financial instruments in favour of risk capital investors or venture capital funds to provide extra capital for investment; and
4. fiscal incentives to investment funds and/or their managers, or to investors to undertake risk capital investment.

Criteria for assessing the compatibility with the common market of aid in the form of risk capital

The starting point for assessing whether State aid in the form of risk capital **3–146** can be declared compatible with the common market is art.87(3)(c) of the EC Treaty. According to this provision, aid to facilitate the development of certain economic activities or of certain economic areas can be considered to be compatible with the common market where such aid does not adversely affect trading conditions to an extent contrary to the common interest. The Commission will apply art.87(3)(c) in accordance with the balancing test referred to above. This means that in the area of risk capital, the Commission will declare State aid measures to be compatible with the common market if they lead to the increased provision of risk capital without at the same time affecting trading conditions in a way which is contrary to the common interest. The more detailed criteria for this balancing test are given below.

General conditions

In principle, the balancing test will lead to a positive outcome if the conditions **3–147** listed below are fulfilled. If an aid measure does not fulfil all the conditions, or if the measure specifically concerns investment companies, the Commission's approval will depend on a detailed assessment; see paras 3–148–3–160.

1. The risk capital measure must provide for tranches of finance, whether wholly or partly financed through State aid, not exceeding €1.5 million per target SME over each period of 12 months. This applies regardless of whether the tranche is financed in whole or in part by means of State aid.

2. In principle, the risk capital measure must provide or promote aid in the form of risk capital, i.e. equity and quasi-equity financing of companies during their early growth stages (seed, start-up and expansion phases). For small enterprises or for medium-sized enterprises located in art.87(3)(a) or art.87(3)(c) regions, the aid measures must be restricted to financing up to the expansion stage. For medium-sized enterprises located outside those regions, the risk capital measures must be restricted to providing financing up to the start-up stage.

3. The risk capital measure must provide at least 70 per cent of its total budget in the form of equity and quasi-equity investment instruments in target SMEs.

4. At least 50 per cent of the funding of the investments made under the risk capital measure must be provided by private investors, or for at least 30 per cent in the case of measures targeting SMEs located in assisted areas.[90]

5. The risk capital measure must ensure that decisions to invest in target companies (SMEs) are profit-driven. The Commission will consider this condition to be fulfilled if the measures have significant involvement of private investors (see point 4 immediately above) providing investments on a commercial basis (for profit) directly or indirectly in the equity of the target enterprises. The investment must also be linked to a business plan for each investment containing details of products, sales and profitability development and establishing the ex ante viability of the project. Finally, there must be a clear and realistic strategy for the liquidation of holdings according to a plan to achieve a maximum return, including trade sale, write-offs, repayment of preference shares/loans, sale to another venture capitalist, sale to a financial institution and sale by public offering (exit strategy).

6. The management of a risk capital measure or fund must be effected on a commercial basis, which means that the management team must behave as managers in the private sector, seeking to optimise the return for their investors. This will be considered to be the case where there is an agreement between a professional fund manager or a management company and participants in the fund, providing that the manager's remuneration is linked to performance and setting out the objectives of the fund and proposed timing of investments. Also, the private market investors must be represented in decision-making, and best practices and regulatory supervision must apply to the management of funds.

[90] Means regions falling within the scope of the derogations contained in art.87(3)(a) or (c) EC.

7. The Commission may accept a sectoral focus for risk capital measures, to the extent that many private sector funds focus on specific innovative technologies or sectors (such as biotechnology, information technology, health etc.). In all events, the sectoral restrictions for the scope of the guidelines must be respected.

Detailed assessment of special situations

The guidelines list a number of situations which will be subject to a special, **3–148** detailed assessment. This is because the evidence of market failure is less obvious and there is a higher potential for crowding out private investment and/or distorting competition. The detailed assessment is made on the basis of the balancing test. The Commission states that in these situations it is not possible to say in advance which elements will be decisive when assessing whether a measure is compatible with the common market. In other words, the assessment must be made on a case-by-case basis, and the decision will be related to the extent of the market failure which is addressed and the risk of crowding out private investment.

   The special situations are as follows:

1. Measures providing for investment tranches beyond the safe-harbour threshold of €1.5 million per target SME over each period of twelve months

The Commission is prepared to consider declaring such situations to be **3–149** compatible with the common market, provided the necessary evidence of the market failure is submitted.

2. Measures providing finance for the expansion stage for medium-sized enterprises in non-assisted areas

The Commission is prepared to consider declaring measures partly covering **3–150** the expansion stage of medium-sized enterprises compatible with the common market in certain cases, provided the necessary evidence is submitted.

3. Measures providing for follow-on investments in target companies that already receive aided capital injections to fund subsequent financing rounds even beyond the general safe-harbour thresholds and the companies' early growth financing

The Commission is prepared to consider declaring follow-on investment com- **3–151** patible with the common market provided the amount of this investment is consistent with the initial investment and with the size of the fund.

4. Measures providing for participation by private investors below 50 per cent in non-assisted areas or below 30 per cent in assisted areas

3–152   In the Community the level of development of the private risk capital market varies from Member State to Member State. In some Member States it may be difficult to find private investors, especially in assisted areas. Therefore, the Commission is prepared to consider declaring measures with a private participation below the thresholds set out to be compatible with the common market, if the Member State concerned submits the necessary evidence.

5. Measures providing seed capital to small enterprises which may involve (i) less or no participation by private investors, and/or (ii) predominance of debt investment instruments as opposed to equity and quasi-equity

3–153   "Seed capital" means financing provided to study, assess and develop an initial concept, preceding the start-up phase. Undertakings in the start-up phase have a higher risk of market failures due to the high degree of risk involved by the potential investment and the need to closely mentor the entrepreneur in this crucial phase. This is also reflected by the reluctance and near absence of private investors to provide seed capital. In such situations State aid implies no or very limited risk of crowding-out private investors. There is also a reduced risk of distortion of competition due to the significant distance from the market of these small-size enterprises. For these reasons, and in the light of the potentially crucial importance of SMEs in generating growth and jobs in the Community, the Commission may adopt a more favourable stance towards measures targeting the seed stage.

6. Measures specifically involving an investment vehicle

3–154   An investment vehicle may facilitate matching between investors and target SMEs. It may thereby improve SMEs' access to risk capital. In case of market failures affecting the enterprises targeted by the vehicle, the vehicle may not function efficiently without financial incentives. Investors may therefore target their investments elsewhere. Therefore, the Commission is prepared to consider declaring measures specifically involving an investment vehicle to be compatible with the common market, provided the necessary evidence of a clearly defined market failure is submitted.

7. Costs linked to the first screening of companies in view of the conclusion of the investments, up to the due diligence phase ("scouting costs")

Risk capital funds or their managers may incur "scouting costs" in identifying **3–155** SMEs, prior to the due diligence phase. Grants covering part of these scouting costs must encourage the funds or their managers to carry out more scouting activities than would otherwise be the case. Even if the search does not lead to an investment, this may be beneficial for the SMEs concerned, since it enables them to gain more experience with risk capital financing. The Commission will therefore have a favourable view of grants covering part of the scouting costs of risk capital funds or their managers. However, this is subject to the following conditions: the eligible costs must be limited to the scouting costs related to SMEs mainly in their seed or start-up stage where such costs do not lead to investment, and the costs must exclude the legal and administrative costs of the funds. In addition, the grant must not exceed 50 per cent of the eligible costs.

Detailed assessment—positive effects of the aid

Evidence of market failure
State aid given in connection with risk capital measures can only be declared **3–156** compatible with the common market if there is a market failure which the aid is intended to correct. In situations where the desired investment tranches go beyond the conditions for the Commission's approval (see above), the Commission will require additional evidence of market failure. Such evidence must be based on a study showing the level of the lack of equity with regard to the enterprises and sectors targeted by the risk capital measure. This study will include the supply of risk capital, as well as the significance of the venture capital industry in the local economy. The study should cover the period of three to five years preceding the implementation of the proposed risk capital measure and should also, if possible, take account of how the market is expected to develop. In the guidelines the Commission lists a number of factors which, depending on the situation, can be relevant for assessing whether the Member State's evidence of market failure is sufficient:

- the development of fundraising over the past five years, compared with the national and/or European averages;
- the current overhang of money;
- the share of government aided investment programmes in the total of venture capital investment over the preceding three to five years;
- the percentage of new start-ups receiving venture capital;
- the distribution of investments by categories of amount of investment; and

- a comparison of the number of business plans presented with the number of investments made by segment.

If the proposed measure is targeted at SMEs located in assisted areas, the relevant information must be supplemented by evidence proving the regional specificities which show the increased degree of market failure and which can justify the features of the measure envisaged. In this connection, depending on the circumstances, the following elements may be relevant:

- the significance of the circumstances of the region due to the lack of equity (in particular in terms of total amount of risk capital invested, number of funds or investment vehicles present in the territory or at a short distance, availability of skilled managers, number of deals and average and minimum size of deals);
- specific local economic data; and
- social and/or historic reasons for an under provision of risk capital, in comparison with the relevant average data.

Appropriateness of the instrument, incentive effect and necessity of aid

3–157   As its starting point, the Commission will evaluate whether State aid is an appropriate instrument for tackling the market failure in question compared with other options, as well as the advantages of the chosen solution. With regard to the incentive effect, the measure must affect market behaviour so that there is a net increase in risk capital for SMEs. The idea is that the increase must be on the basis of increased private investment. In special situations the Commission will also take into account additional criteria showing the profit-driven character of investment decisions and the commercial management of the measure.

Proportionality

3–158   The key to determining whether a measure is proportional is whether the desired change in behaviour could be achieved by using less aid than is proposed. In this connection it is important that there should be sufficiently commercial management of the measure, including that the risks of loss should not be borne by the Member State alone, just as the gains should not go solely to private investors.

Detailed assessment—negative effects of the aid

What is decisive in the assessment of the negative effects of State aid is the   **3–159**
extent of any distortion of competition and risk of crowding-out private
investment. These potentially negative effects have to be analysed at each of
the three levels where aid may be present. Aid to investors, to investment vehicles and to investment funds may negatively affect competition in the market
for the provision of risk capital. Aid to target enterprises may negatively affect
the product markets on which these enterprises compete.

At the level of the market for the provision of risk capital, State aid may
result in private investors waiting until the State provides aid for such investments. It is important for Member States to show that there is no risk of such
crowding-out. In this respect the following elements may be relevant:

- the number of national/regional venture capital firms/funds/investment
  vehicles and the segments in which they are active;
- the targeted enterprises by size, growth stage and business sector;
- the average transaction size, and possibly the minimum transaction size
  which the funds or investors would scrutinise; and
- the total amount of venture capital available for the target enterprises,
  sector and stage targeted by the relevant measure.

Depending on the circumstances, there can also be distortion of competition at the level of the target enterprises (SMEs) which are invested in. In
general, State aid at this level is not assumed to have a significant distorting
effect on competition. This is because the undertakings in question are new on
the market and they will probably not have a strong market position. In the
guidelines the Commission states that it is possible that risk capital measures
may keep alive ineffective undertakings or sectors which, in the absence of
aid, would disappear from the market. Furthermore, an over-supply of risk
capital funding to inefficient enterprises may artificially increase their valuation and thus distort the risk capital market at the level of fund providers,
which would have to pay higher prices to buy these enterprises. There is also
a risk that sector-specific aid may maintain production in non-competitive
sectors. Region-specific aid may lead to the inefficient allocation of production
factors between regions.

There are thus risks of other forms of distortion of competition. In the light
of this, the Commission will examine the following factors:

- overall profitability of the firms invested in over time and prospects of
  future profitability;
- rate of enterprise failure targeted by the measure;
- maximum size of investment tranche envisaged by the measure as compared to the turnover and costs of the target SMEs; and
- over-capacity of the sector benefiting from the aid.

The Commission's balancing and decision

3–160   In the light of the above positive and negative elements, the Commission will balance the effects of the risk capital measure and determine whether the resulting distortions adversely affect trading conditions to an extent contrary to the common interest. For that purpose the Commission will not use the criteria set out in these guidelines mechanically but will make an overall assessment of their relative importance.

The Commission will deal with a notified aid measure following the rules laid down in Regulation (EC) No.659/1999 (see Ch.2) and, for example, it can make its decision conditional on the investment tranches being for lesser amounts than those notified or on a different allocation of profits and losses between the Member State and the private investors.

Cumulation

3–161   Where capital which falls within the scope of the guidelines is used to finance initial investment or other costs eligible for aid under other rules on State aid, the relevant aid ceilings or maximum eligible amounts will be reduced by 50 per cent in general and by 20 per cent for target enterprises located in assisted areas (see Ch.6 of the guidelines). However, this reduction does not apply to aid intensities provided for in the Community framework for State aid for research and development.

Monitoring and reporting

3–162   The Member States must submit annual reports to the Commission giving information about their use of risk capital measures. These reports are published by the Commission. In addition, the Member States themselves must publish the full texts of their risk capital aid schemes on the internet, so that interested parties can easily get hold of them. This increases transparency (and thereby control). Publication of schemes is essential, as they cannot be implemented before they have been published on the internet.

Finally, the Member States must maintain detailed records necessary to establish that the conditions laid down in the guidelines have been observed. This information must be maintained for 10 years.

STATE AID AND TAX

3–163   In its notice on the application of the State aid rules to measures relating to direct business taxation (OJ C 384, December 10, 1998, p.3), the Commission has given a detailed set of directions as to what forms of tax provisions and practice can constitute State aid.[91]

The reader is also referred to paras 1–020 to 1–046, on the conditions under which a tax measure is subject to the prohibition in art.87(1) of the EC Treaty.

In connection with State aid in the area of tax, the application of the rules on State aid does not depend on whether actual companies are involved, e.g. public and private limited companies. According to the practice of the ECJ, in the area of competition law, including the application of art.87(1), the term "undertaking" covers all entities which carry on commercial activities, i.e. offer goods or services on a market, regardless of their legal status or the method of their financing.[92]

It is clear that taxation measures which exempt certain sectors can be equivalent to aid to the commercial sectors concerned.[93]

First, in order to constitute State aid, a tax measure must give the taxpayer **3–164** an advantage which reduces the burden which they would otherwise have. Such an advantage can consist of various ways of reducing the tax burden, namely by:[94]

- a reduction in the tax base (such as special deductions, special or acceler-ated depreciation arrangements or the entering of reserves on the balance sheet),[95]
- a total or partial reduction in the amount of tax (such as exemption or a tax credit), and
- deferment, cancellation or even special rescheduling of tax debt.[96]

Secondly, the advantage must be given by the State or through State resources. A loss of tax revenue corresponds to a use of State resources in the form of the use of tax expenditure. This criterion also applies to aid provided

[91] On the application of the notice, see e.g. Pierpaolo Rossi, " The Italian tax premium in favour of newly listed companies and the notion of selectivity relative to direct business taxation", in *Competition Policy Newsletter*, No.3, Autumn 2005 p.109. For a detailed analysis of the problems of State aid and tax, see also Schön, CML Rev., Vol.36, No.5, September 1999 pp.911-936. See also Pierpaolo Rossi, "State aid and preferential tax regimes for financial hold-ings The Luxembourg's Exempt 1929 Holdings case (1)", in *Competition Policy Newsletter*, No.3, Autumn 2006, p.66. See further Kim Lundgaard Hansen, "A taxing subject", in Liber Amicorum en l'honneur de Bo Vesterdorf/Liber Amicorum in honour of Bo Vesterdorf, Bruxelles, Éditions juridiques Bruylant, 2007.

[92] Case C-222/04, *Ministero dell'Economia e delle finanze v Cassa di Risparmio di firenze and Others*, [2006] E.C.R. I-289.

[93] See Case C-53/00, *Ferring*, [2001] E.C.R. I-9067, where the ECJ found that a special tax advantage allowed to certain undertakings (distributors/wholesalers) in the pharmaceutical sector was compatible with art.86(2) of the Treaty, in so far as the advantage in question did not exceed the additional costs they had as a consequence of their public service obligations.

[94] Further examples are given in the Commission's Annual Report on Competition Policy 2004.

[95] For a case on tax advantages for the promotion of investment see Case C-156/98, *Germany v Commission*, [2000] E.C.R. I-6857.

[96] For examples of cases on State aid, taxation and insolvency, see Case C-200/97, *Ecotrade*, [1998] E.C.R. I-7907; and Case C-295/97, *Rinaldo Piaggio*, [1999] E.C.R. I-3735.

by regional or local authorities. State intervention can also be evidenced by laws or administrative decisions, as well as in the practice of the tax authorities.

Thirdly, the measure in question must affect the terms of competition and trade between Member States. If the aid strengthens the position of an undertaking compared with competing undertakings in the EU, this in itself is enough for trade to be considered as being affected. This finding is not altered by the fact that the aid is limited, that the undertaking is small, or that the beneficiary undertaking has a very small market share in the EU; nor is it altered by the fact the beneficiary undertaking does not export, or that nearly all its exports are to countries outside the EU.

3–165   Fourthly, the tax measure must be selective; i.e. it must benefit certain undertakings or certain productions. According to the ECJ, what is decisive in this respect is whether a national measure, as part of a specific legal arrangement, can benefit certain undertakings or certain productions compared with other undertakings which, given the purpose of the arrangement, find themselves legally or actually in a corresponding situation.[97] However, a system may be justified "by the nature or general scheme" of the tax system, and so fall outside the prohibition of State aid in art.87(1). This will be the case if the measure is a direct consequence of the fundamental principles or the main structure of the tax system of the Member State in question. If this is not the case, then State aid will be found to exist; see the discussion of selectivity below.

General national technical tax rules which apply to all undertakings, such as the setting of tax rates, the rules on depreciation, and rules on the carrying forward of losses, provision on double taxation or tax avoidance, do not constitute aid.

The same applies to measures pursuing general economic policy objectives through a reduction of the tax burden related to certain production costs (research and development (R&D), the environment, training, employment).

It does not matter that some firms benefit more than others from some of these tax measures, for example that measures designed to reduce the taxation of labour for all firms have a relatively greater effect on labour-intensive industries.

3–166   Only measures whose scope extends to the entire territory of the State can escape the prohibition of State aid. Measures which are regional or local in scope may favour certain undertakings.[98] However, this is not always the case. The point of reference for assessing whether a regional tax measure is selective can in principle be the region in question in the Member State. This

---

[97] See Case C-88/03, *Portugal v Commission*, [2006] E.C.R. I-7115, with references to further cases on this question.

[98] In Joined Cases T-92/00 and T-103/00, *Territorio Histórico de Álava and Others v Commission*, [2002] E.C.R. II-1385, concerning tax rules in the Basque region, the CFI deliberately refrained from deciding whether a general tax arrangement in an autonomous tax region falls within the concept of State aid, but the CFI found that there was de facto selectivity, and therefore State aid, because the tax advantages were linked to investment thresholds which could, in reality, only be reached by large undertakings.

presumes that the decision, for example to reduce the tax rate within a region in a Member State, is taken in the exercise of sufficient autonomy. According to the ECJ, this will be the case if the decision is taken by a regional or local authority which has political or financial authority under the constitution which distinguishes it from the central government. In addition, the decision must have been taken without the central government being able to intervene over its content. Finally, the economic consequences of the decision, for example to reduce tax rates for undertakings in the region, must not be made good by contributions from other regions or from the central government.[99]

Tax measures which benefit one or more specific sectors, but not all, fall under the prohibition of State aid. The same applies to tax measures which are primarily aimed at benefiting exports of national products. The same will apply, for example, to tax rules that only benefit national undertakings which produce physical goods (as opposed to services), or which benefit all sectors which are exposed to international competition.[100]

A derogation from the base rate of corporation tax for an entire section of the economy will therefore constitute State aid.

Any administrative tax practice which departs from the generally applicable tax rules for the benefit of individual undertakings will in principle lead to an assumption that State aid may be present.[101]   **3–167**

The differential nature of some measures does not necessarily mean that they must be considered to be State aid. This is the case with measures whose economic rationale makes them necessary to the functioning and effectiveness of the tax system. Such tax differences can on the face of it seem selective, but if there is the rationale referred to, the measure will not be considered selective within the meaning of art.87(1). However, it is up to the Member State to provide such justification.

In recent years both the ECJ and the CFI have had the opportunity to judge the conditions on selectivity in relation to taxation measures. In this area two Italian cases are of particular interest.

The *Unicredito* case arose out of the reform of the Italian banking system.[102] This reform enabled credit institutions governed by public law to be   **3–168**

---

[99] See Case C-88/03, *Portugal v Commission*, [2006] E.C.R. I-7115, which is also discussed in paras 1–041 to 1–043.

[100] See Case C-143/99, *Adria-Wien Pipeline v finanzlandesdirektion für Kärnten*, [2001] E.C.R. I-8365. On the *Adria-Wien Pipeline* case, see *Madeleine Infeldt*, "Eco-tax reliefs for companies in Denmark, finland and Sweden after the Court ruling in Adria-Wien Pipeline GmbH case", in *Competition Policy Newsletter*, No.1, Spring 2003 p.103.

[101] See e.g. Case C-480/98, *Spain v Commission*, [2000] E.C.R. I-8717, where the ECJ reviewed its practice concerning tax and insolvency. In the case in question, undertakings which had suspended payments had been insolvent, and which had debts to public authorities in respect of tax and social contributions, had nevertheless been able to continue in business for several years without paying their public debts, and this amounted to State aid. See also Case C-256/97, *DMT*, [1999] E.C.R. I-3913, where the ECJ held that payment facilities in respect of social security contributions granted in a discretionary manner to an undertaking by the body responsible for collecting such contributions constituted State aid.

[102] Case C-148/04, *Unicredito Italiano v Agenzia delle Entrate, Ufficio Genova 1*, [2005] E.C.R. I-11137.

restructured as limited companies. With a view to this, a public credit institution could transfer its banking undertaking to a limited company. Thereafter, the banking undertaking was placed in a limited company whose share capital was owned by a banking foundation (the previously public credit institution in restructured legal form). The banking foundation's purpose was to administer the capital in the company (i.e. the banking undertaking) and to apply the income from this for social purposes. Provided some further conditions were fulfilled, banks which undertook such restructuring received a tax advantage in the form of a reduction of their income tax for five consecutive tax years.

The ECJ stated that this tax reduction could not be considered to be a general measure of tax or economic policy, because it did not apply to all undertakings, and it had to be characterised as selective, as only undertakings in the banking sector which carried out restructuring could benefit from the tax reduction.

The ECJ went on to state that the tax reduction in fact constituted a departure from the ordinary tax scheme. This was because the beneficiary undertakings enjoyed tax relief to which they would not be entitled under the normal application of the Italian tax laws. In addition, undertakings in sectors other than the banking sector which carried out similar restructuring, or undertakings in the banking sector which did not carry out such operations could not claim such tax reductions. The ECJ therefore found that the tax reduction was not justified by the nature and overall structure of the tax system, and added that the tax reduction was not an adaptation of the general scheme to the particular characteristics of banking undertakings.

3–169   A second case, which also arose from the restructuring of the banking sector in Italy referred to, concerned the relief from direct tax on dividends received by banking foundations which exclusively pursued the aims of social welfare, education, teaching, and study and scientific research.[103]

It was the view of the ECJ that the tax relief was not a general measure of tax or economic policy. The ECJ then stated that the tax advantage was accorded to certain undertakings on account of their legal form (a legal person governed by public law or a foundation) and of the sectors in which they carried on their activities. The tax relief was therefore selective. In extension of this, the ECJ found that the tax advantage derogated from the ordinary tax regime without being justified by the nature or scheme of the tax system of which it formed part. It was the ECJ's view that the derogation was not based on the measure's logic or the technique of taxation. The measure resulted from the national legislature's objective of financially favouring organisations which were regarded as socially deserving.

In the area of charges and duties, the three cases discussed in the following illustrate the selectivity criterion in art.87(1).[104]

---

[103] Case C-222/04, *Ministero dell'Economia e delle finanze v Cassa di Risparmio di firenze*, [2006] E.C.R. I-289.
[104] Reference can also be made to Case C-526/04, *Laboratoires Boiron v Urssaf*, [2006] E.C.R. I-7529.

The *Adria-Wien Pipeline* case arose from a major reform of duties in   **3–170**
Austria which included the law disputed in the case, according to which a duty
had to be paid on the consumption of electricity and natural gas.[105] However,
the law provided that the taxes would be reimbursed on application in so far
as they exceed, in total, 0.35 per cent of net production value. However, only
undertakings whose activity consisted primarily of the production of goods
were entitled to a rebate of energy taxes. Adria-Wien Pipeline's principal
activity was the construction and operation of oil pipelines, i.e. the provision
of services, and the undertaking had thus had its application to the Austrian
authorities for a tax rebate of the energy taxes refused.

In its decision the ECJ referred to the fact that a measure which, although
conferring an advantage on its recipient, is justified by the nature or general
scheme of the system of which it is part does not fulfil that condition of
selectivity. The ECJ found that although objective, the criterion (production
of goods) applied by the national legislation at issue was not justified by
the nature or general scheme of that legislation. The ECJ reasoned that the
ecological considerations underlying the national legislation did not justify
treating the consumption of natural gas or electricity by undertakings supplying services differently than the consumption of such energy by undertakings
manufacturing goods. In the view of the ECJ, energy consumption by both
sectors is equally damaging to the environment.

The second example is the judgment of the CFI in the *British Aggregates
Association* case.[106] The case concerned an environmental tax on aggregates
in the United Kingdom. The scope of the arrangement was limited so that a
levy was only imposed on virgin aggregates, that is to say granular material on
first extraction. However, the levy was not imposed on aggregates extracted
as a by-product or waste from other processes (secondary aggregates), nor
on recycled aggregates. According to the British authorities, the aim of this
restriction was to promote the use of these as building materials by excluding
them from the scope of the arrangement, and thereby reduce the quarrying
of virgin aggregates by reducing demand for them, and thereby promote the
rational use of resources.

In this case the CFI stated that the basis for assessing the selectivity of   **3–171**
an arrangement should be whether the different treatment of undertakings
as regards the advantages or *burdens* introduced by the measure in question, arises from the nature or the general system of the overall scheme
which applies. It was the view of the CFI, among other things by reference
to the *Adria-Wien Pipeline* case, that where such a differentiation is based
on objectives other than those pursued by the overall scheme, the measure
in question will, in principle, be considered as satisfying the condition of
selectivity. It was also the view of the CFI that it was necessary to distinguish between cases where the question of selectivity arises on the basis

---

[105] Case C-143/99, *Adria-Wien Pipeline v finanzlandesdirektion für Kärnten*, [2001] E.C.R. I-8365;
see also case T-233/04 under appeal, see para.3–054..
[106] Case T-210/02, *British Aggregates Association v Commission*, [2006] E.C.R.II-2789.

of a partial exemption from the payment of an environmental tax (the *Adria-Wien Pipeline* case) and cases which restrict the scope of application of an environmental tax. It was the latter which the CFI was required to consider.

According to the CFI, an environmental levy is an autonomous fiscal measure which is characterised by its environmental objective and its specific tax base. It seeks to tax certain goods or services so that the environmental costs may be included in their price and/or so that recycled products are rendered more competitive and producers and consumers are oriented towards activities which better respect the environment. On this basis the CFI found that in principle an environmental tax cannot be seen as part of an overall system of taxation. The CFI held that in the current state of Community law Member States retain their powers in relation to environmental policy and are free, subject to balancing the various interests involved within their environmental policy, to set their priorities as regards the protection of the environment and, as a result, to determine which goods or services they decide to subject to an environmental levy. In extension of this, the CFI noted that the mere fact that an environmental levy constitutes a specific measure, which extends to certain designated goods or services, and cannot be seen as part of an overall system of taxation which applies to all similar activities which have a comparable impact on the environment, does not mean that similar activities, which are not subject to the levy, benefit from a selective advantage. The CFI went on to say that it is for the Commission, when assessing an environmental levy under art.87(1) of the Treaty, to take account of the environmental protection requirements referred to in art.6 of the Treaty, which provides that those requirements are to be integrated into the definition and implementation of, inter alia, arrangements which ensure that competition is not distorted within the internal market.

Against this background, the CFI decided that the decisive question in the case was whether the tax scheme was justified by the environmental purposes which lay behind it. In the case in question the CFI found that there was not compatibility between the restrictions and the environmental goals.

3–172   In this case the CFI seems to be suggesting that there is something special about environmental taxes, among other things because, in the absence of Community legislation, the Member States are free to decide what environmental policies to adopt and therefore have relatively wide discretion to determine the scope of environmental tax measures, as long as any differences in treatment under such measures are justified by their purposes.

The CFI's judgment has been appealed to the ECJ in Case C-487/06 P. where the British Aggregates Association has argued that the ECJ should overturn the CFI's judgment and annul the Commission's decision.

Another case which is interesting with regard to the possible selectivity of taxes is the *GIL Insurance* case which concerned a tax on insurance premiums.[107]

In accordance with the relevant national rules, this tax was imposed on the receipt of insurance premiums by an insurer or taxable insurance intermediary. The general tax rate was 4 per cent, but this was raised to 17.5 per cent in connection with insurance premiums relating to domestic appliances, motor cars and travel. The higher rate corresponded to the normal VAT rate in the United Kingdom. The objective of the higher rate of tax was to counteract the trend for suppliers of domestic appliances in particular to progressively replace service contracts for the repair and maintenance of appliances sold or rented (which were subject to VAT at the standard rate of 17.5 per cent) with insurance contracts ancillary to the contracts for sale or rental, so as to benefit from the exemption from VAT of insurance transactions.

In the first instance the British authorities imposed a 2.5 per cent tax on   **3–173**
insurance agreements. However, this did not succeed in reversing the trend referred to, and the tax authorities experienced a fall in revenue. For this reason the tax on premiums for ancillary insurance agreements was raised to the normal level for VAT. The reason given for the introduction of the higher rate was to prevent "value shifting", since the British tax authorities considered that suppliers of domestic appliances could, by manipulating the prices attributed to the appliances and the corresponding insurance, take advantage of the exemption from VAT of insurance services. This had the consequence of changing the behaviour of suppliers, who reverted to ordinary service contracts for the appliances they supplied.

In this case GIL Insurance and a number of other insurance companies argued that the two different tax rates meant that there was State aid which benefited the undertakings which were subject to the ordinary rate.

The ECJ started from the position of the *Adria-Wien Pipeline* case, according to which a measure which, although conferring an advantage on its recipient, is justified by the nature or general scheme of the system of which it is part, does not fulfil the criteria in art.87(1) of the Treaty on selectivity. The decisive question for the ECJ was therefore whether the application of the higher rate to a specific category of insurance agreements (ancillary insurance agreements), which had hitherto been subject to the standard rate, was justified by the nature or general scheme of the system of which it was part.

In answering this question the ECJ laid weight on the fact that the differenti-   **3–174**
ated rates had been introduced to counteract the practice of taking advantage of the difference between the standard rate of insurance tax and the standard rate of VAT by manipulating the prices of rental or sale of appliances and of the associated insurance on the one hand, and the ancillary insurances on the other hand, depending on the tax rates. According to the ECJ, this gave rise to a loss of VAT revenue and to shifts in the conditions of competition in the

---

[107] Case C-308/01, *GIL Insurance Ltd and Others v Commissioners of Customs & Excise*, [2004] E.C.R. I-4777.

domestic appliance sector. In addition, the ECJ emphasised that the introduction of higher rates on certain contracts was intended to alter behaviour by specifically eliminating ancillary insurance, that it had not been introduced in order to confer an advantage on operators who offered insurance contracts subject to the standard rate, and that the standard rate of insurance tax did not constitute a derogation from the general system of taxation of insurance in the United Kingdom and that the taxes were in accordance with the Sixth VAT Directive.[108]

On this basis the ECJ found that the application of the higher rate of insurance tax to specific kinds of insurance contracts previously subject to the standard rate must be regarded as justified by the nature and the general scheme of the national system of taxation of insurance.

The cases referred to above seem to illustrate a difference of approach to the assessment of selectivity between tax measures and measures dealing with charges or levies.

3–175   In respect of taxes, it seems that the assessment of selectivity should be made in relation to the national tax system as a whole. A measure which is a natural or logical consequence of the nature and overall structure of the Member State's tax system will presumably not be judged to be selective. If, conversely, there is an exception to the normally applicable tax rules, whereby the undertakings affected receive specially favourable treatment in the national tax system, there will presumably be found to be a selective measure.

As for duties or levies which are intended to alter behaviour, including environmental taxes, it seems that the assessment of selectivity should be made on a narrower basis in the sense that a difference in the treatment of undertakings in a provision on charges or levies can be accepted if the different treatment arises from the purpose of the measure in question. Thus, in the *Adria-Wien Pipeline* case the Austrian Government argued that the charges concerned should not be looked at in isolation, but as part of a larger package which was intended to consolidate the budget. According to the Government, this package consisted of general socially balanced measures which affected all groups in society and which should therefore be seen as a whole. The ECJ did not seem to accept this argument. On the contrary, it chose to see the taxes only in relation to the one law of which they were a part. It should be remembered, as the CFI said in the *British Aggregates Association* case, that the Member States have the competence to establish their own priorities in matters of economic policy, taxation policy and environmental policy.

A progressive scale of taxation for income and earnings is, for example, a consequence of a systems redistributive logic, and is thus not selective within the meaning of art.87(1) of the Treaty. The conditions for reducing

---

[108] Sixth Council Directive 77/388/EEC of May 17, 1977 on the harmonization of the laws of the Member States relating to turnover taxes—Common system of value added tax: uniform basis of assessment (OJ L 145, 13.6.1977, p.1).

tax debts or the rules for depreciation or the valuation of stocks differ from Member State to Member State, but they can be justified by the nature or general scheme of the system of which they are part. Furthermore, some circumstances can be justified by objective differences between taxable entities. However, if the authorities have discretion to apply different depreciation periods or methods for valuing assets for individual undertakings or sectors, it will be assumed that this constitutes State aid. This will also be the assumption if the tax authorities deal with individual cases of tax debts on the basis of consideration for optimising the collection of the debt of the undertaking in question.

Differences in the tax treatment of undertakings based in the Member State and undertakings based outside the Member State can give rise to an assumption of the existence of State aid. The same can apply if tax advantages are given to companies with their head offices located in the Member State.   **3–176**

Specific taxation provisions which do not include an element of discretion can be justified, particularly with regard to special accounting requirements or the significance of the role of real property in certain sectors (e.g. agriculture), and these do not constitute State aid.

Also provisions concerning the taxation of SMEs, including smaller farms, can be of such a character that they do not constitute State aid, as they can be compared to the logic of progressive tax rates.

The Commission will not approve aid, even if it could otherwise be acceptable under one of the exceptions to art.87, if it is contrary to one of the fundamental principles of the Treaty (e.g. the prohibition of discrimination on the grounds of nationality and the right of establishment) or against rules on taxation derived from the Treaty.   **3–177**

Provisions on tax reliefs are usually of a permanent nature and in such a case they constitute operating aid which is prohibited in principle, though with certain exceptions in the form of aid for environmental protection and regional aid for the outermost regions; see e.g. the aid for transport in the thinly populated Nordic regions. Operating aid cannot be approved if it constitutes aid for exports between Member States.

Paragraph 33 of the notice on the application of the State aid rules to measures relating to direct business taxation addresses tax advantages for the benefit of certain regions.[109]

Taxation measures which have the character of State aid must be notified to the Commission in accordance with art.88(3) of the Treaty. Unjustified aid provided by means of tax measures can be required to be repaid, just as with other State aid. Each year the Member States must send a report on their aid measures. With regard to tax measures which constitute aid, the report must give information about lost revenue.

---

[109] On the relationship of art.87(1) of the Treaty and regional tax measures, see Case C-88/03, *Portugal v Commission*, [2006] E.C.R. I-7115, discussed above in this section and in paras 1–041 to 1–043.

STATE GUARANTEES AND OTHER FINANCIAL INSTRUMENTS

Introduction

3–178   Commission Notice on the application of arts 87 and 88 of the EC Treaty to
State aid in the form of guarantees (OJ C 155, June 20, 2008, p.10) provides
guidance for the Member States as to determining whether guarantee schemes
and/or individual guarantees contain State aid elements within the meaning
of art.87(1) and therefore should be notified to the Commission according
to art.88(3) prior to giving the guarantee.[110] The notice explains how the
Commission will interpret art.87 in relation to *State guarantees.*

By means of the Notice, the Commission also intends to communicate its
policy in this area to the public and in so doing observing principles concerning transparency, equal treatment and legal certainty. The Notice is in
continuation of recent EC State aid policy particularly transparent in relation
to SMEs because it introduces what might be called "the safe-harbour principle". According to that principle, a State guarantee does not involve State aid
if a minimum annual premium ("safe-harbour premium") is charged on the
amount actual guaranteed by the state. Accordingly, a guarantee in favour of
a SME does not contain State aid elements if the credit rating of the undertaking concerned is known and the undertaking pays the corresponding annual
safe-harbour premium. On the other hand, if the SME pays a lower premium
than the one corresponding to its credit quality, a presumption for State aid
in favour of the SME is present. More details on the safe-harbour principle
are provided below.

The application of article 87(1) EC to financial instruments

3–179   At the outset the contents of art.87 should be recalled. According to art.87 (1)
any aid granted by a Member State (e.g. by central, regional or local authorities of the Member State) or through State resources in any form whatsoever
(e.g. by an undertaking controlled by the Member State) which threatens to
distort competition by favouring certain undertakings or the production of
certain goods shall, in so far it affects trade between Member States, be incompatible with the common market. Article 87 (2) and (3) states the conditions
under which State aid within the meaning of art.87 (1) nevertheless may or
shall be compatible with the common market.

The ECJ has in the Stardust-case elaborated on how and when to apply
art.87 (1) to financial instruments as e.g. State guarantees and, furthermore,
on the notion "through State resources".[111]

According to the ECJ, the expression "State resources" covers all the

---

[110] The new notice replaces the Commission Notice on the application of arts 87 and 88 to the EC
Treaty to State aid in the form of guaranties (OJ C 71, 11.3.2000, p.14).
[111] C-482/99, *French Republic v Commission of the European Communities,* [2002] E.C.R. I-4397.

financial means by which the public authorities may actually support under-takings, irrespective of whether or not those means are permanent assets of the public sector. Therefore, even if the sums corresponding to a State aid measure are financial resources of public undertakings and are not perma-nently held by the Treasury, the fact that they constantly remain under public control, and are therefore available to the competent national authorities, is sufficient for them to be categorised as State resources. That is the case where the State is perfectly capable, by exercising its dominant influence over public undertakings, of directing the use of their resources in order, as occasion arises, to finance specific advantages in favour of other undertakings.

The condition that, for a measure to be capable of being classified as State **3–180** aid within the meaning of art.87 (1), it must be imputable to the State, cannot be interpreted in such a way that such imputability is inferred from the mere fact that that measure was taken by a public undertaking controlled by the State. Even if the State is in a position to control a public undertaking and to exercise a dominant influence over its operations, actual exercise of that control in a particular case cannot be automatically presumed. It is thus nec-essary to examine whether the public authorities must be regarded as having been involved, in one way or another, in the adoption of that measure.

In that respect, the imputability to the State of an aid measure taken by a public undertaking may be inferred from a set of indicators such as, in particu-lar, its integration into the structures of the public administration, the nature of its activities and the exercise of the latter on the market in normal condi-tions of competition with private operators, the legal status of the undertak-ing (in the sense of it being subject to public law or ordinary company law), the intensity of the supervision exercised by the public authorities over the man-agement of the undertaking, or any other indicator showing, in the particular case, an involvement by the public authorities in the adoption of a measure or the unlikelihood of their not being involved, having regard also to the compass of the measure, its content or the conditions which it contains.

In order to determine whether *investment by the public authorities in the* **3–181** *capital of an undertaking, in whatever form, may constitute State aid within the meaning of art.87(1)*, it is necessary to assess whether, in similar circum-stances, a private investor of a dimension comparable to that of the bodies managing the public sector could have been prevailed upon to make capital contributions of the same size, having regard in particular to the information available and foreseeable developments at the date of those contributions.

In order to examine whether or not the State has adopted the conduct of a prudent investor operating in a market economy, it is necessary to place oneself *in the context of the period during which the financial support measures were taken* in order to assess the economic rationality of the State's conduct, and thus to *refrain from any assessment based on a later situation*.

It may consequently be inferred from the above, that inter alia a guarantee provided by the State or by State controlled bodies or undertakings provided the State aid measure is imputable to the State may constitute State aid within the meaning of art.87(1). That assessment should be based on the private investor principle as the situation was at the time when the guarantee was given.[112]

How can a State guarantee involve State aid within the meaning of art.87 (1) EC?

3–182   Normally a guarantee is attached to a loan arrangement in the sense that the guarantor gives a guarantee that the borrower will repay a loan given by a lender. A guarantee may be an advantage to both the borrower and the lender. It is an advantage to the borrower because the borrower gets a loan which he would not have received in the absence of the guarantee or he gets the loan at a lower interest rate or by offering less security. The guarantee is an advantage to the lender because the guarantee serves as a security that the loan will be repaid—in the worst case by the guarantor. On the part of the guarantor, the guarantee involves a risk that the borrower will be in default and that the lender therefore will draw on the guarantee. A guarantor will under normal business conditions not assume such a risk without—in return—being paid by the borrower. That consideration is called a premium.

A guarantee provided by a State is a very good security and it may enable the borrower to raise money and thereby facilitate the creation of new business. However, it may also serve as helping hand to a failing undertaking which thereby stays in business with distortion of competition as a possible consequence.

A State guarantee involves State aid to the borrower if the risk-carrying by the State is not remunerated by an appropriate premium, i.e. market based premium. Whether or not that is the case must—as mentioned above—be assessed at the time when the guarantee is given. Therefore, it is immaterial that the guarantee is never invoked.

A State guarantee may also involve State aid to the lender. This could, e.g. be the case when a State guarantee is given after (ex post) a loan arrangement has entered into force without the terms of the arrangement being adjusted.[113]

Overview of various types of guarantees

3–183   The relationship between art.87(1) and State guarantees described above has for the sake of clarity been illustrated with a normal loan guarantee. However,

---

[112] See paras 6–004–6–010 of this book where the private investor principle is explained in relation to other types of financial transactions.

[113] The fact that a guarantee involves illegal State aid may affect the legal relations between the State and third parties. Whether that is the case, is a matter for national law to decide. However, attention should be drawn to point 2.3.2. of the Notice where the Commission expresses some views on this issue. The Commission suggests inter alia that lenders—as a standard precaution—check if guarantees live up to the State aid rules.

guarantees may also come in other forms depending on their legal basis, the underlying transaction, their duration, etc.[114] For example, a guarantee may be *general* whereby the guarantee is granted to an undertaking as such and not to a specific transaction. Guarantees may also come in the form of *counter guarantees* provided to a first level guarantor. Normally, guarantees are limited in amount and/or time. However, guarantees may also be *unlimited*.[115] In principle a guarantee may come in a somewhat invisible form as e.g. side letters or oral commitments. This could be the case if no premium is being paid. It should of course be stressed that a guarantee normally originates from a formal contract or a letter of comfort.

Further on the Commission Notice on the application of articles 87 and 88 of the EC Treaty to State aid in the form of guarantees

Scope of application of the Commission Notice, terminology and the legal status of the Notice

The Notice applies to State guarantees in all sectors save otherwise provided in rules relating to guarantees in the sector concerned (the *lex specialis* principle). However, the Notice does not apply to export credit guarantees.[116]   **3 184**

The Notice applies not only to loan guarantees but also to any guarantee with a similar transfer of risk such as investments in equity provided the relevant risk profile (including the possible lack of collateralisation) is taken into account. Therefore, when the Notice refers to "the borrower" that should be understood as the principal beneficiary of the guarantee and references in the Notice to "the lender" should be understood as the body whose risk is diminished by the guarantee. Within its scope of application the Notice defines, on the one hand, "guarantee scheme" as any tool on the basis of which, without further implementing measures being required, guarantees can be provided to undertakings respecting certain conditions of duration, amount, underlying transaction, type or size of undertakings (such as SMEs), and, on the other hand, "individual guarantee" as any guarantee provided to an undertaking and not awarded on the basis of a guarantee scheme.

A Commission Notice is a non-binding text as opposed to a binding legislative text cf. art.249 EC, see further Ch.6 in this book. The Notice should especially be seen in connection with the obligation of the Member States to notify to the Commission State aid measures according to art.88(3) EC. This obligation becomes effective if there is any doubt as to whether a planned individual

---

[114] The Commission lists in point 1.2. of the Notice a number of different types of guarantees.

[115] The Commission considers in principle that unlimited guarantees are incompatible with art.87, see point 4.1. of the Notice, and Ch.4, para.4–086 on unlimited guarantees in the railway sector.

[116] Regarding export credit, see s.4.6. and Dagmar Heinisch, "EU-rules on State aid do not allow for export aid", *in Competition Policy Newsletter*, No.2, Summer 2003, p.81.

guarantee or guarantee scheme may involve State aid within the meaning of art.87(1). Any potential doubt on the part of the Member State may be verified or rejected on the basis of the guidance provided by the Commission in its Notice. An arrangement deviating from the conditions ruling out the existence of State aid set in the Notice is not necessarily in violation of art.87. Such an arrangement may still be allowed under EC State aid rules but that conclusion must be reached by the Commission subject to notification and on completion of the notification procedures in art.88.

Conditions ruling out the existence of State aid

As mentioned above it follows from the case law of the ECJ that guarantees do not contain elements of State aid if the terms of the guarantee are acceptable to an investor operating in a market economy ("the market economy investor principle") under the given circumstances.[117] In s.3 of the Notice, the Commission lists a number of conditions which make that principle operational. Hence, if these conditions are fulfilled the market economy investor principle has been complied with and the guarantee does not involve State aid within the meaning of art.87 (1).

1. Individual guarantees in favour of large undertakings as well as SMEs

3–185   Individual guarantees which fulfil the following conditions are provided in accordance with the market economy investor principle and they are not subject to notification according to art.88(3) EC and may be implemented by the Member State concerned without involving the Commission, cf. point 3.2. of the Notice:

A. The borrower is not in financial difficulty.[118] A SME is within a period of three years from its establishment immune with respect to being classified as in difficulty.

B. The guarantee must be attached to specific financial transaction, limited in time and for a fixed maximum amount because it must be possible to measure the guarantee at the time when it is provided.

C. The guarantee must not—at any time—cover more than 80 per cent of the outstanding loan or other financial obligations.[119] Furthermore, any losses and recoveries must be distributed equally between the lender and

---

[117] Other variants of that principle are described in Ch.6 of this book.

[118] When determining if this is the case reference should be made to the Community guidelines on State aid for rescuing and restructuring firms in difficulty, see paras 3–089 to 3–117.

[119] The reason for the limit of 80% is that a coverage exceeding 80% might lead the lender to be less interested in assessing, securing and minimizing the risks associated with the transaction.

guarantor. It should be noted that the 80 per cent limit does not apply to situations where a State authority entrusts a company with the performance of *services of general economic interest* and grants a guarantee to finance that company provided the company in question does not perform other services.

D. A market-oriented price (premium) is paid for the guarantee.

All undertakings

As mentioned above, the State must be remunerated by an appropriate premium on the (counter-)guaranteed amount. Whether the premium is appropriate and hence constitutes a market-oriented price is subject to a concrete assessment. A number of considerations are relevant to that assessment, e.g. the amount and duration of the transaction, the security given by the borrower and other circumstances affecting the recovery rate assessment, the probability that the borrower fails to fulfil his obligations due to his financial situation, his line of business and future situation as well as other economic factors. This assessment should result in a classification of the borrower in terms of a risk rating.[120]   **3–186**

If the contemplated premium is in line with the premium similarly rated undertakings on the relevant market are being charged, a market-oriented price will be paid for the guarantee and no State aid is involved. However, if no corresponding premium benchmark can be found on the financial markets, the total financial costs, including the interest rate of the loan and the premium, should be compared to the interest rate of a *similar* non-guaranteed loan.

Certain SMEs

As indicated, the Notice—as an exception to the otherwise required concrete assessment—provides for a simpler evaluation of whether the premium charged for State guarantees in favour of SMEs is market-oriented. Hence, if the annual premium charged on the amount guaranteed by the State at least corresponds to the safe-harbour premiums shown in the table below, the existence of State aid is ruled out. Still, the undertaking concerned must be subjected to a risk assessment whereby its risk rating is found. It is on the basis of that risk rating the annual safe-harbour premium is found. The table below shows the rating classes of Standard & Poor's, fitch and Moody's. Other systems may be used, see point 3.3. of the Notice. The definition of SMEs is found in annex I to the General Block Exemption Regulation, see s.2.   **3–187**

---

[120] This rating may also be performed by an internationally recognized rating agency (which would be convincing) or the bank giving the loan in question.

Credit quality	Standard & Poor's	fitch	Moody's	Annual safe-harbour premium
Highest quality	AAA	AAA	Aaa	0.4%
Very strong payment capacity	AA + AA AA –	AA + AA AA –	Aa 1 Aa 2 Aa 3	0.4%
Strong payment capacity	A + A A –	A + A A –	A 1 A 2 A 3	0.55%
Adequate payment capacity	BBB + BBB BBB –	BBB + BBB BBB –	Baa 1 Baa 2 Baa 3	0.8%
Payment capacity is vulnerable to adverse conditions	BB + BB BB –	BB + BB BB –	Ba 1 Ba 2 Ba 3	2.0%
Payment capacity is likely to be impaired by adverse conditions	B + B B –	B + B B –	B 1 B 2 B 3	3.8% 6.3%
Payment capacity is dependent upon sustained favourable conditions	CCC + CCC CCC – CC	CCC + CCC CCC – CC C	Caa 1 Caa 2 Caa 3	No safe-harbour annual premium can be provided
In or near default	SD D	DDD DD D	Ca C	No safe-harbour annual premium can be provided

3–188 *Example:* If a bank gives a SME a rating corresponding to BB –/Ba 3, the matching premium is 2.0 per cent. This means that the SME must be charged a premium of (at least) 2.0 per cent on the amount effectively guaranteed (or counter guaranteed) at the beginning of each year. However, a single upfront guarantee premium is also an option in case the premium is at least equal to the present value of the future guarantee premium, see point 3.3. of the Notice.

Not all SMEs may benefit from the simplified method. This is the case with respect to SMEs which get a credit rating to which no safe-harbour annual premium can be provided, cf. the table above. They must be dealt with concretely, cf. D. above. The safe-harbour premium for SMEs with no credit history or a rating based on a balance sheet approach is set at 3.8 per cent.

The flow chart below illustrates the different steps when determining if a market-oriented price is charged on individual State guarantees:

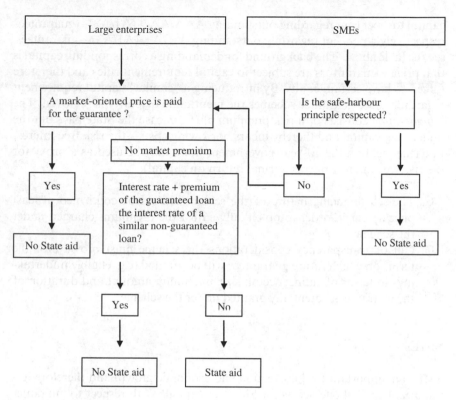

2. Guarantee schemes

All undertakings

A guarantee scheme (see definition above) will not be contrary to art.87 (1)   **3–189**
if the following conditions all are fulfilled, cf. point 3.4. of the Notice:

A. The conditions A–C. regarding individual guarantees must be fulfilled,
    cf. above para.3–185.
B. The premiums charged for guarantees under the scheme should be in line
    with market prices (premiums). This presupposes that guarantees issued
    under the scheme are subjected to a realistic risk assessment, so that premi-
    ums paid by beneficiaries make—in all probability—the scheme *self-financ-
    ing*. Regarding that risk assessment, see conditions D. above. The premiums
    should consequently cover: (1) the risks associated with guarantees issued
    under the scheme, (2) the administrative costs incurred by running the
    scheme, and (3) a yearly remuneration of an adequate capital.

The Commission considers that an *adequate capital* corresponds to 8 per cent
of the outstanding guarantees with the possibility to reduce the corresponding

capital to 2 per cent regarding outstanding AAA/AA—(A1/A3)—guarantees respectively 4 per cent regarding outstanding A +/A – (A1/A3)—guarantees, see the table above. The background for demanding a corresponding capital is that private guarantors are subject to capital requirement rules and therefore forced to have certain equity. By introducing a "similar" capital requirement regarding State guarantee schemes the mentioned disparity is removed. The *remuneration* consists of a risk premium plus—in case the State pays out the underlying capital and thereby incurs borrowing costs—the risk free interest rate (the yield on the 10-year government bond may be used as a proxy for the risk free interest rate as normal return on capital).

C. The self-financing nature of the scheme should be confirmed at least once a year in order to potentially adjust the premiums charged under the scheme.

D. Out of transparency considerations the scheme must provide for the terms on which future guarantees will be granted (e.g. eligible undertakings in terms of rating, sector, size, maximum amount and duration of the guarantees potentially granted under the scheme).

SMEs

3–190   SMEs are important for job creation and economic growth and therefore it is important to facilitate access for SMEs to capital. With respect to guarantee schemes for SMEs the Notice opens up for two options with attached conditions. The fulfilment of these conditions will rule out the existence of State aid.

i. The use of safe-harbour premiums as defined for individual guarantees to SMEs (option 1).

The conditions explained above under para.3–187 regarding SMEs apply equally and the scheme in question lives up to the transparency requirements explained in s.D. above at para.3–185. If these conditions are met, the scheme is deemed self-financing and hence not within the ambit of art.87(1) EC.

ii The valuation of a guarantee scheme as such by allowing the application of a single premium and avoiding the need for individual risk ratings of beneficiary SMEs (option 2).

3–191   If the Member State concerned does not find an individual risk assessment of each SME feasible (e.g. because the scheme covers many small loans), it is possible to apply a single premium to all guarantees under the scheme. This is conditional upon the scheme only being open to SMEs and contains a limit of €2.5 million as to the guaranteed amount per company. The use of a single premium is only possible if the scheme remains self-financing. The above stated conditions regarding exclusion of firms in difficulty, proper measurement of the guarantees and the limit on 80 per cent coverage of the outstanding loan apply equally, cf. A – C at para.3–185. Furthermore the conditions consisting of a yearly review in order to determine if the scheme is self-financing, that premiums must cover the normal risk associated with granting the guarantee, that the administrative costs and a yearly remuneration of an adequate capital and the application of the scheme must be transparent also apply equally, cf. B – D at para.3–185.

The flow chart below illustrates—in a summarised form—the approach of the Notice to guarantee schemes.

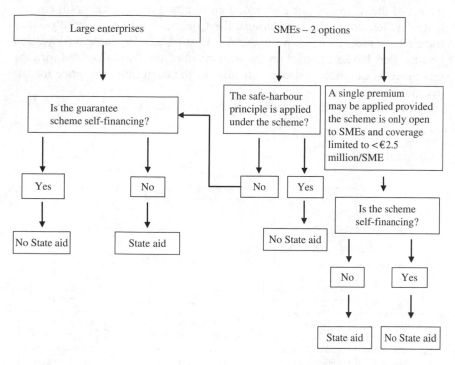

Guarantees containing State aid within the meaning of art.87(1)

The pivotal point of the assessment of guarantees under art.87(1) is the market economy investor principle which the Notice makes operational. In cases that the principle has been neglected, the State guarantee or guarantee scheme is deemed to contain an element of State aid which would be in violation of art.87(1). This is not the same as to say the guarantee or scheme is incompatible with the common market. It could—on the contrary—be possible that the aid element meets the conditions set out in, e.g. a block exemption regulation (in case no notification is required) or in Community guidelines or frameworks on the compatibility of certain aid measures with the common market (in case

3–192

notification is required). When determining if this is the case it is necessary to quantify the aid amount (because aid intensity is an important aspect to this end together with the objectives of the aid and status of the beneficiary). The Notice also provides guidance on how to calculate the State aid element in guarantees and guarantee schemes which do not meet the market economy investor test, cf. s.4 of the Notice. The underlying principle for this calculation is that the State aid element is equal to the difference between the appropriate market price of the guarantee issued individually or through a guarantee scheme and the actual price paid by the beneficiary. In this respect the resulting yearly cash grant equivalents should be discounted to their present value by means of the reference rate and added up resulting in the total grant equivalent.[121] When doing the calculations, the Commission will—naturally—take the circumstances listed above under A – D at para.3–185 into consideration because they have an impact on the assessment of the risk associated with the guarantee in question and consequently on the corresponding price for the guarantee.

The calculations are summarised in the charts below:

Individual guarantees:

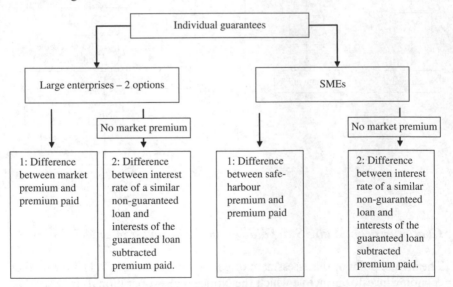

[121] Information on the reference rate is found at: *http://ec.europa.eu/comm/competition/state_aid/legislation/reference.html*

Guarantee schemes:

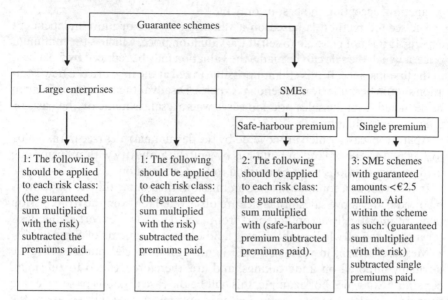

Closing remarks

The Commission requests the Member States to adjust their existing guarantee   **3–193**
measures to the stipulations of the Notice by January 1, 2010 regarding new
guarantees.

PRIVATISATION

The sale of land and buildings by public authorities

In 1997 the Commission issued a Communication on State aid elements in   **3–194**
sales of land and buildings by public authorities (OJ C 209, July 10, 1997, p.3).
The Communication did not deal with the public purchase of real property or
its letting or renting thereof.[122]
   The Communication refers to two methods for ensuring that an assumption
does not arise that a sale involves State aid to the purchaser.
   One method is for the authorities to carry out a sale following a

---

[122] For a case on the sale of land at a low price see Commission Decision 92/11/EEC of July
   31, 1991 concerning aid provided by the Derbyshire County Council to Toyota Motor
   Corporation, an undertaking producing motor vehicles (OJ L 6, 11.1.1992, p.36), concerning
   Toyota's purchase of a site for building a factory in England. The local authority was required
   to claim repayment of GBP 4.2 million from Toyota.

well-publicised, open and unconditional bidding procedure, comparable to an auction, accepting the best or only bid.[123]

3–195   The second method is based on a valuation by one or more independent experts. If it is not possible to sell at the valuation price, which is the minimum price at which the sale can be made, the valuation may be reduced by 5 per cent in the first instance. If it is still not possible to sell at the new price, a new valuation should be made by independent experts. Disadvantages for the buyer can be deducted from the sales price, in cases where a sale is made on the basis of independent valuation.

Apart from cases which are covered by the de minimis rules (see paras 3–001 to 3–006), the sale of land or buildings by a public authority without using one of these two methods must be notified to the Commission.

In the event of a complaint, the Commission will assume that no State aid is involved if the above sales principles are observed. However, the Commission may not uncritically accept a report from an independent expert as the basis for its decision of whether the sale of land contains elements of State aid.[124]

3–196   Measures which, in various forms, lighten the financial burdens that are normally imposed on undertakings, and are, therefore, related to subsidies, constitute State aid. For example, this will be the case if goods or services are provided on advantageous terms. This principle means that, in the case of the sale of land by a public authority to an undertaking, among other things it must be decided whether the buyer could have got the same sale price under normal market conditions.[125] If for this purpose the Commission reviews expert reports which are prepared *after* the transaction in question, the Commission must compare the price actually paid with the prices in various expert reports, and assess whether the price actually paid deviates from the prices in these reports to such an extent as to indicate that there is a basis for considering there to have been State aid.[126]

Privatisation and the sale of public assets

3–197   As with the sale of publicly owned land or buildings, State aid can be involved when a public body wishes to sell some other form of property or carry out a privatisation. If the privatisation takes place by means of the sale of shares on a stock exchange, then this is assumed to be on market terms and without aid. If, prior to the sale of the shares, there is a write-off or reduction of debt,

[123] The term "unconditional" means that in principle any party should be able to buy and use the property for their own purposes. However, it is possible to apply conditions to prevent speculative buying and with regard to compliance with environmental conditions etc. and general provisions relating to town planning etc. do not make the sale conditional. If a buyer has to fulfil special conditions in order to be allowed to buy, the conditions in question must apply to all potential buyers and be fulfilled by them.
[124] Case T-274/01, *Valmont v Commission*, [2004] E.C.R. II-3145.
[125] Case T-274/01, *Valmont v Commission*, [2004] E.C.R. II-3145.
[126] Case T-274/01, *Valmont v Commission*, [2004] E.C.R. II-3145.

this can occur without there being an assumption of aid, as long as the revenue from the sale exceeds the reduction in the debt.

If the privatisation docs not take place via the sale of shares on a stock exchange, but via the sale of a public undertaking as a whole or in parts to other undertakings, the following conditions must be fulfilled in order for it to be assumed, without further investigation, that the sale does not involve State aid:

- there must be use of a public tendering procedure which is open to all, transparent and not dependent on other commitments, such as the acquisition of assets other than those bid for or the continued operation of certain undertakings;
- the undertaking must be sold to the highest bidder; and
- sufficient time and sufficient information must be given to bidders so they can make a thorough evaluation before they bid.

With privatisation by the sale of shares on a stock exchange or by tendering, there is no requirement for notification to the Commission with a view to the examination of any State aid involvement. However, notification can be made for the sake of certainty.

In other cases than those just referred to there must be notification with a **3–198** view to determining whether State aid is involved. This applies in the following cases:

- when the sale is made after negotiation with a single potential buyer or a number of selected bidders;
- when the State, other public authorities or public bodies have made a prior write-off of debt;
- when there has been a prior restructuring of the debt in the form of shares or capital expansion; and
- when the sale is made on terms that are not usual for corresponding transactions between private parties.

Discrimination on the grounds of nationality is never allowed.

If a sale takes place on unusual terms, there must first be an evaluation by an independent expert. Privatisation in sensitive sectors (synthetic fibres, textiles, the motor vehicle industry, etc.) must always have prior notification to the Commission.

When a public body makes infrastructure available only for the benefit of one or some undertakings of a particular kind, this can constitute State aid.[127]

---

[127] Case C-225/91, *Matra v Commission*, [1993] E.C.R. I-3203.

CHAPTER 4

SECTORAL AID

Owing to the special circumstances in certain sectors, special provisions have **4–001** been adopted at EU level with regard to the provisions of aid to the sectors in question which may, for example be characterised by overcapacity.

The general view of the Commission is unfavourable towards sectoral aid, and it seeks to do away with sectoral aid schemes over time.

COAL AND STEEL

As with the EC Treaty, the European Coal and Steel Community (ECSC) **4–002** Treaty contained a prohibition of State aid in the coal and steel sectors. The prohibition was absolute, but it was not complied with in practice and the Commission has thus approved various exceptions to it over time. Until the expiry of the ECSC Treaty on July 23, 2002 certain forms of State aid were approved on the basis of special decisions of the Commission which were made under the authority of the ECSC Treaty. In the steel sector Commission Decision No.2496/96/ECSC of December 18, 1996 establishing Community rules for State aid to the steel industry (OJ L 338, December 28, 1996 p.42) applied. In the coal sector Commission Decision No.3632/93/ECSC of December 28, 1993 establishing Community rules for State aid to the coal industry (OJ L 329, December 30, 1993, p.12) applied, together with Commission Decision No.341/94/ECSC of February 8, 1994 implementing Decision No.3632/93/ECSC establishing Community rules for State aid to the coal industry (OJ L 49, February 19, 1994, p.1).

As stated, the ECSC Treaty expired on July 23, 2002, in accordance with its art.97. In connection with this the Commission adopted a Communication concerning certain aspects of the treatment of competition cases resulting from the expiry of the ECSC Treaty (OJ C 152, June 26, 2002, p.5). According to this, as from July 24, 2002 the sectors previously covered by the ECSC Treaty and the procedural rules and other secondary legislation derived from the ECSC Treaty are subject to the rules of the EC Treaty as well as the procedural rules and other secondary legislation derived from the EC Treaty. In relation to procedural rules, the coal and steel sectors are subject to Regulation (EC) No.659/1999, which is discussed in Ch.2. However, it should be noted that Regulation (EC) No.659/1999 can be supplemented by other legislation, as is the case for example with art.9 in Council Regulation (EC) No 1407/2002 of July 23, 2002 on State aid to the coal industry (OJ L 205, August 2, 2002, p.1). The substantive rules for the coal and steel sectors are discussed below.

Steel

4–003 The General Block Exemption, the GBER, concerning forms of aid that need not be notified to the Commission applies also in the steel sector with the exception of regional aid favouring activities in this sector, see Paras 3–007 to 3–027. The steel sector is defined in annex B of the Multisectoral framework on regional aid for large investment projects (OJ C 70, March 19, 2002, p.8), with reference to the combined nomenclature code.

In the Commission's communication concerning certain aspects of the treatment of competition cases resulting from the expiry of the ECSC Treaty, para.2.3 gives a brief summary of the criteria for the assessment of compatibility of State aid with the common market. The communication referred to the rules for the steel sector then in force in block exemption regulations, guidelines and framework provisions, etc. Some of these have since been amended, so that the communication has to some extent become obsolete. However, the principle in the communication still applies, namely that the steel sector is dealt with individually in the applicable guidelines, frameworks etc., cf. Ch.3.

4–004 The Communication from the Commission on rescue and restructuring aid and closure aid for the steel sector (OJ C 70, March 19, 2002 p.21) states that rescue aid and restructuring aid for firms in difficulty in the steel sector are not compatible with the common market.[1] Nor can investment aid be given in accordance with the rules in the guidelines for regional aid. On the other hand, aid can be given for certain structural adjustments in the steel industry. The reason for this is that there is overcapacity in the steel industry which leads to lack of effectiveness. Thus, the forms of aid which can be given to the steel industry must contribute to creating a healthier steel industry.

According to the communication, by virtue of art.87(3)(c), aid can be given which leads to the following forms of reduction of capacity in the steel industry:

1. Aid to cover payments payable by steel firms to workers made redundant or accepting early retirement provided that:

---

[1] On the rules for the steel industry in the new (and future) Member States, see Max Lienemeyer, "State aid for restructuring the steel industry in the new Member States", in *Competition Policy Newsletter*, No.1, Spring 2005 p.94; and Ewa Szymanska, "Aid in favour of Trinecké Zelezárny, a.s. a steel producer in the Czech Republic", in *Competition Policy Newsletter,* No.1, Spring 2005 p.105.

- the payments actually arise from the partial or total closure of steel plants (aid must not have been given for closure),
- the payments do not exceed those customarily granted under the rules in force in the Member States.

The aid given may not exceed 50 per cent of these payments.

2. The permanent cessation of production of steel products by steel under-   **4–005** takings can be aided, provided that the amount of the aid does not exceed the residual book value of the plants to be closed, and that:

- the undertakings became legal entities before January 1, 2002,
- they regularly produced steel products up to the date of notification of the aid concerned,
- they have not reorganised their production or plant structure since January 1, 2002,
- they close and scrap the installations used to manufacture steel products within six months of the cessation of production or approval of the aid by the Commission, and
- the closure of the plants has not already been taken into account for the approval of aid.

The communication contains provisions on aid for the closure of steel undertakings which fulfil the criteria in point 2 above, but which are part of a corporate group.

The communication lays down that all plans to grant aid for rescuing and restructuring firms in difficulty belonging to the steel industry and for closure aid to the sector must be notified individually.

The communication is in force until December 31, 2009.

Coal

At the outset it should be noted that the General Block Exemption, the   **4–006** GBER, concerning forms of aid that need not be notified to the Commission also applies to activities in the coal sector with respect to training aid, research, development and innovation aid and environmental aid, see paras 3–007 to 3–027.

The coal sector is covered by Council Regulation (EC) No.1407/2002 of July 23, 2002 on State aid to the coal industry (OJ L 205, August 2, 2002, p.1). According to the preamble to the Regulation, the European coal sector is characterised on the one hand by not being competitive against imported coal, and on the other hand it is an important element of energy security. According to the rules on State aid, an uncompetitive activity should not be kept going by means of State subsidies. Nevertheless, the Regulation allows certain forms of aid to the coal industry. This is because it is important to secure access to the European coal reserves. It is also acknowledged in the preamble that, in accordance with the proportionality principle, the provision of public means for coal production should be limited to what is strictly necessary to make an effective contribution to the objective of energy security. The aid given by Member States must thus be limited to covering investment costs or operating losses where mining is part of a plan for accessing coal reserves. Such State aid to help maintain access to coal reserves to ensure energy security should be earmarked for production units which can contribute to this objective on satisfactory economic conditions. The application of these principles will help the gradual reduction of aid to the coal industry.

The aim of the Regulation is thus to promote the restructuring of the coal industry. According to art.3(2), the aid which the Regulation makes it possible to grant should only cover costs in connection with coal for the production of electricity, the combined production of heat and electricity, the production of coke and the fuelling of blast furnaces in the steel industry. It is a condition that such use is within the EU. In addition, it is a condition that the aid should be covered by one of the aid categories listed in Ch.2 (arts 4–8) of the Regulation.

4–007   The first aid category is aid for the reduction of activities; see art.4. According to this provision, aid can be given if it is specifically intended to cover the situation where the operating costs exceed the sales price which the beneficiary can obtain given the conditions of the world market. However, the production units concerned had to form part of a closure plan whose deadline did not extend beyond December 31, 2007. The aid must be adjusted so as to cover the actual losses, and the aid must not lead to any distortion of competition; see art.4(1)(b)–(e). Aid could not be given after December 31, 2007 and was to also be progressively reduced; see art.8.

The second category of aid concerns aid for accessing coal reserves; see art.5. Such aid must be specifically intended for production units or groups of production units, for contributing to maintaining access to coal reserves. Article 5(2) and (3) allows the possibility, under certain circumstances, of granting aid for initial investment costs and for current production losses. These two kinds of aid may not be cumulated.

"Initial investment costs" is defined in art.2(d) of the Regulation as fixed capital costs directly related to infrastructure work or to the equipment necessary for the mining of coal resources in existing mines. Aid to cover these costs may be compatible with the common market if it satisfies the conditions in art.5(2). The aid must be given to existing production units, and the aid notified and actually paid must not exceed 30 per cent of the total costs of the relevant investment project. In addition, the production units must draw up an operating plan and a financing plan showing that the aid for the investment project in question will ensure the economic viability of the production units. Also, aid for initial investments must not lead to any distortion of competition; see the conditions in art.4(c), (d) and (e). Finally, art.5(2) contains a prohibition on the payment of initial investment aid after December 31, 2010. This applies regardless of whether the aid is in the form of a single payment or spread over several years.

"Current production losses" is defined in art.2(f) as the positive difference   **4–008** between the coal production cost and the delivered selling price freely agreed between the contracting parties in the light of the conditions prevailing on the world market. As stated, operating losses can be subject to aid under art.4 in the form of aid for a reduction of activities, if the production units concerned form part of a closure plan.

In contrast to this, art.5(3) concerns the situation where the production units or the group of production units in the same undertaking forms part of a plan for accessing coal reserves. In other words, they are part of a plan for the minimum production of indigenous coal intended to make it possible to ensure access to coal reserves. The aid must be given to the production units in the Member State concerned which offer the best economic prospects, and it may not exceed the difference between the expected production costs and the expected revenues for a coal production year. In addition to this, the conditions in art.4(c)–(e) must be observed so that the aid does not lead to distortion of competition. As with aid for the reduction of activities, operating aid must be progressively reduced so that the overall amount of aid to the coal industry is significantly reduced; see art.6(1).

Finally, under the Regulation aid can be given to cover exceptional costs;   **4–009** see art.7. Undertakings which carry out or have carried out activities in connection with coal production may be entitled to aid. Aid may be paid to cover the costs of rationalisation and restructuring of the coal industry that are not related to current production ("inherited liabilities"). The amounts paid may not exceed the exceptional costs. The categories of costs that are a consequence of the rationalisation and restructuring of the coal industry, and which may therefore be eligible for aid, are set out in the annex to the Regulation. These costs include the cost of paying social welfare benefits resulting from the pensioning-off of workers before they reach statutory retirement age and the costs of retraining workers so they can seek work outside the coal industry.

The amount of aid that can be given in accordance with arts 4, 5 or 7 must be calculated by taking account of the aid granted for the same purposes, in whatever form, by virtue of any other national resource; see art.8(1). Moreover, art.8(2) of the Regulation lays down a rule that all aid received by undertakings must be shown in the accounts as a separate item. All aid received by undertakings (including aid received other than under the regulation) must be shown as a separate item of revenue distinct from turnover. Costs other than those covered by the Regulation can be eligible for aid, as long as this is allowed in accordance with the State aid schemes for research and technological development, the environment and training; see art.3(1). Where an undertaking which receives aid under the Regulation is engaged in other economic activities as well as coal mining, the aid granted must be entered in separate accounts so that aid given under the Regulation can be clearly identified. The aid must be managed in such a way that there is no possibility of cross-subsidy, i.e. of the aid being transferred to the other activities.

SHIPBUILDING

4-010   The General Block Exemption, the GBER, that concerns forms of aid that need not be notified to the Commission also applies in the shipbuilding sector with the exception of regional aid favouring activities in this sector, see paras 3–007 to 3–027.

In the shipbuilding sector, over a number of years the Council of Ministers has issued directives on the basis of art.87(3)(e) of the EC Treaty, making it possible to approve State aid to the shipbuilding industry both in the form of operating aid and rescue aid.[2] More recently these have been replaced by Council Regulation (EC) No.1540/98 of June 29, 1998 establishing new rules on aid to shipbuilding (OJ L 202, July 18, 1998, p.1). The authority for the regulation was art.92(3)(e) (now art.87(3)(e)), art.94 (now 89) and art.113 (now 133) of the EC Treaty, as art.87(3)(e) was the only exception to art.87 which could be relevant to the kind of aid granted to shipbuilders, and which allowed for the levelling out of competitive differences between EU shipbuilders and shipbuilders in third countries.[3]

The Regulation expired on December 31, 2003. The shipbuilding industry is now regulated by the framework on State aid to shipbuilding (OJ C 317, December 30, 2003, p.11). The framework is in force from January 1, 2004 until December 31, 2008, as its duration was extended by the Commission Communication concerning the prolongation of the framework on State aid to shipbuilding (OJ C 260, October 28, 2006, p.7). According to this communication, Council Regulation (EC) No.1177/2002 of June 27, 2002 concerning a temporary defensive mechanism to shipbuilding expired on March 31, 2005. For this reason references to this regulation in the framework are no longer relevant. Thus, according to the communication, point 9 and point 12(e) of the framework are no longer applied by the Commission with effect from January 1, 2007.

4-011   The objectives of the framework are, as far as possible, to remove the differences between the rules applicable to the shipbuilding industry and to other industrial sectors. As stated in the introduction to this chapter, the Commission would like to see all sectors of industry regulated by the same horizontal rules. This is also made clear in the Commission's State Aid Action Plan, where it is stated that the Commission must assess whether there is still a need for sector-specific rules for the shipbuilding sector. Before the

---

[2] Case C-71/04, *Administración del Estado v Xunta de Galicia*, [2005] E.C.R. I-7419.

[3] For a case on aid for shipbuilding, see Case T-72/98, *Astilleros Zamacona v Commission*, [2000] E.C.R. II-1683. See also Case T-266/94, *Skibsværftsforeningen v Commission*, [1996] E.C.R. II-1399.

Commission makes such an assessment, it wants more information about the application of the framework provisions for the specic circumstances which apply to the shipbuilding industry. This is also why the framework has been continued in force.

It is acknowledged in the framework that there are factors which are specific to the shipbuilding sector and which ought to be reflected in the Commission's policy for control of State aid in this area. These factors include overcapacity, low prices and trade distortions on the global market.

It is thus the aim of the framework to encourage greater efficiency and competitiveness of Community shipyards, in particular through the promotion of innovation, by facilitating the reduction of economically non-viable capacity, and by respecting applicable international obligations in the field of export credits and development aid.[4]

According to para.11 of the framework, "aid to shipbuilding" should **4–012** include aid to any shipyard, related entity, shipowner and third party which is granted, whether directly or indirectly, for building, repair or conversion of ships. What seems to be decisive for the application of the framework is whether there is direct or indirect State aid for building, repair or conversion of ships. It is stated in para.8 that aid to shipbuilding, etc. will only be considered compatible with the common market if it complies with the provisions of the framework.

Accordingly, in principle under the framework aid can be given to shipbuilding in accordance with arts 87 and 88 of the EC Treaty and the laws and provisions issued in accordance therewith, including the horizontal measures discussed in Ch.3.

However, there are a number of exceptions to this starting position which are based on the special factors which apply in the shipbuilding sector; see above.

For a start, para.15 of the framework contains special rules on aid for inno- **4–013** vation.[5] Accordingly, aid granted for innovation in existing shipyards may be deemed compatible with the common market up to a maximum aid intensity of 20 per cent gross. This is on condition that the aid relates to the industrial application of innovative products and processes, i.e. technologically new or substantially improved products and processes compared to the current state of the art in this industry in the Community, which carry a risk of technological or industrial failure. Furthermore, in principle the aid is limited to covering expenditure on investment, design, engineering and testing activities directly and exclusively related to the innovative part of the project. However, the framework exceptionally allows aid for additional production costs. This will only be allowed for costs that are strictly necessary to validate the technological innovation and if the additional costs are limited to the minimum necessary.

---

[4] Sabine Crome and Charlotte Dupuis, "Regional investment aid to the shipbuilding industry: How to deal with capacity increases?—Experience with the Volkswerft Stralsund and Rolandwerft cases", in *Competition Policy Newsletter,* No.1, Spring 2007 p.109.

[5] See the discussion of this by Jörg Köhlis in *Competition Policy Newsletter* No.2, 2005 p.73 .

The customary costs for the whole or partial closing down of a shipyard can be eligible for aid in accordance with paras 17 and 18 of the framework. An undertaking that has received rescue or restructuring aid in the past 10 years will only receive partial closure aid under the most extraordinary and unforeseeable circumstances. It is a condition for the grant of aid for closure that there must be genuine and irreversible capacity reduction. In order to ensure the irreversible nature of aided closures, para.21 requires the Member State concerned to ensure that the closed shipbuilding facilities remain closed for at least 10 years.

Employment aid can be given within the scope of the framework, as long as the substantive rules in the General Block Exemption Regulation are complied with, see paras 3–007 to 3–027.

4–014   Finally, para.26 of the framework contains rules on regional aid for shipbuilding etc. It is a requirement that the aid must be granted for investment in upgrading or modernising existing yards, with the aim of improving the productivity of existing installations. The aid must not be linked to financial restructuring of the yard concerned, and may only be used to support eligible expenditure as defined in the applicable Community guidelines on regional aid. The aid intensity may not exceed 22.5 per cent in the regions referred to in art.87(3)(a) and covered by the regional aid map. For the regions referred to in art.87(3)(c) the aid intensity may not exceed 12.5 per cent or the applicable ceiling for regional aid, whichever is lower.

The aid ceilings stated in the framework apply, regardless of whether the aid in question is financed wholly or in part from State resources or from Community resources. Furthermore, aid which is authorised under the framework may not be combined with other forms of State aid if this would lead to higher aid intensity higher than that laid down in the framework; see para.29. If aid is granted for different purposes involving the same eligible costs, the most favourable aid ceiling will apply; see para.30.

If a Member State plans to grant new aid to shipbuilding etc., the plan must be notified to the Commission. However, the Member State need not notify the Commission if the plan fulfils the conditions of the General Block Exemption, see paras 3–007 to 3–027.

SYNTHETIC FIBRE (TEXTILES) AND MOTOR VEHICLES

4–015   In the area of State aid, the synthetic fibre industry has always been treated as a special sector with its own special rules. The same was the case with the motor vehicle industry. These sectors were covered by the Commission's Communication on the Multisectoral framework on regional aid for large investment projects (OJ C 70, March 19, 2002, p.8) so questions about the compatibility of State aid for the synthetic fibre industry and the motor vehicle industry were solved by applying the Multisectoral framework.

The rules applicable to the synthetic fibre industry and the motor vehicle industry are in part 5 of the Multisectoral framework on investment projects in sectors with structural problems other than steel. This part has been amended by Commission Communication on the modification of the Multisectoral framework on regional aid for large investment projects (2002) with regard to the establishment of a list of sectors facing structural problems and on a proposal of appropriate measures pursuant to art.88(1) of the EC Treaty, concerning the motor vehicle sector and the synthetic fibres sector (OJ C 263, November 1, 2003, p.3). Following this amendment, according to para.31 of the framework, sectors where serious structural problems prevail may be specified in a list of sectors to be annexed to the framework. This list had to be published before March 31, 2006. For the period January 1, 2004 to December 31, 2006, para.42 laid down some rules for aid to the synthetic fibre industry and the motor vehicle industry. However, the multisectoral framework does not apply to aid which is granted or notified after December 31, 2006. The provisions of the framework are now integrated in the Guidelines on national regional aid for 2007–2013 (OJ C 54, March 4, 2006, p.13). According to fn.59 in these guidelines, the Commission decided not to proceed with the establishment of this list. Thereafter there are no special rules for the motor vehicle industry, and according to para.8 of the guidelines, no regional investment aid may be granted in the synthetic fibres sector as defined in annex II to the guidelines.

The General Block Exemption, the GBER, concerning forms of aid that need not be notified to the Commission applies to synthetic fibres sector with the exception of regional aid favouring activities in this sector, see paras 3–007 to 3–027.

AIR TRANSPORT

With the EU's increasing liberalisation of the air transport sector, in a number   **4–016** of cases the Member States have found it necessary to use various forms of State aid for restructuring their national airlines.

Guidelines for the air transport sector

Among other things in the light of increasing aid to airlines, in 1994 the   **4–017** Commission adopted a set of guidelines for aid in this area.[6]

In principle, operating aid is not compatible with the EC Treaty and it will not normally be approved on the basis of the exceptions in art.87(3). However, there are various possibilities for having aid approved in the air transport sector. This applies in particular to aid for airlines for restructuring and aid of a very modest extent. Aid for airlines cannot be justified

---

[6] OJ 1994 C350, 10.12.1994, p.5.

merely by reference to the dumping prices of airlines from outside the EEA.

Among other things the guidelines state that the Commission will examine the capital investments, loans and guarantees from the point of view of the market economy investor principle, to assess whether there is State aid; on this principle see paras 6–004 to 6–010.

4–018   If after such an examination it appears that there has been recapitalisation under circumstances which would not have been accepted by a private investor, the Commission will conclude that there is State aid, and it will then examine whether the State aid can benefit from one of the exceptions from the prohibition of State aid in art.87(1). It is possible that one of the exceptions in art.87(3) may apply, namely if subpara.(a) or (c) is relevant. Subparagraph (a) allows State aid for areas where the standard of living is abnormally low (for example for the building of airport facilities in a remote region). Subparagraph (c) allows aid with a view to promoting the development of certain economic activities (for example in the form of restructuring aid).

If aid is to be granted for restructuring under subpara.(c) which, according to the guidelines, can only be approved under very strict conditions, a restructuring plan must be presented to the Commission which must be comprehensive and viable. Restructuring aid must be temporary and it must be expected to re-establish the undertaking within a reasonably short period. The aim of the aid must not be to increase the airline's capacity or services (and with regard to aircraft and airports, the restructuring plan may not lead to an increase above the general level of growth in the area.)[7]

There must be reasonable proportionality between the aims and means of the plan, the government of the Member State in question may only intervene in the management of the company in its capacity as owner or co-owner, and the company must be managed on commercial principles.

4–019   Restructuring aid may not adversely affect competing airlines (see the provisions in the guidelines on capacity referred to above), and during the restructuring period the beneficiary may not acquire shares in other airlines.

In principle, aid for retraining and for retirement before the normal pensionable age will be favourably regarded by the Commission as part of a restructuring plan.

As an overriding rule, restructuring aid may only be given once, and when it is given it must be intended to avoid the need for further aid. The Commission does seem to be willing, in exceptional circumstances, to accept operating aid as part of a restructuring programme, but only in a sector which is characterised by rapid growth.[8]

4–020   Apart from aid given in connection with a restructuring plan, according

---

[7] Case T-296/97, *Alitalia and Another v Commission*, [2000] E.C.R. II-3871, and the subsequent Commission Decision 2001/723/EC: of July 18, 2001 concerning the recapitalisation of the company Alitalia (OJ L 271, 12.10.2001, p.28) illustrate the application of the market economy investor principle and the rules on restructuring in the air transport sector.

[8] See Bellamy & Child, *Common Market Law of Competition*, 5th ed. p.1132.

to the guidelines the Commission can approve aid which is given in connection with unforeseeable circumstances which cannot be ascribed to the
undertaking,[9] or in the form of de minimis aid which is referred to below.

In its examination of a restructuring plan, the Commission will look closely
at the sales prospects on the relevant routes, at rationalising, effectiveness and
productivity, as well as any reduction of activities (e.g. cutting out unprofitable
routes), expected returns on capital etc.

The guidelines also include the possibility of approval of de minimis aid for
up to €1 million over three years, and such aid can be approved by an acceler-
ated process within 20 working days.

With regard to capital investments and guarantees by public bodies, refer-   **4–021**
ence is made to in the guidelines to the general rules, and especially to the
Transparency Directive, which also applies to the transport sector; this is
discussed in paras 2–066 and 2–067.

According to the guidelines, compensation can be given, under more
detailed rules, to airlines which undertake certain public service obligations,
such as flying to remote areas where there is not a commercial basis for flying;
see Council Regulation (EEC) No.2408/92 of July 23, 1992 on access for
Community air carriers to intra-Community air routes (OJ L 240, August 24,
1992, p.8), especially art.4. There are special provisions in the guidelines on
the right of Member States to license certain routes to be flown by an airline
for up to three years. In such cases a tendering procedure must be used to
select the airline which is to have the exclusive right; see Regulation (EEC)
No.2408/92.

According to the guidelines, aid of a social nature for consumers (e.g. chil-
dren, handicapped persons, low income groups) as well as, depending on the
circumstance, island inhabitants will be accepted by the Commission, as long
as there is no discrimination between airlines with regard to the possibility of
providing such services.

The guidelines also contain rules on the privatisation of airlines, which   **4–022**
broadly follow the provisions on open tendering and independent valuation
referred to in paras 3–194–3–189 on the sale of shares, land, buildings, etc. by
a public body.

According to the guidelines, the Commission will monitor any favouring
of one or more airlines by airports (e.g. with regard to tax-free sales, slots—
arrival and departure times, and ground handling, etc. which are now the
subject of separate EU regulation).

The guidelines cover the whole of the EEA.

---

[9] See the special circumstances surrounding the terror attack on the World Trade Centre in New
    York on September 11, 2001, in connection with which the Commission approved aid to the
    sector.

Community guidelines on financing of airports and start-up aid to airlines departing from regional airports

4-023   Since 1994 the air transport sector has undergone significant changes. There has been a restructuring of the sector, with increased liberalisation. New airlines have been set up, with a European dimension, offering favourable prices on the basis of a low cost structure. Some airports have been very active in attracting new air routes.

The Commission's 1994 guidelines for the air transport sector which have been dealt with above do not cover all aspects of the financing of airports and start-up aid for new routes.

In order to make good for this, in 2005 the Commission issued Community guidelines on financing of airports and start-up aid to airlines departing from regional airports (OJ C 312, December 9, 2005, p.1). These guidelines entered into force on December 9, 2005. As for the existing schemes for State aid which is covered by the new guidelines, Member States were required to bring such schemes into line with the new guidelines by June 1, 2007.

These new guidelines do not replace the 1994 guidelines which are therefore still in force, but they lay down supplementary rules with a view to determining how the competition rules should be applied to the different forms of financing of airports and start-up aid to airlines which operate from regional airports. Part 3.1 of the guidelines state that the Commission will examine the financing of airports and State aid for starting up air routes in the light of Community rules and procedures on State aid in art.86(2) or art.87(3)(a), (b) or (c) of the Treaty, noting that the compatibility of regional aid with art.87(3) (a) and (c) is dealt with under separate rules. If none of these rules is applicable, the Commission will assess the aid for financing airports and start-up aid to airlines in accordance with art.87(3)(c), using the principles expressed in the new guidelines and below.

Financing of airports

4-024   The financing of airports and any State aid given in connection with this is dealt with in part 4 of the guidelines. According to this, airport activities can be divided into four categories; see para.53 of the guidelines and below.

The first category is the construction of airport infrastructure and equipment (runways, terminals, aprons, control towers) or facilities that directly support them (fire-fighting facilities, security or safety equipment). The second category concerns the operation of the infrastructure, comprising the maintenance and management of airport infrastructure. The third category covers the provision of airport services ancillary to air transport, such as ground handling services and the use of related infrastructure, fire-fighting services, emergency services, security services, etc. The fourth category consists of the commercial activities not directly linked to the airport's core (transport) activities. This includes the construction, financing, use and renting of land and buildings, not only for offices and storage but also for the hotels and industrial enterprises located within the airport, as well as shops, restaurants and car parks. These non-transport activities are not covered by the guidelines, but any public financing of them will be assessed on the basis of the relevant sectoral and general rules. Also, the guidelines do not apply to activities which are the responsibility of the Member State in its role and under its powers as a public authority. These types of activities include safety, air traffic control, police, and customs and immigration. Such activities are not commercial activities within the meaning of the State aid rules; see paras 30–33 and 54 of the guidelines.

Financing of airport infrastructure

Aid for the financing of airport infrastructure (the first category of activities) is dealt with in part 4.1 of the guidelines. According to this, an airport operator carries on an economic activity (an economic activity consisting in offering goods and services on a given market).[10] Paragraph 57 of the guidelines states that an airport operator should finance the costs of using or building the infrastructure it manages from its own resources. Thus, if the airport infrastructure is made available to an operator by a Member State other than in accordance with the market economy investor principle,[11] or if the infrastructure is financed by means of public aid, this can give the airport operator an economic advantage to the detriment of its competitors. This must therefore be notified to the Commission; see para.57 of the guidelines. According to be the guidelines public aid for the financing of airport infrastructure can take a number of forms, and such measures should be notified to the Commission if they do not comply with the market economy investor principle; see paras 58–61. It is also clear from the guidelines that even if it is shown that a particular measure is in the nature of State aid, it is still possible for the Commission to declare the aid compatible with the common market on the basis of art.87(3)(a), (b) or (c) of the Treaty, or art.86(2) and any implementation measures thereto. Among other things, the Commission will examine whether the construction and operation of the infrastructure meets a clearly defined objective of general interest (e.g. regional development), whether the infrastructure is necessary and proportional to the stated objective, whether the infrastructure has satisfactory medium-term prospects for use, in particular as regards the use of existing infrastructure, whether all potential users of the infrastructure have access to it in an equal and non-discriminatory manner, and whether the development of trade is not affected to an extent contrary to the Community interest; see para.61.

4–025

---

[10] Case C-35/96, *Commission v Italy*, [1998] E.C.R. I-3851.
[11] The principle of a private investor in a market economy, which is dealt with in paras 42-52 of the guidelines.

The operation of airport infrastructure

4–026   The second category of activities concerns aid for the operation of airport infrastructure. The Commission's view is that, in principle, airport operators must cover the normal costs for managing and maintaining airport infrastructure from their own resources; see para.62. Otherwise, any public financing of these services would mean that the airport operator would be relieved of the expenses which it would normally have in carrying out its current operations. According to para.63 of the guidelines and the judgment in the *Altmark* case[12] financing of the kind referred to does not constitute State aid within the meaning of the Treaty if it is compensation for carrying out some obligation in the general interest which is imposed on the airport management under the conditions laid down in the *Altmark* case, and if this is the case, the compensation is not required to be notified to the Commission. Such compensation will not constitute State aid if:

1. the recipient undertaking does actually have clearly defined public service obligations to discharge;
2. the criteria for calculating the compensation is established in advance in an objective and transparent manner;
3. the compensation does not exceed what is necessary to cover all or part of the costs incurred in the discharge of public service obligations, taking into account the relevant receipts and a reasonable profit for discharging those obligations; and
4. except where the undertaking which is to discharge public service obligations is chosen by a public procurement procedure, the level of compensation needed must be determined on the basis of an analysis of the costs which a typical undertaking, well run and adequately provided with means of transport so as to be able to meet the necessary public service requirements, would have incurred in discharging those obligations, taking into account the relevant receipts and a reasonable profit for discharging the obligations.

In other cases operating subsidies will constitute State aid including operating aid (i.e. including aid aimed at reducing an undertaking's current costs). In principle, this kind of aid is covered by the prohibition in art.87(1) of the Treaty, and can only be considered compatible with the common market on the basis of art.87(3)(a) or (c) or art.86(2) (on compensation for the provision of services in the general economic interest); see para.63.

4–027   In principle, all forms of compensation to airports for the provision of services in the general interest must be notified to the Commission. However, according to paras 40–41 and 64, the Commission has decided exceptionally to allow exemptions from the obligation to give prior notification and to

---

[12] (Case C-280/00, *Altmark Trans v Nahverkehrsgesellschaft Altmark*, [2003] E.C.R. I-7747)

regard compensation for public service obligations which constitutes State aid to be compatible with the common market, provided that the provisions in Commission Decision of July 13, 2005 on the application of art.86 of the Treaty to State aid granted in the form of public service compensation to certain undertakings entrusted with management of services in the general economic interest are complied with. This exemption only applies in cases where the aid is given to small regional airports ("Category D" airports). These are airports with annual passenger volumes of less than 1 million; see para.15.

Aid given to larger airports (see para.64) must be notified and assessed according to art.86(2) of the Treaty if compensation is paid for the performance of public service obligations. To this end, the Commission will verify that the airport really has been entrusted with the operation of a service of general interest and that the compensation does not exceed what is necessary to cover the costs incurred in discharging the public service obligations, taking into account the relevant receipts and a reasonable profit; see paras 65–67.[13] It is up to the Member States to entrust the public service obligation to the airport in question by means of one or more official acts. It is left to the Member States to determine the form of these official acts, but regardless of their form, they must contain all the information necessary for identifying the specific costs arising in connection with the public service obligation, and namely:

- the precise nature of the public service obligation,
- the operators and the territory in question,
- the nature of any special or exclusive rights granted to the airport,
- the arrangements for calculating, monitoring and reviewing compensation, and
- the means of preventing and correcting any over- or under-compensation.

Aid for the provision of airport services

Ground handling services are a commercial activity open to competition over a threshold of two million passengers annually according to Council Directive 96/67/EC of October 15, 1996 on access to the ground handling market at Community airports (OJ L 272, October 25, 1996, p.36). Up to the threshold of two million passengers, airport operators may offset various sources of revenue and losses between purely commercial activities, such as its ground handling activities or car parking facilities. However, it is not possible to offset public resources granted to an airport authority or operator for a service of general economic interest. Above the threshold of two million

4–028

---

[13] In this connection it is stated in the guidelines that Commission Decision of July 13, 2005 on the application of art.86 of the Treaty to State aid granted in the form of public service compensation to certain undertakings entrusted with management of services in the general economic interest can be advisory for the application of paras 65-67.

passengers, ground handling services must be self-financing and must not be cross-subsidised by the airport's other commercial revenue,

Start-up aid

4–029 Start-up aid is dealt with in part 5 of the guidelines. The aim of start-up aid is to help smaller airports achieve passenger volumes which make the airport profitable. It is difficult for these airports to achieve passenger numbers which are sufficient to ensure profitable operations. The reason for this is that the airlines prefer well operated suitably located main airports, which their customers have easy access to, are used to using, and where the airlines have arrival and departure slots which they do not want to lose. In addition, recent airport and air transport policy has often led to the concentration of traffic around major cities. The airlines are thus unwilling to run the risk of opening up routes from unknown and untested airports. At the same time, there is a need to improve access to outlying regions, improve competitiveness and promote regional integration. One means for doing this is start-up aid, which can encourage airlines to set up new routes or increase the number of flights to and from regional airports. Start-up aid must be temporary and must make it possible to attract passenger numbers which enable airports to reach the level of profitability within a limited period.

According to the guidelines, aid can be given for the extra start-up costs connected with the launch of new routes or new departures which the air operator will not have to bear once it is up and running. Examples of such costs are the marketing and advertising costs incurred for publicising a new link. They may also include the installation costs incurred by the airline at a regional airport in order to launch the route, provided the airport falls within category C or D (i.e. it is a regional airport with annual passenger numbers of up 5 million; see para.15). However, normal operating costs, such as hire or depreciation of aircraft, fuel, crew salaries, airport charges or catering costs are not start-up costs in this context. The eligible costs must correspond to real costs under normal market conditions. If a Member State wishes to grant such start-up aid, it must notify the Commission, unless the Member State acts in accordance with the market economy investor principle; see para.77.

4–030 State aid can be approved by the Commission if the conditions in paras 79-81 of the guidelines are followed. Briefly, the main rule is that aid can only be given to airlines with a valid operating licence if they establish genuinely new routes or departures which contribute to an increase in the net number of passengers, and which in the long term will cover their costs without public financing and which connect an airport in Category C or D with another airport in the EU. As stated above, the idea behind start-up aid is that it should encourage the setting up of new routes. Conversely, it is not the idea of State aid to help keep unprofitable routes going. For this reason, before

State aid is granted, it must be shown that the route will remain viable for a significant period after aid is no longer paid. Furthermore, start-up aid, which is an incentive aid, must be associated with an actual increase in passenger numbers, for example so that the aid is reduced as the traffic increases. If it appears that the route will be profitable earlier than planned, or the goals in terms of passenger numbers are reached earlier than expected, then the aid must be terminated. This applies even if the three year period in which progressively decreasing aid is paid has not expired. During this three year period, in principle aid may not be paid which exceeds 50 per cent of the eligible costs, and over the whole period may not exceed an average of 30 per cent of the eligible costs. For routes to disadvantaged areas (i.e. the EU's outermost regions, thinly populated areas and regions covered by art.87(3)(a) of the Treaty) progressively decreasing aid can be paid for up to five years. The aid paid may not exceed 50 per cent of the eligible costs, and for the whole aid period it may not exceed an average of 40 per cent of the eligible costs. In the first three years the level of aid intensity may be held at 50 per cent if the aid is to be paid over the permitted five year period. The three-and five-year periods referred to in which start-up aid can be given can only be used to their full extent if these periods are significantly shorter than the periods for which airline companies have bound themselves to operate from the airport in question.

The guidelines also contain some procedural rules to the effect that a public **4–031** body which plans to grant start-up aid to an airline for a new route, must make its plans public with adequate publicity to enable all interested airlines to offer their services; in other words, there must be non-discriminatory allocation. There must also be an appeals procedure to ensure that there is no discrimination in the granting of aid.

Start-up aid may not be cumulated with other kinds of aid provided for the operation of a route, nor can start-up aid be given if access to a route is restricted to a single airline in accordance with art.4 of Council Regulation (EEC) No.2408/92. Furthermore, such aid may not be added together with other forms of aid for the financing of the same costs; this applies even if the aid is paid by another Member State.

MARITIME TRANSPORT

State aid for the maritime transport sector is regulated by Commission com- **4–032** munication—Community guidelines on State aid to maritime transport (OJ C 13, January 17, 2004, p.3). These guidelines replaced Community guidelines on State aid to maritime transport (OJ C 205, July 5, 1997, p.5).

The new guidelines, like the previous ones, lay down the criteria by which the Commission will assess and, depending on the circumstances, approve State aid in the maritime transport sector. The authority for approval is to be found in art.87(3)(c) and/or art.86(2) of the EC Treaty.

According to point 2.2 of the guidelines, they are intended to clarify what

State aid schemes may be introduced to support the Community maritime interests, with the aim of:

- improving a safe, efficient, secure and environmentally friendly maritime transport,
- encouraging the flagging or re-flagging to Member States' registers,
- contributing to the consolidation of the maritime cluster established in the Member States while maintaining an overall competitive fleet on world markets,
- maintaining and improving maritime know-how and protecting and promoting employment for European seafarers, and
- contributing to the promotion of new services in the field of short sea shipping following the White Paper on Community transport policy.

4–033 All new proposals for measures notified to the Commission must include a calendar indicating the expected quantified effects for each of the objectives referred to above for the six succeeding years; see Ch.12 of the guidelines.

The guidelines are applicable to maritime services concerned with the transport of goods and passengers by sea.[14] Specific parts of the guidelines also relate to towage and dredging. The guidelines do not cover aid to shipbuilding, which is covered by Council Regulation (EC) No.1540/98 or subsequent legislation. In its notification, the Commission recalls that State investment in infrastructure, which can also be relevant for maritime transport, will not normally constitute State aid if all operators concerned are given free and equal access to the infrastructure. The Commission also recalls that it will not constitute State aid if a public body invests in an undertaking on terms that would be acceptable to a private investor under normal market economy terms (the market economy investor principle).

In principle, only ships which are registered in the Member State concerned will be entitled to receive State aid. Only in exceptional circumstances will it be compatible with the guidelines to provide aid for ships which are registered in the registers referred to in point 3 of the annex to the guidelines, for example, the Dutch Antilles register, and then only if the ships are managed from the Community by a shipowner established in the Community, and if they comply with international standards and Community rules. The Member State in question must also show that the register concerned directly contributes to the aims referred to in point 2.2 of the guidelines, for example encouraging

---

[14] Maritime services are defined in Council Regulation (EEC) No.4055/86 of December 22, 1986 applying the principle of freedom to provide services to maritime transport between Member States and between Member States and third countries (OJ L 117, 5.5.1988, p.33), and Council Regulation (EEC) No.3577/92 of December 7, 1992 applying the principle of freedom to provide services to maritime transport within Member States (maritime cabotage) (OJ L 364, 12.12.1992, p.7).

the flagging or re-flagging to Member States' registers. Flag-neutral aid measures may also be approved in certain exceptional cases where a benefit to the Community is clearly demonstrated.

The guidelines cover eight areas where, depending on the circumstances and subject to certain conditions, the Commission will allow State aid to the maritime transport sector. These areas are discussed below.

Fiscal and social measures to improve competitiveness

In the guidelines in relation to the fiscal treatment of shipowning companies **4–034** it is stated that the tax climate in third countries is considerably milder than in the Member States. This means that shipowners have an incentive to flag out their vessels and even to consider corporate relocation where there is also an attractive infrastructure in the third country concerned. There are no effective international rules at present to curb such tax competition and few administrative, legal or technical barriers to moving a ship's registration from a Member State's register. It is the Commission's view that the best way forward, and the best way to protect the Community fleets, is to create conditions allowing fairer competition with flags of convenience.

In the guidelines the Commission recognises that many Member States have taken special measures to improve the fiscal climate for shipowning companies. For example, they have allowed accelerated depreciation on investment in ships or the right to reserve profits made on the sale of ships for a number of years on a tax-free basis, provided that these profits are reinvested in ships. These special tax relief measures for shipping and the system of "tonnage tax" are considered to be State aid.[15]

However, the Commission is of the view that in general these kinds of tax incentives can be allowed. This can safeguard high quality employment in the maritime sector in the Community and the maritime sector in the Member State in question can be stimulated in a competitive direction. A combination of fiscal incentives with other initiatives on training and enhancement of safety will facilitate the development of Community shipping in the global market.

The objective of State aid within the common maritime transport policy is **4–035** to promote the competitiveness of the Community fleets in the global shipping market. Consequently, tax relief schemes should be linked with an EU flag.

---

[15] A tonnage tax means that the shipowner pays an amount of tax linked directly to the tonnage operated. The tonnage tax will be payable irrespective of the shipowner's actual profits or losses. Tonnage tax is calculated by applying a notional profit rate to the tonnage and the national corporation tax is applied to the amount so determined. So far the notional profit rates used by the Member States have been homogeneous, but corporation tax rates may vary significantly across the Community. This means that the tonnage taxes to be paid for the same tonnage can vary widely in the different Member States. In order to keep the present equitable balance, the Commission will only approve schemes giving rise to a tax-burden for the same tonnage which is fairly in line with the schemes already approved.

However, even if this requirement is not satisfied, tax reliefs may nevertheless exceptionally be approved where they apply to the entire fleet operated by a shipowner established within a Member State's territory and liable to corporation tax there. In this case it must also be demonstrated that the strategic and commercial management of all the ships concerned is actually carried out from within the territory of the Member State, and that this activity contributes substantially to economic activity and employment within the Community. In addition, evidence must be given showing compliance with the relevant international and Community safety standards, including those relating to onboard working conditions. At the same time Member States must ensure that shipowners in receipt of State aid whose vessels fly non-EU flags commit themselves to increasing or at least maintaining the share of tonnage under the flag of one of the Member States. The tonnage of any subsidiary company is included in this.[16] The Community-tonnage share requirement does not apply to undertakings operating at least 60 per cent of their tonnage under a Community flag.

The Member States must notify the Commission where they allow the above exception, and every three years, with the help of the beneficiary undertakings, they must prepare a report showing that the conditions for allowing the exception have been fulfilled. Should beneficiary undertakings fail to provide such evidence, they will not be allowed to continue to benefit from the tax scheme; see point 3.1 and Ch.12 of the guidelines.

4–036   Shipowners based in the EU are a natural target for the above tax rules. However, according to the guidelines, ship management companies established in the Community may also qualify for advantageous tax schemes in accordance with the same rules, provided certain further conditions are fulfilled; see point 3.1 of the guidelines. Ship management companies are legal entities providing different kinds of services to shipowners, such as technical surveys, crew recruitment and training, crew management, and vessel operation.

It had previously been unclear whether towage and dredging are included under the heading of maritime transport. For example, there is the question of whether tugboats which are constructed so as to be able to work at sea but which seldom operate there are covered by an aid scheme for the maritime transport sector. The guidelines seek to clarify this. Thus, towage is covered by the guidelines only if more than 50 per cent of the towage activity carried out by a tug during a given year constitutes maritime transport. For the purposes of the guidelines, towage activities which are carried out in ports, or which consist of assisting vessels to berth do not constitute maritime transport. Dredging activities do not constitute maritime transport. However, dredgers can also transport extracted materials at sea. If these vessels transport the extracted materials at sea, and if these transport activities exceed than 50 per cent of their annual operational time, the tax arrangements can be applicable

---

[16] See the determining influence of the Seventh Council Directive 83/349/EEC of June 13, 1983 based on the art.54(3)(g) of the Treaty on consolidated accounts (OJ L 193, 18.7.1983, p.1).

to dredgers in respect of their transport activities. There is no derogation from the flag-linking requirement for dredgers.

Labour-related costs

According to point 3.2 of the guidelines, support measures for the maritime sector should aim primarily at reducing fiscal and other costs and burdens borne by Community shipowners and Community seafarers towards levels which are in line with world norms. On this basis it is permitted to reduce the rates of contributions for social insurance and income tax for Community seafarers employed on board ships registered in a Member State. These possibilities are also applicable to Community seafarers working on board seagoing, self-propelled tugs and dredgers, registered in a Member State, carrying out maritime transport at sea for at least 50 per cent of their operational time.   **4–037**

Maritime transport is also covered by the General Block Exemption Regulation and its provisions for employment aid: see Ch.3 of this book.

Crew relief

According to the guidelines, aid can be granted in the form of payment of the costs of repatriation of Community seafarers working on board ships entered in Member States' registers. The aid is subject to the ceiling which is discussed below.   **4–038**

Investment aid and regional aid

Investment aid is governed by Council Regulation (EC) No.1540/98 of June 29, 1998 establishing new rules on aid to shipbuilding (OJ L 202, July 18, 1998, p.1), or legislation which may replace it. Within the framework of the guidelines, aid may be permitted which provides incentives to upgrade Community-registered ships to standards which exceed the mandatory safety and environmental standards, thereby enhancing safety and environmental measures. Such aid must comply with the applicable Community provisions on shipbuilding.   **4–039**

In the context of regional aid schemes, the Commission will apply the general rules on regional aid on the basis of art.87(3)(a) and (c).

Training

Aid for the training of seafarers is covered by provisions in the General Block Exemption Regulation on training, paras 3–007 to 3–027. Training schemes   **4–040** which are supported by the State and are of a general nature are not considered to be State aid. However, if a scheme is regarded as including State aid it must be notified to the Commission. The guidelines refer to the example of schemes which involve training on board ship. Depending on the circumstances, the Commission takes a positive view of training on board ships, as long as the trainee is an extra member of the crew. Aid aimed at enhancing and updating Community officers' skills may be allowed as long as the schemes are designed so as to prevent the aid for training being directly or indirectly diverted into a subsidy for officers' wages. According to the guidelines, aid aimed at the professional retraining of high-sea fishermen who are willing to work as seafarers may also be allowed.

Restructuring aid

4–041   According to Ch.8 of the guidelines, the Commission will apply the Community guidelines on restructuring and rescuing firms in difficulty to the maritime transport sector. The reader is referred to the discussion of such aid in Ch.3 of this book.

Public service obligations and contracts

4–042   In accordance with art.4 of Council Regulation (EEC) No.3577/92 of December 7, 1992 applying the principle of freedom to provide services to maritime transport within Member States (maritime cabotage), Member States may enter into public service contracts with or impose public service obligations, as a condition for the provision of cabotage services, on shipping companies participating in regular services to, from or between islands. Such public service contracts or obligations must be entered into on a non-discriminatory basis.

When imposing public service obligations, Member States must limit such obligations to concern ports to be served, regularity, continuity, frequency, capacity to provide the service, rates to be charged and manning of the vessel. If compensation is given for public service obligations, it must be available to all Community shipowners.

Under the guidelines, the Commission accepts that if an international transport service is necessary to meet imperative public transport needs, public service obligations may be imposed or public service contracts may be entered into.

In Ch.9 of the guidelines the Commission notes that compensation for public service obligations or public service contracts must fulfil the conditions of the Treaty rules and procedures governing State aid, as interpreted by the Court of Justice. Refer to paras 4–141 to 4–151 for further discussion of compensation.

The duration of public service contracts should be reasonable and not over-long, normally about six years.

Aid to short sea shipping

Short sea shipping is dealt with in Ch.10 of the guidelines. There is no legal **4–043** definition of "short sea shipping", but as the term suggests, it concerns the transport of goods and passengers between harbours situated within the territories of the Member States. Such transport is an alternative to road transport and should be promoted for this reason among others. However, the establishment of near shipping connections can be expensive so that it is not an attractive alternative to other forms of transport. One way to overcome this obstacle and to promote short sea shipping can be by giving State aid to some extent.

For this reason State aid can be given to certain ship operators[17] for setting up short sea shipping connections for ships that sail under the flag of a Member State. Such aid must be notified to the Commission and must fulfil the following conditions:

- the aid must not be for more than three years and its purpose must be to finance a shipping service connecting ports situated in the territory of the Member States,
- the service must permit transport (primarily of cargo) by road to be carried out wholly or partly by sea, without diverting maritime transport in a way which is contrary to the common interest,
- the aid must be aimed at implementing a detailed project with a pre-established environmental impact, concerning a new route or the upgrading of services on an existing route, if necessary involving several shipowners, with no more than one project financed per line and with no renewal, extension or repetition of the project in question,
- the purpose of the aid must be to cover either up to 30 per cent of the operational costs of the service in question, or to finance the purchase of trans-shipment equipment to supply the planned service, up to a level of 10 per cent of such investment,
- the aid for a project must be granted on the basis of transparent criteria applied in a non-discriminatory way to shipowners established in the Community. The aid should normally be granted for a project selected by the authorities of the Member State through a tender procedure in compliance with applicable Community rules,
- the service which is the subject of the project must be commercially viable after the period in which it is eligible for public funding, and

---

[17] In other words, shipowners covered by art.1 of Council Regulation (EEC) No.4055/86 of December 22, 1986 applying the principle of freedom to provide services to maritime transport between Member States and between Member States and third countries.

- such aid must not be cumulated with compensation for public service obligations or contracts.

Ceiling

4–044 The exemption of seafarers from the payment of taxation and social charges, and a reduction of corporate taxation of shipping activities (the Commission will only allow arrangements which tax the same tonnage in a way which is reasonably in line with existing approved arrangements) is the maximum level of aid permitted.

Moreover, the Commission considers that the total amount of aid granted under Chs 3–6 of the guidelines should not exceed the total amount of taxes and social contributions collected from shipping activities and seafarers.[18]

The reader is also referred to the discussion in paras 6–016 to 6–018 of this book.

EXPORT AID

4–045 Export aid is referred to in the De minimis Regulation and in other block exemption regulations, but the regulations do not allow for giving export aid.

Export aid for trade within the EU is prohibited and is contrary to art.87(1) of the EC Treaty.[19]

In recent years the Commission has also examined aid for direct investments in third countries, because of possible effects on trade within the EU, and has regarded such aid as permissible for small and medium-sized enterprises if it is within the rules on aid to SMEs, but it requires individual notification for investments by large enterprises.[20] Thus, aid for investment in a ski-lift factory in China was prohibited by the Commission; see the Commission's decision of October 14, 1998. In general it is unlikely that the Commission will approve export aid to large enterprises.[21]

4–046 To the extent that aid for exports to countries outside the EU is at all compatible with arts 132 and 133 of the EC Treaty, as well as other international rules (WTO and OECD), such aid will be assessed in the light of the prohibition of State aid in art.87(1) of the Treaty. This is because it is possible that export aid for trade with countries outside the EU can indirectly affect trade within the EU (see among others the *Tubemeuse* case).[22]

---

[18] Chapters 3–6 deal with fiscal and social measures to improve competitiveness, crew relief, and investment aid and regional aid under art.87(3)(a) and (c).

[19] See, e.g. Dagmar Heinisch, "EU-rules on State aid do not allow for export aid", in *Competition Policy Newsletter,* No.2, Summer 2003, p.81.

[20] See Giorgio Perini, "No export aid to large firms outside the EU", in *Competition Policy Newsletter*, 2005, No.2, p.69.

[21] Perini, "No export aid to large firms outside the EU", in *Competition Policy Newsletter*, 2005, No.2, p.69.

[22] Case C-142/87, *Belgium v Commission*, [1990] E.C.R. I-959, para.35.

Over the years, the Commission has found the following forms of aid in relation to trade within the EU to be incompatible with the common market: price guarantee systems, preferential rediscount rates for exports (see Joined Cases 6 and 11/69, *Commission v France*, [1969] E.C.R. 523), tax advantages for establishing a business abroad, contributions for advertising abroad (see the Commission's XI and XII Annual Reports on Competition Policy, 1981 and 1982), aid for export credits and exchange rate guarantees, as well as the repayment of other than direct costs (see the Commission's XV Annual Report on Competition Policy, 1985).

On the other hand, the Commission has found the following forms of aid to be compatible with the common market: aid given for participating in trade fairs, and aid for research and consultancy with a view to introducing a new product to the market or to an existing market which is new market for an SME. These situations are incorporated in the secondary law regarding State aid.

EXPORT CREDIT INSURANCE AND STATE AID

The Commission has published a Communication on short-term export credit insurance and State aid; see OJ C 281, September 17, 1997, p.4. The purpose of the communication is to remove distortions due to State aid in the export-credit insurance business where there is competition between public or publicly supported export credit insurers and private export credit insurers. Commercial export credit insurance relates to the insurance of short-term export credit risks in trade within the Community and with OECD countries outside it; see the annex to the communication.   **4–047**

According to point 4.1 of the communication, State aid given to public or publicly supported export credit insurers which cover marketable risks may distort competition and is therefore ineligible for exemption under the State aid rules of the Treaty. This also means that the policies for export credit insurance of marketable risks can only be written by public or publicly supported export credit insurers if the factors discussed below which can distort competition are removed.

Public or publicly supported export credit insurers are defined in point 2.1 of the communication. According to this, the definition includes export credit insurance undertakings which, for the account of or with the guarantee of the State provide short-term export credit insurance. These undertakings can be government departments, State-owned or State-controlled companies or wholly privately-owned and controlled companies. Private export credit insurance undertakings are defined as undertakings which provide short-term export credit insurance that do not operate for the account of or with the guarantee of the State.

Factors which can distort competition in this area and which are covered by the communication include: State guarantees, differences in the requirements   **4–048** as to the reserves of insurance undertakings, relief or exemption from taxes normally payable (such as corporation taxes and taxes levied on insurance policies), and awards of aid or provisions of capital by the State.

"Marketable risks" are defined in point 2.5 of the communication. This definition was amended in 2001 and more recently in 2005.[23] Marketable risks are thus now defined as commercial and political risks for a period of up to two years in connection with debtors established in a country listed in the annex to the communication (EU/EEA and OECD countries). Regardless of this definition, and to the extent that there is no private insurance market in a Member State, the risks referred to are considered non-marketable if they are incurred by small and medium-sized enterprises with a total annual export turnover not exceeding €2 million; see point 2.5 following the 2005 amendment.[24] This means that public or publicly supported export credit insurers must as far as possible align their premiums for these types of risks with the premiums for other export credit insurers for a similar risk; see point 2.5 of the communication. This is a specific application of the general exemption in point 4.4 of the communication. According to this provision, there is a derogation from the principle that export credit insurance of marketable risks can only be written by public or publicly supported export credit insurers if the factors referred to above are eliminated. However, this presupposes that otherwise marketable export credit risks cannot be covered by a private export credit insurer, or by a public or publicly supported export credit insurer acting on its own account, because of lack of capacity in the market. In such a case, insurance cover can be provided by a public or publicly supported export credit insurer which insures non-marketable risks on the State's account or with a State guarantee, but the premium must as far as possible be at the same level as premiums required by private export credit insurance undertakings for risk of the same kind. If a Member State wishes to make use of this exemption, the Commission must be given a prior opportunity to assess whether the actually intended use of the exemption is compatible with the EC Treaty. This procedure also applies to named, specific exemptions relating to SMEs.

To a large extent medium and long term risks constitute non-marketable risks and in certain cases only States will undertake to insure such risks. The communication does not concern such risks.

---

[23] Communication of the Commission to Member States amending the communication pursuant to art.93(1) of the EC Treaty applying arts.92 and 93 [now arts 87 and 88] of the Treaty to short-term export-credit insurance (OJ C 217, 2.8.2001, p.2). Points 2.5, 2.6 and 4.5 as well as the annex to the 1997 Communication were amended, and the Communication was extended to January 1, 2005. In 2005 points 2.5, 2.6 and 4.5 were amended by Communication of the Commission to Member States amending the communication pursuant to art.93(1) of the EC Treaty applying arts 92 and 93 [now arts 87 and 88] of the Treaty to short-term export-credit insurance (OJ C 325, 22.12.2005, p.22).

[24] As for the definition of small and/or medium sized enterprises and the calculation of annual export turnover, see Commission Recommendation of May 6, 2003 concerning the definition of micro, small and medium-sized enterprises (notified under document number C(2003) 1422) (OJ L 124, 20.5.2003, p.36).

DEPRIVED URBAN AREAS

In 1997 the Commission issued Guidelines on State aid for undertakings in **4–049** deprived urban areas (OJ C 146, May 14, 1997, p.6). The guidelines expired on May 14, 2002 and the Commission decided not to extend or amend them, as they had not been used in the period 1997–2002. However, this does not mean that it is no longer possible to give State aid to deprived urban areas. Such aid can be regarded as being compatible with the common market under the existing State aid rules or, depending on the circumstances, on the basis of art.87(3)(c) of the Treaty. On this basis, and in order to retain a certain measure of transparency of the Commission's work in this area, on March 1, 2006 the Commission published a working document on the regeneration of deprived urban areas This working document gives an overview of the State aid rules that are relevant to the assessment of urban regeneration measures.[25]

THE ELECTRICITY SECTOR

On July 26, 2001, the Commission published a Communication relating to the **4–050** methodology for analysing State aid linked to stranded costs.[26] "Stranded costs" means the costs which, as a result of the liberalisation of the electricity market, electricity undertakings cannot recover.[27]

Directive 96/92/EC of the European Parliament and of the Council of December 19, 1996 concerning common rules for the internal market in electricity allows Member States to delay the implementation of some of its provisions during a transitional period. Some Member States have also wished to introduce State aid mechanisms on advantageous terms to allow their electricity companies to adjust to the new competitive situation.

The aim of the Commission's communication is to indicate how the Commission will apply the rules of the EC Treaty with regard to such State aid. In the communication the Commission states that State aid measures

---

[25] Commission staff working document, State aid control and regeneration of deprived urban areas, Vademecum is available at: *http://ec.europa.eu/comm/competition/state_aid/studies_reports/vademecum.pdf*. See also Wouter Pieké and Amir Ghoreishi, "State aid control and regeneration: rubber straitjacket or passepartout", in *Competition Policy Newsletter*, No.3, Autumn 2003, p.17.

[26] The Communication is referred to in the Commission's XXXI Annual Report on Competition Policy, 2001, paras 346-353, and is available at *http://ec.europa.eu/comm/competition/state_aid/legislation/stranded_costs_en.pdf*

[27] The principles for the liberalisation of the electricity market were laid down in Directive 96/92/EC of the European Parliament and of the Council of December 19, 1996 concerning common rules for the internal market in electricity (OJ L 27, 30.1.1997, p.20). On the Directive's arts 7(5), 16 and 24, see the ECJ's preliminary ruling in Case C-17/03, *Vereniging voor Energie, etc. v Directeur van de Dienst uitvoering en toezicht energie*, [2005] E.C.R. I-4983, where among other things it is stated that it is only permissible to allow an undertaking priority access to a portion of the capacity for the cross-border transmission of electricity if this is in compliance with the procedure set out in art.24 of the Directive.

which cannot be approved on the basis of art.87 of the EC Treaty may possibly be analysed in the light of art.86(2), which concerns undertakings entrusted with the operation of services of general economic interest, which may justify public compensation being paid.

4–051   The communication deals with aid which is intended to compensate for costs incurred in connection with obligations or operating guarantees which cannot be fulfilled under Directive 96/92/EC.[28] This can involve long term purchase contracts, investments made in the light of direct or indirect sales guarantees, investments above normal for the activity levels, etc.

An example of aid for an operational guarantee can be where there has been investment in the expansion of generating capacity based on the expectation that the electricity generator would continue to have a monopoly of the supply of a given area. If there is then liberalisation of the area for electricity generation, in other words the price for buying and selling electricity is determined by the open market, then the electricity generator has no certainty that it will be able to achieve sales that will make use of the extra capacity invested in, which clearly imposes a serious burden on the finances of that company.

In this situation it is clear that some Member States will be willing to provide aid for a period with a view to levelling out the situation until the financial effects of the stranded costs are no longer felt.

4–052   The communication lists 12 conditions which must be fulfilled before the Commission will approve State aid with a view to compensating an undertaking for stranded costs. Among other things there must be a risk that a commitment or operational guarantee cannot be honoured on account of the provisions in Directive 96/92/EC. In order to qualify as stranded costs, commitments or guarantees must become non-economical on account of the effects of the Directive and must significantly affect the competitiveness of the undertaking concerned. Among other things, this must result in the undertaking making accounting entries (e.g. provisions) which reflect the foreseeable impact of the commitment or guarantee.

The most important reason why the commitments or guarantees in question may be considered as fulfilling the conditions is that, in the absence of aid or any transitional measures, the viability of an undertaking might be jeopardised.

The stranded costs must be calculated on the basis of the most economic solution (not including aid) seen from the point of view of the undertaking in question. Among other things this can be by revoking the commitments or guarantees which create the stranded costs, or by the disposal of all or some of the assets giving rise to stranded costs (where this does not run counter to the principles of the commitments or guarantees).

Costs which some undertakings may have to bear after the period indicated in the Directive cannot, as a rule, constitute eligible stranded costs within the meaning of the methodology laid down in the communication. However,

---

[28] See e.g. in the wake of the *PreussenElektra* case the Commission's positive Decision No.6a/2001 on the stranded costs in connection with electricity liberalisation (Irish peat), where there was an obligation for Irish electricity generators to use a certain percentage of Irish peat for generation.

the communication does state that exceptions can be made in certain cases; see point 3.12 of the communication which can allow a postponement of the deadline.

Directive 96/92/EC has now been replaced by Directive 2003/54/EC.

AID FOR TRANSPORT BY RAIL, ROAD AND INLAND WATERWAY

The general provisions in art.87 of the EC Treaty do not apply directly in the **4–053** area of transport. Article 73 applies instead, which is a derogation from the general State aid rules. This article provides that: "Aids shall be compatible with this Treaty if they meet the needs of co-ordination of transport or if they represent reimbursement for the discharge of certain obligations inherent in the concept of a public service." Article 73 is part of the Treaty's Title V, and art.80 provides that the provisions of Title V only apply to transport by rail, road and inland waterway. The relationship between art.73 and 87(1) is discussed further in Ch.5.

The starting point for rules in this area is Regulation (EEC) No.1191/69 and Regulation (EEC) No.1107/70. However, 2007 saw the adoption of Regulation (EC) No.1370/2007 of the European Parliament and of the Council of October 23, 2007 on public passenger transport services by rail and by road and repealing Council Regulations (EEC) Nos 1191/69 and 1107/70 (OJ L 315, December 3, 2007, p.1) – the so-called "PSO-regulation".

These new rules enter into force on December 3, 2009, and the Regulation contains transitional provisions which means that both existing sets of rules will be relevant for some years to come.

The PSO-regulation has subsequently been complemented with a set of guidelines, cf. below.

Public passenger transport services by rail and by road

As stated above, Regulation (EC) No.1370/2007 of the European Parliament **4–054** and of the Council of October 23, 2007 on public passenger transport services by rail and by road repeals Regulations (EEC) Nos 1191/69 and 1107/70 with effect from December 3, 2009. However, Regulation (EEC) No.1191/69 in respect of goods transport is applicable until December 3, 2012.

Article 8 of Regulation (EC) No.1370/2007 contains a number of transitional provisions. The starting point of these transitional provisions is that the award of public service contracts for rail and road transport must comply with art.5 of the Regulation by December 3, 2019. During the transitional period the Member States can adopt the regulation's provisions on different dates. This is because of the needs of Member States and operators of traffic services for a certain period to adapt to the new rules introduced by the Regulation.

Under the Regulation a new contractual arrangement is introduced by which passenger transport services are to be provided within the framework of a contract between the competent authorities and an operator. In this connection, the Regulation lays down certain requirements as to the content and procedure for the contract which the competent authority must follow prior to entry into the contract (tendering procedure). Finally, the Regulation lays down rules for the calculation of compensation for operators for the provisions of public transport services.

4–055   If a Member State provides compensation for public transport services and compliance with the regulation is observed, the compensation will be exempted from the obligation to notify in art.88(3) of the EC Treaty; see art.9 of the Regulation. The structure of the Regulation is thus similar to the structure of the block exemption Regulations.

The Regulation also lays down non-exhaustive possibilities for providing aid to the transport sector. The Member States can provide aid which meets transport co-ordination needs or which is reimbursement for the discharge of certain obligations inherent in the concept of a public service.

The scope of the Regulation

4–056   The scope of the Regulation is laid down in its art.1. According to this, the Regulation applies to the national and international operation of public passenger transport services by rail and other track-based modes and by road. In this connection, "public passenger transport" is defined as passenger transport services of general economic interest provided to the public on a non-discriminatory and continuous basis. The Member States have considerable discretion to determine what constitutes passenger transport services of general economic interest.

In contrast to Regulation (EEC) No.1191/69, Regulation (EC) No.1370/2007 does not directly include passenger transport services on inland waterways. However, the Member States may choose to make the regulation applicable to passenger transport services on inland waterways and in national waters. In the absence of the use of this option the general rules of the EC Treaty (and any secondary legislation) will apply in this area. A second difference in the scopes of Regulation (EEC) No.1191/69 and Regulation (EC) No.1370/2007 is that the latter does not cover contracts for public transport services for goods. Such transport services for goods must comply with the general principles of the EC Treaty by December 3, 2012 (three years after the entry into force of the Regulation).

The Member States can also exclude from the scope of the Regulation general rules which only concern financial compensation for public service obligations which provide for maximum fares for pupils, students, apprentices and persons with reduced mobility. The Member States must give notice of any such compensation to the Commission. Thereafter the general rules of the EC Treaty apply.

The Regulation exempts from its scope services which are operated mainly for their historical interest or their tourist value.

The introduction of public service contracts and general rules

Article 3 of the Regulation lays down that a competent authority (meaning a   **4–057** public authority which has the power to intervene in public passenger transport in a given geographical area) which wishes to ensure public passenger transport must do so within the framework of a public service contract.

In principle, the competent authorities must enter into contracts with operators (which can be either public bodies/undertakings or private undertakings) on public passenger transport. The contract will include an agreement between a competent authority and an operator of public passenger transport services entrusting the management and operation of public passenger transport services to the operator. Article 2(i) of the Regulation lays down that, depending on the law of the Member State, the contract may also consist of a decision adopted by the competent authority. This decision can take the form of an individual legislative or regulatory act, or it can merely state that under certain conditions the competent authority will itself provide the services or entrust the provision of such services to an internal operator (i.e. an independent legal entity over which the competent local authority exercises control).

The requirement for a contract between the competent authority and the operator applies both when the public transport services is ensured by the grant of an exclusive right, and when it is ensured by means of compensation for the performance of a public service obligation.

However, the competent authority can choose that public service obligations, in the form of maximum tariffs for all passengers or for specific categories of passengers, should be covered by the general rules (i.e. measures which apply without discrimination to all public passenger services of the same kind within a specific geographic area for which the competent authority is responsible). The tariff obligations based on general rules must be compensated for under the provisions of the Regulation on this; see below.

Procedures for the award of contracts for public transport services

Contracts for public transport services must be entered into in accordance   **4–058** with art.5 of the Regulation.[29]

According to art.5, the starting point is that any competent authority which enters into a contract with an external operator, must award public service

---

[29] Service contracts or contracts for public transport services as defined in Directive 2004/17/EC or Directive 2004/18/EC for public passengers services by bus or by tram must be entered into in accordance with the procedures in these directives.

contracts on the basis of a competitive tendering procedure. Contracts entered into by competent local authorities are dealt with below.

The only requirements for the competitive tendering procedure are that it must: (1) be open to all operators, (2) be fair, and (3) observe the principles of transparency and non-discrimination. The use of the term "fair" is unfortunate, because the Regulation does not say what is meant by "fair". As the provision is worded, authorities responsible for applying the law could have the impression that the procedures which they plan in connection with the purchase of public transport services must be open to all, must respect the principles of transparency and non-discrimination (i.e. the principle of equality), and that in addition to this they must be fair. If the procedure is open to all, transparent and non-discriminatory the assumption must be that the procedure is also fair.

4–059   The principles of openness, transparency and equal treatment in connection with public procurement are derived from the rules of the EC Treaty, including art.12 on the prohibition of discrimination on grounds of nationality, and the ECJ's interpretation of the Treaty. In this connection see Commission interpretative communication on the Community law applicable to contract awards not or not fully subject to the provisions of the Public Procurement Directives (OJ C 179, August 1, 2006, p.2). In this communication the Commission seeks to shed light on the understanding of the principles of openness, transparency and equal treatment in the area of public procurement, and to suggest best practices for their application. The Commission interpretative communication is therefore relevant for the arrangements for the public procurement procedure that is required for contracts for public transport services.

The Regulation authorises the competent authorities to negotiate with operators once tenders have been received. However, such negotiation must be restricted to the determination of how best to meet specific or complex requirements. The principles of transparency and non-discrimination must be respected during such negotiations.

However, there are a number of exceptions to the above starting point. Firstly, competent authorities may decide to make direct awards of public service contracts without following a prior tendering procedure for transport by rail, other than other track-based modes such as metro or tramways. This exception only applies if national law does not require a tendering procedure. Such contracts entered into without a tendering procedure may be for a maximum of 10 years; however see point 4 below.

4–060   Secondly, and subject to contrary provisions under national law, the requirement for prior tendering can be derogated from if the average annual value is estimated at less than €1 million or where it concerns the annual provision of less than 300,000 kilometres of public passenger transport services. There is no time restriction for contracts which fall within this exception. These limits on the value of the contract or the distance of the service provided can be increased to €2 million and 600,000 kilometres if the contract is with a small or medium sized undertaking which operates a maximum of 23 vehicles.

Thirdly, a competent authority may take emergency measures. This applies if there is a disruption of services or the immediate risk of such a disruption. Emergency measures can take three different forms: (1) award of a contract without tendering, (2) a formal agreement to extend an existing contract, or (3) a requirement to provide certain public service obligations. The award of a contract by emergency measure may not exceed two years.

Under the Regulation the Member States have a duty to implement an appeal procedure to ensure that decisions taken by the competent authorities under the procedure for entering into contracts for public transport services can be brought before a review body. The review body should either be a court, which can make a reference to the ECJ for a preliminary ruling in accordance with art.234 of the EC Treaty, or it must be possible to refer the decisions of the review body to such a court. This ensures the uniform interpretation and application of the Regulation.

The entry by competent local authorities into contracts for public transport **4-061** services is dealt with in art.5(2) of the Regulation. A competent local authority may decide to provide public passenger transport services itself or to award public service contracts directly to an internal operator (i.e. a legally distinct entity over which the authority exercises control similar to that exercised over its own departments). In other words, art.5(2) of the Regulation gives competent local authorities the possibility of providing public transport services within their areas on their own account. However, this only applies if national law does not require a tendering procedure. Furthermore, it is a condition for the application of art.5(2) that the internal operator operates the public passenger transport service in the geographic area which is subject to the competent local authority, and that it does not take part in competitive tenders for the provision of public passenger transport services outside the territory of the competent local authority.

The rules in art.5(2) also apply to groups of authorities providing integrated public passenger transport services (i.e. interconnected transport services within a determined geographical area with a single information service, ticketing scheme and timetable). If such a group, e.g. a group of local authorities, wishes to enter into a contract with a legally distinct entity, it is sufficient if one of the competent local authorities exercises control over the entity.

How far a competent local authority has control over a legally distinct entity is assessed case-by-case. The assessment of the degree of control can take account of the degree of representation on administrative, management or supervisory bodies, the content of the articles of association, ownership, and the effective influence and control of strategic decisions and individual management decisions.

Mandatory content of public service contracts and general rules

4–062 Article 4 of the Regulation lays down a number of requirements with regard to the content of public service contracts as well as general rules, including:

1. The requirements of a competent authority for public passenger transport services in the general interest that an operator, if it were considering its own commercial interests, would not assume or would not assume to the same extent or under the same conditions without reward (public service obligation), must be clearly defined. The same applies to the geographical areas where the public service is provided.
2. The criteria for calculating any compensation must be established in advance in an objective and transparent manner. The same applies to the nature and extent of any exclusive rights granted (i.e. a right entitling a public service operator to operate certain public passenger transport services on a particular route or network or in a particular area, to the exclusion of any other operator). The criteria must be such as to prevent overcompensation.
3. The arrangements for the allocation of costs connected with the provision of services. These costs may include the costs of staff, energy, infrastructure charges, maintenance and repair of public transport vehicles, rolling stock and installations necessary for operating the passenger transport services, fixed costs and a suitable return on capital.
4. The arrangements for allocating the revenue from the sale of tickets between the operator and the competent authority.

In addition to this, contracts for public transport services must be for a limited period (not more than 10 years for coach and bus services and 15 years for rail services). Contracts for mixed bus and rail transport can be for up to 15 years if the value of the rail service is more than 50 per cent of the overall value of the services. In practice there can be a need for contracts for public transport services to be for a longer period, even though in principle long contracts can be bad for competitiveness. In some cases the Regulation allows contracts to be extended by up to half of their original duration, if the depreciation of assets justifies this. In this case the public service operator must provide assets which are necessary for the performance of the public service contract.

4–063 A similar extension is also possible if justified by costs due to the particular geographical situation in the outermost regions; see the section above on regional aid.

A longer period of a contract will also be allowable to the extent this is justified by the amortisation of capital in relation to exceptional investments in infrastructure, rolling stock or vehicles. However, this will only be allowed if the public service contract is awarded in a fair competitive tendering procedure and if the Commission is notified of the contract and elements justifying its longer duration.

Finally, depending on the circumstances, in contracts and tender documents account must be taken of quality standards, sub-contractors and the transfer of employees.

Compensation for public transport services

Article 6 of the Regulation contains more detailed rules on the compensa-   **4–064** tion which is paid to the operator for providing public transport services. The contract or general rules must always contain the provisions on compensation referred to above. This applies irrespective of how the contract is awarded. If the contract is awarded without a tendering procedure, i.e. without applying one of the exemptions in art.5(3), the compensation must follow the rules laid down in the annex to the Regulation.

According to the annex, compensation may not exceed an amount corresponding to the net financial effect equivalent to the total of the effects, positive or negative, of compliance with the public service obligation on the costs and revenue of the public service operator. The effects must be assessed by comparing the situation where the public service obligation is met with the situation which would have existed if the obligation had not been met.

The net financial effect is calculated by deducting the costs incurred in carrying out the public service obligations from the total of all the positive financial effects generated from carrying out the public service obligations, as well as revenue from ticket sales and any other revenue generated while fulfilling the public service obligations covered by the contract. To this is added a reasonable profit—meaning a rate of return on capital that is normal for the sector, taking account of the risk or absence of risk incurred by the public service operator by virtue of public authority intervention.

Administrative obligations

Under art.7 of the Regulation the Member States are subject to a number   **4–065** of administrative obligations. Thus, each competent authority must publish an annual report on the public service obligations for which it is responsible. In addition, at least one year before the launch of an invitation to tender or before an award without tendering, each competent authority must ensure that the following information is published in the Official Journal of the European Union: (1) the name and address of the competent authority; (2) the type of award envisaged; and (3) the services and areas potentially covered by the award. Such publication does not apply to emergency measures or where a public service contract concerns an annual provision of less than 50,000 kilometres of public passenger transport services. However, considerably more information must be published concerning contracts for rail services which can be entered into without a tendering procedure; see art.5(6) of the Regulation. This information concerns the name of the contracting entity, the duration of the public service contract, the parameters of the financial compensation, the conditions relating to essential assets, quality targets, rewards and penalties applicable, and a description of the passenger transport services to be performed.

Community guidelines on State aid for railway undertakings

Introduction

4–066   The Commission has, on April 30, 2008, adopted a set of guidelines for State aid to railway undertakings, see OJ C 184, July 22, 2008, p.13. They supplement Regulation 1370/2007 (OJ L315, December 3, 2007, p.1) on public passenger transport services by rail and by road. In view of the Union's policy of trying to promote an efficient, clean and safe goods and passenger transport system and alleviate the congestion plaguing the towns and certain areas of the Union the Commission in the guidelines in question, given that the cost of modernisation and adaptation necessitates substantial costs, takes a favourable attitude to the awarding of State aid as a means of furthering a more efficient railway transport sector.

The transport sector, be it rail or road transport or other types of transport, passenger or freight transport, has proved to be one of the most difficult to liberalise and make more effective. Problems in the sector are due to the fact that national railway systems have in many way not been compatible, e.g. due the fact that rail tracks of various countries differ in size or that some trains run on diesel whereas others on electricity, and that railways have been run by national monopolies thus not being subject to competition and for that reason also have faced less incentive to become more efficient.

Against that background the Commission which is the EU institution responsible for State aid policy, is, for good reason, of the opinion that State aid to this sector, in view of the very important costs that liberalisation and modernisation give rise to, should be accepted if certain conditions are fulfilled.

4–067   The awarding of State aid can, however, only be authorised where it contributes to the completion of an integrated European market, open to competition and interoperable and to Community objectives of sustainable mobility. The Commission will make sure that public-sector financial support does not cause distortions of competition contrary to the common interest.

The objective of the guidelines is to provide guidance on the compatibility with the EC Treaty of State aid to railway undertaking as defined in Directive No.91/440/EEC (OJ L 237, July 29, 1991, p.25), i.e. any private or public undertaking whose main business is to provide rail transport services for goods and/or passengers with a requirement that the undertaking should ensure traction. Section 3 of the guidelines also applies to urban, suburban and regional passenger transport undertakings. The guidelines are based in particular on the principles established by the Community legislator in the three successive railway packages (liberalising railway transport) and aim at improving transparency of public financing and legal certainty with regard to the Treaty rules in the context of the opening up of the markets. The guidelines do not concern public financing intended for infrastructure managers.

The guidelines deal with State aid covered by art.87 and art.73 of the EC Treaty, but the guidelines do not cover aspects concerning public service compensation which is, as from December 3, 2009, covered by the new Regulation No.1370/2007 (OJ L 315, December 3, 2007, p.1) on public passenger transport services by rail and by road (the so-called PSO Regulation, see the section above)

After the entry into force of Regulation 1370/2007 art.73 will be directly   **4–068** applicable as a legal basis for establishing the compatibility of aid not covered by the PSO Regulation, and in particular, therefore, of aid for the coordination of freight transport. The present guidelines aim in particular to establish criteria for examining when such aid will be compatible with art.73 and lay down intensity thresholds. The Commission must also make it possible for Member States to show, where appropriate, the need for and proportionality of any aid measure exceeding in the thresholds established.

The guidelines deal with:

- financing of railway undertakings by means of infrastructure funding,
- aid for the purchase and renewal of rolling stock,
- debt cancellation with a view to financial rejuvenation of railway undertakings,
- restructuring aid for railway undertakings,
- aid for the needs of transport coordination, and
- State guarantees for railway undertakings.

Financing of railway undertakings by means of infrastructure funding

Such financing may grant an advantage indirectly and thereby constitute   **4–069** State aid. However, where infrastructure is open to all potential users in a fair and non-discriminatory way, the Commission normally considers that public financing of infrastructure does not constitute aid as such general financing is not selective. But in cases where such financing does constitute aid it may be authorised e.g. on the basis of art.73 of EC Treaty, and as for the problem of compatibility s.6 of the guidelines may constitute a pertinent reference point.

Aid for the purchase and renewal of rolling stock

4–070 As for the purchase and renewal of rolling stock which is necessary in order to make rail transport effective the Commission notes that in principle the need to modernise rolling stock, which is particular high in the new Member States, can be sufficiently taken into account either in implementing the general State aid rules or by applying art.73 where such aid is intended for transport coordination, see s.6 of the guidelines. In assessing the compatibility of aid for rolling stock the Commission therefore generally applies the criteria defined for each of the following aid categories in these guidelines or any other relevant document on State aid:

- aid for co-ordination of transport,
- aid for restructuring railway undertakings,
- aid for SMEs,
- aid for environmental protection,
- aid to offset costs relating to public service obligations and in the framework, of public service contracts, and
- regional aid.

The guidelines specify that, in derogation from the regional aid guidelines, see above in paras 3–123 to 3–137, it shall be possible to award aid for initial investment in transport equipment (movable assets) and thus in rolling stock in certain areas and under certain conditions, but only with regard to rail passenger transport. The derogation will apply to any kind of investment in rolling stock, whether initial or for replacement purposes, as long as it is assigned to lines regularly serving a region eligible for aid under art.87 (3)(a), an outermost region or a region of low population density within the meaning of para.80 and 81 of the regional guidelines.[30]

4–071 In the other regions the derogation only applies for initial investment and, for aid for investment for replacement purposes, only when the rolling stock the aid is aimed at modernising is more than 15 years old.

In order to avoid distortion of competition the Commission requires that the derogation has to be made subject to four conditions which have to be met cumulatively:

(i) such rolling stock must be exclusively assigned to urban, suburban or regional passenger service in a specific region or for a specific line serving different regions (the guidelines contain more detailed definitions of the terms here used);

(ii) the rolling stock must remain exclusively assigned to the specific region

---

[30] The Commission notes that it will, for the sake of equality, apply the same derogation to vehicles used for the public transport of passengers by road where such vehicles meet the latest Community standards applicable to new vehicles.

or the specific line passing through several different regions for which it has received aid for at last 10 years;

(iii) the replacement of rolling stock must meet the latest interoperability, safety and environmental standards applicable to the network concerned; and

(iv) Member States must prove that the project contributes to a coherent regional development strategy.

The Commission will take care to avoid any undue distortion of competition and to that end, the grant of aid may be made subject to an obligation on the recipient to sell on normal market conditions all or part of the rolling stock that it no longer uses, so as to allow its further use by other operators; in such cases the proceeds from the sale of old rolling stock will be deducted from the eligible costs. The other conditions provided for in the regional aid guidelines, e.g. on cumulation and intensity ceilings, will continue to apply.

Where a specific line passes through several regions with different intensity   **4–072**
ceilings the highest will be applied taking into account the regularity of the service.

For projects with eligible expenditure in excess of 50 million euros a derogation from paras 60 and 70 of the regional guidelines will be permitted. However, paras 64 and 67 of the regional aid guidelines will continue to apply when the investment project concerns rolling stock assigned to a specific line serving several regions.

In cases where a railway undertaking is entrusted with providing services of general economic interest that necessitate buying and/or renewing rolling stock and it already receives compensation for such purchases that compensation should be taken into account in the amount of regional aid that may be awarded to that undertaking in order to avoid overcompensation.

Debt cancellation

Railways have in the past experienced a state of imbalance between their   **4–073**
revenues and their costs, especially their investment costs. That has led to major indebtedness, the serving of which represents a very large burden on the railway undertakings and limits their capacity to make the necessary investments in both infrastructure and renewal of rolling stock. Directive 91/440 directly obliges Member States to set up appropriate mechanisms to help reduce the indebtedness of railway undertakings and its art.9(3) envisages State aid to cancel the debts referred to in that article. Such aid must be granted in accordance with arts 73, 87 and 88 of the EC Treaty.

Although there has been a certain improvement in the beginning of the 1990s the Commission notes that the level of indebtedness continues to give cause for concern and that several undertaking are nor capable of self-financing, and/or cannot finance their investment needs from present or future transport operations. The problem is particularly significant in the Member States that joined the EU after May 2004.

Aid cancellation attributable to the State falls within the scope of art.87(1) of the EC Treaty if a railway undertaking receiving such aid is active in markets open to competition and if the aid cancellation strengthens its position in at least one of those markets.

4–074   As Directive No.2001/12/EC (OJ L 75, March 15, 2001, p.1) opened up the international rail freight service to competition over the whole of the European rail freight network from March 15, 2003 the Commission considers that, generally, the market was opened up at the latest on that date.

Cancellation aid must generally be examined on the basis of the Community guidelines on State aid for rescuing and restructuring of firms in difficulty, see paras 3–089 to 3–117.

Cancellation aid must be notified to the Commission.

In specific cases where the debts cancelled exclusively concern transport co-ordination, compensation for public service obligations or the setting of accounting standards, the compatibility of the cancellation aid will be examined on the basis of art.73, the provisions adopted on the basis thereof and the rules for the normalisation of accounts. The Commission will, by analogy, apply the Commission Communication relating to the methodology for analysing State aid linked to stranded costs of July 2001, SEC (2001) 5238.

4–075   According to paras 54 and 55 of the guidelines, in certain cases cancellation aid incurred prior to the entry into force of Directive 2001/12/EC as at March 15, 2001 laying down the conditions for opening up the sector to competition may be authorised without restructuring as such aid may be deemed compatible in so far as it seeks to ease the transition to an open rail market and may thus be compatible with art.87(3)(c) of the EC Treaty. For the new Member States the relevant date is that of their accession to the Community.

Such aid must be linked directly to the activity of rail transport or the activities of management, construction or the use of railway infrastructure. Investment debts incurred for the purpose of investment not directly linked to transport and/or rail infrastructure is not eligible.

The aid to offset the kind of debt in question must be restricted to debt that has been clearly determined and individualised and incurred prior to March 15, 2001 which is the date from which the opening up of the Union rail transport market is set to have occurred, see Directive 2001/12/EC. In the case of new Member States the relevant date is that of their accession to the EU. It goes without syaing that the aid must never exceed the amount of the debts referred to above.

4–076   The cancellation aid must, of course, be necessary to remedy the situation of the undertakings in question, i.e. that such undertakings are burdened by debt to such an extent that they cannot be run on a financially viable basis, and that the undertakings cannot be expected to overcome their problems on their own, The aid must also take into account any productivity improvements which the undertakings can reasonably be expected to achieve. The aid must not go beyond the amount necessary and cancellation of debts must not give an undertaking an advantage to such a point that it prevents the development of effective competition on the market or dissuades outside undertakings or new players from entering the markets in question. In particular, aid for cancelling debts cannot be financed by levies imposed on other rail operators.

Aid for restructuring railway undertakings—restructuring a "freight" division

Normally the Commission, save where otherwise provided for, assesses the   **4–077** compatibility of State aid for restructuring firms in dificulty on the basis of the current restructuring guidelines.

However, in the case of railways the Commission considers that aid to a freight division of a firm, contrary to what is possible under the restructuring guidelines, can be held compatible with the common interest. Given the fact that freight markets are open to competition whereas rail passenger transport is not going to opened up before January 2010 and that several European railway undertakings have not legally separated their passenger and freight transport services, or have only just done so, and that Community legislation does not provide for the obligation to make legal separation of the two forms of transport activities the Commission will require, as part of a restructuring effort and before awarding any aid, the legal separation of the freight division in question by transforming it into a commercial company under common commercial law. Such separation will, in the view of the Commission, help significantly to achieve two goals, namely to exclude all cross-subsidisation between the restructured division and the rest of the undertaking and to ensure that all financial relations between the two are carried out in a sustainable manner and on a commercial basis.

The point of departure is the situation that the freight division in question would, if it had been separated, constitute "a firm in difficulty" within the meaning of the restructuring guidelines. In this connection, also the possibility of such a firm to overcome its difficulties will, of course, be taken into consideration, see para.3–093, of this book and point 10 of the restructuring guidelines. The division must comprise all of the freight transport activities of the railway undertaking in question, and it must be possible to attribute to it a level of losses as well as a level of funds or capital which sufficiently reflects the economic reality the division faces, see point 10 of the restructuring guidelines.

It should be recalled that, under the guidelines on aid to the railway sector,   **4–078** it is possible to give State aid to an enterprise that has been created by means of the splitting up of a railway undertaking in spite of the fact that the guidelines on rescue and restructuring aid to enterprises do not authorise such aid to newly created enterprises.

The guidelines outline in more detail the conditions related to a return of the freight division to long-term profitability, and in para.80 they specify the criteria that need to be fulfilled in order to avoid any excessive distortions of competition, in particular those contained in points 34–37 of the restructuring guidelines, but also that restructuring must ensure that the freight activity will be transformed from a protected activity enjoying exclusive rights into one that is competitive on the open market.

With a view to prevent of excessive distortion of competition the Commission will also have regard to the difference between the economic models for rail and other modes of transport as well as the Community objective of shifting the balance between modes of transport in favour of transport by rail and by sea as well as to the conditions with regard to competition in the transport market.

4–079   Paragraph 82 deals with the question of limiting aid to a minimum necessary to achieve the legitimate goals, but the Commission notes that it may accept lower own contributions in these cases than what is foreseen in the restructuring guidelines of 2004.

The "one time-last time principle" implies that if a railway undertaking as a whole has already received restructuring aid the aid envisaged in this section of the transport guidelines may not be granted to restructure the freight division of the undertaking.

Aid for the needs of transport coordination

4–080   The so-called PSO Regulation will apply only as regards land passenger transport. In so far as coordination of freight transport is concerned only art.73 of the Treaty will apply with regard to aid for coordination purposes. In addition to that the provisions of art.9 of the PSO Regulation concerning aid for coordination of transport and aid for research and development are explicitly without prejudice to art.73. That means that it will be possible to use art.73 directly for justifying the compatibility of aid for coordination of rail passenger transport.

As a consequence of this the guidelines, in s.6, aim at establishing criteria which will allow the Commission to assess the compatibility, on the basis of art.73, of aid for the co-ordination of transport, both generally (para.6–003), and as regards certain types of aid (paras 6–004 to 6–010).

Paragraphs 91-97 explain the reasons why aid for coordination purposes is justified on the basis of art.73 of the EC Treaty as a result of, e.g. disparities between the different modes of transport which ought to be corrected by public authority support for those modes of transport that give rise to the lowest external costs (like congestion and pollution). Further, the problems of achieving a common interoperability standard for rail or difficulties with regard to connections between different modes of transport may justify State aid.

In para.97 the Commission states that aid has to be limited to a period of   **4–081**
five years in order to enable the Commission to re-examine aid in the light of
results obtained.

Co-ordination aid can be provided through:

* aid for infrastructure use, i.e. aid granted to railway undertakings which
  have to pay charges for the infrastructure they use while other undertakings providing transport services based on other modes of transport do
  not have to pay such charges;
* aid for reducing external costs, designed to encourage a modal shift to
  rail because it generates lower external costs than other modes of transport such as road transport;
* aid for promoting interoperability, e.g. to remove technical barriers, to
  promote safety, and to reduce noise; and
* aid for research and development in response to the needs of transport
  co-ordination.

Paragraphs 101–106 of the guidelines define the eligible costs involved in
the types of co-ordination aid outlined above.

According to para.107 the Commission will consider that there is a pre-   **4–082**
sumption of necessity and proportionality when the intensity of the aid stays
below the following values:

* for aid for rail infrastructure use, 30 per cent of the total cost of rail
  transport, up to 100 per cent of the eligible cost;
* for aid for reducing external costs, 30 per cent of the total costs of rail
  transport and 50 per cent of the eligible costs; and
* for aid for interoperability, 50 per cent of the eligible costs.

Above those thresholds Member States must demonstrate the need and the
proportionality of the measures in question.

Paragraph 109 stresses that for both aid rail infrastructure use and aid for
reducing external costs the aid has to be strictly limited to compensation for
opportunity costs with the use of rail transport rather than the use of more
polluting modes of transport. Where there are several competing options
which cause higher levels of pollution than rail transport, the limit chosen
corresponds to the highest differential among the various options.

Paragraph 110 states that where the aid recipient is a railway undertaking   **4–083**
it must be proved that such aid really does have the effect of encouraging a
modal shift to rail. In principle, this will mean that the aid has to be reflected
in the price demanded from the passengers or from the shipper, since it is they
who make the choice between rail and the more polluting transport modes
such as road transport.

In case of this type of aid, like the other types covered by the guidelines, if such aid is needed and proportional it must be considered to be compatible with the common interest.

Eligible costs

4-084   Eligible costs with regard to aid for rail infrastructure use, reducing external costs and interoperability are dealt with in paras 101-106 of the guidelines.

As regards aid for rail infrastructure use the eligible costs are defined as the additional costs for infrastructure use paid by rail transport but not by a more polluting competing transport mode, e.g. such as freight transport by road.

As regards aid for reducing external costs, the eligible costs are the part of the external costs which rail transport makes it possible to avoid compared with competing transport modes.

In this connection the guidelines state that it should be recalled that art.10 of Directive 2001/14/EC explicitly allows Member States to put in place a compensation scheme for the demonstrably unpaid environmental, accident-related and infrastructure costs of competing transport modes in so far as such costs exceed the equivalent costs of rail transport.

4-085   In so far as aid for infrastructure use and aid for reducing external costs are concerned Member States must provide a transparent, reasoned and quantified comparative cost analysis between rail transport and the alternative options based on other modes of transport. The methodology used must be made publicly available.

As regards interoperability aid, the eligible costs cover all relevant investments relating to the installation of safety systems and interoperability, or noise reduction both in rail infrastructure and in rolling stock.

Paragraphs 113–117 of the guidelines state that the Community framework for State aid for research and development and innovation, OJ C 323, December 30, 2006, p.1, is applicable in the railway sector if it does not fall within the scope of art.3(3) of Regulation No.1107/70 (OJ L 130, June 15, 1970, p.1) or art.9 of the PSO Regulation.

It is not excluded that aid for research and development may be assessed directly on the basis of art.73 of the EC Treaty if it is aimed at meeting the need of transport co-ordination.

State guarantees for railway undertakings

4-086   Section 7 of the guidelines concern State guarantees and specify that the Commission Notice on aid in the form of State guarantees apply also to the rail transport field. In this connection the guidelines in particular refer to the existence of unlimited guarantees.

The Commission states that it has been its consistent practice to consider that unlimited guarantees in a sector open to competition is incompatible with the EC Treaty. In accordance with the principle of proportionality such guarantees cannot be justified by tasks of general interest as with unlimited guarantees it is impossible to check whether the amount of aid exceeds the net costs providing the public service in question.

Thus when State guarantees are granted to undertakings with a presence on both competitive and non-competitive markets, the Commission requires the complete removal of the unlimited guarantee to the undertaking as a whole. However, unlimited guarantees do to a large extent constitute existing aid, see art.88(1) of the EC Treaty and as for the procedure concerning existing aid, see Ch.2.

Cumulation

The aid ceilings in the guidelines are applicable regardless of whether the   **4–087** aid in question is financed wholly or in part from State resources or from Community resources. Aid authorised by the railway transport guidelines may not be cumulated with other forms of State aid within the meaning of art.87(1) of the EC Treaty or with other forms of Community financing if such combination produces a level of aid higher than that laid down in the transport guidelines. If aid concerns different purposes and involves the same eligible cost, the most favorable aid ceiling will apply.

Existing aids

Paragraph 128 concerns existing State aid and states that the Commission   **4–088** will propose that Member States amend their existing aid schemes relating to State aid covered by the guidelines on transport so as to comply with them at the latest two years after their publication in the OJ. Member States are invited to confirm that they accept the proposals for appropriate measures at the latest one year after the date of the publication of the guidelines in the OJ.

Entry into force and review

The guidelines apply from July 22, 2008. The guidelines state that the   **4–089** Commission intends to review the guidelines no later than five years after the date of their publication.

AGRICULTURE

Introduction

4–090   In the agricultural sector State aid cases and their regulation are dealt
with by the Commission's Directorate-General for Agriculture and Rural
Development.[31] Agriculture is subject to special rules under the EC Treaty.
These rules are contained in Title II of the Treaty (arts 32 to 38). According
to art.32, the common market extends to agriculture and trade in agricultural products. "Agricultural products" mean the products listed in annex I
to the Treaty, products made of natural cork under CN Codes 4502, 4503
and 4504, processed agricultural products where the processed agricultural
products remain agricultural products, and products which are an imitation
of or substitute for milk and dairy products, other than products covered by
Council Regulation (EEC) No.3759/92 of December 17, 1992 on the common
organization of the market in fishery and aquaculture products (OJ L 388,
December 31, 1992, p.1).

According to art.36 of the Treaty, the provisions of the chapter of the
Treaty relating to rules on competition apply to the production of and trade
in agricultural products only to the extent determined by the Council within
the framework of art.37. This means that the rules in arts 87–89 only come
into play in relation to agriculture if this is specifically decided by the Council.
This also means that the Commission is not directly authorised to control and
monitor State aid in the area of agriculture on the basis of the Treaty. Thus,
the Commission only has such powers if this is stated in legislation adopted
by the Council, and even then only on the premises which the Council lays
down in such legislation.

4–091   Among other things, the Council has adopted Council Regulation (EC)
No.1184/2006 of July 24, 2006 applying certain rules of competition to the
production of, and trade in, agricultural products (OJ L 214, August 4, 2006,
p.7). According to art.3 of the regulation, the provisions of art.88(1) and of
the first sentence of art.88(3) of the Treaty do apply to aid granted for production of or trade in the products listed in annex I to the Treaty. This means
that the Commission, in cooperation with the Member States, keeps under
constant review all existing systems of aid. It also proposes to the Member
States any appropriate measures required by the progressive development
or the functioning of the common market; see art.88(1). In addition the
Commission must be informed in good time about any proposed introduction
of or amendment to aid measures, so that it has an opportunity to comment
on them. Under art.10 of the Treaty, the Member States have a duty to cooperate with the Commission in good faith with a view to facilitating the achievement of the Community's tasks. The consequence of art.3 of Regulation (EC)

---

[31] *http://ec.europa.eu/agriculture/stateaid/index_en.htm* This website gives the rules which are
issued by the Council on State aid for agriculture.

No.1184/2006 is that the procedural rule in art.88(2) does not generally apply. As stated, this will only be the case if the Council has so decided. Such a decision, in the form of a regulation, will constitute a *lex specialis* in relation to Regulation (EC) No.1184/2006. In practice, all the regulations on common market organisations contain provisions on the application of the State aid rules in arts 87, 88 and 89 of the Treaty to the products in question. In addition, in art.88 of Council Regulation (EC) No.1698/2005 of September 20, 2005 on support for rural development by the European Agricultural Fund for Rural Development (EAFRD) (OJ L 277, October 21, 2005, p.1), it is stated that arts 87–89 of the Treaty apply to support for rural development by the Member States. Accordingly, unless otherwise determined in special restrictions or exemptions in the regulation in question, the Treaty rules apply in full to State aid for agriculture, apart from aid that is specifically targeted at the limited number of products that are not covered by common market organisations.[32] This means that arts 87–89 of the Treaty do not take priority over the provisions in the regulation on the common market organisation for the sector in question.[33] Thus the Commission can under no circumstances approve aid which is incompatible with the provisions which regulate a common market organisation, or which may hinder the proper functioning of a common market organisation.

There is in addition a rule that if the Community has adopted a common market organisation for a specific agricultural sector, the Member States are required to refrain from adopting measures which can weaken the market organisation or give rise to exemptions from it.[34] The same principle applies to fisheries.[35]

The agricultural products which are listed in annex 1 to the EC Treaty, **4–092** but which are not yet covered by a common market organisation are potatoes (apart from potatoes for the manufacture of starch), horse meat, coffee, vinegar manufactured from alcohol, and cork.[36] On the other hand, these products are covered by Council Regulation (EC) No.1184/2006 of July 24, 2006 applying certain rules of competition to the production of, and trade in, agricultural products (OJ L 214, August 4, 2006, p.7).[37]

In the following sections there is a discussion of the secondary legislation and guidelines on State aid in the agricultural sector.

---

[32] See para.10 in Community guidelines for State aid in the agriculture and forestry sector 2007 to 2013 (OJ C 319, 27.12.2006, p.1).

[33] Case 177/78, *Pigs and Bacon Commission v McCarren*, [1979] E.C.R. 2161.

[34] Case C-113/00, *Spain v Commission*, [2002] E.C.R I-7601, para.70.

[35] See recital 6 in Commission Regulation (EC) No.1860/2004 of October 6, 2004 on the application of arts 87 and 88 of the EC Treaty to de minimis aid in the agriculture and fisheries sectors (OJ L 325, 28.10.2004, p.4).

[36] See para.21 in Community guidelines for State aid in the agriculture and forestry sector 2007 to 2013 (OJ C 319, 27.12.2006, p.1).

[37] See the Commission's approach to State aid for these products in para.21 in Community guidelines for State aid in the agriculture and forestry sector 2007 to 2013 (OJ C 319, 27.12.2006, p.1).

Community guidelines for State aid in the agriculture and forestry sector 2007–2013

4–093   Community guidelines for State aid in the agriculture and forestry sector 2007 to 2013 (OJ C 319, December 27, 2006, p.1) apply to new State aid from January 1, 2007. There are certain transitional provisions in accordance with the 2003 Act of Accession and the Commission's proposal for suitable measures; see paras 194–196 of the guidelines.

The guidelines apply to all State aid granted in connection with activities related to the production, processing[38] and marketing[39] of agricultural products, unless specific exemptions are laid down in the Treaty or EC legislation.

Chapter VII of the guidelines contains special rules on aid for forestry, including planting forests on agricultural land.

4–094   According to Ch.III of the guidelines, on general principles, in order to be considered compatible with the common market, any aid measure must contain some incentive element or require some counterpart on the part of the beneficiary. Unless otherwise provided by Community legislation, the Commission considers that unilateral State aid measures which are simply intended to improve the financial situation of producers but which in no way contribute to the development of the sector, and in particular aids which are granted solely on the basis of price, quantity, unit of production or unit of the means of production are considered to constitute operating aids which are incompatible with the common market. According to the Commission, the same applies to aid which is granted retrospectively in respect of activities which have already been undertaken by the beneficiary.

In order to maximise the incentive effect of aid, and to facilitate the demonstration of this when notifying the Commission, the eligibility rules of the Member States must provide for the following steps before the granting of aid:

Aid under an aid scheme can only be granted in respect of activities undertaken or services provided after the aid scheme has been set up and approved by the Commission. The same applies if the aid scheme creates an automatic right to receive the aid, requiring no further administrative action. If an aid scheme requires an application to be submitted to a competent authority, the aid itself may only be granted for activities undertaken or services provided on condition that: (1) the aid scheme has been set up and declared compatible with the Treaty

---

[38] In para.7 of the guidelines "processing of an agricultural product" is defined as any operation on an agricultural product resulting in a product which is also an agricultural product, except on-farm activities necessary for preparing an animal or plant product for the first sale. The processing of agricultural products falling within the scope of annex I of the Treaty into non-annex I products therefore falls outside the scope of the guidelines.

[39] In para.8 of the guidelines "marketing of an agricultural product" is defined as holding or displaying with a view to sale, offering for sale, delivery or any other manner of placing on the market, except the first sale by a primary producer to resellers or processors and any activity preparing a product for such first sale. A sale by a primary producer to final consumers is considered as marketing if it takes place in separate premises reserved for that purpose. Aid for advertising of agricultural products is covered by the scope of the guidelines.

by the Commission; (2) an application for aid has been properly submitted to the competent authority; and (3) the application has been accepted by the competent authority in a manner which obliges the authority to grant the aid, clearly indicating the amount of aid to be granted or how this amount will be calculated, and such acceptance by the competent authority may only be made if the budget available for the aid or aid scheme is not exhausted. Individual aid, outside any aid scheme, must only be granted in respect of activities undertaken or services provided after the criteria in points (2) and (3) have been satisfied.

As for aid for export-related activities (namely aid directly linked to the quantities exported, and aid contingent upon the use of domestic over imported goods, or for the establishment and operation of a distribution network or to other current expenditure linked to export activity in other Member States), the Commission emphasises that such aid will not be approved. However, this does not normally apply to aid towards the cost of participating in trade fairs, or for studies or consultancy services needed for the launch of new or existing products in a new market.

In the chapter on general principles it is also stated that State aid rules **4–095** which apply to agricultural processing and marketing companies should be harmonised with the rules that apply to companies that process and market non-agricultural products. This policy should be applied to State aid granted for whatever purpose, for example aid towards the costs of investment, environmental protection or technical support.[40]

As for aid measures which are not covered by the guidelines, according to para.23 of the guidelines, the Commission will assess these on a case-by-case basis, taking into account the principles set out in arts 87–89 of the Treaty and the Community's common agricultural and rural development policies. When proposing support for the agricultural sector which is not covered by the guidelines, Member States have to provide an economic assessment of the positive impact of the measure for the development of the agricultural sector, and of the risks of distortion of competition posed by the measure in question. The guidelines state that the Commission will only approve a measure if the positive contribution to the development of the sector clearly outweighs the risks of distortions of competition.

The measures covered by the guidelines and the conditions for the Commission's approval of them are set out in Chs IV-VII.

Chapter IV concerns measures for the development of rural areas, including **4–096** aid for investment in agricultural holdings (for primary production), aid for investments in connection with the processing and marketing of agricultural products, aid for environmental protection and animal welfare (normally only for primary producers), aid to compensate for disadvantages in certain areas (only for primary production), aid for meeting standards (only for primary production), aid for the establishment of young farmers (only for primary

---

[40] There is an overview of the rules that apply to the agricultural sector, including cross-sectoral horizontal rules at: *http://ec.europa.eu/agriculture/stateaid/leg/index_en.htm*

production), aid for early retirement or for the cessation of farming activities (only for primary production), aid for producer groups, aid for land reparcelling, aid to encourage the production and marketing of quality agricultural products, provision of technical support in the agricultural sector, aid for the livestock sector, and aid for the outermost regions and the Aegean Islands.

Chapter V deals with risk and crisis management, including aid to compensate for damage to agricultural production or the means of agricultural production, aid for closing production, processing or marketing capacity, and aid for rescuing and restructuring firms in difficulty.

Chapter VI deals with other kinds of aid, including aid to promote employment, aid for research and development, horizontal aid instruments applicable to the agricultural sector, aid for the advertising of agricultural products, aid in the form of subsidised short-term loans, aid linked to tax exemptions under Council Directive 2003/96/EC of October 27, 2003 restructuring the Community framework for the taxation of energy products and electricity.

Chapter VII concerns aid for forestry.

4–097 Chapter VIII deals with procedural matters. According to this, all new aid schemes and all new individual aid must be notified to the Commission before they are put into effect in accordance with art.88(3) of the Treaty and the Procedure Regulation (Regulation (EC) No.659/1999 laying down detailed rules for the application of art.88 of the Treaty). However, this does not apply to aid covered by one of the block exemption regulations adopted by the Commission on the basis of Council Regulation (EC) No.994/98 of May 7, 1998 on the application of arts 92 and 93 [now arts 87 and 88] of the Treaty establishing the European Community to certain categories of horizontal State aid. Article 88(3) of the Treaty on notification to the Commission does not apply to aid which has been notified to and approved by the Commission in accordance with the provisions of Regulation (EC) No.1698/2005 of September 20, 2005 on support for rural development by the European Agricultural Fund for Rural Development (EAFRD). According to art.89 of this Regulation, State aid intended to provide additional financing for rural development for which Community support is granted, must be notified by Member States and approved by the Commission in accordance with the Regulation as part of the programming referred to in art.16.

In order to benefit from this exception from the obligation to notify under art.88(3) of the Treaty, the measures must comply with all conditions of substance set out in the guidelines. The amount of additional State aid must be clearly identified in the rural development plan in accordance with the provisions of the Rural Development Implementing Regulation. The Commission's approval of the plan will cover only measures which have been identified in this way. In this area, schemes should be limited to the duration of the programming period 2007–2013.

Approval of notified schemes presupposes that the relevant conditions of the guidelines have been satisfied. In addition it is stated in para.189 of the guidelines that aid schemes should not apply for more than seven years.

Furthermore, in future all notifications should contain an assessment of the effects which the aided activity is expected to have on the environment; see para.22 of the guidelines. In the same place it is also stated that in many cases, this will involve no more than a confirmation that there is no expected environmental impact.

Small and medium sized enterprises in agriculture

In the light of its experiences of State aid in the agricultural sector, the **4-098** Commission has decided that it is appropriate for small and medium sized enterprises (SMEs) to be covered by a block exemption regulation. For this purpose the Commission has adopted Regulation (EC) No.1857/2006 of December 15, 2006 on the application of arts 87 and 88 of the Treaty to State aid to small and medium-sized enterprises active in the production of agricultural products and amending Regulation (EC) No.70/2001 (OJ L 358, December 16, 2006, p.3).[41]

SMEs in the agricultural sector may find it hard to attract investment and to raise loans. Among other things this is because of their inability to provide satisfactory security. The lack of resources of these undertakings can also mean that their access to information and above all to new technology and potential markets is limited. At the same time SMEs play an important role in creating jobs, and in general they contribute to ensuring social stability and a dynamic economy. It is against this background that it is thought that aid which is exempt from the obligation to notify should be aimed at promoting the economic activities of SMEs. However, such aid must not affect the terms of trade in such a way as to be incompatible with the common interest. Aid must be reasonable in relation to the problems it is intended to solve in order to ensure socio-economic benefits that are regarded as being in the interest of the Community. This is not the case with aid measures which are merely intended to improve the financial situation of the producers but which do not in fact contribute to the development of the agricultural sector. Such aid, in particular aid which is granted solely on the basis of price, quantity, unit of production or unit of the means of production, is considered to be operating aid which is incompatible with the common market. Furthermore, such aid is also likely to interfere with the common organisations of the markets.

The Regulation therefore deals with specific forms of aid. Aid for export-related activities, or aid which is contingent upon the use of domestic over imported goods is not covered by the exemptions; see art.1 of the Regulation. Aid for export-related activities covers aid which is directly linked to the

---

[41] The Regulation replaced Commission Regulation (EC) No.1/2004 of December 23, 2003 on the application of arts 87 and 88 of the EC Treaty to State aid to small and medium-sized enterprises active in the production, processing and marketing of agricultural products (OJ L 1, 3.1.2004, p.1). Aid schemes which were exempted under this Regulation continue to be exempt if the conditions of the new Regulation are met; see art.22 of the new Regulation.

quantities exported, to the establishment and operation of a distribution network or to other current expenditure linked to the export activity. Aid towards the costs of participation in trade fairs or for studies or consultancy services needed for the launch of new or existing products in a new market does not normally constitute export aid.

4–099   According to its art.1(1), the Regulation applies to transparent aid granted to small and medium-sized agricultural holdings (farms) active in the primary production of agricultural products. It does not apply to aid granted in connection with the processing or marketing of agricultural products. Processing and marketing of agricultural products is covered by Regulation (EC) No.70/2001 of January 12 2001 on the application of arts 87 and 88 of the EC Treaty to State aid to small and medium-sized enterprises, as discussed in Ch.3 of this book. The reason is that these activities are similar to normal industrial activities and ought therefore to be covered by the rules for other industrial goods.

The Regulation does not make a distinction between small undertakings and medium sized undertakings, and the definition is the same as that given in annex I to the GBER.

As stated, the Regulation applies to *transparent aid*. This term is defined in art.2(18) as aid measures in which it is possible to calculate precisely in advance the gross grant equivalent as a percentage of eligible expenditure ex ante without the need to undertake a risk assessment (for example are measures which use grants, interest rate subsidies and capped fiscal measures considered to be transparent). Public loans are considered to be transparent, provided that they are backed by normal security and do not involve abnormal risk. If so, they are not considered to contain a State guarantee element. Aid measures involving State guarantees or public loans with a State guarantee element are not considered to be transparent. However, such aid measures are considered transparent if, before the implementation of the measure, the methodology used to calculate the aid intensity of the State guarantee has been notified to and accepted by the Commission after adoption of the Regulation.[42]

4–100   If a State aid measure is not transparent it must be notified to the Commission before it is implemented. The Commission will assess non-transparent State aid measures for the agricultural sector in accordance with the Community guidelines for State aid in the agriculture and forestry sector 2007 to 2013.

Article 3 of the Regulation sets out the conditions for exemption of aid measures that fall within the scope of the Regulation from the obligation to notify in accordance with art.88(3) of the Treaty. Here a distinction is made between transparent individual aid which is not part of any scheme and transparent aid schemes. Both individual aid and aid schemes are compatible with the common market in accordance with art.87(3)(c) and are exempt from

---

[42] The Commission will assess the methodology in accordance with the rules in the Commission's communication on the application of arts 87 and 88 of the EC Treaty to State aid in the form of guarantees. This communication is discussed in Ch. 3 of this book.

the obligation to notify in art.88(3) if a number of conditions are met. First, individual aid and aid schemes (and aid granted under such schemes) must fulfil the conditions laid down in the Regulation, and in particular the conditions in Ch.2; see below. Secondly, according to art.20(1), Member States must forward to the Commission a summary of the information regarding such aid scheme or individual aid with a view to its publication in the Official Journal of the European Union. This information must be sent electronically, in the form laid down in annex I to the Regulation. The information must be sent at least 10 working days before the entry into force of an aid scheme which is not covered by the Regulation. According to art.20(4), as soon as an aid scheme or individual aid exempted by the Regulation enters into force, the Member States must publish on the internet the full text of such an aid scheme, or the criteria and conditions under which such individual aid is granted. The address of websites containing a direct link to the text of the scheme must be communicated to the Commission in accordance with art.20(1). Thirdly, both individual aid and aid schemes must expressly refer to the Regulation, giving its title and a reference to its publication in the Official Journal.

Chapter 2 of the Regulation sets out different aid categories which are covered by the Regulation. For each category there are detailed conditions which must be fulfilled if a Member State is to be exempt from the obligation to notify in accordance with art.88(3) of the Treaty. Chapter 2 contains 14 categories of aid in arts 4–17. The categories are briefly reviewed in the following.

Article 4: Investment in agricultural holdings (the investment must be aimed **4–101** at, e.g. reduction of production costs; improvement and re-deployment of production; improvement in quality; preservation and improvement of the natural environment, or the improvement of hygiene conditions or animal welfare standards).

Article 5: Conservation of traditional landscapes and buildings (aid for investments or capital works intended for the conservation of non-productive heritage features located on agricultural holdings, such as archaeological or historical features, and for investments or capital works intended for the conservation of heritage features of productive assets on farms, such as farm buildings, provided that the investment does not entail any increase in the production capacity of the farm).

Article 6: Relocation of farm buildings in the public interest (the public interest invoked must be specified in the relevant provisions of the Member State, and where the relocation results in the farmer benefiting from more modern facilities or increase in production capacity, the farmer must contribute at least 60 per cent, (or 50 per cent in less favoured areas) of the costs, or if the beneficiary is a young farmer who fulfils the criteria in Regulation (EC) No.1698/2005,[43] this contribution must be at least 55 per cent or 45 per cent respectively).

---

[43] These criteria are that the beneficiary must be under 40 years old and be setting up on their own farm for the first time; they must have sufficient qualifications and competence for the job; and they must submit a business plan for the development of their farming activities.

4–102   Article 7: Aid for the establishment of young farmers (the more detailed criteria for aid for the setting up of young farmers are set out in art.22 of Regulation (EC) No.1698/2005).

Article 8: Aid for early retirement (such aid must fulfil the criteria set out in art.23 of Regulation (EC) No.1698/2005,[44] and the cessation of commercial farming activities must be permanent and definitive).

Article 9: Aid for producer groups (start-up aid can be given for setting up producer groups or producer associations,[45] and the eligible costs include the rental of suitable premises, acquisition of office equipment, including computer hardware and software, administrative staff costs, overheads and legal and administrative fees, and if premises are purchased, the eligible costs for premises are limited to rental costs at market rates).

4–103   Article 10: Aid in respect of animal and plant diseases and pest infestations (aid to compensate farmers for the costs of prevention, for the eradication of animal or plant diseases or pest infestations incurred, and for the losses incurred).

Article 11: Aid for losses due to adverse climatic events (aid to compensate farmers for losses of plants or animals or farm buildings or damage to farm buildings and farm equipment caused by adverse climatic events which can be assimilated to natural disasters provided the adverse climatic event is formally recognised as such by public authorities).

Article 12: Aid towards the payment of insurance premiums (aid for insurance against losses caused by climatic events, animal or plant diseases, or pest infestations; the aid must not constitute a barrier to the operation of the internal market for insurance services).

4–104   Article 13: Aid for land reparcelling (aid can be granted towards the legal and administrative costs, including surveying costs).

Article 14: Aid to encourage the production of quality agricultural products (aid granted in this category must usually be given in the form of subsidised services, such as for the development of quality agricultural products, market research activities, product conception and design, the introduction of quality control schemes and training in their use, certification of quality assurance and similar systems).

Article 15: Provision of technical support in the agricultural sector (aid for education and training, replacement services during the absence of farmers or farm workers, consultancy services, knowledge exchange, etc.).

4–105   Article 16: Support for the livestock sector (aid for the establishment and

---

[44] The beneficiary must be at least 55 years old, but not yet have reached normal pensionable age or be at most 10 years younger than the normal pensionable age in the Member State in question; they must cease all commercial farming activity, finally; and they must have been farming for the previous 10 years.

[45] A "producer group" is a group which, according to art.2 (12), is set up for the purpose of jointly adapting, within the objectives of the common market organisations, the production and output of its members to market requirements, in particular by concentrating supply. A "producer association" is an association which consists of recognised producer groups and pursues the same objectives on a larger scale.

maintenance of herd books, tests to determine the genetic quality or yield of livestock, introduction at farm level of innovative animal breeding techniques or practices (except artificial insemination), the costs of removing and destroying fallen stock, or aid for insurance to cover the costs of removing and destroying fallen stock, TSE tests and BSE tests).

Article 17: Aid provided for in certain Council Regulations (Council Regulation (EC) No.1255/1999, in particular art.14(2)[46]; Council Regulation (EC) No.1782/2003, in particular art.87, art.107(3) and the first subparagraph of art.125(5)[47]; and Council Regulation (EC) No.2200/96, in particular art.15(6)[48]).

The Member States are subject to a number of obligations under art.18 of the Regulation, which must be fulfilled prior to the grant of aid. In this respect the Regulation distinguishes between aid schemes and individual aid. First, art.18 deals with aid schemes which create an automatic right to receive aid, requiring no further action at administrative level. In such cases, aid may only be granted in respect of activities undertaken or services received after the aid scheme has been set up and published in accordance with the regulation; see the discussion of art.20(1) and (4) above. The same applies in respect of aid schemes under which aid is sought. In this situation the aid application must also be correctly submitted to the authorities and it must be approved, with a statement of the aid amount and of how this amount has been calculated. Approval is also conditional on the budget available for the aid scheme not being exhausted. Secondly these further conditions must also be fulfilled before individual aid can be granted for activities or services.

Article 19 of the Regulation deals with the cumulation of aid. According   **4–106** to this, the aid ceilings fixed in arts 4–16 apply regardless of whether the aid is financed entirely from State resources or is partly financed by the Community. Furthermore, aid which is exempted under the Regulation may not be cumulated with any other State aid if such cumulation would result in an aid intensity exceeding the maximum laid down in the Regulation. Aid which is exempted from notification under the Regulation may not be cumulated with de minimis support within the meaning of Regulation (EC) No.1860/2004 in respect of the same eligible expenditure or investment project, if such cumulation would result in an aid intensity exceeding that fixed by the Regulation.

Article 20 of the Regulation lays down a number of administrative duties for the Member States. According to art.20(2), the Member States must keep

---

[46] Aid for supplying certain milk products to school pupils.

[47] Aid to farmers who grow nuts (art.87); aid for 50% of the costs associated with establishing multi-annual crops intended for bio-mass production on set-aside land (art.107(3)); aid for an additional national suckler cow premium, up to a maximum of €50 per animal, provided that no discrimination is caused between stockfarmers in the Member State concerned (art.125(5)).

[48] Article 15 concerns producer organisations setting up an operational fund, and under para. 6, where the degree of organisation of producers is particularly low, Member States may pay financial assistance equal to half the financial contributions of producers.

detailed records of the aid schemes exempted by the Regulation, as well as the individual aid which is exempted by the Regulation. Such records must contain information about the status of the company as an SME, and other information necessary to establish that the conditions for exemption laid down in the regulation are fulfilled. Member States must keep such information for 10 years from the date on which aid is granted. Under art.20(3), the Member States must compile a report on the application of the Regulation, and must submit a separate report relating to payments made under arts 10 and 11.

The Regulation entered into force on January 1, 2007 and remains in force until December 31, 2013, with a supplementary period of a further six months.

De minimis aid in the agricultural sector

4–107   In accordance with Council Regulation (EC) No.994/98 of May 7, 1998 on the application of arts 92 and 93 [now arts 87 and 88] of the Treaty establishing the European Community to certain categories of horizontal State aid, the Commission has adopted Regulation (EC) No.1535/2007 of December 20, 2007 on the application of arts 87 and 88 of the EC Treaty to de minimis aid in the sector of agricultural production (OJ L 337, December 21, 2007, p.35).

The intention of the De minimis Regulation is that aid measures that are below a certain ceiling should not be regarded as fulfilling the criteria in art.87(1) of the EC Treaty on State aid. Such measures are thus also not subject to the obligation to notify them to the Commission as set out in art.88(3) of the Treaty.

On the basis of its experience in the agricultural sector, the Commission decided that very small aid amounts which are provided in this sector do not fulfil the criteria in art.87(1) if certain conditions are met. This is the case both with aid amounts granted to individual producers, and when the accumulated amount of aid granted to the agricultural sector does not exceed a small percentage of the value of the production. The agricultural sector of the Community is normally characterised by the products being produced by a large number of very small producers who mainly produce interchangeable goods within the framework of common organisations of the market. The effect of small aid amounts granted to individual producers in a given period ought thus to relate to the value of agricultural production at the sector level in the same period. A ceiling in the form of an amount per Member State laid down on the basis of the value of production in the agricultural sector makes it possible to ensure a uniform approach in all Member States, based on an objective economic reference value.

4–108   According to art.1, Regulation (EC) No.1535/2007 applies to aid granted to enterprises that are not in difficulty and active in the primary production of agricultural products (i.e. the products listed in annex I of the Treaty apart from products covered by Regulation (EC) No.104/2000, see above). However, the Regulation does not apply to aid the amount of which is fixed on the basis of the price or the quantity of products put on the market. Furthermore, aid to export-related activities (export aid) is not covered by the Regulation.[49] Finally, aid which is conditional on the use of domestic products in preference to imported products is also not covered by the Regulation.

Aid measures which are within the scope of the Regulation are not required to be notified in accordance with art.88(3) of the EC Treaty if the conditions in art.3 are fulfilled:

- The total de minimis aid granted to any one enterprise may not exceed €7,500 over any period of three years, and
- The cumulative amount granted over any three-year period to various enterprises in the agricultural sector may not exceed the value per Member State set out in the annex to the Regulation.

If the threshold of €7,500 is exceeded, the Regulation will be inapplicable to the entire aid measure in question—including that part of the aid which is within the threshold. Consequently, such aid becomes unlawful State aid, cf. Ch.2 of this book.

These ceilings are expressed as a cash grant, and all figures used must be gross, that is, before any deduction or taxes/charges. Where aid is awarded in a form other than a grant it should be possible to calculate in advance the aid amount expressed in gross grant equivalent of the aid without undertaking a risk assessment ("transparent aid"). Aid that is paid in several instalments must be discounted to its value at the date of granting it. In this connection, and with regard to the calculation of the three-year period and the interest, de minimis aid is regarded as being granted when the legal right to receive the aid is conferred on the beneficiary and the interest rate to be used for discounting purposes and to calculate the aid amount in a soft loan must be the reference rate applicable at the time of grant. This presupposes that the loan is backed by normal security and does not involve abnormal risk—otherwise the aid is not transparent and the Regulation would therefore not be applicable at all. The reference rate is periodically fixed by the Commission and published in the Official Journal of the European Union and on the internet.

4–109

Cumulation with respect to the same eligible costs is possible as long as the most favourable threshold in the applicable Community rules is respected.

Article 4 of the Regulation introduces monitoring duties on the Member States which inter alia include providing aid recipients with information that the aid is granted as de minimis aid, publicity concerning implementation of schemes and the set-up of monitoring systems which include information necessary to establish that the Regulation has been adhered to.

---

[49] Export-related activities are discussed in para.3–075 and 3–076.

The regulation applies from January 1, 2008 to the end of 2013. It may also be applied to aid granted before January 1, 2008 provided the Regulation is adhered to. Furthermore, according to art.6(3) the Regulation may be applied for a period of six months after the Regulation expires.

FISHERIES

4–110   According to art.7(1) in Council Regulation (EC) No.1198/2006 of July 27, 2006 on the European Fisheries Fund (OJ L 223, August 15, 2006, p.1), and art.32 in Council Regulation (EC) No.104/2000 of December 17, 1999 on the common organisation of the markets in fishery and aquaculture products (OJ L 17, January 21, 2000, p.22), arts 87, 88 and 89 of the Treaty apply to production of and trade in fishery products. Fishery products are defined in art.1 in Regulation 104/2000.

Attention should be drawn to the fact that art.7 in Regulation No.1198/2006 contains two exceptions to the rule that art.87(1) EC applies to the fisheries sector. First, art.87(1) does not apply to financial contributions from Member States to operations co-financed by the EFF and provided as part of an operational programme (i.e. a programme aiming at attaining some of the objectives of the European Fisheries Fund (EFF) such as promotion of a sustainable balance between resources and the fishing capacity of the Community fishing fleet). This means that such financing is not subject to the notification requirement in art.88(3). If national public financing exceeds what is allowed under the EFF, that financing as a whole will be subject to notification to the Commission who will assess the financing under the guidelines dealt with below.

Guidelines for the examination of State aid to fisheries and aquaculture

4–111   As stated previously in this book, in principle State aid is incompatible with the common market; see art.87(1) of the Treaty. However, according to art.87(2) and (3) of the Treaty there are a number of situations in which State aid either is or can be compatible with the common market.

With a view to administering these exceptions the Commission has issued Guidelines for the examination of State aid to fisheries and aquaculture (OJ C 84, April 3, 2008, p.10). The Guidelines are applied from April 1, 2008.

For the application of the guidelines there must be a measure which constitutes State aid in accordance with art.87(1) and which must therefore be notified to the Commission in accordance with art.88(3). A State aid element may be found in special levies or parafiscal charges, interest subsidies, tax reductions or exemptions etc. provided a financial advantage is transferred from a public authority to a beneficiary. A Member State notifying State aid measures needs to provide the Commission with information on the aid

intensity based on eligible costs and the total amount of aid per measure—
otherwise the aid will not be declared compatible with the common market.
All circumstances are taken into account when the Commission evaluates the
effective benefit to the recipient. In case a State aid scheme should last longer
than 10 years solid justification to that end must be provided.

However, an actual aid measure can be covered by one of the block exemp-   **4–112**
tion regulations; for example, see below on de minimis aid or aid for SMEs
in the fisheries sector, or one of the General Block Exemption Regulation
(GBER) discussed in Ch.3 of this book. There can also be other aid measures
which the Member States are not required to notify to the Commission, see
art.7(2) in Regulation No.1198/2006.

The *scope of the guidelines* is set out in its para.1.1. Accordingly they apply
to the entire fisheries sector and concern the exploitation of living aquatic
resources and aquaculture together with the means of production, processing
and marketing of the resultant products, but excluding recreation and sport
fishing which does not result in the sale of fisheries products. According to
art.3(d) of Regulation 1198/2006 aquaculture means rearing or cultivation of
aquatic organisms using techniques designed to increase the production of the
organisms in question beyond the natural capacity of the environment;
the organisms remain the property of a natural or legal person throughout
the rearing or culture stage, up to and including harvesting.

The Common Fisheries Policy must be complied with. This supplements
the State aid rules so that it is a condition for the compatibility of a State
aid measure with the common market that it complies with the objectives
of the Common Fisheries Policy.[50] The Member States must ensure compliance with the Common Fisheries Policy both before and after the grant of
aid. If it appears that the aid beneficiary does not comply with the rules of
the Common Fisheries Policy during the aid period, the aid must be reimbursed. According to para.3.3 of the guidelines, the grant must be reimbursed
in proportion to the gravity of the infringement. Thus the Member State
will not necessarily be required to reclaim the whole of the aid paid to the
beneficiary.

Further, it is the intention that State aid should promote *the rationalisa-*   **4–113**
tion and efficiency of the production and marketing of fishery products. It
must yield lasting improvements so that the industry can develop solely on
the basis of market earnings. Thus it is not compatible with the common
market to grant aid for activities which the beneficiary has already set in
motion or which the beneficiary would have implemented under normal
market conditions—such State aid has no *incentive effect.* As a consequence
of this, operating aid is incompatible with the common market, to the
extent that the beneficiary is merely relieved of costs and is not subject to
firm obligations which clearly promote the aims of the Common Fisheries
Policy. Such aid may come in the form of aid calculated on product prices

---

[50] See Chs 1–3 of the Common Fisheries Policy.

or quantity produced. Operating aid can—despite of a missing incentive effect—be justified under exceptional circumstance such as to make good damage caused by natural disasters. Export aid and aid for trade in fisheries products within and outside the Community is likewise incompatible with the common market.

Chapter 4 of the guidelines lists eight categories of State aid which can be regarded as compatible with the common market.

1. *Aid for categories of measures covered by a block exemption regulation.*

  • Such measures will be assessed on the basis of the guidelines and the relevant provisions in the applicable regulation.

2. *Aid falling within the scope of certain horizontal guidelines*

  • Such measures may be found compatible with the common market provided the horizontal provisions are respected together with the above mentioned conditions applicable to the fisheries sector. In the case of State aid for rescuing and restructuring firms in difficulty a plan to reduce the fleet capacity concerned must be submitted together with the notification to the Commission.

4–114 3. *Aid for investment on-board fishing vessels*

  • Such aid should as a starting point be granted within the framework of an operational programme covered by the EFF. A deviation from this starting point should be explained. Anyhow, such aid must be directed at investments in equipment and modernisation of *vessels more than five years old*, such as improvements of safety on board, working conditions, hygiene, product quality and energy efficiency, *provided* that it does not increase the ability of the vessels to catch fish. Other possibilities may be mentioned, e.g. aid for reducing the impact of fishing on non-commercial species and aid for reducing the impact of fishing on ecosystems and the sea bottom. More options are mentioned in art.25(2) and (6) of Regulation No.1198/2006. It should also be noted that annex II to that regulation contains *limits as to the amount* of State aid grantable which also must be respected.

4. *Aid to compensate damage caused by natural disasters, exceptional occurrences or specific adverse climate events.*

  • State aid compensating losses caused by natural disasters and exceptional occurrences will be assessed directly on the basis of art.87(2)(b) EC. If in fact the aid falls within the scope of application of art.87(2)(b) it is deemed to be compatible with the common market. This means that if there is a link between the natural disaster/exceptional occurrence and the loss no further assessment is necessary. Hence, aid intensity up to 100 per cent is allowed. The application of art.87(2)(b) is discussed further in Ch.1 of this book.

- In case adverse climate events cannot be classified as natural disasters or exceptional occurrences they are not within the ambit of art.87(2)(b). However, State aid compensating for damage caused by such events may be declared compatible with the common market on the basis of art.87(3)(c). This is conditional upon the State aid being notified to the Commission within one year after the occurrence of the event and that certain thresholds subsequently are observed when the Member State concerned implements the State aid measure. According to those thresholds aid up to 100 per cent may be granted if the extent of damages reaches 30 per cent of the average annual turnover of the undertaking concerned in the previous three years—calculated on the basis of the loss of turnover compared to the average turnover during the last three years.
- In any case the compensation should be assessed individually and it should also be observed that no overcompensation takes place. Losses that could have been avoided by taking reasonable precautions are not eligible for compensation, e.g. losses that could have been covered by a normal insurance.

5. *Tax relief and labour related costs concerning Community vessels operating outside Community waters*

- The underlying rationale for this option is to discourage Community vessels from registering in third countries which do not keep control of their fishing fleet in terms of especially illegal, unreported and unregulated fishing.
- The option is only open to Community vessels fishing exclusively outside Community waters (beyond 200 nautical miles from the baselines of the Member States) for *tuna and tuna-like species*.
- Such vessels may be granted corporate tax reliefs and offered reduced rates of social contributions and income taxes for fishermen employed onboard the vessel.
- Member States are required to prove the existence of the risk for de-registration and to provide a safeguard measure that the State aid—in case de-registration takes place despite the State aid—will be paid back for a period of three years preceding the de-registration.

6. *Aid which is financed through parafiscal charges*   **4–115**

- This refers to situations where an aid scheme is funded by special charges, in particular parafiscal charges, which are imposed on certain fishery and aquaculture products, irrespective of their origin.

Where an aid scheme benefits both domestic and imported products, and otherwise complies with the conditions of the Guidelines, it can be regarded as compatible with the common market.

7. *Aid for marketing of fishery products from the outermost regions (The Azores, Madeira, the Canary Islands and the French departments of Guiana and Réunion)*

- Aid for quantities of fishery products in excess of what is allowed under Council Regulation (EC) No.791/2007 of May 21, 2007 (OJ L 176, December 5, 2007, p.1) introducing a scheme to compensate for the additional costs incurred in the marketing of certain fishery products from the outermost regions is allowed if it is granted in accordance with the conditions laid down in arts 3–5 in the said Regulation and on condition that the annual amounts of such additional aid do not exceed the annual amounts provided for each Member State in the above Regulation.

8. *Aid concerning the fishing fleet in the outermost regions*

- This option is open until December 31, 2008, cf. point 4.7 of the Guidelines.

4–116   Other State aid measures than the above mentioned (points 1–7) are in principle not possible unless a Member State can demonstrate that the contemplated measure is compatible with the common market and clearly in line with the Common Fisheries Policy.

Existing aid schemes throughout the EU relating to State aid to fisheries and aquaculture should be brought in line with the Guidelines no later than September 1, 2008.

Small and medium-sized enterprises active in the production, processing and marketing of fisheries products.

Introduction

4–117   State aid to SMEs producing, processing and marketing fisheries products is covered by Commission Regulation (EC) No.736/2008 of July 22, 2008 on the application of arts 87 and 88 of the Treaty to State aid to small and medium-sized enterprises active in the production, processing and marketing of fisheries products (hereinafter The Regulation).[51] The Regulation entered into force on August 19, 2008 and is applicable until December 31, 2013.

The regulation is a so-called Block Exemption Regulation because it is

---

[51] OJ L 201, 30.7.2008, p.16.

issued on the basis of Council Regulation (EC) No.994/98 of May 7, 1998 on the application of arts 92 and 93 [now 87 and 88] of the Treaty to certain categories of horizontal State aid[52] which empowers the Commission to declare certain categories of State aid, e.g. State aid to SMEs, compatible with the common market and not subject to notification to the Commission prior to its implementation according to art.88(3) EC. Consequently, State aid measures which fulfil the applicable conditions in a block exemption regulation may be granted without consulting the Commission. This is also the case concerning State aid measures within the fisheries sector. However, apart from being in conformity with the Competition Policy such measures in the field of fisheries must also be in conformity with the Common Fisheries Policy as currently expressed in Council Regulation (EC) No.1198/2006 of July 27, 2006 on the European Fisheries Fund[53] and Commission Regulation (EC) No.498/2007 of March 26, 2007.[54] These "double conditions" are incorporated in the SME block exemption regulation and further elaborated upon below. See paras 4–121 to 4–140 concerning general remarks on the application of arts 87, 88 and 89 in the fisheries sector.

The regulation is divided into three chapters. The first chapter contains common conditions stemming from the Competition Policy. The second chapter lists 16 categories of State aid measures. Each category is attached with references to special conditions stemming from the Common Fisheries Policy. It is only those 16 measures which are exempted from notification to the Commission according to art.88(3) provided the measure in question fulfils the common conditions and the attached special conditions derived from the Common Fisheries Policy. Chapter 2 also contains a 17th category of aid in the form of tax exemptions in accordance with Directive 2003/96/EC. The third chapter contains common and final provisions. It should be stressed that only State aid measures fulfilling *all* the conditions of the Regulation are exempted from the requirement of prior notification to the Commission which calls for some caution because State aid granted contrary to the Regulation must be recovered.

Scope of application

Article 1 of the Regulation states its scope of application. Accordingly, the Regulation applies to State aid within the meaning of art.87(1) EC granted to SMEs[55] active in the production, processing or marketing of fisheries products, i.e. products caught at sea or in inland waters and the products of **4–118**

---

[52] OJ L 142, 14.5.1998, p.1.
[53] OJ L 223, 15.8.2006, p.1.
[54] OJ L 120, 10.5.2007, p.1
[55] Small and mediums-sized enterprises are defined in annex I to The General Block Exemption Regulation, See paras 3–007 to 3–027.

aquaculture.[56] Furthermore, the Regulation is inapplicable to operating aid[57], export aid[58] and State aid which is conditional upon the use of domestic goods over imported goods and to SMEs in difficulty. When it comes to State aid within the scope of the Regulation, a simplified definition of "undertaking in difficulty" is given in art.2(i)[59] as an exception to the definition given in Community guidelines on State aid for rescuing and restructuring firms in difficulty. Moreover, SMEs which are incorporated since less than three years should not be considered as being in difficulty for this period for the purposes of the Regulation, unless it fulfils the criteria under domestic law for being the subject to collective insolvency proceedings.

The Regulation excludes from its scope of application State aid exceeding certain *thresholds*. Accordingly, the Regulation does not apply to individual projects with eligible expenses exceeding €2 million, or where the amount of State aid exceeds €1 million per beneficiary per year. When calculating these thresholds, art.6 on cumulation provides guidance to that end. First of all, art.6 prescribes that when calculating if the individual notification threshold is respected (and the maximum aid intensities which is the aid amount expressed as a percentage of the eligible costs, see below), the total amount of public support for the aided activity or project shall be taken into account, irrespectively of whether the support stems from local, regional, national or Community sources or not. Cumulation with different aids exempted under the Regulation is, however, allowed as long as those aid measures concern *different* identifiable eligible costs. It is not allowed to cumulate aid exempted under the Regulation with any other aid exempted under the Regulation or with de minimis aid according to Commission Regulation (EC) No.875/2007 or with other Community funding in relation to the *same*—partly or fully overlapping—eligible costs if the result

---

[56] The definition of "products of aquaculture" is given in art.1 of Council Regulation (EC) No.104/2000 of December 17, 1999 on the common organisation of the markets in fishery and aquaculture products (OJ L 17, 21.1.2000, p. 22). It comprises, e.g. live fish; fresh, chilled and frozen fish; dried, salted and smoked fish; fish fillets and other fish meat; molluscs; crustaceans; animal products; prepared or preserved fish; flours, meals and pellets, of meat or of meat offal, of fish or molluscs or other aquatic invertebrates; a number of different pastas provided they contain more than 20% by weight of fish, crustaceans, molluscs or other aqua aquatic invertebrates.

[57] i.e. the amount of aid is fixed on the basis of price or quantity of products put on the market, or the aid is granted solely on the basis of unit of production or unit of the means of production.

[58] i.e. aid to export-related activities, namely directly linked to the quantities exported, to the establishment and operation of a distribution network or to other current expenditure linked to the export activity. However, State aid towards the cost of participating in trade fairs, or of studies or consultancy services needed for the launch of a new or existing product on a new market is normally not considered to constitute export aid.

[59] "a undertaking in difficulty" means an undertaking (1) which has lost more than half of its registered capital and more than quarter of that capital has been lost over the preceding 12 months (in case of a limited company), or (2) which has lost more than half of its capital as shown in the company accounts and more than quarter of that capital has been lost over the preceding 12 months (in case of a company where at least some members have unlimited liability for the debt of the company), or (3) fulfilling the criteria under domestic law for being the subject of collective insolvency proceedings (all types of companies).

is the highest aid intensity or aid amount applicable to that aid under the Regulation is exceeded.

In line with Commission policy following the Deggendorf case law, see Ch.7, ad hoc aid ("individual aid not awarded on the basis of an aid scheme") to undertakings which is subject to an outstanding recovery order following a previous Commission decision declaring an aid unlawful and incompatible with the common market is excluded from the scope of application of the Regulation. The same is true for aid schemes which do not explicitly exclude the payment of aid to the such undertakings.

General conditions

Article 3 of the Regulations contains the overall conditions for exemp-   **4–119**
tion from the notification requirement of art.88(3) EC. It follows that if State aid granted as ad hoc aid or as individual aid[60] under an aid scheme[61] fulfils all the conditions of the Regulation the aid shall be compatible with the common market within the meaning of art.87(3)(c) EC and thus exempted from the notification requirement. This is further-more conditional upon the summary information according to art.25(1) cf. below having been submitted and the aid being accompanied by an express reference to the title of the Regulation ("Commission Regulation (EC) No.736/2008 of July 22, 2008 on the application of arts 87 and 88 of the Treaty to State aid to small and medium-sized enterprises active in the production, processing and marketing of fisheries products") *and* its publication in the Official Journal of the European Union (OJ L 201, July 30, 2008, p.21). State aid schemes are under similar condi-tions exempted from the notification requirement if any individual aid that could be granted under the scheme fulfils the conditions of the Regulation.

Article 25(1) places Member States under a duty to submit summary infor-mation regarding aid schemes or the awarding of ad hoc aid exempted under the Regulation. The information must forwarded—on the entry into force of the measure in question—to the Commission electronically (using the established Commission IT application, See Ch.2) and in the form provided in annex I. The information required is inter alia the amount of aid granted or in case of an aid scheme the planned annual expenditure, the maximum aid intensity, the category of aid concerned, objective of and motivation for the aid, and according to art.25 (2) also the web address leading directly to

---

[60] Meaning ad hoc aid and notifiable awards of aid on the basis of an aid scheme.
[61] Meaning any act on the basis of which, without further implementing measures being required, individual aid awards may be made to undertakings defined within the act in a general and abstract manner and any act on the basis of which aid which is not linked to a specific project may be awarded to one or several undertakings for an indefinite period of time and/or for an indefinite amount.

the full text of the aid measure. The Commission is under a duty to acknowl-edge the receipt of the information without delay and to publish it on the Commission's website and in the Official Journal.

It furthermore follows from art.3 that Member States, on the one hand, shall verify—before any aid is granted under the Regulation—that the sup-ported measure and its effect are in accordance with Community law, and on the other hand, explicitly inform the beneficiaries *that* they must comply with the Common Fisheries Policy during the grant period and *that* the con-sequence of non-compliance is recovery of the State aid in proportion to the gravity of the infringement.

Other general conditions

4–120 The Regulation only applies to State aid which is transparent and has an incen-tive effect. Transparent aid is defined as aid in respect of which it is possible to calculate precisely the gross grant equivalent ex ante without undertaking a risk assessment. According to art.5 the following types of aid instrument shall be considered transparent respectively non-transparent.

As mentioned the Regulation only exempts State aid with a so-called incen-tive effect cf. art.7. The entire aid measure shall have an incentive effect. The background for introducing such a condition is a wish to ensure that the aid is necessary and acts as an incentive to develop certain activities (cf. below regarding aid categories).

An aid measure has an incentive effect if it enables the beneficiary to carry out activities or projects which it would not have carried out as such (under normal market conditions) in the absence of the aid. This condition is considered to be fulfilled if the beneficiary has submitted an application for the aid to the national authority concerned *before* the work on the project or activ-ity has started. The condition does not apply to fiscal measures establishing a legal right to aid in accordance with objective criteria and without the Member State having to exercise discretion if those fiscal measures have been adopted before work on the aided project or activity has started.

Categories of aid

4–121 As mentioned in the introduction the Regulation provides for 16 categories of State aid with special conditions attached. If these conditions—together with the general conditions described above—are fulfilled, the State aid measure shall be compatible with the common market within the meaning of art.87(3)(c) EC and shall be exempt from the notification requirement of art.88(3) EC.

It is a condition with respect to all 16 categories that the amount of aid, in grant equivalent, does not exceed the total rate of public contribution fixed in annex II (on aid intensities) to Council Regulation (EC) No.1198/2006 of

Transparent	Non-transparent
1. Direct grants.	1. Capital injunctions.
2. Interest rate subsidies.	2. Risk capital measures.
3. Aid comprised of guarantee schemes provided: • The Commission has after a notification approved the methodology to calculate the gross grant equivalent and that methodology directly addresses the type of guarantee and underlying transaction being applied in the context of the Regulation, or • The gross grant equivalent has been calculated on the basis of the safe-harbour principle, See paras 3-154 to 3-168.	
4. Fiscal measures provided: • The measure includes a cap ensuring that the applicable threshold is not exceeded.	
5. Loans provided • The gross grant equivalent is calculated on the basis of the applicable reference rate at the time of grant and taking into account the security and/or abnormal risk associated with the loan.	
6. Repayable advances if: • The total amount of repayable advance does not exceed the individual notification thresholds and aid intensities[62] (total amount of repayable advance as a percentage of the eligible costs) under the Regulation.	3. Repayable advances if: • The total amount of repayable advance exceeds the individual notification thresholds and aid intensities (total amount of repayable advance as a percentage of the eligible costs) under the Regulation.

July 27, 2006 on the European Fisheries Fund.[63] The above mentioned rule on cumulation also applies when calculating the maximum aid intensities under each category of aid. The Regulation furthermore contains rules on calculation of aid intensities and determination of eligible costs cf. art.4. The eligible costs shall be supported by clear and itemised documentary evidence and be in accordance with art.55(2) and (5) in Regulation 1198/2006 and art.26 of

---

[62] See below regarding calculation of aid intensities and determination of eligible costs.
[63] OJ L 223, 15.8.2006, p.1.

Commission Regulation (EC) No.498/2007 of March 26, 2007 laying down detailed rules for the implementation of Council Regulation (EC) 1198/2006 on the European Fisheries Fund.[64] When calculating aid intensities the figures used shall be before deduction of taxes or other charges. Apart from State aid in the form of grants, the aid amount shall be the grant equivalent of the aid. For discounting purposes the applicable interest rate is the reference rate.

Categories of aid with attached special conditions:

4–122

Aid category—Aid in favour of:	Conditions in reg.1198/2006	Conditions in reg.498/2007
1. Permanent cessation of fishing activities.	Art.23	Art.4
2. Temporary cessation of fishing activities (for fishers and owners of fishing vessels).	Art.24	None
3. Socioeconomic compensation for the management of the fleet.	Art.26(3) and 27	Art.8
4. Productive investments in aquaculture.	Arts 28 and 29	Arts 9 and 10
5. Aqua-environmental measures (compensation for the use of aquaculture production methods helping to protect and improve the environment and conserve nature).	Arts 28 and 30	Art.11
6. Public health measures (to mollusc farmers for the temporary suspension of harvesting of farmed mollusc).	Arts 28 and 31	None
7. Animal health measures.	Arts 28 and 32	Art.12
8. Inland fishing.	Art 33	Art.13
9. Processing and marketing.	Arts 34 and 35	Art.14
10. Collective actions (for measures of common interest which are implemented with the active support of operators themselves or by organisations acting on behalf of producers or other organisations recognized by the Member States.	Arts 36 and 37	Art.15
11. Measures intended to protect and develop aquatic fauna and flora (of common interest and enhancing the aquatic environment).	Arts 36 and 38	Art.16
12. Investment in fishing ports (public or private), landing sites and shelters.	Arts 36 and 39	Art.17

[64] OJ L 120, 10.5.2007, p.1.

13. Development of new markets and promotional campaigns (of common interest intended to implement a policy of quality and value enhancement, development of new markets or promotional campaigns for fisheries and aquaculture products).	Arts 36 and 40	Art.18
14. Pilot projects	Arts 36 and 41	Art.19
15. Modification for reassignment of fishing vessels (under the flag of a Member State and registered in the Community for training or research purposes inside the fisheries sector or for other activities outside fishing).	Arts 36 and 42	Art.20
16. Technical assistance	Arts 46(2) and (3)	None

The Regulation exempts furthermore an additional 17th aid category regarding tax exemptions applicable to the whole fishing sector introduced by Member States pursuant to and in accordance with art.14 of Council Directive 2003/96/EC of October 27, 2003 restructuring the Community framework for the taxation of energy products and electricity.[65] Environmental aid in the form of tax exemptions or reductions applicable to inland fishing and piscicultural works introduced by Member States pursuant to art.15 of Directive 2003/96/EC are also exempted from the notification requirement provided it is not granted for periods exceeding 10 years. The recipients of tax reductions shall at least pay the Community minimum tax level set by the directive.

Transparency and monitoring requirements

Chapter 3 (art.25) of the Regulation contains administrative requirements **4–123** which the Member States must observe. According to art.25(2), which is concerned with *aid schemes* and ad hoc aid, the Member States must—upon the entry into force of the mentioned aid measures—publish on the internet the full text of the aid measure in question. The text has to indicate the criteria and conditions for granting aid and the identity of the granting authority. The text is to be accessible on the internet as long as the measure concerned is in force. The act by which *individual aid* is granted according to the Regulation (apart from aid in the form of fiscal measures) shall contain an explicit reference to the specific provision of the Regulation concerned by the granting act and to the national law ensuring respect of the relevant provisions of the Regulation. The act must furthermore include a reference to the above mentioned Internet address.

[65] OJ L 283, 31.10.2003, p.51.

Member States are furthermore under a duty to keep records on the application of the Regulation and keep those for 10 years. The records shall contain all information necessary for the Commission to conclude whether the Regulation has been adhered to and be provided to the Commission on written request. Non-compliance on the part of the Member States with this duty may ultimately lead the Commission to adopt a decision stating that all future individual aid granted under the scheme has to be notified to the Commission.

De minimis aid in the fisheries sector

4–124 When the Commission adopted Regulation (EC) No.1860/2004 of October 6, 2004 on the application of arts 87 and 88 of the EC Treaty to de minimis aid in the agriculture and fisheries sectors (OJ L 325, October 28, 2004, p.4), the agricultural and fisheries sectors were considered as one. The Commission has now acknowledged that this approach is no longer suitable. The Commission has thus already dealt with the processing and marketing of agricultural products in the horizontal de minimis regulation.

De minimis aid in the fisheries sector is now regulated by Commission Regulation (EC) No.875/2007 of July 24, 2007 on the application of arts 87 and 88 of the EC Treaty to de minimis aid in the fisheries sector and amending Regulation (EC) No.1860/2004 (OJ L 193, July 25, 2007, p.6).

Scope

4–125 According to its art.1, the Regulation applies to aid for undertakings whose activities concern the production, processing or marketing of fisheries products.[66] However, the Regulation does not apply to aid for export-related activities, aid which is contingent upon the use of domestic over imported goods, or where the amount of the aid is fixed on the basis of price or quantity of products put on the market.[67]

The scope of the Regulation is further limited by the rules in its art.3(7), where it is stated that the Regulation only applies to transparent aid, i.e. aid where the gross grant equivalent has been calculated on the basis of market interest rates prevailing at the time of the grant. This will be relevant if the aid is provided in any form other than as a cash subsidy.

---

[66] "Fisheries products" are defined in art.1 of Regulation (EC) No.104/2000. "Processing and marketing" means all operations, including handling, treatment, production and distribution, performed between the time of landing or harvesting and the end product stage.

[67] Aid for the expansion of fishing capacity, expressed as tonnage of the power of machinery, other than aid for the modernisation of the main deck, is also not covered by the Regulation; see art.3(n) and art.11(5) of Council Regulation (EC) No.2371/2002 of December 20, 2002 on the conservation and sustainable exploitation of fisheries resources under the Common Fisheries Policy (OJ L 358, 31.12.2002, p.59).

If aid is provided in the form of a loan it will be considered as transparent if the gross grant equivalent has been calculated on the basis of market interest rates prevailing at the time of the grant. Aid in the form of capital injections by public bodies will be considered as transparent if the total does not exceed the de minimis ceiling. Aid consisting of risk capital is considered to be transparent as long as the risk capital provided does not exceed the de minimis ceiling. Aid in the form of repayable advances is not considered transparent aid to the extent that the total amount of repayable advances exceeds the de minimis threshold under the Regulation. Aid under a guarantee arrangement to undertakings which are not undertakings in difficulty is assumed to be transparent if the guaranteed part of the underlying loan provided under such scheme does not exceed €225,000 per undertaking. If the guaranteed part of the underlying loan only accounts for a given proportion of this ceiling, the gross grant equivalent of the guarantee will be deemed to correspond to the same proportion of the de minimis ceiling of €30,000 over three years. The guarantee may not exceed 80 per cent of the underlying loan.

The de minimis ceiling in the fisheries sector

Article 3(1) and (2) of the Regulation provides that if the total de minimis aid per undertaking does not exceed a ceiling of €30,000 over a period of three fiscal years, the aid will not fall within the ambit of art.87(1) of the EC Treaty and will thus be exempt from the obligation to notify laid down in art.88(3) of the Treaty. However, the rules on monitoring and the transitional provisions discussed below must also be complied with. The Member States are also restricted in their scope for providing de minimis aid by art.3(4) of the Regulation, whereby the cumulative amount granted to undertakings in the fisheries sector over any period of three fiscal years may not exceed the value per Member State set out in the annex to the Regulation.   **4–126**

If the ceiling of €30,000 is exceeded, the total amount of aid cannot benefit from the exemption in the Regulation; see art.3(3).

The ceilings referred to in the Regulation are expressed as cash grants, and all figures used must be gross figures (i.e. before deductions for taxes and other duties). In other cases the aid amount is the gross grant equivalent.

If aid is paid in instalments, it must be discounted to its value at the date of its grant, using the reference rate applicable at the time of the grant.

Cumulation

Under art.3(8) of the Regulation, de minimis aid may not be cumulated with aid in respect of the same eligible costs if such cumulation would result in an aid intensity exceeding that fixed in the specific circumstances   **4–127** of each case by a block exemption regulation or decision adopted by the Commission.

Monitoring

4–128   Article 4 of the Regulation provides that where a Member State grants de minimis aid to an undertaking, it must inform the undertaking in writing about the amount of the aid (expressed as the gross grant equivalent) and about its de minimis character, making express reference to the Regulation (citing its title and publication reference in the Official Journal of the European Union). Also, before aid is granted, the Member States must make a declaration (in writing of electronically) about all other de minimis aid which the undertaking has received in the current and two previous fiscal years.[68] Member States can avoid this if they set up a central register containing all the information about de minimis aid granted in the Member State in question, and if the register covers a period of three fiscal years. Thereafter the Member States can monitor that the ceilings referred to are not exceeded.

Member States must also collect and register all information necessary for establishing that the Regulation is complied with. The information must be kept for 10 years and must be made available to the Commission upon request.

Transitional arrangements

4–129   Article 5 of the Regulation lays down some transitional rules. According to this, the Regulation is also applicable to aid granted before its entry into force, if the aid fulfils all the conditions laid down in the Regulation. Any aid which does not fulfil those conditions will be assessed by the Commission in accordance with the relevant frameworks, guidelines, etc.

SERVICES OF GENERAL ECONOMIC INTEREST

The concept of Services of general economic interest

4–130   Services of general economic interest are referred to in art.16 in part one of the EC Treaty on the Community's principles. According to art.16, without prejudice to arts 73, 86 and 87, the Community and the Member States, each within their respective powers and within the scope of application of this Treaty, must ensure that such services operate on the basis of principles and conditions which enable them to fulfil their missions.

---

[68]   In this respect art.4(1) contains special rules for what constitutes aid granted in accordance with schemes.

These services of general economic interest will often be provided on special conditions, so that their aims can be achieved. Thus, in order for the purposes to be achieved, it can be necessary for the Member States to provide financial support to cover all or part of the special costs associated with the perform-ance of services of general economic interest. In accordance with art.295 of the Treaty, it makes no difference whether these services are provided by public or private undertakings.

The starting point for undertakings which have been entrusted with the provisions of services of general economic interest is art.86(2) of the Treaty. According to this, such undertakings are:

> "subject to the rules contained in this Treaty, in particular to the rules on competition, in so far as the application of such rules does not obstruct the performance, in law or in fact, of the particular tasks assigned to them. The development of trade must not be affected to such an extent as would be contrary to the interests of the Community."

Thus, under art.86(2), undertakings which have been entrusted with the provisions of services of general economic interest are subject to the com-petition rules of the Treaty, and the Treaty rules on State aid apply to such undertakings. Furthermore, the application of the rules can be limited to the extent that this may be necessary for the achievement of the purposes of the services of general economic interest. This means that it is possible to grant exemptions from the Treaty rules under art.86(2). **4–131**

However, art.86(2) is only applicable if a number of conditions are fulfilled. First, the task must be explicitly entrusted by the State through an act of public authority.[69] The act of public authority whereby the task is entrusted must at least contain a precise statement of what obligations of general eco-nomic interest the undertaking in question has specifically been entrusted with, including their extent and duration, and the undertaking itself must be clearly identified. Secondly, the task which is entrusted must concern a service of general economic interest. Unless otherwise specifically provided under Community law, the Member States have wide discretion in determining which services are of general economic interest.[70] This discretion may only be set aside if it is manifestly wrong.[71] Thirdly, an exemption from the Treaty rules must be necessary for the performance of the service entrusted, and the exemption must be reasonable in relation to the obligation. Compensation to an undertaking which carries out a service of general economic interest must not exceed what is necessary for carrying out the service. Finally, trade

---

[69] For the meaning of "entrust" and "act of public authority", see Case T-17/02, *Fred Olsen v Commission*, [2005] E.C.R. II-2031, with references to further cases..

[70] Case T-17/02, *Fred Olsen v Commission*, [2005] E.C.R. II-2031, with references to further cases..

[71] e.g. it is possible that helping employees fill out their tax returns correctly could be a service of general economic interest; see Case C-451/03, *Servizi Ausiliari Dottori Commercialisti v Giuseppe Calafiori*, [2006] E.C.R. I-2941.

must not be distorted to such an extent as to be contrary to the interests of the Community.

4–132   In the postal services sector, the notice from the Commission on the application of the competition rules to the postal sector and on the assessment of certain State measures relating to postal services (OJ C 39, February 6, 1998, p.2) sets out how the Commission intends to act when applying the competition rules to the sector, including assessing certain State measures in relation to the provision of postal services.

Among other things, the notice is concerned with the cross-subsidisation between profitable and not profitable parts of the activities of postal services. A directive has now laid down the upper limit for what individual Member States can consider as a reserved domain, i.e. not open to free competition. This concerns the universal postal service, while other services, such as courier services, must be open to competition and may not receive funds passed over from the non-competition domain.

The notice on postal services also deals with State aid and it emphasises that there is an obligation to give notice of any State aid and any changes to such aid in this area. Moreover, the Transparency Directive (Directive 80/723/EEC) applies, so that postal service providers must comply with its provisions on providing the Commission with information about financial relations between the State and the postal service provider on request.

The Commission will decide on cases of State aid for postal services on a case-by-case basis, including taking into account the need for compensation, proportionality, and the boundaries between the reserved domain and the area in which services should be open to free competition.[72]

The Altmark case

4–133   In the *Altmark* case the ECJ decided that compensation for discharging public service obligations does not constitute State aid, as long as a number of conditions are fulfilled.[73] To some extent the case clears up the doubt that

---

[72] On the situation for postal services see Case 367/95 P, *Sytraval*, [1998] E.C.R. I-1719. The judgment in Case T-106/95, *FFSA and Others v Commission*, [1997] E.C.R. II-229 and not least the decisions in the *UFEX* cases can be authoritative with regard to cross-subsidies; see Case T-613/97, *UFEX v Commission*, [2000] E.C.R. II-4055; Joined Cases C-83/01 P, C-93/01 P and C-94/01 P, *Cronopost and Others v Commission*, [2003] E.C.R. I-6993; and Case T-613/97, *UFEX v Commission*, [2006] E.C.R. II-1531 (this last appealed to the ECJ—see C-342/06 P). In 2002 the Commission decided cases in relation to the Italian and the Irish postal service providers; see IP/02/390 and IP/02/391 of March 12, 2002.

[73] Case C-280/00, *Altmark Trans, Regierungspräsidium Magdeburg v Nahverkehrsgesellschaft Altmark*, [2003] E.C.R. I-7747. See also, e.g. Joined Cases C-34/01—C-38/01, *Enirisorse v Ministero delle finanze*, [2003] E.C.R. I-14243, where the decision in the *Altmark* case was followed. The *Altmark* case is discussed in *Competition Policy Newsletter*, 2003, No.3 p.1, and in The Commission Report on Competition Policy XXXII, p.150 et seq. See also Sandro Santamato and Nicola Pesaresi: "Compensation for services of general economic interest: some thoughts on the Altmark ruling", in *Competition Policy Newsletter*, No.1, Spring 2004, p.17. On the *Altmark* case and public funding of broadband see Monika Hencsey, Olivia

had existed about the relationship between compensation for the discharge of public service obligations and the prohibition on State aid in art.87(1) of the Treaty. In the *Altmark* case certain conditions are laid down which, if they are complied with, exclude State aid. However, the *Altmark* case does not necessarily clear up all questions on the conditions for when compensation for discharging public service obligations does not constitute State aid within the meaning of art.87(1) of the Treaty.[74]

According to the judgment, a public payment does not fall within the ambit of art.87(1) of the Treaty in so far as such payment can be regarded as a fee paid to the recipient for the fulfilment of public service obligations. This is the case if the following conditions are satisfied:

- First, the recipient undertaking must actually have public service obligations to discharge, and the obligations must be clearly defined.
- Second, the parameters on the basis of which the compensation is calculated must be established in advance in an objective and transparent manner.
- Third, the compensation may not exceed what is necessary to cover all or part of the costs incurred in the discharge of public service obligations, taking into account the relevant receipts and a reasonable profit for discharging those obligations.
- Fourth, where the undertaking which is to discharge public service obligations is not chosen pursuant to a public procurement procedure which would allow for the selection of the tenderer capable of providing those services at the least cost to the community, the level of compensation needed must be determined on the basis of an analysis of the costs which

Reymond, Sandro Santamato and Jan Gerrit Westerhof: "State aid rules and public funding of broadband", in *Competition Policy Newsletter,* No.1, Spring 2005, p.8; Lambros Papadias, Alexander Riedl and Jan Gerrit Westerhof: "Public funding for broadband networks—recent developments", in *Competition Policy Newsletter,* No.3, Autumn 2006, p.13; and Pedro Dias and Jan Gerrit Westerhof: "State aid in the broadcasting sector: two decisions regarding ad hoc aid to public service broadcasters in Portugal and the Netherlands", in *Competition Policy Newsletter*, No.3, Autumn 2006, p.86. On the *Altmark* case and hazardous waste, see Anne Theo Seinen: "State aid for hazardous waste treatment: the case of AVR, the Netherlands", in *Competition Policy Newsletter*, No.3, Autumn 2005, p.97. See also Daniel Boeshertz and Paola Icardi: "Poste Italiane: a market fee can fulfil the Altmark criteria", *Competition Policy Newsletter*, No.1, Spring 2007, p.121. The *Altmark* case is also dealt with in The Commission Report on Competition Policy, 2003, pp.149 and 152.

[74] Claus Gulmann, previously a judge at the European Court of Justice has commented on the *Altmark* case in his article "State aid and compensation for public services", in a festschrift for the former President of the Court of first Instance, Bo Vesterdorf; see Liber Amicorum en L'Honneur de Bo Vesterdorf / Liber Amicorum in Honour of Bo Vesterdorf, 2007, Bruylant. In his article Gulmann questions whether the four conditions which the ECJ listed in its *Altmark* judgment are generally applicable. Gulmann argues that public service obligations should not be treated differently from other services which public bodies buy, e.g. cleaning services. He also points to some problems for judges in the Member States in the situation where they have to decide whether compensation for the provision of a service in the general economic interest fulfils the criteria in the *Altmark* case and need not therefore be notified to the Commission in accordance with art.88(3) of the Treaty, particularly in relation to the question of reimbursement of compensation.

a typical undertaking, well run and adequately provided with means so as to be able to meet the necessary public service requirements, would have incurred in discharging those obligations, taking into account the relevant receipts and a reasonable profit for discharging the obligations.

4–134   In furtherance of the *Altmark* judgment, the Commission has issued some new rules, with a view to implementing the *Altmark* criteria in practice.[75] These are Commission Decision of November 28, 2005 on the application of art.86(2) of the EC Treaty to State aid in the form of public service compensation granted to certain undertakings entrusted with the operation of services of general economic interest (OJ L 312, November 29, 2005, p.67) and Community framework for State aid in the form of public service compensation (OJ C 297, November 29, 2005, p.4).

The framework referred to details the costs to be taken into account when calculating compensation. The Decision contains rules which must be complied with in order to be exempted from the requirement for prior notification of compensation under certain threshold amounts and for specified public services. The Transparency Directive (Directive 80/723/EEC) is amended so that following the *Altmark* case it is clear that undertakings that have been entrusted with public service obligations and which carry on other activities must keep separate accounts for their different activities, even if the compensation in question does not constitute State aid. Separate accounts are a prerequisite for the correct calculation of the amount of compensation.

The framework and the Decision are discussed below, and the reader is also referred to the discussion of the Transparency Directive in paras 2–066 to 2–067 of this book.

Commission Decision on the application of art.86(2) of the EC Treaty to State aid in the form of public service compensation granted to certain undertakings entrusted with the operation of services of general economic interest

4–135   The Decision deals with the conditions under which State aid in the form of compensation paid to an undertaking for the discharge of public service obligations should be regarded as being compatible with the common market and exempt from the notification requirement under art.88(3) of the Treaty. The decision was adopted under the authority of art.86(3) of the Treaty, and has the same effect as a block exemption regulation, as it exempts certain measures from the requirement to notify in art.88(3).

The scope of the Decision is set out in its art.2. According to this, the

---

[75] See the Commission's Report on Competition Policy 2004, Vol.1 p.133 et seq. See also *Lars Peter Svane*: "Public service compensation in practice: Commission package on State aid for Services of General Economic Interest", in *Competition Policy Newsletter*, No.3, Autumn 2005, p.34.

Decision does not apply to land transport, and it only applies to sea and air transport to the extent that the conditions in Regulation (EEC) No.2408/92 and Regulation (EEC) No.3577/92 apply.

Apart from these situations, the Decision applies to compensation granted to undertakings in connection with services of general economic interest as referred to in art.86(2) of the Treaty in so far as the compensation falls within one of the following categories:

- Compensation granted to undertakings with an average annual turnover before tax, all activities included, of less than €100 million (for credit institutions, the threshold is €800 million in terms of balance sheet total) during the two financial years preceding that in which the service of general economic interest was assigned, and which receive annual compensation for the service in question of less than €30 million. The threshold of €30 million may be determined by taking an annual average representing the value of compensation granted during the contract period or over a period of five years;
- Compensation granted to hospitals and social housing undertakings carrying out activities qualified as services of general economic interest by the Member State concerned;
- Compensation for air or maritime links to islands on which average annual traffic during the two financial years preceding that in which the service of general economic interest was assigned does not exceed 300,000 passengers; and
- Compensation for airports and ports for which average annual traffic during the two financial years preceding that in which the service of general economic interest was assigned does not exceed 1,000,000 passengers, in the case of airports, and 300,000 passengers, in the case of ports.

Within the areas defined above, State aid in the form of compensation **4–136** for public service obligations which fulfils the conditions laid down in the Decision (see below) is compatible with the common market and exempt from the requirement to notify set out in art.88(3) of the Treaty. However, there is an exception to this, that the principle of *lex specialis* can lead to a different result, as restrictive provisions of Community law may apply in relation to specific sectors.

According to art.4 of the Decision, responsibility for operation of the service of general economic interest must be entrusted to the undertaking concerned by way of one or more official acts. It is up to each Member State to determine the form of these official acts. In contrast, the Member States are not free to determine the content of such official acts. Among other things, they must clearly specify the undertaking and territory concerned, the nature and the duration of the public service obligations, and the nature of any exclusive or special rights assigned to the undertaking. In addition, such official acts must state the parameters for calculating, controlling and reviewing the compensation and the arrangements for avoiding and repaying any overcompensation. According to art.6, the Member States must ensure that regular checks are carried out, to ensure that undertakings are not receiving overcompensation. If a Member State finds that an undertaking has been overcompensated, it must claim reimbursement. However, if the amount of overcompensation does not exceed 10 per cent of the annual compensation the claim for reimbursement need not be made. In such a case the overcompensation may be carried forward to the next annual period and deducted from the amount of compensation payable in respect of that period. In respect of undertakings in the social housing sector which exclusively carry out services of general economic interest, any overcompensation of up to 20 per cent of the annual compensation may be carried forward to the next period. The Member States must carry out regular checks of such undertakings. Even though, in certain circumstances, it is possible to carry forward some overcompensation, the Member States must regularly update the parameters for calculating if the control of these shows that they lead to the compensation being too high.

Article 5 contains detailed rules for the calculation of compensation. The principle is that the amount of compensation must not exceed what is necessary to cover the costs incurred in discharging the public service obligations. This must take into account the relevant receipts and a reasonable profit on any own capital necessary for discharging those obligations. The amount of compensation must include all the advantages granted by the State or through State resources, regardless of their form.

4–137   The revenue to be taken into account must include at least the entire revenue earned from the service of general economic interest. An undertaking may have been granted special or exclusive rights linked to some other service of general economic interest. If the undertaking thereby obtains a profit in excess of a reasonable profit, this must be included in its revenue. The same applies to other advantages which may have been granted to the undertaking by the Member State. The profits accruing from activities other than the service of general economic interest are to be assigned to the financing of the service of general economic interest, to the extent determined by the Member State.

On the costs side, art.5(2) states that all the costs incurred in the operation of the service of general economic interest are to be taken into consideration. They are to be calculated as follows:

- Where the activities of the undertaking in question are confined to the service of general economic interest, all its costs may be taken into consideration.
- Where the undertaking also carries out activities falling outside the scope of the service of general economic interest, only the costs associated with the service of general economic interest may be taken into consideration. These can include all the variable costs incurred in providing the service of general economic interest, and a proportionate contribution to fixed

costs common to both the service of general economic interest and other activities and a reasonable profit; see more on this below. The costs linked to any activities outside the scope of the service of general economic interest cover all the variable costs, an appropriate contribution to common fixed costs and an adequate return on capital. No compensation may be granted in respect of those costs.

- The costs linked with investments may be taken into account when necessary for the operation of the service of general economic interest. For example, these can include costs for investment in infrastructure.

The allocation of costs and receipts associated with the service of general economic interest and those of other services (if such are carried out), as well as the parameters for allocating costs and revenues must be shown separately in the internal accounts of the undertaking; see art.5(5) of the Decision. The same applies if an undertaking carries out more than one service of general economic interest which is of a different kind or has been entrusted by a different authority. This enables controls to be made of whether there is overcompensation or cross-subsidising, though the undertaking has a right to make a reasonable profit. Furthermore, such undertakings must comply with the provisions of the Transparency Directive, which takes precedence.

"Reasonable profit" is defined in art.5(4). It means a rate of return on own   **4–138**
capital that takes account of the risk, or absence of risk, incurred by the undertaking by virtue of the intervention by the Member State. This applies particularly if an undertaking has been granted exclusive or special rights. The profit is regarded as reasonable if it does not exceed the average rate for the sector concerned in recent years. In sectors where there is no basis for making such a comparison, a comparison may be made with undertakings in other Member States or in other sectors. Naturally the particular characteristics of each sector must be taken into account. In determining what constitutes a reasonable profit, the Member States may introduce incentive criteria relating, for example to the quality of service provided and productivity gains.

As stated, compensation which is in accordance with the Decision need not be notified to the Commission. However, the Member States must keep available, for at least 10 years, all the information necessary to determine whether the compensation granted is compatible with this Decision. This information must be made available to the Commission upon request. The Member States must also send periodic reports to the Commission on the implementation and application of the Decision.

Community framework for State aid in the form of public service compensation

As stated above, compensation for services of general public interest does not   **4–139**
constitute State aid falling within the ambit of art.87(1) of the Treaty as long

as the conditions stated in the *Altmark* case are fulfilled. Where this is not the case, provided that the case otherwise falls under the terms of art.87(1), compensation must, in principle, be notified to the Commission in accordance with art.88(3) of the Treaty. However, there is no duty to notify compensation which is covered by art.87(1) if the compensation falls within the scope of the Decision discussed above and fulfils its conditions.

In cases where compensation must be notified to the Commission, the framework lays down the conditions under which compensation can be compatible with the common market in accordance with art.86(2) of the Treaty. However, the framework does not apply to the transport sector, see Chs 4 and 5 of this book, or the public service broadcasting sector (see the section below). The framework is also subject to more restrictive provisions on services of general economic interest which are laid down in Community legislation for specific sectors. The framework applies for six years from the date of its publication in the Official Journal on November 29, 2005.

Chapter 2 of the framework contains the conditions under which compensation for a public service which constitutes State aid can be considered as being compatible with the common market.

4–140   For a start, the service must be a service of general economic interest as referred to in art.86(2) of the Treaty. As stated above, each Member State has wide discretion to determine the nature of the service which is regarded as being of general interest in its territory. The Commission can only request the discretion to be set aside if it is manifestly wrong, but it can encourage Member States to consult widely when defining public service obligations and in assessing whether those obligations are met by the undertakings concerned. Such consultation is not obligatory but, depending on the outcome of the consultation, it will support the categorisation of the service as being of general interest and of its necessity.

In addition to this, there are some requirements as to the official act by which the service of general interest in the Member State is entrusted (by central, regional and local authorities) to an undertaking, and the framework contains requirements for the calculation of the amount of compensation. These requirements for the official act, and how the service of general interest is entrusted and compensated, correspond to the requirements in the Decision which are discussed above.

Chapter 3 of the framework contains rules on overcompensation. There will be overcompensation when an undertaking is given more compensation than is necessary for carrying out the service of general economic interest. Thus, compensation which is in excess of the amount calculated under the rules in Ch.2 will be incompatible State aid and must be repaid to the State. Member States must check regularly to ensure that there is no overcompensation, and if there is the parameters for calculating the compensation must be updated. However, it is possible to carry forward overcompensation of up to 10 per cent to the following year, as long as the undertaking is not overcompensated overall. Some services of general economic interest may have costs that vary significantly each year. For example, it may be necessary to make special investments at the start of the period in which the undertaking is entrusted with a public service obligation. In such cases, exceptionally, overcompensation in excess of 10 per cent in certain years may prove necessary. However, such a period is limited, as any overcompensation which is outstanding after four years must be repaid. If a Member State assesses that there is a need for overcompensation of more than 10 per cent, it must explain the circumstances of this in a notification to the Commission.

Depending on the circumstance, overcompensation may be used to finance another service of general economic interest operated by the same undertaking; see para.22 of the framework. However, it is not possible to justify overcompensation on the grounds that it is State aid which is compatible with the Treaty on some other grounds. In principle such aid must be notified to the Commission before it is paid. But it is possible for such aid to be paid if it is covered by a block exemption regulation. If so, the conditions of the relevant regulation must be fulfilled.

RADIO AND TELEVISION AND COMPENSATION FOR PUBLIC SERVICE OBLIGATIONS

In its document of October 17, 2001 on services of general economic interest which it prepared for the European Council Meeting in Laeken in December 2001, the Commission indicated that it would propose further guidelines or similar measures for public service obligations for specific sectors. In fact, shortly afterwards it published Communication from the Commission on the application of State aid rules to public service broadcasting (OJ C 320, November 15, 2001, p.5).

4–141

The communication points out that private operators have made the Commission aware that increased competition, together with the presence of State-funded operators, has led to growing concerns about the possibility of competing on equal terms. The majority of the complaints concerned infringements of art.87 of the Treaty in relation to public funding schemes established in favour of public service broadcasters. The communication sets out the principles to be followed by the Commission in the application of arts 87 and 86(2), of the EC Treaty to State funding of public service broadcasting.

The communication describes the role of public service broadcasting, and refers to art.16 of the EC Treaty which states:

> "Without prejudice to Articles.73, 86 and 87, and given the place occupied by services of general economic interest in the shared values of the Union as well as their role in promoting social and territorial cohesion, the Community and the Member States, each within their respective powers and within the scope of application of this Treaty, shall take care

that such services operate on the basis of principles and conditions which enable them to fulfil their missions."

The communication also refers to the interpretation in Protocol 32 (to the Amsterdam Treaty) which states that:

"The ... Treaty ... shall be without prejudice to the competence of Member States to provide for the funding of public service broadcasting insofar as such funding is granted to broadcasting organisations for the fulfilment of the public service remit as conferred, defined and organised by each Member State, and insofar as such funding does not affect trading conditions and competition in the Community to an extent which would be contrary to the common interest, while the realisation of the remit of that public service shall be taken into account."

4–142   The communication states that the legal basis for the application of the State aid rules to radio and television undertakings is art.87 of the Treaty (in particular art.87(3)(d), which permits aid to promote culture), art.86(2) and art.16 (both of which concern services of general economic interest), art.151 on culture, and Council Directive 89/552/EEC of October 3, 1989 on the co-ordination of certain provisions laid down by Law, Regulation or Administrative Action in Member States concerning the pursuit of television broadcasting activities (OJ L 298, October 17, 1989, p.23), as well as the Transparency Directive (now Directive 2006/111/EC on the transparency of financial relations between Member States and public undertakings as well, OJ L 318, November 17, 2006, p.17).

In its para.19, the communication states that any transfer of State resources to an undertaking for carrying out public service obligations has to be regarded as State aid, even when the payment only covers the net costs of the public service obligations. In this connection the Commission relies on the view of the CFI in Case T-106/95, *FFSA and Others v Commission*, [1997] E.C.R. II-229. The communication was published just a few days before ECJ's decision in Case C-53/00 *Ferring v Agence centrale des organismes de sécurité sociale*, [2001] E.C.R. I-9067 was given, and of course before the decision in the *Altmark* case.[76] In the light of these cases, the view of the Commission, as expressed in para.19 of the communication, is no longer the applicable law. Paragraph 19 must be interpreted in accordance with the practice of the ECJ as expressed in the *Altmark* case.[77]

The communication explains that, since the financing arrangements in the radio and televisions sector were established a long time ago, the Commission must first assess whether the financing should be considered as existing aid

---

[76] Case C-280/00, *Altmark Trans, Regierungspräsidium Magdeburg v Nahverkehrsgesellschaft Altmark*, [2003] E.C.R. I-7747.
[77] See Stefaan Depypere, Jérôme Broche and Nynke Tigchelaar, "State aid and broadcasting: state of play", in *Competition Policy Newsletter*, No.1, Spring 2004, p.71.

within the meaning of art.88(1) of the Treaty (see para.2-012 of this book on existing aid). The Commission will examine whether the legal framework for the aid has been changed since its introduction.

According to art.151 of the EC Treaty, the Community must take cultural aspects into account when acting under other provisions of the Treaty, in particular in order to respect and to promote the diversity of cultures; and art.87(3)(d) of the Treaty expressly allows for the exemption of cultural aid from the prohibition of State aid in art.87(1). However, the communication also states that unless a Member State provides for the separate definition and the separate funding of State aid to promote culture alone, such aid cannot generally be approved under art.87(3)(d). On the other hand, it can normally be assessed on the basis of art.86(2) on services of general economic interest. **4–143**

In order to satisfy the requirements of art.86(2), as interpreted by the ECJ, i.e. in order for there to be a service of general public interest clearly defined by a Member State, it is necessary to establish an official definition of the public service mandate. Only then can the Commission decide. According to the communication, the definition of the public service mandate falls within the competence of the Member States, which can decide at national, regional or local level, but in exercising that competence account must be taken of the Community concept of "services of general economic interest".

According to the communication it is normally possible to use a "wide" definition, entrusting a given broadcaster with the task of providing balanced and varied programming in accordance with the remit, in view of the inter- pretative provisions of Protocol 32 referred to above, while retaining a certain size of audience. Such a definition must be consistent with the objective of fulfilling the democratic, social and cultural needs of a particular society and guaranteeing pluralism, including cultural and linguistic diversity. The public service remit can also include certain services that are not programmes in the traditional sense, such as on-line information services, provided that, while taking into account the development and diversification of activities in the digital age, they address the same democratic, social and cultural needs of the society.

The role of the Commission is limited to checking for manifest error. It is not for the Commission to decide whether an individual programme is to be provided as a service of general economic interest, nor to question the nature or the quality of a certain product. However, according to the communica- tion e-commerce and commercial activities such as the sale of advertising space would not normally be regarded as being part of a public service remit. According to the communication, the definition of the public service remit must be as precise as possible. If it is not, the Commission cannot approve aid under art.86(2). **4–144**

The communication includes a further condition that the public service remit should be entrusted to one or more undertakings by means of an official act (for example, by legislation, contract or terms of reference). The public service must also in fact be supplied as designated, and there must be an appropriate authority or appointed body (independent of the public service undertaking) to monitor its application. If this is not the case, the Commission will not grant an exemption under art.86(2).

As laid down by Communication from the Commission to the Council, the European Parliament, the Economic and Social Committee and the Committee of the Regions Principles and guidelines for the Community's audiovisual policy in the digital age (COM(1999) 657 final), it is not for the Commission to assess the fulfilment of any quality standards, it must rely on the Member States to ensure the necessary supervision.

4–145   Funding schemes can either be "single-funding" or "dual-funding", i.e. either financing solely through public funds, or financing by different combinations of State funds and revenues from commercial activities, such as advertising revenue. The choice of funding scheme is a matter for the Member States.

The Commission's evaluation of funding is based on a proportionality test. The Commission must ensure that the aid does not affect trade or competitive conditions in the Community to such an extent as would be contrary to the interests of the Community, while having regard to the fulfilment of the public service obligations. This requires a clear separation between public service tasks and others. It is necessary to keep separate accounts in order to enable the Commission to examine and assess whether there is a cross-subsidisation (on this concept, see paras 6-011 to 6-014 of this book).[78] The State aid must not exceed the net costs of the public service mission. On this, the communication refers to the Transparency Directive (discussed in paras 2–066 and 2–067), which lays down requirements for cost accounting principles for the separate accounts. The communication refers to the fact that in the broadcasting sector, separation of accounts poses no particular problem on the revenue side, but may not be straightforward or, indeed, feasible on the cost side.

The Commission requires detailed accounts to be presented for all revenues derived from activities that are not public service activities. On the cost side, all costs that are specific for other activities must be clearly identified. When the same resources are used—personnel, equipment, fixed installations etc., for carrying out both public service and other tasks, such costs must be allocated on the basis of the difference to the undertaking's total costs with and without such activities.

4–146   In paras 56-62 the communication goes into more detail on the proportionality test, and emphasises among other things that distortion of competition can occur which is not necessary for the fulfilment of the public service obligation. Thus, in so far as lower revenues are covered by State aid, a public service broadcaster might be tempted to depress its prices for advertising or

---

[78] For a more detailed review of this, see Stefaan Depypere and Nynke Tigchelaar, "The Commission's state aid policy on activities of public service broadcasters in neighbouring markets", in *Competition Policy Newsletter*, No.2, Summer 2004, p.19.

other non-public service activities on the market, so as to reduce the revenue of competitors. If such an undertaking were to set prices for commercial activities below the level necessary to cover the stand-alone costs which an effective operator in an equivalent situation would normally have to cover, this will amount to overcompensation of the public service obligations, and thus an infringement of the EU's State aid rules.

The Commission emphasises that cases on aid to public service undertakings in the radio and television sector will all be dealt with by individual assessment on a case-by-case basis, among other things because the prices charged by broadcasting companies cannot be determined on the basis of general criteria for the whole EU/EEA, since the market structures and other characteristics vary from Member State to Member State. But the Commission's starting point will, of course, be the principles referred to in the communication.[79]

---

[79] For a case on State aid and public service obligations, see Case T-46/97, *SIC-Sociedade Independente de Comunicação v Commission*, [2000] E.C.R. II-2125, on the Portuguese broadcaster Radiotelevisão Portuguesa. The case was brought by a competitor. The CFI annulled the Commission's decision to approve the measures objected to without having opened a formal investigation procedure; see art.88(2) of the Treaty.

CHAPTER 5

THE RELATIONSHIP BETWEEN THE TREATY STATE AID RULES, AND BETWEEN THESE RULES AND OTHER TREATY RULES

THE RELATIONSHIP BETWEEN ART.87 AND ART.73 ON AID TO THE TRANSPORT SECTOR

Article 73 which is in Title V of the EC Treaty states as follows: **5–001**

> "Aids shall be compatible with this Treaty if they meet the needs of coordination of transport or if they represent reimbursement for the discharge of certain obligations inherent in the concept of a public service."

According to art.80(1) of the Treaty, the provisions in Title V, including art.73, apply to transport by rail, road and inland waterway.

Article 87 of the Treaty (containing the prohibition of State aid and certain exceptions to that prohibition) also applies to the transport sector, but only in so far as other provisions in the Treaty do not provide otherwise.[1] Such provisions which provide otherwise are found in art.36 (on agriculture), art.76 (on transport tariffs), art.77 (on charges or dues in respect of crossing frontiers), and art.86(2) (on undertakings entrusted with the operation of services of general economic interest). However, the definition of State aid, as expressed in art.87, applies horizontally across the different rules in the Treaty so that the definition of State aid in the various special provisions of the Treaty has the same meaning as that contained in art.87.[2]

It is also necessary to be aware of the special exceptions in art.296 relating **5–002** to trade in arms etc. and the provisions in art.132 on commercial policy in relation to exports to third countries.

The starting point for art.73 is that the provision only governs the compatibility of State aid with the common market, as expressly referred to in the provision. This concerns coordination aid and compensation for public service obligations.

---

[1] Case 156/77, *Commission v Belgium*, [1978] E.C.R. 1881.
[2] Case 156/77, *Commission v Belgium*, [1978] E.C.R. 1881.

Article 73 is a provision which, in principle, does not leave much discretion to the Commission. It states that coordination aid and compensation for public service obligations are compatible with the Treaty. Aid of the kind referred to in art.73 is either compatible with the Treaty or not. It does not allow scope for aid to be *declared* compatible with the Treaty.

5–003   Article 3 of Regulation (EEC) No.1107/70 of the Council of June 4, 1970 on the granting of aids for transport by rail, road and inland waterway (OJ L 130, June 15,1970, p.1) provides that:

"Without prejudice to the provisions of Council Regulation (EEC) No 1192/69... and of Council Regulation (EEC) No 1191/69... Member States shall neither take co-ordination measures nor impose obligations inherent in the concept of a public service which involve the granting of aids pursuant to Article 77 [now Article 73] of the Treaty except in the following cases or circumstances".

On this basis, in the *Altmark* case[3] the Court of Justice (ECJ) held that the Member States are no longer authorised to rely on art.73 of the Treaty other than in the cases referred to in Community secondary legislation. Thus, the implication was that art.73 had been exhausted by Community secondary legislation, i.e. the regulations referred to above. It also followed from the *Altmark* case, as well as the *Combus* case[4], that to the extent that Regulation (EEC) No.1191/69 did not apply, and the subsidies at issue fell within art.87(1), Regulation (EEC) No.1107/70 exhaustively listed the circumstances in which the authorities of the Member States were entitled to grant aid under art.73.

However, Regulation (EC) No.1370/2007 of the European Parliament and of the Council of October 23, 2007 on public passenger transport services by rail and by road and repealing Council Regulations (EEC) Nos 1191/69 and 1107/70 (OJ L 315, December 3, 2007, p.1) changes the possibilities for applying art.73. The new Regulation is discussed above in paras 4–054 to 4–100. As stated, the Regulation repeals Regulations (EEC) Nos 1191/69 and 1107/70. This is with effect from December 3, 2009. Thereafter the provisions of art.73 will not have been exhausted by secondary legislation. This is because the new Regulation does not pretend to exhaust the possibilities for providing aid in the transport sector which meets transport coordination needs or which represents reimbursement for the discharge of certain obligations inherent in the concept of a public service; see art.9(2) and recital 37 of the Regulation.[5]

---

[3] Case C-280/00, *Altmark Trans, Regierungspräsidium Magdeburg v Nahverkehrsgesellschaft Altmark*, [2003] E.C.R. I-7747.
[4] Case T-157/01, *Danske Busvognmænd v Commission*, [2004] E.C.R. II-917.
[5] See the Community framework for State aid for railway undertakings, para.20, and Ch.4 in this book.

THE RELATIONSHIP BETWEEN ART.87 AND ART.76 ON THE PROHIBITION
OF FARES, ETC. IN RESPECT OF TRANSPORT INVOLVING ANY ELEMENT
OF SUPPORT OR PROTECTION OF ONE OR MORE PARTICULAR
UNDERTAKINGS OR INDUSTRIES

Article 76 of the EC Treaty states as follows: **5–004**

> "1. The imposition by a Member State, in respect of transport opera-
>   tions carried out within the Community, of rates and conditions
>   involving any element of support or protection in the interest of
>   one or more particular undertakings or industries shall be prohib-
>   ited, unless authorised by the Commission.
> 2. The Commission shall, acting on its own initiative or on application
>   by a Member State, examine the rates and conditions referred to in
>   paragraph 1, taking account in particular of the requirements of an
>   appropriate regional economic policy, the needs of underdeveloped
>   areas and the problems of areas seriously affected by political cir-
>   cumstances on the one hand, and of the effects of such rates and
>   conditions on competition between the different modes of trans-
>   port on the other.
>   After consulting each Member State concerned, the Commission
>   shall take the necessary decisions.
> 3. The prohibition provided for in paragraph 1 shall not apply to
>   tariffs Wxed to meet competition."

Article 76 is thus a special provision that takes precedence over the prohibition of State aid in art.87(1).

The provisions of art.76 are taken from the European Coal and Steel   **5–005**
Community (ECSC) Treaty. Article 70(4) of the ECSC Treaty applied to
special tariffs for the coal and steel sectors until the Treaty expired in July
2002, since when art.76 of the EC Treaty has been applicable also to the
coal and steel sector.[6] When there is a preferential tariff arrangement, the
Commission decides solely on the basis of art.76. Article 76 does not provide
for a notification requirement, so the notification requirement in art.88 does
not apply.

In order for there to be an arrangement, as referred to in art.76, there must
be a preferential arrangement which is not aimed at supporting the transport
undertaking, but rather has the aim of supporting one or more undertakings
that are customers of the transport undertaking which has been required to
apply the preferential tariff.

The preferential tariffs referred to here are tariffs that are imposed on

---

[6] The German state railways has special tariffs for Saarland's industries approved in Commission
Decision 78/975/ECSC of November 16, 1978 on the authorization of special Deutsche
Bundesbahn tariffs in favour of coal and steel producers in the Saar (OJ L 330, 25.11.1978,
p.34); see *Groeben, Thiesing, Ehlermann, 5. Auflage,* 1/1726.

transport undertakings as public service obligations. They are, therefore, covered by the EU's rules on their permissibility and financial rewards or compensation from the State.[7]

In contrast to the tariffs referred to in art.76(1) and (2), the competitive tariff referred to in art.76(3) is intended to regulate competition between transport undertakings.[8]

5–006   The scope given in art.76 for the Commission to authorise a Member State to apply preferential tariffs for the benefit of certain undertakings or industries was aimed in particular at the development of regional policy, for example, the situation in the previously divided Germany. Special legislation has not been adopted with a view to implementing art.76.

The Treaty has by art.76 conferred on the Commission a large measure of discretionary power, not only as regards the tariffs to be authorized, but also as regards the details of the authorisation to be granted.[9] It can grant authority with retrospective effect, it can grant authority subject to conditions, it can make grant authority for a limited period, and it can grant authority subject to revocation.

Especially in connection with setting time limits and reservations for revocation, the Commission must take into account the nature of its decision-making powers as an exception to the prohibition of tariff preferences; i.e. only granting permission as an exception and, if so, subject to strict conditions. Permits are most often granted for a limited period, among other things in order to create an incentive for restructuring the undertakings which benefit.[10]

5–007   The possibility of permitting preferential tariffs has seldom been used in the EU. But it has occasionally been used for the transport of agricultural products from remote areas, for example artichokes from Brittany.[11]

It is natural to assume that following the enlargement of the EU, with a number of less economically advanced Member States joining, the need would arise for permitting preferential tariffs in the new Member States, for example for the transport of coal and iron.

Permission is normally given upon a request being made by a Member State. The Commission also has a duty to examine the special tariffs which have not been referred to it but which it receives information about, perhaps after a reference by another Member State.

---

[7] See Council Directive 91/440/EEC of July 29, 1991 on the development of the Community's railways (OJ L 237, 24.8.1991, p.25) with subsequent amendments.
[8] Joined Cases 27-58, 28-58 and 29-58, *Compagnie des hauts fourneaux et fonderies de Givors v High Authority of the ECSC*, E.C.R. English special edition p.241.
[9] Case 1/69, Government of the Italian Republic, [1969] p.277.
[10] See Groeben, op. cit., I-1730, with a reference to Wägenbaur, "Unterstützungstarife, Regionalpolitik und Wettbewerb im Gemeinsamen Markt", in ZHR 1965, p.180.
[11] See Groeben, op. cit., I-1725.

THE RELATIONSHIP BETWEEN ART.86 AND ART.73.

The relationship between art.86 and art.73 is referred to in recital 17 of   **5–008**
Commission Decision of November 28, 2005 on the application of art.86(2)
of the EC Treaty to State aid in the form of public service compensation
granted to certain undertakings entrusted with the operation of services of
general economic interest (OJ L 312,November 29, 2005, p.67). According to
this, art.73 of the Treaty constitutes a *lex specialis* with regard to art.86(2).

Article 73 contains rules on compensation for discharging public service
obligations in the transport sector; see art.80(1).

Article 86(2) constitutes an exception to the prohibition on State aid in
art.87(1). In other words, art.86(2) makes it possible to legitimise "[u]nder-
takings entrusted with the operation of services of general economic interest
or having the character of a revenue-producing monopoly", if the provision
of financial aid is necessary for such undertakings to carry out the tasks in
question.

The aid can constitute compensation for the necessary additional costs   **5–009**
which are incurred in providing the service. For example, aid can be given in
the form of financial support for an electricity producer which has an obligation to supply all consumers at the same price, regardless of where they are
situated. There will unquestionably be State aid if the undertaking is over-
compensated.

If the matter concerns a transport undertaking, art.86(2) will not be the
relevant provision on aid to compensate for the additional costs or aid for
coordination of transport; it will be art.73. According to the decision in the
Altmark case,[12] compensation for public service obligations in the transport
sector which does not fall within the ambit of art.73 cannot be declared compatible with the common market on the basis of art.86(2) or any other Treaty
provision; see also recital 17 of the Decision referred to above. Since secondary
legislation in this area is exhaustive with respect to art.73, it can no longer have
direct effect. Article 73 will first have direct effect from December 3, 2009; see
paras 5–001 to 5–003 above.

THE RELATIONSHIP BETWEEN THE NOTIFICATION REQUIREMENT IN
ART.88(3) AND ART.86(2) ON COMPENSATION FOR THE OPERATION OF
SERVICES OF GENERAL ECONOMIC INTEREST

The Commission's powers with regard to the control of State aid also apply   **5–010**
to aid covered by art.86(2) on undertakings that have been entrusted with the
operation of services of general economic interest. This was made clear in the
Banco Exterior de Espana case in the mid 1990s.[13]

---

[12] Case C-280/00, *Altmark Trans, Regierungspräsidium Magdeburg v Nahverkehrsgesellschaft Altmark*, [2003] E.C.R. I-7747.

[13] Case C-387/92, *Banco Exterior de España v Ayuntamiento de Valencia*, [1994] E.C.R. I-877.

The distinction between existing aid and new aid also applies to undertakings that are covered by art.86(2).

The notification procedure referred to in art.88 also applies to aid granted to undertakings on the basis of art.86(2). In Case C-332/98, *France v Commission*, [2000] E.C.R. I-4833, the ECJ held that the obligation to suspend temporarily the implementation of aid, as set out in art.88(3), also applies to aid which is covered by art.86(2).

5–011   As for the obligation to notify in art.88(3), the ECJ has ruled that there must also be notification in cases concerning aid to an undertaking covered by art.86(2), i.e. an undertaking entrusted with the operation of services of general economic interest.

It is not enough merely to notify the aid and then proceed to pay it, with a view to avoiding breaking the continuity in providing the service concerned. The obligation to suspend payment laid down in art.88(3) covers the actual payment of aid, and it is not permitted to notify the Commission with a view to getting its approval while at the same time actually paying out the aid.[14]

As a consequence of the *Altmark* case[15] the Commission adopted its Decision of November 28, 2005 on the application of art.86(2) of the EC Treaty to State aid in the form of public service compensation granted to certain undertakings entrusted with the operation of services of general economic interest (OJ L 312, November 29, 2005, p.67); the Decision is discussed in more detail in paras 4–141 to 4–151. The Decision provides that certain cases where State aid is given in the form of compensation for public service obligations are to be regarded as compatible with the common market and exempt from the requirement to notify under art.88(3). Accordingly, compensation granted to undertakings with an average annual turnover of less than €100 million and which receive annual compensation of less than €30 million need not be notified. Public service compensation granted to hospitals and social housing undertakings need not be notified under art.88(3) and, subject to certain conditions, compensation for air or maritime links and for airports and ports can also be exempt from the notification requirement.

THE RELATIONSHIP BETWEEN ART.87 AND ART.86(2) ON UNDERTAKINGS WITH PUBLIC SERVICE OBLIGATIONS

5–012   Article 86(2) is regarded as constituting an exception to the prohibition in art.87(1). In art.86(2) it is stated that:

> "Undertakings entrusted with the operation of services of general economic interest or having the character of a revenue-producing monopoly shall be subject to the rules contained in this Treaty, in particular to

---

[14] Case C-332/98, *France v Commission*, [2000] E.C.R. I-4833.
[15] Case C-280/00, *Altmark Trans, Regierungspräsidium Magdeburg v Nahverkehrsgesellschaft Altmark*, [2003] E.C.R. I-7747.

the rules on competition, in so far as the application of such rules does not obstruct the performance, in law or in fact, of the particular tasks assigned to them. The development of trade must not be affected to such an extent as would be contrary to the interests of the Community."

According to the judgment in Case C-174/97 P, *FFSA v Commission*, [1998] E.C.R. I-1303, an undertaking of the kind referred to in art.86(2), for example an electricity company, can receive compensation for the special tasks which it is entrusted to carry out in the general interest and which give rise to additional costs for the undertaking, without being affected by the prohibition in art.87(1). Such an undertaking therefore receives State aid, but as compensation for the additional costs for carrying out the tasks entrusted, a form of compensation which does not have the net effect of benefiting the undertaking and which is, therefore, compatible with art.87(1).

However, according to the judgment in the *FFSA* case, such aid may only be intended to compensate for the additional costs incurred by the undertaking in carrying out the public service, and the aid must be judged necessary for enabling the undertaking to fulfil its public service obligations on reasonable financial terms.[16]

Aid to an undertaking entrusted with the operation of services of general economic interest, as referred to in art.86(2), and which merely serves to bring financial stability to the undertaking, regardless of whether the need for it is due in whole or in part to poor management and not to the special character of the services incurring extra costs for the undertaking, will not be approved on the basis of art.86(2).   **5–013**

According to the judgment in the *FFSA* case, aid which is compensation for additional costs may not be used to cross-subsidise other commercial activities.

According to the judgment, the Commission has some discretion concerning the method used to investigate whether the aid involves a risk of cross-subsidisation. For example, cross-subsidisation can occur if a public monopoly undertaking or an undertaking which has received State aid and is entrusted with carrying out certain public services, transfers funds from the part of the undertaking's activities which are not exposed to competition to parts of the undertaking which are in competition with private undertakings which do not receive aid.

The judgment in Case C-53/00, *Ferring v Agence centrale des organismes de sécurité sociale*, [2001] E.C.R. I-9067 cast doubt on the tenability of judgment in the *FFSA* case, as in the *Ferring* case the ECJ held that compensation paid to undertakings for the special costs associated with their carrying out certain operations of general economic interest does not constitute State aid at all, and is, therefore, not required to be notified. The case concerned a tax   **5–014**

---

[16] For an interesting case on compensation, see Commission Decision 2002/149/EC of October 30, 2001 on the State aid awarded by France to the Société nationale maritime Corse-Méditerranée (SNCM) (OJ L 50, 21.2.2002, p.66).

exemption for certain wholesalers of medicines, which in return undertook certain public service obligations.

The *Altmark* case,[17] which was an extension of the *Ferring* case, must now be considered to be the established precedent. Consequently the decision in the *FFSA* case must be regarded as not expressing the now applicable Community law on the question of the extent to which compensation for operations of general economic interest constitutes State aid. The conclusion in the *Altmark* case was as follows:

Public subsidies do not fall within the ambit of art.87 in so far as such subsidies are to be regarded as compensation for the services provided by the recipient undertakings in order to discharge public service obligations, provided the following conditions are satisfied:

1. The recipient undertaking is actually required to discharge public service obligations and those obligations have been clearly defined.
2. The parameters on the basis of which the compensation is calculated have been established beforehand in an objective and transparent manner.
3. The compensation does not exceed what is necessary to cover all or part of the costs incurred in discharging the public service obligations, taking into account the relevant receipts and a reasonable profit for discharging those obligations.
4. Where the undertaking which is to discharge public service obligations is not chosen in a public procurement procedure, the level of compensation needed has been determined on the basis of an analysis of the costs which a typical undertaking, well run and adequately provided with means of transport so as to be able to meet the necessary public service requirements, would have incurred in discharging those obligations, taking into account the relevant receipts and a reasonable profit for discharging the obligations.

THE RELATIONSHIP BETWEEN ART.87 AND ART.36 ON AID TO AGRICULTURE

5–015 The agricultural sector is subject to special rules in the EC Treaty. These rules are set out in Title II of the Treaty, on Agriculture (art.32–38).

Article 36 is a *lex specialis* in relation to art.87. It states that the EC Treaty's competition rules apply to production of and trade in agricultural products only to the extent determined by the Council within the framework of art.37(2) and (3) and in accordance with the procedure laid down therein (i.e. the Treaty rules on the Council's adoption of rules on the Common Agricultural Policy,

---

[17] Case C-280/00, *Altmark Trans, Regierungspräsidium Magdeburg v Nahverkehrsgesellschaft Altmark*, [2003] E.C.R. I-7747.

common market organisations, etc.), account being taken of the objectives set out in art.33 (i.e. the objectives of the Common Agricultural Policy).

Among other things, the Council has adopted Council Regulation (EC) No.1184/2006 of July 24, 2006 applying certain rules of competition to the production of, and trade in, agricultural products (OJ L 214, August 4, 2006, p.7). According to art.3 of this Regulation, the provisions of art.88(1) and of the first sentence of art.88(3) of the Treaty apply to aid granted for production of, or trade in, the products listed in annex I to the Treaty. This means that the Commission, in cooperation with the Member States, keeps under constant review all systems of aid existing in those States, and that the Commission proposes to the Member States any appropriate measures required by the progressive development or by the functioning of the common market; see art.88(1). In addition to this, the Commission must be informed, in sufficient time to enable it to submit its comments, of any plans to grant or alter aid. Under art.10 of the Treaty, the Member States have a duty to cooperate with the Commission in good faith with a view to the achievement of the Community's tasks. The effect of art.3 of the Regulation referred to is that the procedural rule in art.88(2) does not generally apply. As stated, this is only the case if the Council has adopted a decision thereon. Such a decision, in the form of a regulation, will constitute a *lex specialis* in relation to Council Regulation (EC) No.1184/2006. In practice, the regulations on common market organisations contain provisions on the application of the State aid rules in arts 87, 88 and 89 to the products concerned.

To the extent that there is a common market organisation, which is the case   **5–016** for the great majority of agricultural products, arts 87, 88 and 89 of the Treaty apply, unless specifically provided otherwise in the relevant regulation.

In addition to this, aid is normally an element of the common market organisations, thus preventing the Member States from applying national State aid to the same sectors, again unless provided otherwise in the relevant regulation.[18]

It is clear that art.36 contains greater scope for derogating from the general State aid rules in art.87 in relation to the agricultural sector than art.73 does in relation to the transport sector. Article 36 contains a general authorisation for the Council to derogate from art.87. Article 73 does not contain such an authorisation. Article 73 only allows some exemptions in relation to specific forms of aid which are related to parts of the transport sector's traditional functions and *modus operandi* and, other than that, the State aid rules of art.87 apply in general to the transport sector, without the possibility of further exemptions being granted by the Council or the Commission.

In Case T-82/96, *ARAP v Commission*, [1999] E.C.R. II-1889, the Court of First Instance (CFI) considered the application of the Treaty's State aid rules when there is co-financing, i.e. aid from both the Community and the State, and the CFI found that the application of arts 87 and 88 of the EC Treaty

---

[18] Case C-86/89, *Italy v Commission*, [1990] E.C.R. I-3891.

would be incompatible with the precedence over the rules on competition accorded by the Treaty to the common agricultural policy.[19]

THE RELATIONSHIP BETWEEN ART.87 AND ART.81 ON AGREEMENTS RESTRICTING COMPETITION, AND ART.82 ON ABUSE OF DOMINANT POSITION

5–017   According to Case C-225/91, *Matra v Commission*, [1993] E.C.R. I-3203, paras 41–42, even though arts 87 and 88 leave considerable discretion to the Commission (and under certain circumstances to the Council), the State aid procedures must never produce a result which is contrary to the specific provisions of the Treaty, in particular where those other provisions also pursue the objective of undistorted competition in the common market.

In the judgment it was emphasised that the procedures under art.81 and art.87 of the Treaty are independent procedures governed by specific rules. Consequently, when taking a decision on the compatibility of State aid with the common market, the Commission is not obliged to await the outcome of a parallel procedure initiated under Regulation No.17/62 (on the procedure for cases under art.81), which has now been replaced by Council Regulation (EC) No.1/2003 of December 16, 2002 on the implementation of the rules on competition laid down in arts 81 and 82 of the Treaty (OJ L 1, January 4, 2003, p.1), once it has reached the conclusion, based on an economic analysis of the situation and without any manifest error in the assessment of the facts, that the recipient of the aid is not in breach of the provisions of the Treaty prohibiting agreements which restrict competition, or the abuse of a dominant position. If the Commission were unable to do this, it would risk a decision taken to approve State aid as being compatible with the common market without having entered into a formal procedure under art.88(2) being overruled by the CFI.[20]

5–018   In Case C-225/91, *Matra v Commission*, [1993] E.C.R. I-3203, which concerned State aid for a motor vehicle factory for the production of multi-purpose vehicles (MPVs) within the terms of a joint venture between Ford and Volkswagen, and which was to be assessed under the Treaty rules on agreements which restrict competition, the ECJ held that "it is clear from the general scheme of the Treaty that that procedure [the State aid procedure] must never produce a result which is contrary to the specific provisions of the Treaty."

---

[19] For other cases on agriculture and State aid see, e.g. Case C-280/93, *Germany v Council*, [1994] E.C.R. I-4973; and Case C-311/94, *IJssel-Vliet Combinatie v Minister van Economische Zaken* [1996] E.C.R. I-5023. According to the practice of the ECJ, the competition rules of the Treaty must be applied in such a way as to respect the goals of art.33 of the Treaty, i.e. the Common Agricultural Policy; see Case C-177/78, *Pigs and Bacon Commission v McCarren*, [1979] E.C.R. 2161.

[20] Case T-49/93, *SIDE v Commission*, [1995] E.C.R. II-2501, paras 67–76; and Case C-164/98 P, *DIR International film v Commission*, [2000] E.C.R. I-447.

The ECJ has also held that implementation measures for aid which contravene specific provisions of the Treaty, other than arts 87 and 88, may be so indissolubly linked to the object of the aid that it is impossible to evaluate them separately (see Case 74/76 *Iannelli & Volpi v Meroni* [1977] E.C.R. 557). This obligation of the Commission to have sufficient regard for the connection between arts.87 and 88 on the one hand, and on the other hand other Treaty provisions applies especially in cases where the other provisions are also intended to prevent distortion of competition within the Community.[21]

In para.6–003 there is a discussion of the special circumstances which can apply to the relationship between State aid and the merger of undertakings.

THE RELATIONSHIP BETWEEN ART.87 AND ART.28 ON QUANTITATIVE RESTRICTIONS ON IMPORTS AND ALL MEASURES HAVING EQUIVALENT EFFECT

This restriction is important, if for no other reason because art.28, in contrast to art.87, has direct effect and can be relied upon directly in cases brought before the national courts. Furthermore, while a State aid measure can be approved by the Commission, it does not have the authority to approve quantitative restrictions on imports and measures having equivalent effect.   **5–019**

State aid which is granted to a body whose purpose is to promote the use of domestic products over imported products can both be an infringement of art.28 and of art.87; see for example the *Buy Irish* and the *Apple and Pear Development Council* cases.[22] In these cases, as well as some French and Italian measures which concerned the reservation of public contracts to local undertakings, aid for the purchase of domestically manufactured motor vehicles, and State aid for newspapers which were printed in the Member State concerned,[23] even though there could be said to be State aid involved, the ECJ decided on the basis of the principal provision in the Treaty prohibiting quantitative restrictions on imports and all measures having equivalent effect; see art.28.

Apart from possible theoretical speculation about the relationship between

---

[21] In Commission Decision 93/337/EEC of May 10, 1993 concerning a scheme of tax concessions for investment in the Basque country (OJ L 134, 3.6.1993, p.25), the Commission agreed with the incompatibility with the Treaty rules on discrimination with regard to the right of establishment (art.43 of the Treaty) and thereby avoided having to decide whether or not the autonomous tax system of the Basque region constitutes State aid. The question of the autonomy of regional tax systems in relation to art.87(1) is dealt with in paras 1–020 to 1–046 and in paras 5-025 and 5-026 below; see Case C-88/03, *Portugal v Commission*, [2006] E.C.R. I-7115.

[22] Case 249/81, *Commission v Ireland (Buy Irish)*, [1982] E.C.R. 4005; and Case 222/82, *Apple and Pear Development Council v K.J. Lewis Ltd and Others*, [1983] E.C.R. 4083.

[23] See respectively Case C-21/88, *Du Pont de Nemour Italiana v Unità sanitaria locale No.2 di Carrara*, [1990] E.C.R. I-889; Case C-263/85, *Commission v Italy*, [1991] E.C.R. I-2457; and Case 18/84, *Commission v France*, [1985] E.C.R. 1339.

art.87 and art.28, it might be thought that the outcome of these cases and similar cases would be obvious, since the aid element was clearly combined with an attempt to promote the sales of national products instead of foreign products. However, this is far from always being so in cases of State aid. Moreover, in none of these cases was there prior notification to the Commission with a view to the measures being treated as State aid.

5–020   There are grounds for believing that, in cases where a State aid has been notified as such, priority should be given to the State aid procedure, and that the directly applicable prohibition of quantitative restrictions on imports and measures having equivalent effect in art.28 should await the Commission's decision on the notification of State aid with a view to its possible approval, but this depends on how the State aid measure is in fact composed; see below. If such a measure is not approved it is unlawful, and if aid is nevertheless paid, the case can be brought before the national courts, which can suspend payment and require the reimbursement of aid already paid.

Even where a case is dealt with on the basis of art.28 and is found to be incompatible with the Treaty, this does not mean that the aid measure as such is annulled, other than those elements that are covered by art.28; see, for example, Case 74/76, *Iannelli & Volpi v Meroni*, [1977] E.C.R. 557. In the *Iannelli* case the ECJ held in para.17:

> "the aids referred to in Articles 92 and 93 [now Articles 87 and 88] of the Treaty do not as such fall within the field of application of the prohibition of quantitative restrictions on imports and measures having equivalent effect laid down by Article 30 [now Article 28] but those aspects of aid, which are not necessary for the attainment of its object or for its proper functioning and which contravene this prohibition, may for that reason be held to be incompatible with this provision; (c) the fact that an aspect of aid, which is not necessary for the attainment of its object of for its proper functioning , is incompatible with a provision of the Treaty other than Article 92 and Article 93 [now Articles 87 and 88] does not in fact invalidate the aid as a whole or for that reason vitiate by reason of illegality the system of financing the said aid."

Furthermore, in para.12 of its judgment in the *Iannelli* case the ECJ stated:

> "The effect of an interpretation of Article 30 [now Article 28] which is so wide as to treat an aid as such within the meaning of Article 92 [now Article 87] as being similar to a quantitative restriction referred to in Article 30 [now Article 28] would be to alter the scope of Articles 92 and 93 [now Articles 87 and 88] of the Treaty and to interfere with the system adopted in the Treaty for the division of powers by means of the procedure for keeping aids under constant review as described in article 93 [now Article 88]" (i.e. State aid control).

If the competitive advantage which the grant of aid gives to national prod-   **5–021**
ucts were to be treated in all cases as a measure having equivalent effect to
quantitative restrictions on imports, the direct applicability of the provision in
art.28 would effectively make the provisions in arts 87 and 88 superfluous.

It is obvious that if national courts were, purely on the basis of the directly
applicable art.28, to annul an aid measure because it had a tendency to hinder
imports, many general State aid measures would become impossible, since
they typically put domestic undertakings in a better position vis-à-vis international competition than they would otherwise be. The system of the Treaty
is therefore that State aid must be notified with a view to its control by the
Commission which, on the basis of its overall responsibility for the proper
functioning and development of the common market, can approve State aid,
even if to some extent it has distorting effects on competition which can affect
trade between Member States. On the other hand, quantitative restrictions
on imports and measures having equivalent effect cannot be regarded as a
means for promoting the interests of the Community, and therefore cannot
be approved.

The *Iannelli* case introduced a form of test to distinguish between cases.[24]
According to this, implementing measures for an aid which contravene specific
provisions of the Treaty (for example art.28) other than arts 87 and 88 may be
so indissolubly linked to the object of the aid that it is impossible to evaluate
them separately so that their effect on the compatibility or incompatibility of
the aid viewed as a whole must therefore of necessity be determined in the light
of the procedure prescribed in art.88. It is different if, when a system of aid
is being analysed, it is possible to separate those conditions or factors which,
even though they form part of this system, may be regarded as not being
necessary for the attainment of its object or for its proper functioning. In the
latter case there are no reasons under arts 87 and 88 to prevent the isolated
conditions or elements being assessed under other Treaty provisions which
have direct effect, including the prohibition on quantitative restrictions on
imports and measures having equivalent effect in art.28.

In the *Du Pont de Nemour Italiana* case, on the obligation of public authori-   **5–022**
ties in Italy to make at least 30 per cent of their purchases from undertakings
in Southern Italy, the ECJ indicated that the arrangement was an infringement
of art.28, but that the arrangement could also be considered as State aid; see
Case 21/88, [1990] E.C.R. 889. In this case in para.20 of the judgment, the
ECJ referred to the fact that the Court has consistently held that art.87 may
in no case be used to frustrate the rules of the Treaty on the free movement
of goods. It is clear from the case law that these rules and the Treaty provisions relating to State aid have a common purpose, namely to ensure the free
movement of goods between Member States under normal conditions of
competition.[25]

---

[24] Case 74/76, *Iannelli & Volpi v Meroni*, [1977] E.C.R. 557, para.14.
[25] See also Case 18/84, *Commission v France*, [1985] E.C.R. 1339, on aid to French newspapers
which were printed in France, where the ECJ ruled that the mere fact that a measure was

The ECJ's ruling in the *Du Pont de Nemour Italiana* case should presumably be seen in the light of the question which the referring court laid before the ECJ for a preliminary ruling and the facts of the case, whereby Italy had been given the right, in a directive, to maintain certain provisions in its national legislation. This legislation, which was the subject of the case, had subsequently obtained a different and more comprehensive complexion which was clearly contrary to art.28. On this basis the national court did not need an interpretation of the boundaries between arts 28 and 88.

THE RELATIONSHIP BETWEEN ART.87 AND ART.31 ON STATE MONOPOLIES OF A COMMERCIAL CHARACTER

5–023   Article 31 on State monopolies of a commercial character states as follows:

"1. Member States shall adjust any State monopolies of a commercial character so as to ensure that no discrimination regarding the conditions under which goods are procured and marketed exists between nationals of Member States.

The provisions of this Article shall apply to any body through which a Member State, in law or in fact, either directly or indirectly supervises, determines or appreciably influences imports or exports between Member States. These provisions shall likewise apply to monopolies delegated by the State to others.

2. Member States shall refrain from introducing any new measure which is contrary to the principles laid down in paragraph 1 or which restricts the scope of the articles dealing with the prohibition of customs duties and quantitative restrictions between Member States.

3. If a State monopoly of a commercial character has rules which are designed to make it easier to dispose of agricultural products or obtain for them the best return, steps should be taken in applying the rules contained in this article to ensure equivalent safeguards for the employment and standard of living of the producers concerned."

5–024   Commercial State monopolies can, but may not, restrict trade. In Case 91/78, *Hansen v Hauptzollamt flensburg*, [1979] E.C.R. 935, the ECJ held that the prohibition on discrimination in art.31 also covers cases where, by using State aid, a State commercial monopoly sold alcohol so as to price national products below imported products. In this case the ECJ established that art.31 constitutes a *lex specialis* in relation to arts 87 and 88, i.e. the general State aid rules in the Treaty.

From this it appears that the fact that certain measures taken by a

classified as State aid was not sufficient reason to find that it was not covered by the prohibition in art.28.

commercial State monopoly can, for example, entail that the producers who can only sell via the monopoly obtain especially high prices, does not in itself constitute State aid to the producers in question such as must be regarded as prohibited in accordance with art 87's prohibition on State aid. It is only if there is discrimination against imports, for example if the monopoly's sales price is not only lower than its purchase price guaranteed to the producer but also than the price, before tax, of spirits of comparable quality imported from another Member State that such a monopoly's pricing will be considered contrary to art.31.

   Thus, art.31 and art.87 on State aid are not mutually exclusive. The business of a commercial State monopoly will not be contrary to art.31 merely on the ground that its business or parts of business can be regarded as State aid, while the fact that a measure taken by a commercial State monopoly, and which can constitute State aid, is not prohibited under art.31, need not necessarily mean that the measure does not fall within the ambit of and cannot be assessed on the basis of art.87.[26]

THE RELATIONSHIP BETWEEN ART.87 AND ART.90 ON DISCRIMINATORY INTERNAL TAXES AND ART.25 ON CUSTOMS DUTIES ON IMPORTS AND EXPORTS AND CHARGES HAVING EQUIVALENT EFFECT

According to art.25, customs duties on imports and exports and charges having equivalent effect are prohibited between Member States. This prohibition also applies to customs duties of a fiscal nature (i.e. a duty which is imposed to raise revenue for the State rather than to protect domestic production). Article 25 is supplemented by art.90, according to which no Member State may impose, directly or indirectly, on the products of other Member States any internal taxation of any kind in excess of that imposed directly or indirectly on similar domestic products. Furthermore, no Member State may impose on the products of other Member States any internal taxation of such a nature as to afford indirect protection to other products.

5–025

   Articles 25 and 90 supplement each other and cannot both be applied to the same facts. In other words, there is no overlap between their respective areas of application.[27] Articles 25 and 90 are both directly applicable, so that private citizens can rely on the rights given under these provisions before the national courts.[28] The consequence of an arrangement for the collection of tax being contrary to art.25 is naturally that the tax provision in question must removed from the national tax legislation. The consequence of internal taxation either

---

[26] See the judgment in Case 253/83, *Sektkellerei C.A. Kupferberg & Cie v Hauptzollamt Mainz*, [1985] E.C.R. 157, which states in para.16 that a price reduction made by a commercial State monopoly must be assessed on the basis of art.87 on the prohibition of State aid.

[27] This was laid down in Case 57/65, *Alfons Lütticke v Hauptzollamt Sarrelouis*, [1965–1968] E.C.R. 205, and it has been the firmly established practice ever since.

[28] See Case 28/67, *firma Molkerei-Zentrale Westfalen/Lippe v Hauptzollamt Paderborn*, [1965–1968] E.C.R. 143; and the famous Case 26/62, *Van Gend en Loos*, [1963] E.C.R. 3.

discriminating or having the effect of protecting national products is that the discriminatory/protective part of the tax scheme must be removed from the national tax legislation. In the latter case it is not the whole of the tax scheme which is required to be repealed.[29] On this basis it is necessary to define the boundaries between the areas where the provisions apply.

The starting point for defining the boundaries is the ECJ's interpretation of art.25, according to which a charge having equivalent effect to a customs duty is any pecuniary charge which is not a customs duty in the strict sense, whatever its designation and mode of application, which is imposed unilaterally on goods by reason of the fact that they cross a frontier.[30] A charge is internal taxation within the meaning of Article 90, if it relates to a general system of internal dues applied systematically to categories of products in accordance with objective criteria irrespective of the origin or destination of the products.[31]

5–026   The starting point for defining the boundary between art.25 and art.90 is thus whether the charge arises as the result of goods crossing a frontier. In several cases the ECJ has made it clear that a charge forming part of a general system of internal charges applying systematically to both domestic and imported products may none the less constitute a charge having an effect equivalent to a customs duty on imports, if the revenue from it is *exclusively* intended to finance activities which specifically benefit domestic products and offset in full the burden on them. In such a case it must be assumed that the charge does indeed constitute a net financial burden for imported products, whereas for domestic products it represents only consideration for advantages received.[32] However, even if there is partial offsetting, the charge will be contrary to art.90 as being discriminatory.

The charges referred to are interesting in the present context because, regardless of the factual circumstances, they can constitute State aid in the sense of the definition in art.87. The charges will namely be able to finance an aid scheme. What is interesting is that both art.25 and art.90 are directly applicable, so that the financing of an aid scheme can be challenged before the national courts. It has also been established by the case law of the ECJ that the fact that a national charge is intended to finance an aid scheme that has been approved by the Commission in accordance with the Treaty's provisions on State aid, does not prevent a national court from examining the compatibility of the charge with other Treaty provisions which have direct effect.[33] However, this situation will only arise if the method of financing is not an integral part of the notifiable State aid measure and therefore not covered by the obligation to notify. If this is the case, the compatibility of the charge with art.25 or art.90 can be tried by a national court. However, if the charge

[29] Case 46/80, *Vinal v Orbat*, [1981] E.C.R. 77.
[30] Case C-313/05, *Maciej Brzezi ski v Dyrektor Izby Celnej w Warszawie*, 2007 E.C.R. I-513.
[31] Case C-72/03, *Carbonati Apuani v Comune di Carrara*, [2004] E.C.R. I-8027.
[32] Case C-266/91, *Celulose Beira Industrial v Fazenda Pública*, [1993] E.C.R. I-4337.
[33] Case C-234/99, *Niels Nygård v Svineafgiftsfonden*, [2002] E.C.R. I-3657.

in question is an integral part of the aid measure, then art.88(3) applies in full; see paras 2–015 to 2–021 in this book. This thus means that if the obligation to notify is disregarded and the aid measure involves making a charge, in principle this should be reimbursed.[34]

If an arrangement that involves aid also constitutes a discriminatory internal taxation which is prohibited under art.90, as stated the aid scheme will not normally be approved by the Commission. The corresponding result must apply with regard to any repayment of internal taxation which exceeds the internal taxation imposed on products, whether directly or indirectly, when those products are exported to the territory of another Member State; see art.91.[35]

[34] Joined Cases C-261/01 and C-262/01, *Belgische Staat v Eugène van Calster and Felix Cleeren*, [2003] E.C.R. I-12249.
[35] Case 73/79, *Commission v Italy*, [1980] E.C.R. 1533. See also the Opinion of Advocate General Mischo in Case C-234/99, *Niels Nygård v Svineafgiftsfonden*, [2002] E.C.R. I-3657, where he argued that the fact that a national levy is part of a system of aid authorised by the Commission under the rules on State aid is immaterial in regard to the applicability to that levy of the prohibitions laid down in arts 23 and 25 on measures having an equivalent effect to customs duties, and art.90 on discriminatory internal taxation. In the opinion of the Advocate General, where a national court takes the view that any of those prohibitions applies to a levy that has been so authorised, it is for that court to make a reference to the ECJ for a preliminary ruling on the correct application of these provisions.

CHAPTER 6

SELECTED TOPICS

ON THE LEGAL NATURE OF THE COMMISSION'S FRAMEWORK PROVISIONS, GUIDELINES, NOTICES AND LETTERS ON STATE AID

The Commission's guidelines and frameworks constitute what is known as **6–001** "soft law", as they have not been subject to the proper legislative procedure.[1] They are provisions which, by issuing them, the Commission has made public that it will follow them in its assessment of State aid cases under art.87(3) of the EC Treaty which gives the Commission wide discretion, as has been confirmed by the Court of Justice (ECJ). In other words, they establish the norms for the Commission's exercise of its discretion and they are a form of guidance—also for the Commission itself—on how it will decide concrete State aid cases within the terms of the Treaty's State aid provisions.[2] Once the Commission has adopted such guidelines, etc. it is bound by them.[3] It would be contrary to the principle of equal treatment for the Commission to derogate from them arbitrarily, i.e. without an explanation based on objective facts and differences between cases.

Such guidelines etc. are not binding on the ECJ, which can overrule them in specific cases and thereby give the Commission cause to adjust the guidelines in question. This thus means that plaintiffs in cases before the ECJ can plead that the guidelines etc. concerned ought not to form the basis of a specific decision, since they may be contrary to and ought to be interpreted in accordance with art.87(3). However, when the Commission's exercise of its discretion—possibly clarifying guidelines etc. which it has adopted—involves a complex economic or social assessment carried out on the basis of Community policies, the examination of such a decision by the ECJ, or by the Court of First Instance (CFI), is limited to examining whether the procedure and the legal principles have been complied with, whether the material facts are true, whether there is a manifestly wrong exercise of discretion, or whether there has been a misuse of power.[4]

[1] These guidelines, framworks, notices etc. are dealt with in Ch.4 of this book.
[2] Case T-17/03, *Schmitz-Gotha Fahrzeugwerke v Commission*, [2006] E.C.R. II-1139.
[3] Case T-171/02, *Regione autonoma della Sardegna v Commission*, [2005] E.C.R. II-2123.
[4] Case T-171/02, *Regione autonoma della Sardegna v Commission*, [2005] E.C.R. II-2123.

6–002   The ECJ can examine whether the Commission has complied with the guidelines etc. which it has itself issued, or whether by failing to follow them it is in breach of the principle of equal treatment.[5]

In cases where the Commission has entered into a formal agreement with a Member State, according to the case law (see Case C-311/94, *IJssel-Vliet Combinatie v Minister van Economische Zaken*, [1996] E.C.R. I-5023) the guidelines or framework in question can obtain the status of binding provisions for that Member State, in other words it is not able to challenge the provisions in a case on State aid before the ECJ, provided the provisions are not contrary to the Treaty.[6] Thus, the Commission's proposals for measures in accordance with art.88(1) will be binding on Member States if they accept them.[7]

It is clear that if guidelines conflict with the provisions of a regulation, it is the latter that prevails.[8]

STATE AID AND MERGERS OF UNDERTAKINGS

6–003   In a case from Germany (on the so called Kohler compromise),[9] where there was a merger of undertakings in the coal sector (the *RJB Mining* case), there was a question of whether there was State aid in the form of the purchase price of DM 1. The case concerned the coal sector, so that questions about mergers and State aid were to be dealt with under the provisions of the European Coal and Steel Community Treaty (ECSC Treaty) which corresponded substantially to the rules on these issues under the EC Treaty. Since the expiry of the ECSC Treaty, the EC Treaty has applied to the coal sector.

As merger cases have to be dealt with particularly quickly, it would be a problem if the approval of a merger had to await the outcome of a State aid case which, because of the applicable rules, including procedural rules, necessarily takes a relatively long time, and in any case some months.

In the *RJB Mining* case the CFI found that, in connection with deciding on a merger, the Commission did not need to make an exhaustive examination of whether State measures constituted State aid within the meaning of art.87(1). According to the judgment, the Commission need not await the result of a parallel State aid case, but under the merger procedure it must only consider whether possible State aid has in fact strengthened the merged undertaking's financial position and thereby its market position. In other words, the Commission must assess the quantitative effect of the possible State aid for the undertaking which results from the merger, and not whether

---

[5] Case T-171/02, *Regione autonoma della Sardegna v Commission*, [2005] E.C.R. II-2123.
[6] Case C-91/01, *Italy v Commission*, [2004] E.C.R. I-4355.
[7] Case C-242/00, *Germany v Commission*, [2002] E.C.R. I-5603.
[8] Case C-110/03, *Belgium v Commission*, [2005] E.C.R. I-2801.
[9] Case T-156/98, *RJB Mining v Commission*, [2001] E.C.R. II-337.

any State aid is compatible with the common market. Following this, the State aid procedure can be initiated.[10] The CFI has subsequently clarified its judgment in the *RJB Mining* case in the sense that the Commission is not required to carry out State aid proceedings in every merger case, and in particular not in connection with a merger between two private undertakings.[11]

In Case C-156/98, *Germany v Commission*, [2000] E.C.R. I-6857, in a plenary judgment the ECJ held that when the Commission has decided that a measure does not constitute State aid as defined in art.87(1), it could naturally not institute proceedings on the basis of art.88 with a view to deciding that some other provision in the EC Treaty, for example art.43, has been infringed. On the other hand, the ECJ ruled that a State aid procedure may never lead to a result that is in conflict with other procedures under the Treaty. Consequently, according to the ECJ a State aid measure which contains certain elements that are in breach of other Treaty provisions cannot be declared compatible with the common market (para.78).

THE MARKET ECONOMY INVESTOR PRINCIPLE

The market economy investor principle, which is defined in the judgment in   **6–004**
Case C-42/93, *Spain v Commission*, [1994] E.C.R. I-4175, para.13, is a concept that is used when assessing whether State aid exists when a public body invests capital, either directly or indirectly, in a public or private undertaking. The position is that there will be State aid if the investment would not have been made on the same terms and under the factual circumstances by a private investor operating under normal market economy conditions. In other words, if an undertaking on the private capital market would not have made an investment on the same terms, it will be found that there is State aid within the meaning of the Treaty.[12]

However, there is reason to modify this position slightly, since public bodies will not always act in the same way as a private investor, and need not necessarily do so from a commercial point of view. According to the practice of the ECJ (see Case C-305/89, *Italy v Commission (Alfa Romeo I)*, [1991] E.C.R. I-1603, there can be grounds for adopting the view that the State, or public authorities or public undertakings, will have a tendency to view matters from

---

[10] See the discussion of the *RJB Mining* coal compensation case in Europarecht, Vol.5, September-October 2001, p.758.

[11] Case T-114/02, *BaByliss v Commission*, [2003] E.C.R. II-1279.

[12] See, e.g. the judgment in Case C-142/87, *Belgium v Commission (Tubemeuse)*, [1990] E.C.R. I-959. See also Ben Slocock, "The Market Economy Investor Principle", in *Competition Policy Newsletter*, No.2, June 2002, p.23; Stefan Moser and Elke Gräper, "The Judgement of the Court of first Instance concerning the transfer of capital to Westdeutsche Landesbank Girozentrale (WestLB)", in *Competition Policy Newsletter*, No.2, Summer 2003, p.40; and Steffen Suehnel, "The market investor principle in privatisations—European Court of Justice upholds the Commission's decision on Gröditzer Stahlwerke GmbH", in *Competition Policy Newsletter*, No.2, Summer 2003, p.79.

a perspective corresponding to that adopted by a holding company or group of private undertakings.[13]

Such undertakings will often pursue a strategy in which the profitability of a given investment is viewed from a long-term perspective, with a global or sectoral angle; see Joined Cases C-278/92 and others, *Spain v Commission (Hytasa)*, [1994] E.C.R. I-4103. In the same way, consideration for the image of an undertaking, or regard for being able to cease the operations of an undertaking in difficulties at a time when the resulting losses will be minimised as far as possible, can lead to a capital investment being considered commercially justifiable.

6–005   In Case C-278/92, just referred to, the ECJ ruled that in applying the market economy investor principle a distinction must be made between the obligations of the State as owner, and its obligations as a public authority. As owner, it is the value of the assets which it must have regard for if the State decides to provide aid in the hope of avoiding losses as a result of liquidation, while the costs associated with liquidation, for example, the costs of unemployment, cannot be included when applying the market economy investor principle.

If over a longer period the State or some other public authority has accepted losses, so that the undertaking in question has, for that period, been advantageously placed in competition, this can be considered State aid, together with any aid subsequently granted in order to reduce a negative balance, as a private investor would normally have intervened at a much earlier stage in order to restrict their losses. The thought here is that earlier intervention in the loss-making undertaking could have avoided causing distortion of competition during the period in question, and the effects correspond to State aid in giving an advantage to an undertaking over its competitors, whereafter the losses are later made good by subsequent aid, possibly by claiming the application of the market economy investor principle.

The Commission issued a communication on the application of the market economy investor principle in 1984.

6–006   When assessing whether a private investor would have made a corresponding investment, the Commission's practice is to have regard to the following circumstances:

- The profitability and financial strength (debt/equity ratio, indebtedness etc.) of the beneficiary undertaking. The Commission will also look at whether, for example the undertaking has had serious losses or consistent losses in recent years. If this is the case, it will be assumed that a private investor would not have invested.

---

[13] See e.g. the judgment in Case T-234/95, *DSG Dradenauer Stahlgesellschaft v Commission*, [2000] E.C.R II-2603, which concerned State aid in the steel sector, which had hitherto been subject to the ECSC Treaty. However, it was permissible to refer to the case law on State aid derived from the EC Treaty in order to assess the legality of decisions regarding aid covered by the ECSC Treaty; see para.115 of the judgment. Paragraphs 119–122 give a good overview of the ECJ's practice with regard to the market economy investor principle.

- The economic and commercial development in the sector in which the undertaking operates, including whether the sector has overcapacity.[14]
- The extent to which private investors invest in the undertaking at the same time.

The same applies if the State invests an amount which is disproportionately large in relation to the share of the State's ownership of the undertaking.[15]

If an undertaking is in financial difficulties, the Commission will see whether the capital investment is made as part of a restructuring plan that will re-establish the profitability and financial health of the undertaking within a reasonable period. At the date when the investment is made, the restructuring plan must be reliable and sufficient to re-establish the undertaking's profitability.[16]

This last shows that, in the event of an unsuccessful restructuring, the Commission will not consider investment from the State to be State aid, since public investors, like private investors, must have the possibility of investing, even where there is a risk element.   **6–007**

In assessing whether there is State aid, there will be a presumption of the existence of State aid if it would have been cheaper for the public body to have liquidated the undertaking or have allowed it to go bankrupt.

An interesting problem can arise if a private undertaking and a State have joint ownership of an undertaking, for example a train operator, with ownership of an equal number of shares, and with equal influence and control over the undertaking. In such a situation will it constitute State aid if, during a contract period, the State agrees to cover, in whole or in part, the costs of acquiring new rolling stock for the undertaking which, on the basis of a tender, has won the right to operate trains on certain stretches in the Member State in question?[17]

---

[14] See, e.g. Case C-303/88, *Italy v Commission (ENI-Lanerossi)*, [1991] E.C.R. I-1433, in which the ECJ ruled that a public holding company can make its investments with a view to the more long term restructuring of the business, but that if the investment—even in the longer term— has no likelihood of giving a reasonable return, it will be found that State aid is involved; see Commission Decision 1999/658/ECSC of July 8,1999—*Neue Maxhütte Stahlwerke*. In this case the capital investment took place at the same time as the German authorities disposed of their shares in the company, which negated any possibility that the State might have obtained a reasonable return on its investment.

[15] Case C-142/87, *Belgium v Commission (Tubemeuse)*, [1990] E.C.R. I-959. See also Commission Decision 97/753/ EC of March 12, 1997—*Aircraft Services Lemwerder*.

[16] See also the chapter on the Commission's framework for rescue and restructuring in Ch.3, s.5. See also the judgment in Case C-482/99, *France v Commission (Stardust Marine)*, [2002] E.C.R. I-4397, where the ECJ found that by failing to examine loans and guarantees provided to the beneficiary, and considering the date on which they had been given, the Commission had failed to apply the market economy investor principle correctly.

[17] If the State invites tenders for an operating contract and later it buys the rolling stock for the operator that has submitted the winning tender, the advantage to the operator in this context could constitute State aid. If, on the other hand, as part of such tendering procedure it is made clear that new rolling stock will be bought, with operating and financial advantages attaching to it, and made available to the winner of the tendering competition, there will be equality between all those submitting tenders, so this would not be considered State aid.

6–008   If, as in an actual case, there is a situation where it is obvious that a private investor would not normally invest in new rolling stock, since the investor would not be sure of winning a new operating contract after the expiry of the current contract period, would the State incur problems with the State aid rules if it paid for new rolling stock for the use of the undertaking in which it owns a half share? It seems that it would be unlawful if the train operator, i.e. the public body, as an alternative ensured co-financing by the joint owner, against a promise to extend the contract for some years without opening the contract to a new round of tendering, as that would be contrary to the EU's rules on public procurement and presumably also against the State aid rules.

On the facts shown, it would seem that the State would be able to justify its investment on the basis of the market economy investor principle, so that investment or joint investment in new rolling stock before the expiry of the current contract period would not be State aid, even if the purchase involved the transfer of money to the jointly owned train operator. The alternative to the State itself financing the new rolling stock in whole or in part would be to extend the contract with the private operator in question, which would then undertake the necessary investment in the new rolling stock itself. However, as stated, this could constitute a breach of the State aid rules, among other things by pre-selecting a train operator without a tendering procedure. If, on the other hand, the State undertook the necessary purchase of rolling stock, it would presumably immediately improve the train service because of the reduction in delays, and ensure that the next tendering round would be more advantageous for the State, as the operators submitting tenders would be able to make better offers to the State because they would have less risk of incurring fines for bad time-keeping than the existing operator. At the same time, the partly State-owned train operator would also improve its finances due to being fined less for delays during the unexpired portion of the contract.

In a situation such as this, the problem in assessing whether there is State aid is complicated by the fact that a public body owns half the undertaking (and not more), and that the public body is also the contracting authority. In such circumstances it must be clearly required that the State should show that it has acted in accordance with the market economy investor principle. In the case discussed here, it seems that it could be argued that the State's interest as owner coincided with its interest as contracting authority, and that the costs both in relation to the State's interest as owner and as contracting authority can be justified on the basis of the market economy investor principle. If the rolling stock is bought not at the cost of the State, in whole or in part, the State risks that its 50 per cent owned undertaking will become insolvent, and that the next round of tendering will be less advantageous than it would be for the State as contracting authority.

6–009   A State decision that is in accordance with the market economy investor principle cannot be said to favour certain undertakings, as referred to in art.87(1) of the EC Treaty. It cannot therefore constitute State aid. Thus, the market economy investor principle is a tool for determining whether, in connection with making a capital investment, a State infringes art.87(1). However, there is also a question of whether it is possible to use a similar test in situations where the State does not invest capital, but acts for example as a lender.[18] This question can be answered in the affirmative. Thus, conduct by a public authority which is not in accordance with what a private investor would have done can favour an undertaking and will be contrary to art 87(1).[19] There can be similar variants of the market economy investor principle, if a public body acts as a buyer or seller of goods and services. In connection with this it must also be assessed whether the public body does in fact need the goods or services.[20]

The criterion of the private creditor has also been subject to consideration by the CFI in a case concerning aid given by Greece to Olympic Airways.[21] In its judgment, the CFI stated that the mere fact that *discretionary* credit facilities were allowed by a public creditor was insufficient for this to be characterised as State aid. There was also a requirement that the credit facilities provided should clearly be more significant than those which could have been obtained from a private creditor standing in an equivalent position in relation to the debtor, namely with regard to the amount of the debt, the legal remedies available to the public creditor, the prospects for the improvement of the debtor's situation if it were allowed to continue operations, and the risk of the creditor's loss being increased by the debtor undertaking being allowed to continue operations. The assessment of whether the criteria for private creditors are fulfilled can involve complicated financial calculations. In this the Commission has wide discretion. The CFI cannot substitute its own discretion with regard to the financial circumstances for that of the Commission. Furthermore, the CFI's examination of such cases is limited to examining whether the procedure and the legal principles have been complied with, whether the material facts are true, whether there is a manifestly wrong exercise of discretion, or whether there has been a misuse of power.[22]

In relation to agreements made by public undertakings, the ECJ has stated **6–010** that a measure which is adopted by a public undertaking in relation to a private undertaking in the form of a commercial agreement does not automatically fall outside the scope of State aid, as dealt with in art.87(1), just because the two parties have mutual obligations. How far a measure must be regarded as being State aid depends on whether the undertaking to which the measure is addressed obtains an economic benefit which it would not have

---

[18] On different variants of the market economy investor principle, see Ben Slocock, "The Market Economy Investor Principle", in *Competition Policy Newsletter*, No.2, June 2002, p.23; and Leigh Hancher, Tom Ottervanger and Piet Jan Slot, *EC State Aids*, Sweet & Maxwell, 3rd ed., 2006.
[19] Case C-276/02, *Spain v Commission*, [2004] E.C.R. I-8091.
[20] Case T-14/96, *BAI v Commission*, [1999] E.C.R. II-129.
[21] Case T-68/03, *Olympiaki Aeroporia Ypiresies v Commission*, [2007] E.C.R. 0000.
[22] Case T-68/03, *Olympiaki Aeroporia Ypiresies v Commission*, [2007] E.C.R. 0000.

obtained under normal market conditions. This can be the case if an agreement entered into departs from normal commercial agreements between two private undertakings.[23]

The application of the market economy investor principle to State investments in public undertakings is not as straightforward as with public investments in private undertakings. In the former case the market economy investor principle looks theoretically at whether the new investment is profitable for the investors and whether a return on the investment is merely made at the expense of the existing shareholders.[24] In other words, the market economy investor principle is applicable both to the role of the State as a new investor and to the State as owner of the existing undertaking. In such a situation, State aid can arise both directly as a subsidy via a capital investment, and indirectly via a reduction in the value of the public body's ownership of existing shares.[25]

The reader is referred to the *Chronopost* case, where there was not a market operator with which the conduct of the public body could be compared; see paras 6–011 to 6–014.[26]

CROSS-SUBSIDISATION

6–011   Cross-subsidisation can be defined briefly as the incorrect allocation of joint costs between different product or geographic markets.[27] Cross-subsidisation can thus be an expression of the fact that an undertaking which enjoys exclusive or special rights transfers means from the part of its business that is not exposed to competition to parts of its business that are in competition with other undertakings, as alleged by the plaintiffs in Case T-106/95, FF*SA and Others v Commission (La Poste)*, [1997] E.C.R. II-229. However, is can also be an expression of the opposite, namely the transfer of means from the competitive sector to the non-competitive sector.

Cross-subsidisation can naturally be considered equivalent to State aid if there is a situation where a publicly owned undertaking, with a monopoly on the provision of certain services (such as the normal provision of postal services, as distinct from courier services), uses means obtained from the monopoly sector (State means) to support the competitive part of the under-

---

[23] Case T-158/99, *Thermenhotel Stoiser Franz Gesellschaft v Commission*, [2004] E.C.R. II-1.
[24] On this problem, see Hans W. Friederiszick and Michael Tröge, "Applying the Market Economy Investor Principle to State Owned Companies—Lessons Learned from the German Landesbanken Cases", in *Competition Policy Newsletter*, No.1, Spring 2006 p.105.
[25] Friederiszick and Tröge, "Applying the Market Economy Investor Principle to State Owned Companies—Lessons Learned from the German Landesbanken Cases", in *Competition Policy Newsletter*, No.1, Spring 2006 p.105.
[26] Joined Cases C-83/01 P, C-93/01 P and C-94/01 P, *Chronopost and Others v Commission*, [2003] E.C.R. I-6993.
[27] The definition is taken from Hancher and Buendia Sierra, "Cross Subsidization and EC Law", in CML. Rev., Vol.35, No.4, August 1998.

taking's activities.[28] In the *Chronopost* case, which concerned La Poste's provision of logistical and commercial assistance within its reserved area to a subsidiary company, on the question of whether the price paid to La Poste was the market price the ECJ held that the provision of logistical and commercial assistance was indissolubly bound to La Poste's network, since it arose from the availability of the network which had no equivalent on the market. In these circumstances, since it was not possible to compare the situation of La Poste with the situation of a private undertaking on a non-monopoly market, the "normal market conditions" which must necessarily be hypothetical must be judged in relation to such available objective information as can be examined. In this case the ECJ was of the view that the costs which La Poste had borne in connection with providing logistical and commercial assistance to its subsidiary could constitute such objective information. On this basis the ECJ concluded that: "there is no question of State aid to SFMI-Chronopost if, first, it is established that the price charged properly covers all the additional, variable costs incurred in providing the logistical and commercial assistance, an appropriate contribution to the fixed costs arising from use of the postal network and an adequate return on the capital investment in so far as it is used for SFMI-Chronopost's competitive activity and if, second, there is nothing to suggest that those elements have been underestimated or fixed in an arbitrary fashion."[29]

For cross-subsidisation to be found to be present, transfers will normally be made within an undertaking or within a group of undertakings, there will be a monopoly situation for the undertaking in at least one of the markets which it is active in, and there will be shared costs applicable to several of the relevant products or geographic markets. This last typically arises in connection with the existence of some infrastructure or network, for example for telecommunications or postal services, which is used both for the competitive and the non-competitive sectors of the market.

Cross-subsidisation within a monopoly area will not normally cause a **6–012** problem, as it will be in an area where there is no open competition. Such cross-subsidisation goes together with the allocation of costs for the provision of public services in different areas, so that all receive the same universal service for the same price, e.g. the universal postal service. Nor will there be

---

[28] See Case T-613/97, *UFEX and Others v Commission*, [2000] E.C.R. II-4055, which also concerned postal services in France, but the case was overruled by the ECJ in Joined Cases C-83/01 P, C-93/01 P and C-94/01 P, *Chronopost and Others v Commission*, [2003] E.C.R. I-6993, and heard again by the CFI in Case T-613/97, *UFEX v Commission*, [2006] E.C.R. II-1531. This last case was appealed to the ECJ in Case C-342/06 P. The ECJ set aside the judgment of the CFI in so far as the CFI annulled the decision of the Commission and dismissed the application of UFEX and others for the annulment of the contested decision.; see also the well known Case C-320/91, *Corbeau v Belgium*, [1993] E.C.R. I-2533, which concerned the abuse of dominant position contrary to art.82 of the Treaty, and the distinction between the reserved area of the postal services and activities such as express mail which, according to the judgment should be open to competition.

[29] Joined Cases C-83/01 P, C-93/01 P and C-94/01 P, *Chronopost and Others v Commission*, [2003] E.C.R. I-6993.

a problem if there is cross-subsidisation by transferring means from a sector which is open to competition to a monopoly sector unless this is in connection with the abuse of a dominant position, which would be subject to art.82 of the Treaty. For example, there can be an abuse of a dominant position contrary to art.82 where a dominant undertaking, i.e. the monopoly undertaking, does not make the activity which is open to competition, e.g. courier services, bear the full proportion of the overheads shared with monopoly activity. By doing so it can cost the monopoly activity money in the short term, but by under-pricing it may be possible to capture a much greater share of the competitive market than would otherwise have been possible, and thereby generate a profit which can then be used to transfer the money back to the monopoly activity's accounts. Thus the original cross-subsidisation from the monopoly activity to the activity which is exposed to competition can lead to subsidisation in the opposite direction later on. This means that the activity which is exposed to competition supports the monopoly activity unlawfully. This may not be considered cross-subsidisation in a strict sense, but it can constitute abuse of a dominant position.

If, on the other hand, there is cross-subsidisation from a reserved or monopoly area to an activity which is exposed to competition, and if this involves a public undertaking, it can constitute a breach of the Treaty in the form of State aid.[30] However, this presumes that there is a transfer of means or a failure to charge for fixed costs which apply to the undertaking as a whole, without it being possible to document that the allocation of fixed costs between expenditure in the area of the monopoly activity and expenditure in the area of the activity which is exposed to competition is correctly appor-tioned, or alternatively that it can be shown to be probable that a private investor would be prepared to accept a corresponding loss (from transferring the means in question, or from refraining from imposing appropriate fixed costs) for a corresponding period on the market that is not exposed to com-petition.[31] As is shown in the cases of *Sytraval v Commission* and *SFEI v La Poste*,[32] State aid in the form of cross-subsidies can also occur by providing logistical support and commercial assistance to an activity of a monopoly undertaking which is exposed to competition, in so far as such aid relieves the burdens which would otherwise be borne by the activity which is exposed to competition.

6–013   A good example of the problems in relation to cross-subsidies is the cir-

[30] If, on the other hand, it concerns a privately owned undertaking which has special or exclusive rights, it will not involve the use of State funds and will presumably not constitute State aid; on State funds, see paras 1–032 to 1–036.

[31] Case C-39/94, *SFEI and Others v La Poste and Others*, [1996] E.C.R. I-3547. It must be assumed that the undertaking in question does not include in the assessment whether, by making the cross-subsidisation, it can gain an advantage whereby, as a consequence of the transfer, it could abuse or even create a dominant position on the market which is open to competition, and later be able to apply unreasonably high sales prices.

[32] Case T-95/94, *Sytraval and Others v Commission*, [1995] II-2651, confirmed on appeal in Case C-367/95 P, [1998] E.C.R. I-1719; and Case C-39/94, *SFEI and Others v La Poste and Others*, [1996] E.C.R. I-3547.

cumstances connected with the adoption of a new law on electricity supply in Denmark in the 1990s.

The Commission found that it was necessary to avoid cross-subsidies and thus State aid to the ancillary activities of the electricity companies, such as tomato growing or fish farming (based on the recovery of waste heat from the generation of electricity) which competed with private tomato growers or fish farmers. The Commission therefore encouraged the Danish government to change the proposed law in the area in order to ensure that such ancillary activities were put into independent companies with their own accounts, so that it would be possible to monitor if there was a transfer of means from the electricity companies' monopoly activities, i.e. the generation and sale of electricity to consumers, to the ancillary activities.

It is doubtful whether this approach still expresses "good law". At that time the price of electricity in Denmark was the price approved by the Electricity Price Committee. But strictly speaking, the revenue from the electricity was for the most part not public funds (except for some publicly owned power stations). The Electricity Price Committee was, however, appointed by the Minister for Energy. If, through the electricity price, electricity consumers financed ancillary activities (i.e. not the generation or distribution of electricity) which were in competition with similar commercial activities, the Commission's view was that there could be said to be a financial advantage of certain undertakings or the production of certain goods through State resources; art.87(1).[33]

As stated, depending on the circumstances, cross-subsidisation can be governed by either art.82 on the abuse of dominant position or art.87(1), or both. The conditions under which a set of circumstances may fall under one or the other of these two provisions differ. Article 82 has direct effect and can be relied upon before national courts, while this is not the case with art.87(1), though it should be added that non-notified State aid is unlawful aid which can be pleaded before the national courts with the effect that cross-subsidisation can be suspended or required to be reimbursed on an interim basis.[34]   **6–014**

Depending on the circumstances, cross-subsidisation which is contrary to Community law can form the basis for a claim for compensation before the national courts.

Reimbursement in cases where there has been cross-subsidisation within the same activity, e.g. a national public postal service, one part of the activities of

---

[33] The outcome of the Danish decision on electricity supply is put in doubt by the decision of the ECJ in Case C-379/98, *PreussenElektra v Schleswag*, [2001] E.C.R. I-2099. At least following this judgment there can be doubt about whether State aid will be found to be present in cases where, as in the electricity supply case, it is not State resources that are used, but where as a result of a State decision some undertakings are favoured over others.

[34] Termination of suspension and/or definitive reimbursement depends on whether in the case the Commission finds the aid to be compatible with the common market, as referred to in art.87(1), and thus regarded as lawful aid. See also Hancher and Buendia Sierra, "Cross Subsidization and EC Law", in CML. R. Vol.35, No.4, August 1998.

which is not open to competition can be difficult to implement since the cross-subsidisation involves the transfer of funds within the same undertaking. The ECJ has held that the aid must be reimbursed to the State authorities and not just to the State undertaking that has committed the cross-subsidisation in breach of the Treaty.[35]

CUMULATION OF AID

6–015   The guidelines and frameworks, as well as the block exemption regulations issued by the Commission contain more or less complicated provisions on cumulation. Cumulation is normally understood as aid from different sources for the same purpose, and not aid for different purposes.

The adding together of aid can naturally have unacceptable effects. If a single undertaking could simultaneously receive regional aid, research and development aid and environmental aid for the same purpose, just to take a few examples, this could lead to the undertaking being over-compensated for its disadvantages, such as being located in a development region and being a small or medium-sized enterprise (SME), so it could live on the aid alone. This would be contrary to the general purpose of several of the exemptions to the prohibition of State aid found in art.87. For example, this would apply to the aim of supporting business development. If it were possible to obtain too much aid, the incentive to improve, to rationalise, carry out research etc. would be diminished.

For this reason the various frameworks, guidelines, etc. on State aid contain provisions on the maximum permitted aid of the type dealt with by the frameworks, guidelines, etc. as well as the maximum permitted aid in total, i.e. the aid type in question combined with other forms of aid.

AID CEILINGS, AID INTENSITY AND GRANT EQUIVALENT

6–016   The various guidelines, frameworks and block exemption regulations on State aid contain terms such as "aid ceilings" and "aid intensity".

The term "aid ceiling" means the maximum permitted for a given form of State aid or several cumulated forms of State aid, possibly together with EU aid.

The term "aid intensity" indicates how great a proportion of a given investment the aid in question may constitute; for example 50 per cent of the eligible costs in connection with investment in a new industrial installation, or the costs of a research project.

The expression "grant equivalent" is used to determine the value of different

---

[35] Hancher and Buendia Sierra, "Cross Subsidization and EC Law", in CML. R., Vol.35, No.4, August 1998.

forms of aid. The grant equivalent is determined by means of a calculation. If it is necessary to calculate the grant equivalent of a "soft loan", meaning a loan which is given on advantageous terms, a calculation will be made to determine the difference between the interest which would have been paid on a loan provided on open market terms, and the actual interest paid on the soft loan.

Each year the Commission establishes a reference interest rate for use when   **6–017** making this calculation. As per September 1, 2007 it was 5.58 per cent.

The following is an example of a calculation of the grant equivalent of a soft loan with a randomly chosen reference interest rate of 6.21 per cent:

10-year loan of €500,000 on which the borrower is to pay interest of 4 per cent. The loan is repayable in equal instalments from the end of year 1.

The grant equivalent is calculated, as follows, on the basis that the difference between the actual interest paid and the reference rate is 2.21 per cent.

6–018

Year 1	€500,000 × 0.0221/(1.0621)	1	=	€10,403.92
Year 2	€450.000 × 0.0221/(1.0621)	2	=	€8,816.05
Year 10	€50.000 × 0.0221/(1.0621)	10	=	€604.93

The total grant equivalent is the sum of the discounted subsidy in each year.

Guarantees are calculated in the same way as soft loans, but with the deduction of the premium which the beneficiary may have paid for the guarantee.

The grant equivalent can also be calculated as the guaranteed sum multiplied by the risk factor, less any premium paid. The risk factor is determined on the basis of experience of defaults on loans given under similar circumstances, taking account of the commercial sector involved, the size of the undertaking and the general economic circumstances.

For tax reliefs, the grant equivalent is the amount of tax saved in the year in question.

PREFERENTIAL ENERGY TARIFFS

On the basis of, among other things, judgments concerning natural gas tariffs in   **6–019** the Netherlands, it can be stated that according to the practice of the ECJ it is possible, without infringing the State aid rules, for publicly owned and controlled supply undertakings to use preferential tariffs for natural gas (and perhaps also for electricity, etc.). However, this only applies in relation to a preferential tariff, i.e. a tariff which favours some customers more than others, if it is commercially justified and, for example, is a response to advantages which competitors in other countries have received with regard to energy tariffs.[36]

---

[36] See in particular the *Ammonia* case, Case C-56/93, *Belgium v Commission*, [1996] E.C.R. I-723; and Joined Cases 67, 68 and 70/85, *van der Kooy and Others v Commission*, [1988] E.C.R. 219,

Such preferential tariffs must be commercially justified, for example, because the undertaking in question would either switch to other forms of energy or would succumb to competition and would therefore no longer be a customer. The tariff must be necessary and must not go beyond what is required to attain its ends.

The following guidelines can be derived from the practice of the ECJ.

Prices which are below the ordinary tariff for supplies from energy supply companies that are wholly or partially owned by governments or other public authorities, and which are wholly controlled by them,[37] can be justified in one or more of the following circumstances:

6–020
1. if such lower prices are the result of genuine cost savings, such as volume discounts;
2. to the extent that the lower prices are part of a general tariff which is available to the whole of industry;
3. to the extent that there is an objective justification on the basis of the market economy investor principle;[38] and
4. if such lower prices serve a purpose which is recognised in Community law, and to the extent that the tariff is necessary and proportionate.[39]

A deliberate forfeit of profit does not automatically mean that the circumstances constitute State aid. Such forfeit of profit can have good commercial reasons on several grounds, for example because of the longer term expectations.[40]

Whether preferential tariffs granted by a public undertaking fall within the ambit of art.87(1) EC, i.e. encompasses the transfer of State resources, should be assessed on the basis of the indicators provided for in the *Stardust* and *PreussenElectra* judgments of the ECJ. These judgments are explained above under paras 1–032 to 1–034. It must be remembered that the other conditions in art.87(1) EC, namely the selectivity condition, also must be fulfilled before a preferential tariff is contrary to art.87(1) EC.

para.28. Both cases concerned Gasunie, which was 50% owned by the Dutch State and whose tariffs were approved by the State. After the *PreussenElektra* case it must be assumed that if a State did not own the supplying company, but only approved its tariffs, this would not amount to State aid.

[37] This will typically mean that the public authority owns at least 50% of the voting rights on the board of the undertaking.

[38] There is a good example of a commercially justified preferential tariff in Commission Decision 2001/274/EC of April 11, 2000 on the measure implemented by EDF for certain firms in the paper industry (OJ L 95, 5.4.2001, p.18).

[39] See Piet Jan Slot, *Understanding state aid policy in the European Community*, p.143, whose conclusions at p.154 should be modified in the light of the decision in the *PreussenElektra* case.

[40] See the example of DONG, the Danish publicly owned and controlled oil and natural gas company. In 2001, on the basis of the judgments in the Dutch natural gas cases, it decided to offer market gardeners using greenhouses in Denmark a preferential tariff for natural gas on commercial grounds, including the risk of losing customers by their transfer to coal fired heat or as a result of bankruptcies.

CHAPTER 7

REPAYMENT OF STATE AID

The repayment of State aid is the most appropriate way of removing the **7–001** effect of unlawful State aid and to re-establish fair competition.[1] For many years, under the practice of the Court of Justice (ECJ), aid could be required to be repaid by a beneficiary undertaking. The rules on repayment are now contained in Ch.III (arts 14 and 15) of Council Regulation (EC) No.659/1999 of March 22, 1999 laying down detailed rules for the application of art.93 [now 88] of the EC Treaty (OJ L 83, March 27, 1999, p.1) (the "Procedure Regulation"), and in Ch.V of Commission Regulation (EC) No.794/2004 of April 21, 2004 implementing Council Regulation (EC) No.659/1999 (OJ L 140, April 30, 2004, p.1) with amendments. According to this, when it takes a negative decision on unlawful State aid, the Commission must decide that the Member State concerned must take all necessary measures to recover the aid from the beneficiary. The aid must be repaid with interest. The interest is calculated on the basis of the interest rate applicable on the date when the unlawful aid was first made available to the beneficiary up to the date of repayment. The interest is compounded. The interest rate is determined by the Commission, and is published in the Official Journal and on the internet.[2]

However, according to art.14 of the Procedure Regulation, the Commission cannot require the recovery of State aid if this would be contrary to a general principle of Community law. In addition, art.15 contains a rule whereby the powers of the Commission to recover State aid are subject to a limitation period of 10 years.

As stated above in Ch.2, where unlawful aid is paid, i.e. State aid not notified **7–002** to the Commission in accordance with art.88(3) EC, the national courts can take measures for the recovery of the aid. On the other hand, the Commission can only require repayment of aid if it finds that the unlawful aid is incompatible with the common market. In other words, in contrast to the courts of the Member States, it cannot require aid to be repaid merely on the grounds

---

[1] The Commission commissioned the "Study on the Enforcement of State Aid Law at National Level", March 2006, prepared by Jones Day, Lovells, Allen & Overy. Among other things the study deals with the treatment of unlawful aid in the different Member States. The report is available at: *http://ec.europa.eu/comm/competition/state_aid/studies_reports/studies_reports. cfm*

[2] *http://ec.europa.eu/comm/competition/state_aid/legislation/reference.html*

that the obligation to notify the aid has been disregarded, or that the aid has been implemented in spite of the stand-still obligation in art.88(3) of the EC Treaty. However, under art.11 of the Procedure Regulation, the Commission can require a Member State provisionally to recover any unlawful aid; see in more detail below.

It should be borne in mind that the Commission has issued "Notice from the Commission—Towards an effective implementation of Commission decisions ordering Member States to recover unlawful and incompatible State aid" (OJ C 272, November 15, 2007, p.4). While the notice does not constitute a legislative act, it does contain the Commission's statement of the applicable law in this area together with an explanation of the Commissions policy towards the implementation of recovery decisions.

WHAT MUST BE REPAID?

7–003   As stated, Ch.III (arts 14 and 15) of the Procedure Regulation contains rules on the recovery of aid. According to art.14(1), when negative decisions are taken in cases of unlawful aid, the Commission must decide that the Member State concerned shall take all necessary measures to recover the aid from the beneficiary.

Thus, art.14(1) makes it clear that it is the unlawful aid which is the subject of a negative decision that must be repaid. "Unlawful aid" is defined in art.1(f) of the Procedure Regulation as new aid put into effect in contravention of art.88(3) of the Treaty. According to art.1(c), "new aid" is all aid, both aid schemes and individual aid, which is not existing aid, including alterations to existing aid.

In this connection, according to art.4(1) of Regulation (EC) No.794/2004, an alteration to existing aid means any change, other than modifications of a purely formal or administrative nature which cannot affect the evaluation of the compatibility of the aid measure with the common market. An increase in the original budget of an existing aid scheme by up to 20 per cent is not considered an alteration to existing aid.

7–004   Even if aid is not put into effect in contravention of art.88(3) of the Treaty and is the subject of a positive decision by the Commission, such aid can nevertheless be required by the Commission to be repaid if the aid is misused. The Commission's authority to do so is found in art.16 of the Procedure Regulation, which states that art.14 also applies to the misuse of aid. "Misuse" is defined in art.1(g) as aid used by the beneficiary in contravention of a Commission decision.

Article 11 of the Procedure Regulation gives the Commission the authority, after giving the Member State concerned the opportunity to submit its comments, to adopt a decision requiring the Member State provisionally to recover any unlawful aid until the Commission has taken a decision on the compatibility of the aid with the common market. However, according to the established practice of the courts, this possibility only exists if there is no doubt about the measure's character as aid, and there must be a need to act quickly due to the significant risk of considerable and irreparable harm to a competitor. Repayment must include interest, see art.14(2), and must be in accordance with national procedures, see art.14(3).

With regard to existing aid, the Commission can propose that such aid should be amended or abolished, but a Member State is not obliged to follow such a proposal by the Commission. A Member State is only obliged to comply with the wishes of the Commission if a decision is adopted on the basis of art.88(2). As long as the Commission has not adopted a decision under art.88(2), a Member State can implement the aid in question and the Commission cannot require it to be suspended, since the Commission only has powers in relation to new aid. If, on the basis of a complaint, the Commission finds that an existing State aid scheme is incompatible with art.87(1) of the Treaty, it can carry out an examination on the basis of art.88(1) and (2). However, any negative decision taken following such an examination does not have retroactive effect. This means that any aid paid on the basis of an aid scheme which is found incompatible in this way cannot be required by the Commission to be recovered.

This problem will not normally arise in relation to notified aid, even if the **7–005** Commission decides not to approve the aid measure in question. However, it can be that aid which is paid out after approval by the Commission must be recovered if the decision to approve is subsequently annulled by the Court of first Instance (CFI) or the ECJ following a complaint.

The Commission's powers to require recovery of aid are limited by art.15 of the Procedure Regulation which contains rules on a period of limitation. According to this, the period of limitation is 10 years. If the period has expired, the aid is regarded as existing aid. The period of limitation begins on the day on which the unlawful aid is awarded to the beneficiary either as individual aid or as aid under an aid scheme. The period can be interrupted by any action taken by the Commission or by a Member State acting at the request of the Commission with regard to the unlawful aid.

In relation to the interruption of the period of limitation, the ECJ has stated that this can be by the Commission asking the Member State concerned for information, for example in connection with a complaint about allegedly unlawful aid.[3] Thus, this can be a measure of the Commission. In the same case the ECJ ruled that it was not a precondition for the interruption that the beneficiary should receive notice of the measure.

An undertaking's repayment of unlawful aid must normally not be neutral- **7–006** ised by the Member State giving the undertaking new aid. However, art.11(2), third paragraph, of the Procedure Regulation does allow the Commission to authorise the Member State to couple the refunding of the aid with the payment of rescue aid to the firm concerned.

---

[3] Case C-276/03 P, *Scott SA v Commission*, [2005] E.C.R. I-8437.

Finally, the amount, including interest (see below) which must be repaid must be stated in the Commission's decision. This is not a requirement under Community law, but the Commission's decision must at least contain instructions whereby the addressee of the decision can establish the amount to be paid without undue difficulty.[4]

CALCULATION OF INTEREST

7–007   The repayment of aid includes interest calculated according to a rate which is determined by the Commission; see art.14(2) of the Procedure Regulation. Interest is payable for the period from the date on which the unlawful aid was at the disposal of the beneficiary until the date of its recovery.[5] Chapter V of Regulation (EC) No.794/2004 contains more detailed provisions for fixing the interest rate for the repayment of unlawful aid.[6] The interest rate to be used for recovering State aid granted in breach of art.88(3) of the Treaty is an annual percentage rate fixed for each calendar year, unless otherwise provided for in a specific decision. The Commission publishes the interest rate in the Official Journal and on its website.

The interest rate used is the applicable rate at the date on which the unlawful aid was first put at the disposal of the beneficiary. This rate is applied throughout the whole period until the date of recovery, unless more than one year elapses between the date on which the unlawful aid was first put at the disposal of the beneficiary and the date of the recovery of the aid. In this case the interest will be recalculated at yearly intervals; see art.11(3). The interest payable is compounded.

WHO MUST CARRY OUT THE COMMISSION'S DECISION ON REPAYMENT AND UNDER WHAT RULES?

7–008   According to art.14(1) of Regulation (EC) No.659/1999, the Member State in question must take the necessary measures to ensure the repayment of the aid.

According to art.14(3), the Member State must ensure that the recovery is effected without delay and in accordance with the procedures under its national law, provided that they allow the immediate and effective execution of the Commission's decision. In this connection the government authority

---

[4]   Case C-415/03, *Commission v Greece*, [2005] E.C.R. I-3875.
[5]   Sometimes the repayment and the calculation of the interest payable can be left to the national authorities; see Case T-67/94, *Ladbroke Racing v Commission*, [1998] E.C.R. II-1, paras 188 and 189.
[6]   Chapter V has been amended by Commission Regulation (EC) No.271/2008 of January 30, 2008 amending Regulation (EC) No.794/2004 implementing Council Regulation (EC) No.659/1999 laying down detailed rules for the application of art.93 [now 88] of the EC Treaty (OJ L 82, 25.3.2008, p.1).

of a Member State cannot argue that it does not have powers to implement a Commission decision on the ground that, for example, it is a matter for regional authorities.[7] The recovery must be sought under national rules, but a Member State cannot excuse itself on the ground that the national rules do not allow recovery to be made. However, the ECJ or the CFI can decide that the implementation of a legal act that has been challenged can be postponed; see art.242 of the EC Treaty.

The use of national procedures for the recovery of payment requires that they enable immediate and effective repayment, and the compatibility of the effectiveness of national procedures with the Procedure Regulation can be referred to the ECJ, which can decide whether the national procedure is in fact sufficiently effective. In this context, recital 13 of the Regulation states that such procedures should not, by preventing the immediate and effective execution of the Commission decision, impede the restoration of effective competition.[8] For example, a national procedural rule, which has suspensive effect when an action is brought against a requirement for repayment issued with a view to the recovery of aid, cannot be regarded as allowing the immediate and effective execution of a Commission decision for repayment.[9] On the other hand, an aid beneficiary can bring an action to annul the Commission's decision, which is an option it always has under art.230 of the Treaty. An undertaking that receives aid which is declared to be unlawful cannot challenge this decision in a suit before the national courts in connection with measures of the national authorities to implement such a decision.[10]

The CFI has found that the Commission is not obliged to take account of any tax on the amount of aid recovered, but that does not prevent the national authorities from taking account of any tax paid on the aid granted, so that the amount to be recovered pursuant to their internal rules is less than the aid paid, provided that the application of those rules does not make the recovery impossible in practice or discriminate in relation to comparable cases governed by national law.[11]

WHO MUST REPAY?

The purpose of recovering unlawful aid is to remove the distortion of competition caused by the competitive advantage given by the aid. Thus the aim of repayment of aid is to re-establish the circumstances which existed on the market in question prior to the payment of the aid.

7–009

[7] Case C-74/89, *Commission v Belgium*, [1990] E.C.R. I-492.
[8] Case C-232/05, *France v Commission*, [2006] E.C.R. I-10071.
[9] Case C-232/05, *France v Commission*, [2006] E.C.R. I-10071. The case is discussed by Bernadette Willemot and Anne Fort, "ECJ Judgement of October 5, 2006 *Commission v France*: A major step forward for the recovery policy", in *Competition Policy Newsletter*, No.1, Spring 2007 p.101.
[10] Case C-232/05, *France v Commission*, [2006] E.C.R. I-10071.
[11] Case T-459/93, *Siemens v Commission*, [1995] E.C.R. II-1675, para.83.

According to art.14(1) of the Procedure Regulation, the Member State must recover the aid from the *beneficiary*, or in other words from the undertaking or undertakings which have received the State aid in question.[12] This will not usually give rise to problems.

The question of the true debtor in relation to repayment of unlawful aid becomes relevant when the beneficiary undertaking has changed hands, either by a transfer of shares or by a transfer of assets, and especially when the undertaking is insolvent and is in receivership.[13]

7–010   The ECJ has thus stated that it is not material to a Member State's implementation of a Commission decision which orders the recovery of unlawfully paid aid that the beneficiary enters into bankruptcy proceedings following the adoption of the Commission's decision.[14] In such a situation the Member State must make a genuine attempt to recover the aid from the undertaking in question, or it must propose to the Commission an alternative method for carrying out a decision which would make it possible to overcome the problem. This means that the Member State must at least register a claim on the insolvent estate.[15] This will normally be sufficient, but if a company is formed[16] with a view to carrying on the activities of the beneficiary undertaking after it has become bankrupt, it is possible that such a company can also be liable to repay the aid in question. This is on condition that it is established that the successor undertaking does in fact benefit from the competitive advantage given by the aid. Among other things, this can be the case if the successor company acquires assets from the insolvent company without paying a price equivalent to the market price for them, or if it is shown that the formation of the successor company has led to the evasion of the obligation to repay the aid.[17] The Commission has the burden of proof in this instance.

The question of the recovery of aid from the undertaking which has in fact received the State aid can be relevant in those cases where the beneficiary undertaking has been bought by another undertaking, or if the beneficiary undertaking's assets have been transferred to another undertaking.

If there were not recovery of aid in such cases, there would be a significant risk that a requirement that aid must be repaid would be evaded by means of a sales transaction.

---

[12] Case C-277/00, *Germany v Commission*, [2004] E.C.R. I-3925.
[13] These questions are discussed by Vassilios Skouris, "The Recovery of Unlawful State Aid from Successor Companies", in *Festschrift For Carl Baudenbacher*, 2007, Nomos. This article discusses the ECJ's practice on the recovery of State aid from undertakings which are the successors to the original beneficiary undertaking.
[14] Case C-42/99, *Spain v Commission*, [1994] E.C.R. I-4175.
[15] Case C-277/00, *Germany v Commission*, [2004] E.C.R. I-3925; and Case 499/99, *Commission v Spain*, [2002] E.C.R. I-603. See also Case T-324/00, *CDA Datenträger Albrechts v Commission*, [2005] E.C.R. II-4309, which among other things concerned companies in the same corporate group and avoidance measures. The claim for recovery will often be addressed to the beneficiary's insolvent estate (administrator).
[16] It can be interesting for the administrator, with regard to ensuring the fullest possible satisfaction of the claims of the creditors, to continue with any profitable activities of the insolvent company in separate companies.
[17] Case C-277/00, *Germany v Commission*, [2004] E.C.R. I-3925.

A distinction must be made between the purchase of shares and the purchase of assets from the beneficiary undertaking.

When an undertaking which has received unlawful aid is sold via the sale of **7–011** shares at market price, i.e. the highest price which a private investor trading on normal competitive terms would be prepared to pay for the company in the actual situation, including having received State aid, the aid element will have been valued at the market price and taken account of in the purchase price. In these circumstances the purchaser cannot be said to have obtained any advantage over other actors on the market.[18] If an undertaking which has received State aid retains its status as a legal person and continues to carry on the activities for which it was granted State aid, this undertaking usually retains the competitive advantage associated with the State aid, and is therefore obliged to repay an amount corresponding to the aid. Thus, the purchaser cannot be required to repay the aid.[19]

There is not a problem with the purchase of assets, as long as they are bought at the true market price.[20] In such a case there will not be a loss of value in the undertaking against which the claim for repayment is made, so the possibility of making repayment is not reduced.

Regardless of whether a case involves the sale of shares or the sale of assets, it is up to the Commission to show that the transfer has not taken place at the true market price. See Ch.6 where the market investor principle is described further.

If the assets of a public undertaking that is required to make a repayment are sold to another public undertaking, there can be a problem in determining whether the price paid is the proper price. In principle in such a case one should use a form of public tendering or evaluation by an independent expert; on this see the section in this book on the sale by public bodies of land and buildings or the sale of public assets in general. As for the cases where the State sells, at market price, an undertaking which has received State aid which is required to be repaid, the purchaser can be assumed to have paid for the aid element and will not therefore be required to repay the State aid. On the other hand it is the seller, in this situation the State, which must repay the State aid. However, it is not possible to require repayment of aid where the debtor and creditor are one and the same in relation to the claim for repayment.[21]

PROTECTION OF LEGITIMATE EXPECTATIONS

According to art.14(1) of Regulation (EC) No.659/1999, the Commission may **7–012** not require the recovery of aid if this would be contrary to a general principle of Community law.

---

[18] Case C-277/00, *Germany v Commission*, [2004] E.C.R. I-3925. See also Case T-324/00, *CDA Datenträger Albrechts v Commission*, [2005] E.C.R. II-4309.
[19] Case C-277/00, *Germany v Commission*, [2004] E.C.R. I-3925.
[20] Case C-277/00, *Germany v Commission*, [2004] E.C.R. I-3925.
[21] Case C-390/98, *H.J. Banks & Co v The Coal Authority*, [2001] E.C.R. I-6117.

A beneficiary can thus rely on these general principles in an action for annulment of a Commission decision.[22]

It is a general principle of Community law that legitimate expectations must be protected. However, in principle an aid beneficiary cannot have a legitimate expectation that the aid they have received is lawful, unless it has been examined under the procedure referred to in art.88 of the Treaty, and a prudent business person must normally be able to confirm that such a procedure has been followed.[23] It is only when the Commission has given a positive decision under the art.88 procedure, and the deadline for challenging the decision has expired that a beneficiary undertaking can be regarded as having a legitimate expectation of the lawfulness of the aid.[24] This underlines that undertakings that receive aid must be careful and, depending on the circumstance, must undertake their own legal evaluation of the procedures of the granting authority, including whether the law has been correctly applied.

7–013   The ECJ acknowledges that the possibility cannot be excluded that an undertaking that has received unlawful aid can refer to extraordinary circumstances that give it a legitimate expectation that the aid was lawful.[25] In this connection the ECJ has stated that the fundamental requirement for legal certainty means that the Commission cannot postpone the exercise of its powers indefinitely. Because of the lapse of time before the Commission decides whether some State aid is lawful, and because it can be annulled and be recovered by the Member State, under certain circumstances the beneficiary can have a legitimate expectation which can prevent the Commission requiring aid to be recovered.[26] It is up to the national courts to determine whether there are extraordinary circumstances, after consulting the ECJ in the form of a reference for a preliminary ruling on the interpretation of Community law.[27]

The fact that the beneficiary undertakings concerned are small enterprises

---

[22] Joined Cases T-204/97 and T-270/97, *EPAC—Empresa para a Agroalimentação e Cereais v Commission*, 2000 E.C.R. II-2267; and Case T-288/97, *Regione autonoma Friuli Venezia Giulia v Commission*, 1999 E.C.R. II-1871.

[23] Case C-148/04, *Unicredito Italiano v Agenzia delle Entrate, Ufficio Genova 1*, [2005] E.C.R. I-11137. See also the *Mauro Alzetta* case, which was appealed to the ECJ, which rejected the appeal; Case C-298/00 P, *Italy v Commission*, [2004] E.C.R. I-4087. See also Joined Cases T-239/04 and T-323/04, *Italy v Commission*, [2007] E.C.R. 0000.

[24] Case T-171/02, *Regione autonoma della Sardegna v Commission*, [2005] E.C.R. II-2123; and Case C-91/01, *Italy v Commission*, [2004] E.C.R. I-4355.

[25] See Case T-55/99, *Confederación Española de Transporte de Mercancías (CETM) v Commission*, [2000] E.C.R. II-3207, in which the CFI stated that the recipients of the loans concerned in the case, at favourable interest rates, which had been provided by private banks without direct State involvement had no reason to believe that the reduction in interest rates on the loans was derived from the State. See also Case C-5/89, *Commission v Germany*, [1990] E.C.R. I-3437.

[26] Case C-298/00 P, *Italy v Commission*, [2004] E.C.R. I-4087.

[27] Case C-298/00 P, *Italy v Commission*, [2004] E.C.R. I-4087. The ECJ has held that the protection of legitimate expectations under national administrative law, in connection with beneficial administrative acts, cannot mean that recovery is made impossible, since the national rules must not make the implementation of Community law impossible in practice. See Case C-5/89, *Commission v Germany*, [1990] E.C.R. I-3437.

is not sufficient to justify a legitimate expectation that the aid in question is lawful.[28]

A Member State that has not followed the procedural rules referred to in art.88, and has thus paid unlawful aid, cannot refrain from recovering aid by reference to the fact that it would be contrary to the legitimate expectations of the beneficiary undertakings. This would make it impossible to apply art.87 of the Treaty on the prohibition of State aid, and art.88 on notification and Commission approval.[29]

Beneficiaries which want to be sure about the possibility of retaining aid granted to them, can refrain from receiving the aid or refrain from using the aid until the two months period of limitation for actions for annulment under art.230 has expired. Thereafter there cannot be a requirement for repayment.

Another general principle of Community law is the principle of proportionality. The annulment of unlawful aid by repayment is a logical consequence of the aid being found to be unlawful. The recovery of the aid in order to re-establish the original situation cannot, therefore, be considered as a measure which is disproportionate to the purpose of the Treaty provisions on State aid.[30] By making the repayment, the beneficiary loses the advantage obtained in the market in relation to competitors, and the situation which existed prior to the grant of aid is re-established.

REPAYMENT WHICH IS DE FACTO IMPOSSIBLE

According to the case law of the ECJ, the only objection which a Member   **7–014**
State can make against a case brought by the Commission for breach of the Treaty under art.88(2) is that it is absolutely impossible to implement the decision to recover aid correctly.[31] The requirement that it must be absolutely impossible to implement a decision will not be fulfilled if the defendant government merely informs the Commission about the legal, political and practical difficulties in implementing the decision, without having made any proper attempt to recover the aid from the undertakings in question, or proposing to the Commission such alternative methods for implementing the decision as would make it possible to overcome the difficulties.[32]

If, when implementing a Commission decision on the repayment of aid, a Member State meets unforeseen and unforeseeable problems or becomes aware of difficulties which were not anticipated by the Commission, the Member State must refer these problems to the Commission for assessment,

---

[28] Case C-298/00 P, *Italy v Commission*, [2004] E.C.R. I-4087.
[29] Case C-5/89, *Commission v Germany*, [1990] E.C.R. I-3437, para.17.
[30] Case C-148/04, *Unicredito Italiano v Agenzia delle Entrate, Ufficio Genova 1*, [2005] E.C.R. I-11137; and Case C-66/02, *Italy v Commission*, [2005] E.C.R. II-10901.
[31] Joined Cases C-485/90-C490/03, *Commission v Spain*, [2006] E.C.R. I-11887; and Case C-415/03, *Commission v Greece*, [2005] E.C.R. I-3875.
[32] Joined Cases C-485/90 – C490/03, *Commission v Spain*, [2006] E.C.R. I-11887. See also Case C-441/06, *Commission v France*, [2007] E.C.R. I-8887.

together with a proposal for suitable amendments to the decision in question. In this case, in accordance with art.10 of the Treaty the Commission and the Member State must cooperate in taking all appropriate measures to ensure fulfilment of the obligations arising out of the Treaty.[33] Article 10 of the EC Treaty requires the Member States and the Community's institutions (as listed in art.7) to co-operate mutually and loyally in order to realise the aims of the Treaty and to uphold the laws derived from it.

Case C-280/95, *Commission v Italy*, [1998] E.C.R. I-259, is an example of a case where a Member State argued that recovery of payment was de facto impossible to implement correctly. In this case the Italian authorities referred to the enormous administrative difficulties in recovering aid in about 100,000 cases. The ECJ did not find that such considerations could justify refraining from seeking recovery of the aid. Moreover, the Italian government had been warned that the tax exemption (which constituted the aid) was possibly contrary to the Treaty and that recovery of the aid could ensue. The ECJ ruled that to allow, under these circumstances, that it was impossible to implement recovery of the aid, would endanger the effectiveness of Community law in the area of State aid. As stated, a Member State that encounters difficulties in recovering aid should refer the question to the Commission, under the principle of loyal cooperation under the Treaty.[34]

NON-COMPLIANCE WITH A DECISION TO RECOVER STATE AID

7–015   Compliance on the part of the Member State with a Commission decision concluding that State aid must be recovered is established when the Member State concerned has implemented the decision fully and within the required time-limits. That is in case of insolvency when the undertaking has been liquidated on market terms. The question arises what the consequences could be if the Member State does not comply with a Commission decision requiring recovery of State aid. Such non-compliance may have consequences for both the Member State and the beneficiary of the unlawful and non-compatible State aid.

The Member State faces the risk of being brought before the ECJ according to art.88(2). According to that provision, the Commission or any other interested State may, if the State concerned does not comply with a Commission

---

[33] Case C-404/97, *Commission v Portugal*, [2000] E.C.R. I-4897, para.40; and Case C-404/00, *Commission v Spain*, [2003] E.C.R. I-6695, para.46.

[34] See Case C-348/93, *Commission v Italy*, [1995] E.C.R. I-673, para.17; and Case 52/84, *Commission v Belgium*, [1986] E.C.R. 89, paras 12 and 14, where, in relation to a Belgian objection that it could not require repayment of the aid because of the financial situation of the undertaking, the ECJ held that repayment could be made by the undertaking entering into liquidation, which the Belgian State could institute in its capacity as shareholder or creditor. Simple concern for insurmountable difficulties cannot justify the failure to apply Community law correctly; see Case C-404/97, *Commission v Portugal*, [2000] E.C.R. I-4897. On the right of set-off under Community law, see Case T-105/99, *Conseil des communes et régions d'Europe (CCRE) v Commission*, [2000] E.C.R. II-4099.

decision within the prescribed time (in derogation from the provisions of arts 226 and 227) refer the matter to the Court of Justice directly. The consequence of a judgment saying that the Member State in question has failed to fulfil the obligation to recover the State aid concerned is that the Member State shall be required to take the necessary measures to comply with the judgment of the Court of Justice, i.e. implement the recovery decision, cf. art.228(1). If a Member State fails to take the necessary measures, the Commission may bring the Member State before the ECJ one more time, cf. art.228(2). If the Court of Justice finds that the Member State concerned has not complied with its judgment it may impose a lump sum or penalty payment on it according to art.228(2). The procedures mentioned above are explained in more detail in Ch.8.

Non-compliance with at decision ordering recovery of State aid may also **7-016** have an impact on the beneficiary if the Member State has not implemented the mentioned decision correctly because the Commission may refrain from authorizing new State aid to that beneficiary as long as the recovery order is outstanding. The basis for such an approach is the *Deggendorf* case.[35] It follows from the CFI judgment in the *Deggendorf* case that the Commission when authorizing aid may attach conditions to its decision to the effect that the authorized aid does not alter trading conditions in a way contrary to the general interest. The risk of such an alteration must be assessed in the light of all the relevant factors, including the possible cumulative effect of the previous aid and the new aid, and *the non-repayment of the previous unlawful aid*. With reference to the *Deggendorf* judgment the Commission may order a Member State to suspend the payment of a new compatible aid to an undertaking that has at its disposal an unlawful and incompatible aid which is subject to an earlier recovery decision. The suspension is in force until the Member State has reassured itself that the undertaking concerned has reimbursed the old unlawful and incompatible aid.

The Deggendorf case law has been incorporated in, e.g. the General Block Exemption Regulation and the Commission Notice on Guarantees and will be applied by the Commission in all State aid rules and decisions.[36]

---

[35] T-244/93 and T486, *TWD Deggendorf v Commission of the European Communities*, E.C.R. [1995] 2265.
[36] See Notice from the Commission—Towards an effective implementation of Commission decisions ordering Member States to recover unlawful and incompatible State aid (OJ C 272, 15.11.2007, p.4).

CHAPTER 8

JUDICIAL PROTECTION IN STATE AID CASES

CONTROL BY THE COMMUNITY COURTS

Both the ECJ and the national courts help ensure that the EU's State aid rules   **8–001**
are applied and complied with correctly in practice. The Commission has sole
competence to approve measures that benefit from the exemptions in art.87(2)
and (3) of the Treaty.

Direct cases, for example actions for annulment of decisions of the
Commission under art.230 of the EC Treaty, must always be brought before
the Court of First Instance (CFI). According to art.225, first sentence, the
CFI has jurisdiction to deal with cases for annulment brought under art.230
and cases brought for failure to act in accordance with art.232, as regards
a decision or lack of decision by the Commission in a State aid case. This
applies regardless of whether an action is brought by a Member State or
a legal or natural person; see art.51 of the Statute of the Court of Justice.
According to art.225(1), first sentence, the decisions of the CFI can be
appealed to the ECJ on points of law; see art.51 of the Statute of the Court
of Justice. Under the Statute, such an appeal may be brought by any party
which has been unsuccessful, in whole or in part, in their submissions. As
stated, the appeal is limited to points of law. This means that the appellant's grounds for having a case tried by the ECJ are limited to the lack of
competence of the CFI, a breach of procedure before it which adversely
affects the interests of the appellant, or an infringement of Community law
by the CFI; see art.58 of the Statute. If the appellant's intention is to get the
ECJ to judge the facts of the case differently than the CFI, the appeal will
be dismissed.

State aid cases can also be referred to the ECJ by a national court with
a view to obtaining a preliminary ruling on the interpretation or validity
of Community secondary legislation (for example, State aid rules) which is
involved in a case before the national court; see art.234 of the Treaty. It is
also possible to bring an action before the CFI against the Commission for
its failure to act (art.232), and for compensation for non-contractual liability

(art.235, by reference to art.288, second paragraph of the Treaty—see below).

Actions for annulment of Commission decisions

8–002   According to art.230 of the Treaty, the ECJ (and the CFI) can review the legality of acts adopted by the Commission, which includes the Commission's decisions on State aid. In this respect the ECJ has jurisdiction, among other things, in actions brought by a Member State on grounds of lack of competence, infringement of an essential procedural requirement, infringement of the Treaty or of any rule of law relating to its application, or misuse of powers; see art.230, second paragraph. Any natural or legal person may, under the same conditions, institute proceedings against a decision addressed to them or against a decision which, although addressed to another person, is of direct and individual concern to them; see art.230, fourth paragraph. The Commission's decisions on State aid are addressed to the Member State concerned. According to art.230, fifth paragraph, proceedings for annulment must be instituted within two months of the publication of the measure, or of its notification to the applicant, or, in the absence thereof, of the day on which it came to the knowledge of the applicant.

    In an action for annulment in accordance with art.230, the legality of a Community act, for example, a Commission decision, is judged according to the circumstances which existed at the time when the legal act was issued. In other words, the Commission's assessment can only be judged on the basis of the information which was available to the Commission at the time it made its assessment.[1]

    If the ECJ/CFI finds that an action brought under art.230 is justified, the decision will be found void in whole or in part; see art.21 of the Treaty. Furthermore, according to art.233, if a decision of the Commission is declared void, the Commission will be required to take the necessary measures to comply with the judgment of the ECJ/CFI, which will often mean that the Commission is required to make a new decision.

What can be subject to action for annulment?

8–003   At a general level, only legal acts that are legally binding and which affect the applicant's interests because of a significant change in their legal rights can be the subject of an action for annulment under art.230. Any provision adopted by one of the institutions of the Community, including the Commission, that is intended to have legal effects can thus be the subject of

---

[1] Case T-34/02, *EURL Le Levant 001 and Others v Commission*, [2006] E.C.R. II-267.

an action for annulment, and this applies regardless of the nature or form of the legal act.[2] If, for example, the Commission receives a complaint, and the Commission replies to the complainant by means of a letter, the content of this letter may mean that there is in effect a decision in accordance with art.4(2) of Council Regulation (EC) No.659/1999 of March 22, 1999 laying down detailed rules for the application of art.93 [now 88] of the EC Treaty (OJ L 83, March 27, 1999, p.1), and not merely an information to the complainant under art.20(2) of the Regulation that the Commission finds there are insufficient grounds for taking a view on the case. The latter cannot be subject to an action for annulment. On the other hand, the former can be subject to an action for annulment if the Commission gives a clear and reasoned statement for why, for example some measure is not considered to be State aid.[3] Whether a decision has been published, or whether it has been taken by the Commission as a body does not affect the right to bring an action for annulment against a letter or notice addressed to a Member State.[4]

In relation to State aid, according to a number of decisions relating to the State aid procedure, cases can be brought before the CFI in accordance with art.230, and may be annulled on the same basis:

1. Commission decisions in which a national measure is judged to constitute State aid, whether compatible or incompatible with the common market. This applies to new and existing aid, as such decisions are legally binding.
2. Commission decisions in which a national measure is not found to constitute State aid in accordance with art.87(1).[5]
3. Commission decisions to initiate the formal procedure in art.88(2):

    (a) in relation to existing aid, the decision cannot be the subject of an action for annulment;[6] and
    (b) in relation to new aid, the decision can be the subject of an action for annulment.[7]

4. Commission decisions ordering the termination of aid measures or an order for the interim repayment of aid in accordance with art.11(1) and (2) of Regulation (EC) No.659/1999.
5. Council decisions made in accordance with art.88(2), third paragraph.[8]

---

[2] Case T-351/02, *Deutsche Bahn v Commission*, [2006] E.C.R. II-1047.
[3] Case T-351/02, *Deutsche Bahn v Commission*, [2006] E.C.R. II-1047.
[4] Case T-351/02, *Deutsche Bahn v Commission*, [2006] E.C.R. II-1047.
[5] Case C-367/95 P, *Commission v Sytraval*, [1998] E.C.R. I-1719.
[6] Joined Cases C-182/03 and C-217/03, *Belgium and Forum 187 ASBL v Commission*, [2006] E.C.R. I-5479.
[7] Case C-400/99, *Italy v Commission*, [2001] E.C.R. I-7303.
[8] See paras 1–065 and 1–066of this book on the Council's powers under art.88(2), third paragraph.

Commission proposals for appropriate measures,[9] in accordance with art.88(1), are not decisions which can be brought before the courts.[10]

What does the examination by the Community courts involve?

8–004   As stated, the decisions of the Commission can be referred to the CFI, with a view to their annulment in accordance with art.230 of the EC Treaty. The CFI has full jurisdiction, but in relation to the discretionary exemptions in art.87(3), in practice it refrains from examining the Commission's exercise of its discretion,[11] and restricts itself to ensuring that the procedure used by the Commission which has led to the decision in dispute does not suffer from any significant procedural failing (infringement of important procedural requirements, such as the failure to hear the parties, or the lack of or inadequate justification; see art.253 of the Treaty), that there is not a misuse of power, lack of jurisdiction,[12] or manifest error in establishing the facts. This restraint of the CFI's examination of a case applies in particular when the Commission's exercise of its discretion involves complex economic and social evaluations.[13]

In all cases the CFI will itself control the correct application of the law and of the Community law in general.

It can often happen that an applicant obtains the annulment of a decision of the Commission concerning the approval or non-approval of State aid.[14]

[9] Under art.88(1) of the EC Treaty, the Commission must, in cooperation with Member States, keep under constant review all systems of aid existing in those States. It must propose to the Member States any appropriate measures required by the progressive development or by the functioning of the common market. This is described in more detail in arts 17-19 of Regulation (EC) No.659/1999. This states that if, after consulting the Member State concerned, the Commission finds that an existing aid measure is no longer compatible with the common market, it should make a recommendation to that Member State. In such a recommendation the Commission should propose appropriate measures which may concern substantive changes to the aid measure, the introduction of procedural requirements, or the annulment of the aid measure.

[10] Case T-330/94, *Salt Union v Commission*, [1995] E.C.R. II-2881.

[11] On this, see paras 1–051 to 1–064.

[12] See Case T-442/93, *Association des Amidonneries de Céréales (AAC) v Commission*, [1995] E.C.R. II-1329, which concerned the fact that the Commission should, in principle, take the decision as a collegiate body.

[13] Case T-171/02, *Regione autonoma della Sardegna v Commission*, [2005] E.C.R. II-2123; and Case T-34/02, *EURL Le Levant 001 and Others v Commission*, [2006] E.C.R. II-267.

[14] See e.g. Case T-73/98, *Société chimique Prayon-Rupel v Commission*, [2001] E.C.R. II-867, where an applicant obtained the annulment of a decision of the Commission, where it had considered aid as being compatible with the common market without having initiated the procedure in art.88(3) and without consulting the interested parties. The CFI found that the Commission had taken its decision with insufficient knowledge of the facts. See also Case C-204/97, *Portugal v Commission*, [2001] E.C.R. I-3175, where the ECJ annulled the Commission's positive decision concerning aid to French producers of fortified wine, among other things on the ground of the failure to initiate the procedure in art.88(2). In this case, according to the ECJ, the circumstances indicated that it would only be by adopting the procedure in art.88(2) that the Commission would have been able to obtain insight into the connection between the French aid scheme in question and a French tax on wines, and could have assessed whether there was an infringement of art.90 on discriminatory internal taxation,

Cases brought for the annulment of Commission decisions on State aid often involve highly complex issues of law, as well as large amounts of money, and they can also involve claims for the repayment of large sums, and sometimes important questions of principle (such as the right to cross-subsidise in public service undertakings like postal services).[15]

As stated, the CFI has full jurisdiction, and it can even call on external **8–005** experts with a view to establishing that the facts in a case have been correctly laid out.[16]

Among the procedural rules, compliance with which is traditionally a matter of importance for the CFI, and the infringement of which can in practice lead to annulment, is the requirement for a statement of reasons to be given in art.253 of the Treaty. According to the case law, the Commission must state the reasons for its decisions in State aid cases, giving the addressees, the ECJ and CFI, the complainant and others who might be directly and individually concerned a sufficient insight into the basis for the decision taken.[17] The statement of reasons must thus clearly and unambiguously state the considerations which lie behind the decision, regardless of how obvious they may be.[18] There is not a requirement to give all the various relevant facts and legal aspects, but the decision must not only be assessed in relation to its wording, but also in relation to its context, as well as in relation to all the other rules that apply in the area in question.[19] The specific circumstances of a case can make it necessary to give a more detailed statement of reasons.[20]

which would have been incompatible with the common market. It is interesting to note that the ECJ emphasised art.90, while the claim of the Portuguese Government was based on art.87 combined with art.90.

[15] See e.g. Case T-613/97, *UFEX v Commission*, [2000] E.C.R. II-4055; Joined Cases C-83/01 P, C-93/01 P and C-94/01 P, *Chronopost and Others v Commission*, [2003] E.C.R. I-6993; and Case T-613/97, *UFEX v Commission*, [2006] E.C.R. II-1531 (this last case has been appealed to the ECJ as Case C-342/06 P.) These cases concerned the French monopoly undertaking La Poste and its subsidiary courier service company SFEI. The logistical and commercial support from La Poste to SFEI constituted State aid. The Commission's decision not to regard the aid as State aid was annulled. By judgment of July 1, 2008 the Court of Justice set aside the ruling of the Court of First Instance in so far as the CFI annulled the decision of the Commission and dismissed the application of UFEX and others for the annulment of the contested decision.

[16] Case C-169/84, *Cdf Chimie AZF v Commission*, [1990] E.C.R. I-3083.

[17] See para.65 in Case C-105/99, *Italy v Commission*, [2000] E.C.R. I-8855; Case T-34/02, *EURL Le Levant 001 v Commission*, [2006] E.C.R. II-267; and Case T-93/02, *Confédération nationale du Crédit mutuel v Commission*, [2005] E.C.R. II-143, in which the CFI stated that the obligation to state reasons is an essential procedural requirement, as distinct from the question of whether the reasons given are correct, which goes to the substantive legality of the contested measure.

[18] Case T-318/00, *Freistaat Thüringen v Commission*, [2005] E.C.R. II-4179; Joined Cases T-111/01 and T-133/01, *Saxonia Edelmetalle and Others v Commission*, [2005] E.C.R. II-1579; and Case C-88/03, *Portugal v Commission*, [2006] E.C.R. I-7115.

[19] See e.g. para.67 in Case C-156/98, *Germany v Commission*, [2000] E.C.R. I-6857; para.138 in Joined Cases T-111/01 and T-133/01, *Saxonia Edelmetalle and Others v Commission*, [2005] E.C.R. II-1579; and Case T-171/02, *Regione autonoma della Sardegna v Commission*, [2005] E.C.R. II-2123. Another example is Case T-166/01, *Lucchini v Commission*, [2006] E.C.R. II-2875, which concerned the ECSC Treaty, but which is nevertheless relevant under the regime of the EC Treaty.

[20] Case T-613/97, *UFEX v Commission*, [2006] E.C.R. II-1531, which has been appealed to the ECJ as Case C-342/06 P. By judgment of July 1, 2008 the ECJ set aside the judgment of the

The reasons must be stated in the text of the decision, and except in special circumstances, the reasons may not be given later, for example in the course of litigation.[21] According to art.253, both the operative part and the statement of reasons must constitute an indivisible whole, so that if the adoption of a decision falls within the powers of the College of Commissioners, in accordance with the principle of collegiate responsibility it must adopt both elements, since any alteration to the statement of reasons, other than simple corrections of spelling or grammar, belongs to its exclusive province.[22]

It is the practice of the Commission to send complainants a copy of its decisions on complaints, so the requirement for giving a statement of reasons should be satisfied in relation to the complainants.

8–006   The Commission must show, as part of its decision, that the aid can affect trade between Member States and distort or threaten to distort competition, but the Commission is not required to demonstrate that the aid actually affects trade between Member States or distorts competition.[23] The Commission is not required to show that non-notified State aid has had an actual effect, since this is not necessary with regard to notified aid.[24] [25]

Inadequate consultation of interested parties (on the meaning of "interested parties" see paras 2–024 to 2–027, and art.1(h) of Regulation (EC) No.659/1999) can also constitute a significant breach of the procedural rules, and can in principle lead to annulment of a decision. According to the practice of the Community courts, it is only in cases where consultation of an interested party or parties could have led to a substantially different result that inadequate consultation will lead to the annulment in whole or in part of a Commission decision.[26]

CFI in so far as that judgment annulled the decision of the Commission and dismissed the application of UFEX and others for annulment of the decision of the Commission.

[21] Case T-349/03, *Corsica Ferries France SAS v Commission*, [2005] E.C.R. II-2197; para.287 of the judgment refers to the practice of the courts concerning subsequent statements of reasons. Case T-613/97, *UFEX v Commission*, [2006] E.C.R. II-1531, which has been appealed to the ECJ as Case C-342/06 P. By judgment of July 1, the ECJ set aside the judgment of the CFI in so far as that judgment annulled the decision of the Commission and dismissed the application of UFEX and others for an annulment of the decision of the Commission.

[22] Case T-93/02, *Confédération nationale du Crédit mutuel v Commission*, [2005] E.C.R. II-143.

[23] See para.24 of the judgment in Joined Cases 296 and 318/82, *The Netherlands and Leeuwarder Papierwarenfabriek v Commission*, [1985] E.C.R. 809; and Case T-171/02, *Regione autonoma della Sardegna v Commission*, [2005] E.C.R. II-2123.

[24] Case C-301/87, *France v Commission (Boussac)*, [1990] E.C.R. I-307.

[25] A statement of reasons with regard to repayment is also necessary, but it can be assumed when a formal procedure is initiated with a finding that the aid can be subject to repayment and the final decision sets out the effect of the aid; see Case C-303/88, *Italy v Commission (ENI-Lanerossi)*, [1991] E.C.R. I-1433, paras 53 and 54. In its statement of reasons the Commission has merely stated that there was a serious breach of Community law. The ECJ found that, in itself, the statement of reasons could be criticised for being very brief. See also Case C-142/87, *Belgium v Commission (Tubemeuse)*, [1990] E.C.R. I-959, where the ECJ stated that the repayment was a logical consequence of the finding that the aid was unlawful.

[26] See, e.g. on compliance with the right of defence, para.99 of the judgment in Case 288/96, *Germany v Commission*, [2000] E.C.R. I-8237; and Case C-301/87, *France v Commission (Boussac)*, [1990] E.C.R. I-307. See also Case T-171/02, *Regione autonoma della Sardegna v*

Also, any infringement by the Commission of the principle of equal treatment can lead to annulment. Such an infringement could arise, for example if the Commission did not apply frameworks or guidelines issued by itself in relation to aid in a specific case, without there being objective reasons to justify the failure to do so.

Misuse of powers is also referred to in art.230 of the Treaty as being circum-   **8–007** stances which can lead to the annulment of a Commission decision. The term "misuse of powers" refers to the circumstances where, in exercising its powers, an administrative authority pursues some other objective than that for which the powers were given to it. A Commission decision will only be considered a misuse of powers if it appears, on the basis of objective, relevant and consistent facts, to have been taken for some other purpose.[27]

Other recognised principles of Community law, such as the principle of legitimate expectations, can be the basis of a claim, for example, in connection with cases on recovery of unlawful aid, where according to the case law exceptional circumstances are required for an infringement to be recognised by the Community courts.[28] A legitimate expectation of the legality of aid can in principle only apply if the aid has been granted in accordance with the procedure in art.88, unless there are wholly exceptional circumstances.[29] If, for example, the examination procedure referred to in art.88(2) of the Treaty has been initiated, it must have been concluded with a positive decision in accordance with art.7(1) and (3) of Regulation (EC) No.659/1999 (the Procedure Regulation). It is only when the Commission has made such a decision, and the deadline for bringing an action to challenge such a decision has expired, that the beneficiary undertaking can be regarded as having a legitimate expectation of the lawfulness of the decision.[30]

It is possible for the Commission to refuse to approve State aid on the ground that its approval would lead to the infringement of Treaty rules other than the State aid rules; see para.78 in Case C-156/98, *Germany v Commission*, [2000] E.C.R. I-6857.

In practice, cases are brought before the CFI concerning the Commission's   **8–008** decisions to initiate the procedure under art.88(2) or to terminate it, and on whether an aid measure requires notification, on repayment and very often about whether an aid measure is compatible with the common market.[31] In particular, competitors will have an interest in bringing cases for annulment against a Commission decision not to initiate a procedure under art.88(2).

It is clear that any use by the Commission of wrong information as the basis for a decision can lead to the annulment of the decision. Since, according to

Commission, [2005] E.C.R. II-2123, where the claims relating to the setting aside on the right to submit evidence were dismissed.
[27] Case C-400/99, *Italy v Commission*, [2005] E.C.R. I-3657; and Case C-310/99, *Italy v Commission*, [2002] E.C.R. I-2289.
[28] See Case C-183/91, *Commission v Greece*, [1993] E.C.R. I-3131, para.18.
[29] Case T-171/02, *Regione autonoma della Sardegna v Commission*, [2005] E.C.R. II-2123.
[30] Case T-171/02, *Regione autonoma della Sardegna v Commission*, [2005] E.C.R. II-2123.
[31] See *Bellamy & Child* 5th ed. p.1273.

the practice of the courts, it is difficult for the CFI to reject a discretionary decision of the Commission (unless the case involves a manifest error[32]), in some cases the applicant will have more of a chance to succeed by challenging the Commission's statement of the facts and that is often attempted, sometimes with success. The facts can concern the financial circumstances, but also a misunderstanding by the Commission of legal or procedural matters in the Member State concerned.

It is clear that the CFI and, in the event of an appeal, the ECJ will consider whether the Commission has correctly applied Community law. For example this could concern whether a specific Treaty article may have direct effect; see art.73 for example, regardless of the existence of a number of regulations which might be thought to have exhausted art.73. It may also concern the application of the law in a specific case, for example whether a specific measure constitutes State aid at all, as defined in art.87(1).[33]

Cases on State aid brought before the CFI as part of a direct case can only be referred to the ECJ on questions of law; see art.56 of the Statute of the Court of Justice and art.225(1) of the EC Treaty.

Who can bring an action for annulment?

8–009   Any person who is the addressee of a decision of the Commission has the right to challenge it before the CFI. In relation to Commission decisions on State aid, it is always the Member State that is the addressee of the decision, and on this basis it can always bring an action for annulment on the basis of art.230, second paragraph, of the Treaty.[34]

In assessing whether the beneficiary and its competitors can bring an action for annulment of a Commission decision on the basis of art.230, fourth paragraph, a distinction is made between decisions which concern general aid schemes and individual aid measures. However, it must be emphasised that an action for annulment can only be brought by a natural or legal person if, at the time of bringing the action, that person has a legal interest (locus standi) in the annulment of the legal act challenged.[35] There must be an existing and

---

[32] Case C-301/87, *France v Commission*, [1990] E.C.R I-307, para.49; and Case T-126/99, *Graphischer Maschinenbau v Commission*, [2002] E.C.R. II-2427.

[33] See Case C-379/98, *PreussenElektra v Schleswag*, [2001] E.C.R. I-2099, which established that it is only measures which involve the use of State resources (and not a legal act on the obligation to buy electricity from renewable sources, benefiting one group of undertakings at the cost of others) that constitute State aid.

[34] On the question of the legal interest of Member States in actions brought on the basis of art.230, second paragraph, see the Opinion of Advocate General Alber in Case C-409/00, *Spain v Commission*, [2003] E.C.R. I-1487, para.32.

[35] Case T-141/03, *Sniace v Commission*, [2005] E.C.R. II-1197, concerned an undertaking, Sniace, that had received State aid which had been declared by the Commission to be compatible with the common market. Sniace, supported by the Spanish State, brought an action for annulment of the Commission's decision, i.e. against a decision which was in its favour. However, the case was dismissed, as Sniace was unable to show that it had a legal interest in the action. See also Case T-136/05, *EARL Salvat père & fils and Others v Commission*, [2007] E.C.R. 0000.

real interest in the annulment, and the applicant's interest may not be assessed on the basis of future or hypothetical circumstances. If the interest which the applicant claims to have concerns some future right, the applicant must prove that the interference with that right gives the applicant a vested and present interest.[36] In addition to this, art.230, fourth paragraph, contains the requirement that applicants must be directly and individually concerned.

An applicant is directly concerned if the contested decision is capable of affecting the applicant's interests. This may seem problematic in the sense that a decision in State aid cases is addressed to the Member State and, therefore, needs implementing measures at national level before the beneficiary and competitors are affected. However, in practice the requirement that the applicant must be directly concerned does not seem to give rise to problems. Either the Commission's decision does not give the Member State concerned any choice about implementing it, or—in case of, e.g. general measures such as approved aid schemes—there is no doubt that the Member State intends to implement at national level the State aid approved by the Commission. So, where there is no doubt that the national authorities wish to act in a certain way, the possibility of their not making use of the option afforded by the Commission decision is purely theoretical, with the result that the applicant may be directly concerned. [37] In contrast, the requirement that the applicant should be individually concerned is more problematic, and this is dealt with in the following.

As for decisions which declare general aid schemes as being either compatible or incompatible with the common market, an undertaking does not usually have a right to bring an action under art.230, fourth paragraph. According to the established case law, persons other than those to whom a decision is addressed may only claim to be individually concerned if a decision affects them by reason of certain attributes which are peculiar to them or by reason of circumstances in which they are differentiated from all other persons and by virtue of these factors distinguishes them individually just as in the case of the addressee of such a decision. [38] It will usually not be possible for undertakings to fulfil these conditions as in this context the Commission's decisions are generally applicable.

8–010

The ECJ has held that, in principle, an undertaking may not challenge a Commission decision which prohibits an aid scheme for a sector solely on the basis that the undertaking is affected by the decision because it belongs to that

---

[36] Joined Cases T-228/00 and others, *Gruppo ormeggiatori del porto di Venezia Soc. coop. rl & Others v Commission*, [2005] E.C.R. II-787.

[37] On this question, see Case 11/82, *Piraiki-Patraiki and Others v Commission*, [1985] E.C.R. 207; Case T-435/93, *ASPEC and Others v Commission*, [1995] E.C.R. II-1281; Case T-442/93, *AAC and Others v Commission*, [1995] E.C.R. II-1329; Case T-266/94, *Skibsværftsforeningen and Others v Commission*, [1996] E.C.R. II-1399; Case T-380/94, *AIUFASS and AKT v Commission*, [1996] E.C.R. II-2169; and Case T-114/00, *Aktionsgemeinschaft Recht und Eigentum eV v Commission*, [2002] E.C.R. II-5121 (this last judgment was overturned on appeal in Case C-78/03 P, *Commission v Aktionsgemeinschaft Recht und Eigentum eV*, [2005] E.C.R. I-10737).

[38] Case 25-62, *Plaumann & Co v Commission*, E.C.R. English special edition p.95.

sector, and could potentially benefit from the aid.[39] In respect of competitors to an undertaking which falls within the scope of an aid scheme, the CFI has ruled that a positive decision of the Commission is of general application, so that competitors are only affected in their objective capacity as an undertaking in the area which is affected by the aid, and to the same extent as any other undertaking which actually or potentially finds itself in an equivalent situation.[40] In an extension of this, the CFI has stated that a competitor's competitive situation can only be affected potentially and indirectly by a Commission decision.[41] Since this decision concerns the approval of a general aid scheme, and the potential beneficiaries are thus defined in a general and abstract way, it requires that the aid scheme should have been specifically applied by giving individual aid before there can be said to be an actual beneficiary and thus an actual competing undertaking to the aid beneficiary.[42] The mere fact that a potential competitor has submitted a complaint to the Commission, has had an exchange of correspondence and has had discussions on the matter with the Commission cannot be said to constitute special circumstances to make that party individually affected compared to others, so as to give that party the right to bring an action in connection with a general scheme.[43]

In this connection it is irrelevant whether the decision is taken on the basis of art.88(3) or art.88(2) of the Treaty.[44] A decision to initiate proceedings under art.88(2) also appears to be a general decision.

8–011 According to the judgment in Joined Cases 67, 68 and 70/85, *Kwekerij Gebroeders van der Kooy and Others v Commission*, [1988] E.C.R. 219, a market gardener is not regarded as being directly and individually affected by a Commission decision addressed to a Member State prohibiting State aid in the form of a preferential tariff for gas supplied to market gardeners. The contested decision was of concern to the applicants solely by virtue of their objective capacity as growers established in the Member State in question and qualifying for the preferential gas tariff on the same footing as any other grower in the same circumstances. On the other hand, in the same case the ECJ held that the potential beneficiaries' trade association, which had negotiated the matter and had participated in the Commission's administrative procedure under art.88(2), could bring an action for annulment. The trade association was concerned as a negotiator and not as a potential beneficiary.

If an undertaking is an actual beneficiary of aid provided under an aid scheme, it is regarded as being directly and individually concerned, within the

---

[39] Joined Cases C-15/98 and C-105/99, *Italy and Sardegna Lines v Commission*, [2000] E.C.R. I-8855, para.33.
[40] Case T-398/94, *Kahn Scheppvaart v Commission*, [1996] E.C.R. II-477.
[41] Case T-398/94, *Kahn Scheppvaart v Commission*, [1996] E.C.R. II-477.
[42] Case T-398/94, *Kahn Scheppvaart v Commission*, [1996] E.C.R. II-477.
[43] Case T-398/94, *Kahn Scheppvaart v Commission*, [1996] E.C.R. II-477.
[44] Case T-398/94, *Kahn Scheppvaart v Commission*, [1996] E.C.R. II-477; and Case T-69/96, *Hamburger Hafen- und Lagerhaus v Commission*, [2001] E.C.R. II-1037. See also Case C-298/00 P, *Italy v Commission*, [2004] E.C.R. I-4087; and Joined Cases C-15/98 and C-105/99, *Italy and Sardegna Lines v Commission*, [2000] E.C.R. I-8855.

meaning of art.230 of the Treaty, by a Commission decision that aid which is incompatible with the common market must be repaid.[45] In this case annulment proceedings must be brought within two months, as its right to challenge the decision before a national court or to request a preliminary ruling from the ECJ will be precluded once the deadline for bringing an action for annulment under art.230 has expired.[46]

With regard to individual aid measures, in relation to new aid the Commission can take decisions in two stages in its examination of the compatibility of the aid with the common market. The first stage is a preliminary stage under art.88(3). If on the basis of this the Commission decides to open formal proceedings under art.88(2), this decision can be challenged by the undertaking which is the intended beneficiary of the aid measure. In such circumstances the undertaking will be directly and individually concerned. If, on the other hand, on the basis of its preliminary examination under art.88(3), the Commission finds that there is not State aid, or that the aid is compatible with the common market, and therefore decides not to initiate the formal procedure under art.88(2), such a decision can be challenged on the basis of art.230, fourth paragraph, by interested parties that have submitted observations under the art.88(2) proceeding, in order to protect their procedural guarantees under art.88(2).[47] Those interested are persons, undertakings or associations whose interests may be affected by the aid granted, including in particular competing undertakings and trade organisations.[48] According to art.20 of Regulation (EC) No.659/1999 (the Procedure Regulation) a complainant who has made a complaint to the Commission has a right to receive a copy of the Commission's decision in cases where the Commission has not initiated proceedings under art.88(2), but has approved an aid measure. If the complainant challenges the correctness of the decision and the assessment of the aid as such, the mere fact that the complainant can be regarded as an interested party within the meaning of art.88(2) will not be enough for the

---

[45] Case T-136/05, *EARL Salvat père & fils and Others v Commission*, [2007], not yet reported. See also Joined Cases C-15/98 and C-105/99, *Italy and Sardegna Lines v Commission*, [2000] E.C.R. I-8855, para.34.

[46] Case C-188/92, *TWD Textilwerke Deggendorf v Bundesrepublik Deutschland*, [1994] E.C.R. I-833; and Joined Cases T-228/00 and others, *Gruppo ormeggiatori del porto di Venezia and Others v Commission*, [2005] E.C.R. II-787.

[47] Case C-198/91, *William Cook v Commission*, [1993] E.C.R. I-2487; and Case C-367/95 P, *Commission v Sytraval and Brink's France*, [1998] E.C.R. I-1719.

[48] Article 1(h) of Council Regulation (EC) No.659/1999 of March 22, 1999 laying down detailed rules for the application of art.93 of the EC Treaty (OJ L 83, 27.3.1999, p.1), where interested parties are listed; see Case T-395/04, *Air One v Commission*, [2006] E.C.R. II-1343; Case C-78/03 P, *Commission v Aktionsgemeinschaft Recht und Eigentum*, [2005] E.C.R. I-10737; and Case C-198/91, *William Cook v Commission*, [1993] E.C.R. I-2487. The action should be brought against the Commission's decision not to initiate the procedure in art.88(2), not against the written notice which the Commission will have sent, in accordance with good administrative practice, to the complainant who wishes to bring the action for annulment; see the judgment in Case T-82/96, *ARAP and Others v Commission*, [1999] E.C.R. II-1889. The written notice is purely informative and does not constitute a legal act that can be challenged under art. 230. See also Case T-86/96, *Arbeits-gemeinschaft Deutscher Luftfahrt-Unternehmen and Others v Commission*, [1999] E.C.R. II-179.

case to be heard in full. For this, it must be shown that the complainant is directly and individually concerned, which will be the case if the complainant's market position is significantly affected by the aid measure which the decision concerns.[49]

8–012   The aid beneficiary or potential beneficiary will always be entitled to bring an action for annulment of a negative decision under art.230, fourth paragraph, i.e. a decision by the Commission that the aid is incompatible with the common market on the basis of the procedure in art.88(2).[50] The same applies if a decision finds that aid is compatible with the common market, but subject to the beneficiary fulfilling conditions laid down by the Commission.[51]

Depending on the circumstances, undertakings that are not intended beneficiaries of aid can bring an action for annulment against a decision which concludes the procedure in art.88(2) and which declares an aid measure to be compatible with the common market. This presumes that the undertaking is directly and individually concerned, as stated in art.230, fourth paragraph. As indicated above, this will be the case if the contested decision affects the undertaking solely by virtue of its objective capacity or because of its actual situation that distinguishes it from all others, and makes it individually concerned as if it were the addressee of the decision. According to the practice of the ECJ and the CFI, it is not sufficient for an undertaking to rely on the fact that it is a competitor to the undertaking receiving the aid, but it needs to show that, given the level of its involvement in the proceedings and the extent of the risk for its market position, its actual situation will make it individually concerned in the same way as if it were the addressee of the decision.[52] In the area of control over State aid, a decision of the Commission under art.88(2) is of concern to undertakings which have been involved as complainants in the case, as well as those that have made submissions or been involved in the proceedings of the case, as long as their market position is significantly affected by the aid measure which is the subject of the decision which is challenged.[53] The mere fact that the decision is liable to have some influence on competitive conditions on the market in question, and the undertaking concerned competes in some way with the undertaking that benefits under the decision, is not sufficient to establish that there is a significant effect.[54] According to the case law, the fact that an undertaking has

---

[49] Case C-78/03 P, *Commission v Aktionsgemeinschaft Recht und Eigentum*, [2005] E.C.R. I-10737; and Case T-30/03, *Specialarbejderforbundet i Danmark (SID) v Commission*, 2007 E.C.R. II-34. The latter case has been appealed to the ECJ as Case C-319/07 P.

[50] Case 730/79, *Philip Morris Holland v Commission*, [1980] E.C.R. 2671; Case T-395/04, *Air One v Commission*, [2006] E.C.R. II-1343.

[51] Case T-296/97, *Alitalia v Commission*, [2000] E.C.R. II-3871.

[52] Case T-88/01, *Sniace v Commission*, [2005] E.C.R. II-1165, appealed as Case C-260/05 P, *Sniace v Commission*, [2007] E.C.R. 0000. The ECJ rejected the appeal.

[53] Case T-36/99, *Lenzing v Commission*, [2004] E.C.R. II-3597, where reference was made to other cases on this question. This judgment concerned the question of when a market position can be said to be significantly affected. The case was appealed to the ECJ; see Case C-525/04 P, *Spain v Commission*, [2007] E.C.R. 0000. The ECJ rejected the appeal.

[54] Case T-117/04, *Jachthavens Zuidelijke Randmeren and Others v Commission*, [2006] E.C.R. II-3861.

taken the initiative to make the complaint that has prompted the initiation of the examination, that the undertaking has made submissions to the examination, and that its submissions have to a large extent influenced the outcome of the examination, are facts that can support the argument that the undertaking is directly and individually concerned within the meaning of art.230, fourth paragraph.[55] However, it must be emphasised that there can be other concrete circumstances which can make an undertaking directly and individually concerned, even if it has not taken part in proceedings under art.88(2).[56]

If a beneficiary could have challenged an aid decision on the basis of art.230, the beneficiary is precluded from challenging the decision before a national court and from seeking a preliminary ruling from the ECJ once the deadline for bring an action for annulment under art.230 has expired.[57]   **8–013**

As stated previously in this book, individuals and undertakings, as well as organisations, can appear as applicants before the CFI in State aid cases. As for trade or business organisations, it has been established in case law that they can either appear because their own situation is affected (directly and individually concerned—art.230), or as representatives for their members, or appearing jointly with some or all of their members, provided they have an individual interest in the action.[58] As stated, the organisation itself must be directly and individually concerned and therefore have a right to bring an action for annulment. In assessing this, it is necessary to distinguish between decisions concerning the initial examination phase, see art.88(3), and decisions concerning the formal examination procedure, see art.88(2), as discussed above.[59] An organisation can also be individually concerned if in the proceedings leading up to the decision it has been involved as a leading party in negotiations that were clearly limited and closely connected with the subject matter of the Commission decision, and the organisation is in a situation which distinguished it from all others.[60]

---

[55] Joined Cases T-447/93, T-448/93 and T-449/93, *Associazione Italiana Tecnico Economica del Cemento and Others v Commission*, [1995] E.C.R. II-1971.

[56] Case T-435/93, *Association of Sorbitol Producers within the EC (ASPEC) and Others v Commission*, [1995] E.C.R. II-1281.

[57] Case C-188/92, *TWD Textilwerke Deggendorf v Bundesrepublik Deutschland*, [1994] E.C.R. I-833.

[58] To illustrate this, see Joined Cases T-447/93, T-448/93 and T-449/93, *Associazione Italiana Tecnico Economica del Cemento and Others v Commission*, [1995] E.C.R. II-1971, para.60 et seq.; Case T-55/99, *Confederación Española de Transporte de Mercancías (CETM) v Commission*, [2000] E.C.R. II-3207. See also Case T-30/03, *Specialarbejderforbundet i Danmark (SID) v Commission*, 2007 E.C.R. II-34, where it was held that SID was not entitled to bring an action for annulment of a Commission decision. The case has been appealed to the ECJ as Case C-319/07 P.

[59] Case C-78/03 P, *Commission v Aktionsgemeinschaft Recht und Eigentum eV*, [2005] E.C.R. I-10737; and Case T-210/02, *British Aggregates Association v Commission*, [2006] E.C.R. II-2789 (appealed to the ECJ).

[60] Case C-106/98 P, *Comité d'entreprise de la Société française de production and Others v Commission*, [2000] E.C.R. I-3659. See also Case C-313/90, *Comité International de la Rayonne et des fibres Synthétiques and Others v Commission*, [1993] E.C.R. I-1125; and Joined Cases 67, 68 and 70/85, *Kwekerij Gebroeders van der Kooy and Others v Commission*, [1988] E.C.R. 219. Another illustrative example is Case T-117/04, *Jachthavens Zuidelijke Randmeren and Others v Commission*, [2006] E.C.R. II-3861.

Regional bodies of a Member State can also bring an action for annulment before the CFI. According to the established case law of both the ECJ and the CFI, the term "Member State" in the EC Treaty provisions on the institutions and the provisions on proceedings before the Court of Justice only includes central government authorities in the Member States, so that "Member State" does not include regional and autonomous governments or bodies, regardless of their powers.[61] A right for regions, etc. to bring an action thus requires that, even if the Commission's decision is addressed to a Member State, the regional or local body, as a legal person under national law, is directly and individually affected by a decision, and can therefore bring an action for annulment under art.230, fourth paragraph of the Treaty, in the same way as any other party. A region will always fulfil the requirements of art.230, fourth paragraph, if the Commission's decision is a negative decision in relation to individual aid or aid schemes which that region has adopted or decided, in other words if the decision concerns a refusal to approve aid which has been decided on by the regional body in question.[62]

Deadlines for bringing actions for annulment

8–014   According to art.230, fifth paragraph, of the EC Treaty, proceedings for annulment must be instituted within two months of the publication of a measure, or of its notification to the plaintiff, or, in the absence thereof, of the day on which it came to the knowledge of the plaintiff. The criterion as to the date when the plaintiff may have knowledge of the legal act challenged, which is decisive for when the period of limitation begins to run, is of less importance than the date on which the legal act is published or notified.[63] According to the case law, if a legal act has neither been published or notified, those who acquire knowledge that a legal act concerns them, must themselves in reasonable time request notification of the full text of the legal act, and the period of limitation first begins to run from the date on which the third party concerned acquires such precise information about the content and reasons of the legal act as to be able to exercise its right to bring an action. The term "notification" seems to be most relevant with respect to the addressee of a decision.[64]

[61] Case T-214/95, *Het Vlaamse Gewest (Flemish Region) v Commission*, [1998] E.C.R. II-717, which contains references to other cases.
[62] Joined Cases T-269/99, T-271/99 and T-272/99, *Territorio Histórico de Guipúzcoa and Others v Commission*, [2002] E.C.R. II-4217; Joined Cases T-132/96 and T-143/96, *Freistaat Sachsen and Volkswagen v Commission*, [1999] E.C.R. II-3663; Case T-214/95, *Het Vlaamse Gewest (Flemish Region) v Commission*, [1998] E.C.R. II-717; and Case T-288/97, *Regione Friuli Venezia Giulia v Commission*, [1999] E.C.R. II-1871.
[63] Case T-426/04, *Tramarin Snc di Tramarin Andrea e Sergio v Commission*, [2005] E.C.R. II-4765; and Case T-17/02, *Fred Olsen v Commission*, [2005] E.C.R. II-2031, which has been appealed to the ECJ as Case C-320/05 P. The appeal was dismissed.
[64] Case T-17/02, *Fred Olsen v Commission*, [2005] E.C.R. II-2031, which has been appealed to the ECJ as Case C-320/05 P. The appeal was dismissed.

According to the established practice of the Commission, which has been developed since May 1999 following the entry into force of Regulation (EC) No.659/1999 (the Procedure Regulation), the summary of the decision referred to in art.26(1) of the Regulation must refer to the Commission's website and it is stated that the full text of the decision in question, minus any confidential information, is available there in the authentic language(s). The fact that the Commission gives third parties access to the full text of a decision which is posted on the website, combined with a notice in summary form in the Official Journal that makes it possible for interested parties to identify the decision, is to be regarded as publication for the purposes of art.230, fifth paragraph.[65]

Finally, the Community provisions on periods of limitation can only be derogated from under special circumstances which are not foreseeable, or force majeure (see art.45(2) of the Statute of The Court of Justice), or excusable error, and as long as the strict compliance with these provisions is in accordance with consideration for the principles on legal certainty and equal treatment, or arbitrariness in the administration of justice.[66] The term "excusable error" must be interpreted narrowly, and can only apply in unusual circumstances where the conduct of the decision-making body, either alone or to a decisive extent, is such as to give rise to pardonable confusion in the mind of a party acting in good faith and exercising all the diligence required of a normally experienced person.[67] **8–015**

The precise calculation of the two months deadline is made on the basis of the rules in arts 101–103 in the Rules of Procedure of the Court of first Instance including, for example that the prescribed time limits are extended on account of distance by ten days.[68] There is similarly a period of two months for appeals to the ECJ; see art.56 of the Statute of The Court of Justice.

Intervention in an action for annulment

According to art.40, second paragraph, of the Statute of The Court of Justice, which according to its art.53, first paragraph, also applies to the CFI, any other person establishing an interest in the result of any case submitted to the Court may intervene in cases before the Court, except for cases between **8–016**

[65] Case T-321/04, *Air Bourbon SAS v Commission*, [2005] E.C.R. II-3469; and Case T-17/02, *Fred Olsen v Commission*, [2005] E.C.R. II-2031, which has been appealed to the ECJ as Case C-320/05 P. The appeal was dismissed.

[66] Case T-426/04, *Tramarin Snc di Tramarin Andrea e Sergio v Commission*, [2005] E.C.R. II-4765, which contains references to further cases on the topic; and Case T-17/02, *Fred Olsen v Commission*, [2005] E.C.R. II-2031, which has been appealed to the ECJ as Case C-320/05.P. The appeal was dismissed.

[67] Case T-321/04, *Air Bourbon SAS v Commission*, [2005] E.C.R. II-3469; and Case T-17/02, *Fred Olsen v Commission*, [2005] E.C.R. II-2031, which has been appealed to the ECJ as Case C-320/05 P.

[68] The rules of procedure for the ECJ and the CFI are available at *http://curia.europa.eu/da/instit/ txtdocfr/index.htm*.

Member States, between institutions of the Communities or between Member States and institutions of the Communities. An interest in the result of the case for the purposes of art.40 of the Statute of the Court of Justice means a direct, present interest in the grant of the particular form of order sought that the application to intervene is designed to support and not an interest in relation to the pleas or arguments raised.[69]

The Member States and the Community institutions always have a right to intervene in a case before the ECJ or the CFI; see art.40, first paragraph of the Statute of the Court of Justice.

According to the established case law, associations whose purpose is to protect their members' interests have a right to intervene in cases involving matters of principle which can affect their members.[70]

Interveners enter into a case as it stands at the point of intervention, and they are entitled to put forward independent arguments, but only in support of the claims of one of the parties, and they may not depart from the basic issues of the case, as established between the plaintiff and the defendant.[71] Thus, an intervener does not have a right to demand that a case be dismissed when such a claim has not been made by the defendant.[72]

Actions against the Commission for failing to act

8–017   According to art.232 of the Treaty, it is also possible to bring an action on the Commission's failure to act in State aid cases. Under this provision, should the European Parliament, the Council or the Commission fail to act on an infringement of the Treaty, the Member States and the other institutions of the Community may bring an action before the Court of Justice to have the infringement established. Such an action can only be accepted by the court if the institution in question has been asked to take action. If the institution in question has not taken action within two months after being asked to do so, the complainant can bring an action within a deadline of a further two months. According to the third paragraph of the article, any natural or legal person may, under conditions corresponding to those discussed above, complain to the ECJ that an institution of the Community has failed to address to that person any act other than a recommendation or an opinion. Under art.225(1) of the Treaty and art.51 of the Statute of the Court of Justice, cases against the Commission for failure to act are brought before the CFI, with appeal on points of law to the ECJ.

If under art.232 judgment is given against the Commission for failing to act, then according to art.233, the Commission is required to take the necessary measures to comply with the judgment of the ECJ, i.e. to act.

---

[69] Case T-227/01, *Territorio Histórico de Álava and Others v Commission*, 2006 E.C.R. II-1.
[70] Case T-227/01, *Territorio Histórico de Álava and Others v Commission*, 2006 E.C.R. II-1.
[71] Case T-171/02, *Regione autonoma della Sardegna v Commission*, [2005] E.C.R. II-2123.
[72] Case C-225/91, *Matra v Commission*, [1993] E.C.R. I-3203.

There is a close connection between art.230 on actions for annulment and art.232 on actions for failure to act. The ECJ has stated that arts 230 and 232 are in fact expressions of the same legal remedy. Accordingly, just as art.230, fourth paragraph, gives citizens the possibility of instituting annulment proceedings in respect of a legal act issued by an institution which is not addressed to them if the legal act is of direct and individual concern to them, art.232, third paragraph, should be interpreted so that it gives citizens the possibility of bringing an action against an institution which has failed to issue a legal act that would similarly have affected them.[73]

Actions for failing to act are a possibility if an undertaking which is a competitor to an undertaking which has received aid, wishes to obtain a decision from the Commission where the Commission may be sitting on a case for political reasons. If the Commission then takes a decision to approve the aid, the competing undertaking can bring an action to annul the decision.[74] **8–018**

What is decisive in relation to art.232 is whether, at the time when it received an express request to act, the Commission had a duty to act. It is the established law that the Commission has sole competence to assess the compatibility of State aid with the common market. This means that, having regard for good administrative practice and the correct application of the Treaty rules on State aid, the Commission has an obligation to carry out a thorough and impartial examination of a complaint which challenges some aid as being incompatible with the common market.[75] Once it has agreed to initiate an examination on the prompting of a complaint, for example by requesting information from the Member State concerned, the Commission cannot allow the examination once initiated to continue indefinitely. An assessment must be made from case to case on whether the duration of the examination, including preliminary examinations, can be considered reasonable. This assessment must be made on the basis of the context of the case, the different steps in the administrative procedure, and the complexity of the case.[76] Thus if the Commission has had reasonable time to carry out a thorough and impartial examination, it has a duty to act. If the Commission does not decide within two months of being

---

[73] Case C-68/95, *T. Port GmbH v Bundesanstalt für Landwirtschaft und Ernährung*, [1996] E.C.R. I-6065; and Case T-395/04, *Air One v Commission*, [2006] E.C.R. II-1343.

[74] Case T-95/96, *Gestevision Telecinco v Commission*, [1998] E.C.R. II-3407; and Case T-46/97, *SIC—Sociedade Independente de Comunicação v Commission*, [2000] E.C.R. II-2125.

[75] Case T-395/04, *Air One v Commission*, [2006] E.C.R. II-1343; and Case T-95/96, *Gestevision Telecinco v Commission*, [1998] E.C.R. II-3407.

[76] The following cases illustrate when the duration of the Commission's examination is considered reasonable or unreasonable: Case T-167/04, *Asklepios Kliniken v Commission*, [2007], not yet reported; Case T-395/04, *Air One v Commission*, [2006] E.C.R. II-1343; and Case T-95/96, *Gestevision Telecinco v Commission*, [1998] E.C.R. II-3407. Case T-167/04, *Asklepios Kliniken v Commission*, [2007], not yet reported, illustrates the problem of determining how long the Commission can sit on a complaint before an action can be brought for its failure to take action. In this case the CFI acknowledged that the Commission needed time to digest the consequences of the *Altmark* case before it decided on the case which was the subject of the complaint concerning compensation for a public service obligation; see Case C-280/00, *Altmark Trans v Nahverkehrsgesellschaft Altmark*, [2003] E.C.R. I-7747.

requested to do so, an action can be brought for its failure to act within a deadline of a further two months.

However, where notification of aid is made bringing an action for failure to act is not particularly relevant, as the consequence of the rules in the Procedure Regulation on notified aid and the period of limitation for the preliminary procedure (two months) will be that a notified aid measure will be regarded as approved.[77]

Claims against the Commission for compensation

8–019   According to art.288, second paragraph, of the Treaty, the Community must, in accordance with the general principles common to the laws of the Member States, make good any damage caused by its institutions or by its servants in the performance of their duties. Under art.235, the Court of Justice has jurisdiction in disputes relating to compensation for damage provided for in the second paragraph of art.288, which are referred to the CFI under art.225(1).

Briefly, the conditions under which the Commission can be found liable are that the conduct of the Commission which is the subject of a claim is contrary to the law, that some loss has occurred, and that there is a causal connection between the conduct and the loss claimed.[78]

Under art.46 of the Statute of the Court of Justice, proceedings against the Community institutions in matters arising from non-contractual liability are barred after a period of five years from the occurrence of the event giving rise to them. The period of limitation can be broken either by submitting a claim to the CFI, or by the injured party taking the claim directly to the Community institution concerned. In the latter case, the claim must be made within the deadline of two months referred to in art.230 of the Treaty.

Suspensory effect and provisional provisions

8–020   According to art.242 of the Treaty, actions brought before the Court of Justice do not have suspensory effect unless the Court of Justice considers the circumstances require it and issues an order that the application of the contested act be suspended. art.243 allows the Court of Justice to prescribe any necessary interim measures.[79]

---

[77] Of course, a Member State can bring an action against the Commission for failure to act, in order to obtain the Commission's final decision, as the Member State will not be able to implement aid before the Commission has taken a decision; see art.88(3) of the Treaty.

[78] Case T-230/95, *Bretagne Angleterre Irlande (BAI) v Commission*, [1999] E.C.R. II-123.

[79] Case T-455/05 R, *Componenta Oyj v Commission*, [2006] E.C.R. II-38, and the Rules of Procedure of the ECJ and of the CFI.

The Commission's scope for enforcement via the ECJ

The adoption of Regulation (EC) No.659/1999 (the Procedure Regulation) **8–021**
has created clarity on a number of procedural matters which were previously only regulated by the practice of the Court. Furthermore, the Rules of Procedure of the Community courts contain detailed and reasonably clear procedural rules which are a help for plaintiffs and others who may be interested in participating in cases before the courts.

Under art.88(2), if a Member State does not comply with a decision of the Commission that some State aid is incompatible with the common market or is being misused, the Commission may refer the matter directly to the ECJ. By the same provision, a Member State has the same right as the Commission to go directly to the ECJ to force another Member State to comply with a decision of the Commission that some aid is incompatible with the common market.

Under art.12 of Regulation (EC) No.659/1999, the Commission can also refer directly to the CFI cases concerning a Member State's failure to comply with a Commission decision based on art.11 of the Regulation, to suspend aid or require aid to be repaid. According to art.11, both decisions require that the Member State should have had an opportunity to submit arguments. A decision on the repayment of aid also requires that there should be no doubt about the nature of the measure as aid, that it is necessary to act quickly, and that there is a significant risk of serious and irreparable harm to a competitor.

Article 226, on breach of the Treaty, can also be the basis for an action **8–022**
brought by the Commission. According to the procedure in art.88(2), all interested parties have some guarantees which are particularly framed for the problems which State aid causes for competition in the common market, and which are much more comprehensive than the guarantees which can be obtained by the procedure under art.226, and which only the Commission and the Member State in question rely on. Even if the special procedure referred to does not necessarily mean that the compatibility of an aid measure with Community provisions, other than the provisions in art.87, is considered under the art.226 procedure, it is nevertheless the procedure in art.88(2) which must be used by the Commission if it wishes to establish that a measure is *incompatible* with the common market.[80] If, for example, a Member State does not notify an aid measure in accordance with art.88(3), that Member State will not have complied with its obligations under the Treaty, and the Commission can therefore institute proceedings for breach of the Treaty under art.226.[81]

In a case brought against it by the Commission in accordance with art.88(2), on the grounds of deficient implementation of a Commission

---

[80] Case 290/83, *Commission v France*, [1985] E.C.R. 439.
[81] Case C-61/90, *Commission v Greece*, [1992] E.C.R. I-2407.

decision, a Member State cannot argue that the decision is unlawful. Such a claim must be brought by the Member State under art.230. The reason for this is that the Treaty distinguishes between causes of action under arts 226 and 227, where the objective is to establish that a Member State has not complied with its obligations, and causes of action under arts 230 and 232, where the objective is to ensure the lawfulness of the acts or omissions of the Community's institutions. These remedies have different purposes and are subject to different conditions.[82] However, it will be otherwise if the legal act challenged contains "particularly serious and manifest defects such that it could be deemed non-existent".[83] According to the case law, the only real defence that a Member State can make in a case of deficient implementation of a Commission decision under art.88(2) is that it is in fact entirely impossible to implement a decision correctly.[84] If, when implementing a Commission decision a Member State encounters unforeseen and unforeseeable difficulties or becomes aware of consequences not contemplated by the Commission, it must submit those problems for consideration by the Commission, together with proposals for suitable amendments to the decision in question. In such a case, in accordance with art.10 of the Treaty, the Commission and the Member State concerned must work together in good faith with a view to overcoming difficulties whilst fully observing the Treaty provisions.[85] Article 10 of the Treaty requires the Member States and the Community's institutions (as listed in art.7) to abstain from any measure which could jeopardise the attainment of the objectives of the Treaty. The Commission has wide discretion as to whether to bring an action under art.88(2).[86]

If the ECJ finds that a Member State has not complied with its obligations, the Member State is required to take the necessary measures in accordance with art.228(1). In order to satisfy the judgment of the ECJ the necessary measures must be put in place immediately, and implemented as quickly as possible.[87] If, in spite of this, a Member State does not take the necessary measures, the Commission will institute the procedure under art.228(2), and ultimately bring the matter before the ECJ which can impose a fine or a periodic penalty payment.

---

[82] Case C-404/97, *Commission v Portugal*, [2000] I-4897, para.34; and Case C-404/00, *Commission v Spain*, [2003] E.C.R. I-6695, para.40.

[83] Case C-404/97, *Commission v Portugal*, [2000] I-4897, para.35; and Case C-404/00, *Commission v Spain*, [2003] E.C.R. I-6695, para.41.

[84] Case C-404/97, *Commission v Portugal*, [2000] I-4897, para.39; and Case C-404/00, *Commission v Spain*, [2003] E.C.R. I-6695, para.45.

[85] Case C-404/97, *Commission v Portugal*, [2000] I-4897, para.40; and Case C-404/00, *Commission v Spain*, [2003] E.C.R. I-6695, para.46.

[86] Case T-277/94, *Associazione Italiana Tecnico Economica del Cemento (AITEC) v Commission*, 1996 E.C.R. II-351.

[87] Case C-375/89, *Commission v Belgium*, [1991] E.C.R. I-383.

CONTROL BY THE NATIONAL COURTS

It was stated in Ch.2 in this book that the national courts have an important **8–023**
role to play in the enforcement of the EU's State aid rules.[88] They must ensure
(if necessary on their own initiative) that the art.88(3) of the Treaty is correctly
applied by the national authorities. If a national court finds that art.88(3) has
not been complied with, it must use whichever measures it can under national
law to counter the infringement of art.88(3).

A national court can decide whether a State aid measure within the meaning
of art.87(1) has been notified to the Commission according to art.88(3), but
it is only the Commission that can decide that a State aid measure is compatible with the common market according to art.87(2) or (3). If a national
court has doubts as to whether a measure falls within the ambit of art.87(1),
the national courts can seek assistance from the Commission, by asking for
legal or financial information,[89] just as it can, and sometimes must (in the
case of national courts of last instance), refer questions of interpretation of
Community law to the ECJ for a preliminary ruling, i.e. a decision which is
binding on the national court in respect of the interpretation of EU law; see
art.234 of the Treaty. In the area of State aid, art.234 means that national
courts can/must refer questions on the interpretation of the Treaty, in particular arts 87(1) and 88, to the ECJ,[90] as well as the validity and interpretation
of legal acts issued by the Community's institutions (as listed in art.7 of the
Treaty), including of course the Commission. In this connection the block
exemption regulations issued by the Commission in accordance with Council
Regulation (EC) No.994/98 of May 7, 1998 on the application of arts 92 and
93 [now 87 and 88] of the Treaty establishing the European Community to
certain categories of horizontal State aid (OJ L 142, May 14, 1998, p.1), has
direct effect; see art.249 of the Treaty and recital 5 in the Regulation. The
national courts have to apply these block exemption regulations subject to preliminary rulings given in accordance with art.234. The national courts cannot
refer a question to the ECJ for a preliminary ruling under art.234 about a State
aid measure's compatibility with the common market.[91]

Even if unlawful aid is subsequently found by the Commission to be compatible with the common market, the national court's ruling with respect to

[88] See Commission Notice on cooperation between national courts and the Commission in the
State aid field (OJ C 312, 23.11.1995, p.8). In September (22nd) the Commission issued a draft
guidance for State aid enforcement by national courts. The powers of the national courts in
State aid cases is also described in Case C-119/05, *Ministero dell'Industria, del Commercio e
dell'Artigianato v Lucchini*, [2007] E.C.R. I-6199.

[89] Jan-Gerrit Westerhof, "State aid and 'private litigation': practical examples of the use of Article
88(3) EC in national courts", in *Competition Policy Newsletter*, No.3, Autumn 2005, p.97.

[90] The national court must presumably decide whether the conditions of art.87 are fulfilled before
deciding whether art.88(3) is relevant; see Case C-345/02, *Pearle and Others v Hoofdbedrijfschap
Ambachten*, [2004] E.C.R. I-7139; Case C-172/03, *Wolfgang Heiser v Finanzamt Innsbruck*,
[2005] E.C.R. I-1627; and Case C-71/04, *Administración del Estado v Xunta de Galicia*, [2005]
E.C.R. I-7419.

[91] Case C-297/01, *Sicilcassa v IRA Costruzioni and Others*, [2003] E.C.R. I-7849.

art.88(3) will be definitive, since at the time in question the aid had not been found compatible and was unlawful and a Commission decision does not have retrospective effects. A decision by the Commission, for example on the basis of a complaint, to approve aid that has not been notified, cannot make implementation measures lawful after the event if they were invalid because they were adopted in contravention of the prohibition in art.88(3).[92] The proceedings of a national court concerning a case of unlawful State aid will not be interrupted because the Commission initiates proceedings in the same case. The national courts have, however, a duty to respect the decisions of the Commission which have not been challenged in due time on the basis of an action for annulment under art.230 and they must thus refuse to refer a question to the ECJ on the validity of such a decision after the expiry of the period for bringing an action under art.230. This applies to those who would have had standing in an action for annulment according to art.230 EC.[93] However, the possibility of challenging the validity of a Commission decision by way of a procedure in national courts using art.234 EC seems to remain open to those who could not have availed themselves of a direct action on the basis of art.230 EC.

8–024   If a national court finds a measure is within the scope of application of art.87(1) it must consider whether the aid is new aid or existing aid, see Ch.2. As stated there, new aid is covered by the stand-still requirement in art.88(3) (naturally with the exception of cases concerning aid covered by a block exemption regulation). Existing aid is covered by art.88(1), and the national court must therefore evaluate whether there have been such changes as to make art.88(3) relevant (see for example art.4 of Commission Regulation (EC) No.794/2004 laying down detailed rules for the application of art.93 [now 88] of the EC Treaty on amendments to existing State aid measure; see para.2–021, above).

The national courts thus are under a duty to deal with non-notified (i.e. unlawful) aid, even though they may be aware that the Commission is in the process of examining the compatibility of the aid with the common market.[94] The national courts must protect the rights of citizens against any setting aside by national authorities of the prohibition of implementing an aid measure before the Commission has taken its decision to approve the aid. In this connection, in the absence of Community provisions in this area, it is up to each Member State within its national legal order to appoint competent courts and lay down procedural rules to secure the rights of citizens under Community law. However, these rules may not be less favourable than those that apply to corresponding rights under national rules (the principle of equivalence), and they must not make it impossible or unreasonably difficult in practice to

---

[92] Case C-368/04, *Transalpine Ölleitung in Österreich GmbH and Others v finanzlandesdirektion für Tirol and Others*, [2006] E.C.R. I-9957; Case C-354/90, *Fédération Nationale du Commerce Extérieur des Produits Alimentaires v France*, [1991] E.C.R. I-5505.

[93] C-188/92, *TWD Textilwerke Deggendorf v Bundesminister für Wirtschaft*, [1994] E.C.R. I-833.

[94] Case C-354/90, *Fédération nationale*, [1991] E.C.R. I-5505; and Case C-39/94, *SFEI*, [1996] E.C.R. I-3547 para.44.

exercise the rights granted under the Community's legal order (the principle of effectiveness).[95]

Furthermore, the ECJ has held that national courts must offer to individuals entitled to rely on the obligation of notification the certain prospect that all appropriate conclusions will be drawn, in accordance with national law, with regard to both the validity of the acts giving effect to the aid and the recovery of financial support granted in disregard of that provision or possible interim measures. The national courts must ensure that whatever remedies they grant are such as to *negate* in fact the effects of the aid granted in breach of art.88(3).[96] In this respect it will not be sufficient merely to extend the circle of beneficiaries. This would not respect the consideration for the Community that requires art.88 to be complied with.

National courts can order that the granting of aid should be suspended **8–025** or even repaid, and they can also award damages.[97] In fact national courts must—in principle—allow an application for repayment of State aid implemented in breach of art.88(3). However, the ECJ has held that the national court is *not bound* to order the recovery of aid implemented contrary to the last sentence of art.88(3) where the Commission has adopted a final decision declaring the aid in question compatible with the common market.[98] Instead the national court must—based on community law—order the beneficiary *to pay interest in respect of the period of unlawfulness.* This case law originated from the following factual circumstances: the beneficiary of the State aid in question was CELF which was to process directly orders from abroad and the French overseas territories and departments for books, brochures and any other communication media together with promoting French culture throughout the world. CELF's obligations were reaffirmed in agreements concluded with the French Ministry of Culture and Communication. From 1980 to 2002, CELF received non-notified operating subsidies from the French State to offset the extra costs of handling small orders placed by booksellers established abroad. In 1993 the Commission concluded that the aid was compatible with the common market. That decision was annulled by the CFI in 1995.[99] The Commission decided again—in 1998—that the aid was compatible with the common market. Also that decision was—in 2002—annulled by the CFI[100] Afterwards the Commission approved the aid in 2004. That decision was also challenged and subsequently annulled by the CFI.[101] Particularly under such circumstances the question on how to calculate the interests becomes

---

[95] Case C-368/04, *Transalpine Ölleitung in Österreich GmbH and Others v Finanzlandesdirektion für Tirol and Others*, [2006] E.C.R. I-9957.
[96] *Transalpine Ölleitung in Österreich GmbH and Others v Finanzlandesdirektion für Tirol and Others*, [2006] E.C.R. I-9957.
[97] Case C-354/90, *Fédération nationale du commerce exterieur*, [1991] E.C.R. I-5505; and Case C-39/94, *SFEI*, [1996] E.C.R. I-3547.
[98] C-199/06, Centre d'exportation du livre français (CELF), *Ministre de la Culture et de la Communication v Société internationale de diffusion et d édition* (SIDE), not yet reported.
[99] See T-49/93, SIDE *v* Commission, [1995] E.C.R.II-2501.
[100] T-155/98, SIDE *v* Commission, [2002] E.C.R.II-1179.
[101] T-348/04, SIDE *v* Commission, not yet reported.

substantial. The ECJ has on that question ruled that the obligation to remedy the consequences of the aid's unlawfulness extends also, for the purposes of calculating the interests, and save for exceptional circumstances, to the period between a Commission decision declaring the aid to be compatible with the common market and the annulment of that decision by the Community court.[102]

Also, in the case of aid which may have been granted, regardless of a decision on interim measures taken by the Commission, it is up to the national courts either to order suspension of payment or repayment, depending on the circumstances. In contrast to the powers of the Commission, a national court can order the repayment of unlawful (i.e. non-notified) aid, solely on the grounds that the aid has been paid in breach of art.88(3), last sentence.

National courts can also consider whether there is cause for adopting interim measures with a view to protecting the interests of the parties pending a final decision.

8–026   In this connection it is also emphasised that a national court may be required to set aside a national rule if the rule would prevent the court from taking the necessary interim measures.[103] For example, this may concern a national authority which does not have discretionary powers with regard to recovery and may be unable to supply the supplementary information relating to the Commission's decision, but which can nevertheless be obliged to seek recovery of unlawfully paid aid, even if it may exceed the limitation period under national law and even if such recovery is not permitted under national law on the grounds that the beneficiary has not acted in bad faith.[104]

However, apart from questions of damages, the decisions of the national courts on unlawful, i.e. non-notified, aid can only be provisional, as it is only the Commission that can decide on the compatibility of a State aid measure with the common market (subject to any involvement of the Community courts).

In principle it is the national legal order which determines *who can rely on art.88(3)*, as procedural rules, such as on the interests of plaintiffs and the locus standi of interested parties in connection with proceedings before national courts which concern the protection of citizens' rights under Community law, fall within the competence of the Member States. However, these rules may not be less favourable than those that apply in cases brought under national law, and they may not, in practice, make it impossible to exercise the right which the national court is required to protect. In connection with art.88(3), the ECJ has stated that a citizen not only can have an interest in the national courts applying the direct effect of the prohibition in art.88(3), last sentence, with a view to removing the negative effects of distortion of competition that

---

[102] C-199/06, Centre d'exportation du livre français (CELF), *Ministre de la Culture et de la Communication v Société internationale de diffusion et d édition* (SIDE), not yet reported.

[103] See the seminal Case C-213/89, *The Queen v Secretary of State for Transport,* Ex p.: *Factortame,* [1990] E.C.R. I-2433.

[104] Case C-24/95, *Land Rheinland-Pfalz v Alcan Deutschland,* [1997] E.C.R. I-1591.

is a consequence of unlawful aid, but can also have an interest in the repayment of a charge imposed in connection with the aid. In the latter case the question of whether the citizen has been affected by the distortion of competition that is a consequence of the aid measure is not relevant for assessing their interest in the case. It is only necessary to have regard to the fact that the citizen has been required to pay a charge that is an integral part of the aid measure which has been implemented in contravention of the prohibition.[105] This will be the case if there is a fixed connection between the charge imposed and the aid granted under national legislation, so that the revenue from the charges is used to finance the aid and has a direct effect on its amount and therefore the assessment of the aid's compatibility with the common market.[106]

---

[105] Case C-174/02, *Streekgewest Westelijk Noord-Brabant v Staatssecretaris van financiën*, [2005] E.C.R. I-85. See also Joined Cases C-266/04 to C-270/04 and others, *Nazairdis, now Distribution Casino France and Others v Organic*, [2005] E.C.R. I-9481.

[106] Joined Cases C-393/04 and C-41/05, *Air Liquide Industries Belgium v Ville de Seraing*, [2006] E.C.R. I-5293. See also Joined Cases C-266/04 to C-270/04 and Others, *Nazairdis, now Distribution Casino France and Others v Organic*, [2005] E.C.R. I-9481.

INDEX